The Wisdom of the Romantics

Michael K. Kellogg

Essex, Connecticut

Prometheus Books
An imprint of The Globe Pequot Publishing Group, Inc.
64 South Main Street
Essex, CT 06426
www.globepequot.com

Distributed by NATIONAL BOOK NETWORK

Copyright © 2025 by Michael K. Kellogg

All rights reserved. No part of this book may be reproduced in any form or by any electronic or mechanical means, including information storage and retrieval systems, without written permission from the publisher, except by a reviewer who may quote passages in a review.

British Library Cataloguing in Publication Information available

Library of Congress Cataloging-in-Publication Data
Names: Kellogg, Michael K., 1954– author.
Title: The wisdom of the Romantics / Michael K. Kellogg.
Description: Essex, Connecticut : Prometheus, [2025] | Includes bibliographical references and index. | Summary: "In this book, Michael Kellogg profiles such disparate authors as Rousseau and Balzac, Goethe and Hegel, Wordsworth and Jane Austen, revealing that classifying Romantic thinkers is a highly subjective enterprise—which is the whole Point"— Provided by publisher.
Identifiers: LCCN 2024040533 (print) | LCCN 2024040534 (ebook) | ISBN 9781493087112 (cloth) | ISBN 9781493087129 (epub)
Subjects: LCSH: Romanticism.
Classification: LCC PN603 .K45 2025 (print) | LCC PN603 (ebook) | DDC 809/.9145—dc23/eng/20241118
LC record available at https://lccn.loc.gov/2024040533
LC ebook record available at https://lccn.loc.gov/2024040534

∞™ The paper used in this publication meets the minimum requirements of American National Standard for Information Sciences—Permanence of Paper for Printed Library Materials, ANSI/NISO Z39.48-1992

To Baird, Cole, and Camille.

To finish the moment, to find the journey's end in every step of the road, to live the greatest number of good hours, is wisdom.

—RALPH WALDO EMERSON

CONTENTS

Introduction 1

1: Rousseau and Sensibility 9

2: Goethe: Poetry and Truth 41

3: Hegel: The World Spirit Realizing Itself 75

4: Wordsworth: Meaning and Memory 105

5: Jane Austen's Heroines 139

6: Stendhal on Love and Death 173

7: Alessandro Manzoni and the Great Italian Novel 197

8: John Keats and the Great Odes 225

9: Alexander Pushkin and the Descent into Prose 257

10: Balzac and the *Comédie Humaine* 285

Acknowledgments 313

Notes 315

Suggestions for Further Reading 345

Index 353

v

Introduction

In my last book, I noted that "Enlightenment . . . is more an idea than a period."[1] I am tempted to reverse that statement for the post-Enlightenment movement generally known to us as Romanticism. The constellation of concepts and themes that constitutes the Romantic period is not as readily circumscribed as the Enlightenment's dedication to reason and progress. From Descartes on, Enlightenment thinkers were inclined to believe that all genuine questions, even on ethics and politics, could be answered by applying the same methods that drove the Scientific Revolution and that the answers to these questions were not only knowable through reason and experiment but also compatible with one another.[2] There was, in other words, a single, coherent universe of knowledge accessible to us through the application of scientific methods. Even Immanuel Kant, who wanted to circumscribe claims to knowledge in order to make room for faith, contended that within the realm of the empirical and the purely conceptual, knowledge formed a complete and comprehensible whole. Indeed, for Kant, contradiction was the surest sign that we had exceeded those limits and were seeking a form of transcendent knowledge beyond our capabilities.

There were, of course, exceptions. Most notably, David Hume rejected the common Enlightenment assumption that we can use abstract reasoning to uncover the foundations of human knowledge and experience. Yet even Hume's skepticism reveals that the search for such foundations was a defining preoccupation of Enlightenment thought.

Romanticism was a much messier business—so messy, in fact, that many scholars eschew any attempt to define it. In reaction to the overreliance on reason, Romantics emphasized sensibility, inspiration, individual freedom, emotional intensity, introspection, sincerity, and heightened imagination. They sought out nature at its wildest and most sublime: tall mountains, steep gorges, and resounding cataracts. They dabbled in the gothic and grotesque, in mythology, the sacred, and the mystical. Romanticism was a turning inward into subjectivity. Hegel called it "absolute inwardness."[3]

In his lectures on the *Roots of Romanticism*, Isaiah Berlin has a wonderful two-page paragraph giving a nonexhaustive list of all the things that "Romanticism is."[4] The list is full of deliberate inconsistencies:

> It is beauty and ugliness. It is art for art's sake, and art as an instrument of social salvation. It is strength and weakness, individualism and collectivism, purity and corruption, revolution and reaction, peace and war, love of life and love of death.[5]

What Romanticism "is" includes many contradictions, precisely what the rationalists rejected.

Most Romantics, by contrast, embraced contradictions as inevitable. Indeed, acknowledging a lack of the sort of conceptual clarity that was considered a desideratum of the Enlightenment was a frequent feature of the Romantic era and illustrates an important philosophical point later developed by Ludwig Wittgenstein.[6] Consider the word *game*. There are many kinds of games: board games, card games, ball games, Olympic Games, and all varieties of children's games (hopscotch, kick-the-can, tag). We can even talk of the "games people play" in relationships. What do all these games have in common that make them "games"? What are the necessary and sufficient conditions for being a game? Wittgenstein explains that "these phenomena have no one thing in common which makes us use the same word for all."[7] When you look at how the word *game* is actually used, you see "a complicated network of similarities overlapping and criss-crossing: sometimes overall similarities, sometimes similarities of detail."[8] Wittgenstein characterizes these similarities as "'family resemblances'; for the various resemblances between members of a family: build, features, color of eyes, gait, temperament, etc. etc. overlap and criss-cross in the same way."[9]

Introduction

Romanticism is just such a "family resemblance" concept.[10] There is no set of necessary and sufficient conditions that lead us to use the same label for such disparate authors as Rousseau and Balzac, Goethe and Hegel, or Wordsworth and Jane Austen. Indeed, many would dispute the word's application to at least one member of each of these pairings. When we study certain writers, we may see similarities that make us call them all Romantics; others may see differences sufficiently important to withhold the term. It is a highly subjective enterprise, which is the whole point.

> That thinkers, historians and academics have failed to agree on one succinct definition of Romanticism would have pleased the [early Romantics], who liked this indefinability of the concept. They themselves never attempted to provide rigid rules—in fact, it was the very absence of rules that they celebrated. They were not interested in an absolute truth but in the *process* of understanding. They tore down boundaries between disciplines, thereby transcending the divisions between the arts and the sciences, and pushed against the Establishment.[11]

Scholars, accordingly, feel a strong impulse to cabin their study by a pair of dates that largely encompass what we call the Romantic period.[12] Most of the works we consider quintessentially Romantic were written between the Storming of the Bastille on July 14, 1789, through the Napoleonic Wars and the heyday of the Industrial Revolution, to the political upheaval that spread rapidly across Europe in 1848. There are obvious exceptions. Jean-Jacques Rousseau died more than a decade before the French Revolution. Victor Hugo wrote *Les Misérables* in 1862 and was active as a novelist, poet, and playwright until at least 1874. Still, such dates allow us to set the social, intellectual, and historical context for what Berlin called "the greatest single shift in the consciousness of the West"[13] and what Eric Hobsbawm dubbed "the greatest transformation in human history since the remote times when men invented agriculture and metallurgy, writing, the city and the state."[14]

REVOLUTION, WAR, AND ECONOMIC GROWTH

The Industrial Revolution marked a dramatic departure from the agrarian, feudal economy that had held sway across Europe for centuries. Significant improvements in agricultural methods, particularly in England, were already underway in the eighteenth century, including crop rotation, better plows, and improved means of transportation. Greater productivity led to increases in the food supply and population. It also led to a decrease in the number of workers needed for agriculture. The timing was fortuitous, because many of these excess workers were quickly absorbed by the factories and mills of the Industrial Revolution.

The flying shuttle (1733) and the spinning jenny (1764) boosted England's textile business. But it was the invention of the steam engine in 1769 that sounded the factory whistle signaling the beginning of the Industrial Revolution in England. The steam engine powered the mills and factories, as well as the boats and trains, that quickly transformed the economy and everyday life. It also led to a dramatic shift of people from the country to the cities. The population of London increased four-fold between 1780 and 1850. Wealth, too, soared dramatically, but its distribution was far from equitable. Typical mill workers barely earned subsistence wages, and the urban landscape was often blighted by smog and poverty. Child labor was common. The world as depicted in Charles Dickens's *Hard Times* and William Hogarth's engravings was all too real.

In France, the revolution was political rather than industrial.[15] In 1780, almost every state in continental Europe was ruled by an absolute monarch. There had been revolutions in the United States, Spain, and Portugal, but those were against outside control by other countries. The French Revolution was internal and far more radical. Urban laborers, artisans, and the peasantry eventually joined forces with the business and professional classes that made up the bourgeoisie. This so-called Third Estate rebelled not just against the king, Louis XVI, but also against the privileges afforded to nobles and the clergy. The fall of the infamous Bastille triggered a widespread reaction against oppression and injustice, which drew strong support from intellectuals in England and Germany as well as in France. Feudalism was abolished, and a "Declaration of the

INTRODUCTION

Rights of Man and Citizen" was proclaimed. Rousseau's ideals of equality, liberty, and fraternity seemed within reach.

But Europe's remaining monarchs were not ready to be mothballed. To contain the contagion, they sent troops to the borders of France. A series of European-wide military conflicts known as the Wars of the French Revolution ensued between 1792 and 1802. These wars had two consequences. First, they radicalized the revolution. Moderate reforms were no longer possible. The Jacobins took control, abolished the monarchy, and launched the Reign of Terror of 1793/1794. The king and his queen, Marie Antoinette, were executed in 1793, along with numerous nobles, clergymen, and suspected royalist sympathizers.

Second, the wars led to the rise of Napoleon Bonaparte, from an obscure second lieutenant to first consul of the French Republic in 1799 to emperor in 1804. The mostly defensive wars to preserve the revolution evolved into wars of conquest and oppression, which replaced one absolute ruler with another. Napoleon engineered a series of stunning victories in Italy, Spain, the Low Countries, and Austria, usually against more numerous opponents. A united Europe seemed a real possibility—until, that is, he made the fatal decision to invade Russia in 1812.

Napoleon, the brilliant tactician, was outsmarted by the crude rope-a-dope tactics of the Russian army, which constantly retreated and drew the French deeper and deeper into the interior as winter loomed. Napoleon, repeatedly frustrated by his inability to provoke a decisive engagement, lost more than 80 percent of his army, mainly due to bad weather, poor provisioning, and disease. The remaining French forces suffered a decisive defeat at Leipzig in 1813. Coalition members occupied France and forced Napoleon to abdicate and go into exile on Elba, a Tuscan island six miles from the mainland. A year later, he was welcomed back by the French before a final defeat at Waterloo in 1815. This time, Napoleon was exiled to the remote volcanic island of Saint Helena in the South Atlantic Ocean, where he died in 1821. Decades of peace followed among the great powers of Europe.

Internal affairs, however, were still volatile. The House of Bourbon returned to the throne of France in 1815. The Bourbon Restoration lasted only until the July Revolution of 1830. After "Three Glorious Days" of fighting, Charles X, last of the Bourbon kings, fled the country, and a constitutional monarchy was established, headed by Louis-Philippe of the House of Orléans. Universal male suffrage was declared. But the hunger for political freedom, freedom of the press, and economic rights for workers remained. Tightening repression, along with widespread unemployment and food shortages, triggered a cascading series of revolts against the European monarchs that began in Sicily in January 1848 and almost simultaneously spread throughout the continent, including France, Germany, Italy, and Austria. England, which had long since adopted the gradual reforms of a constitutional monarchy, was largely spared.

In France, Louis-Philippe was forced to abdicate, and a Second Republic was proclaimed. It did not last long. The French exercised their new democracy by electing as president Louis Napoleon, nephew of the former emperor. In 1851, he declared himself emperor of the Second French Empire. Throughout Europe, the various democratic revolutions were harshly suppressed. Some hard-won reforms, such as the abolition of serfdom and universal male suffrage, remained. But the revolutionaries uniformly failed to establish the liberal (or socialist) democracies they sought. As the French socialist Pierre-Joseph Proudhon sadly conceded, "We have been beaten and humiliated . . . scattered, imprisoned, disarmed and gagged. The fate of European democracy has slipped from our hands."[16]

THE ROMANTICS

Romanticism, of course, made its mark beyond poetry and prose. The transition from Haydn and Mozart to Beethoven and Chopin could not have been more dramatic. The passionate, iconoclastic Beethoven—who first dedicated his 1803 *Eroica* symphony to Napoleon but withdrew the dedication after Napoleon declared himself emperor—became a model of the Romantic hero. Opera, too, exploded in the nineteenth century as a quintessentially Romantic genre. The German-born composer Giacomo Meyerbeer, working largely in France, brought grand opera to new heights maintained by the great Italian *bel canto* trio of Gioachino Rossini, Gaetano Donizetti, and Vincenzo Bellini. The paintings of Francisco Goya, William Blake, Caspar David Friedrich, J. M. W. Turner, and

Eugène Delacroix were all part of the transition away from a classical, academic style, which emphasized the "calm repose of beauty," to the "emotive extremes" that heralded the coming of impressionism in the latter part of the century.[17] Friedrich's 1818 *Wanderer Above the Sea of Fog* is an iconic painting of the Romantic era. Even science took a romantic turn away from the mathematics of matter in motion beginning in 1768 when Captain James Cook left on his first voyage around the world. In 1831, Charles Darwin sailed to the Galapagos on the famous HMS *Beagle*, a trip that ultimately resulted in his religion-shattering theory of evolution, as detailed in *On the Origin of Species*, published in 1859. In what became known as the "Second Scientific Revolution," biology, botany, and anthropology were studied along with more "fluid" phenomena such as chemistry, electricity, and magnetism. Science itself was rebelling against the straitjacket of Newtonian physics.[18]

Even within the realm of poets, playwrights, and novelists, which will necessarily be our focus, the list of those regrettably left out is necessarily long. A case could readily be made for separate chapters on, among others, William Blake, Samuel Taylor Coleridge, Lord Byron, Percy Bysshe Shelley, Mary Shelley, Sir Walter Scott, Victor Hugo, Alexander Dumas, Emily Brontë, Elizabeth Barrett Browning, Giacomo Leopardi, William Hazlitt, Alphonse de Lamartine, Mme de Staël, and Arthur Schopenhauer, as well as members of the "Jena Set"—Friedrich Schiller, Friedrich Schelling, the Schlegel brothers—so compellingly portrayed by Andrea Wulf in her study *Magnificent Rebels: The First Romantics and the Invention of the Self*. One can question the Romantic credentials of some of the ten authors I have chosen but not, I think, their importance in the history of Western thought. In each chapter, I will try to make the case for both.

Goethe notoriously pronounced the Classical as healthy and the Romantic as diseased. Yet his historical drama, *Götz von Berlichingen*, and his epistolary novel, *The Sorrows of Young Werther*, were among the founding texts of Romanticism. There is a similar, if less pronounced, degree of ambivalence in each of the "Romantics," but that is an important part of the "family resemblance" that warrants their inclusion.

I

Rousseau and Sensibility

Since I have undertaken to reveal myself absolutely to the public, nothing about me must remain hidden or obscure. I must remain incessantly beneath his gaze, so that he may follow me in all the extravagances of my heart and into every least corner of my life.[1]

Jean-Jacques Rousseau is one of the pivotal figures in the history of Western thought. Saint Augustine embodied the turn from secular Rome to the all-encompassing religious framework that shaped the Middle Ages. Petrarch rode in the vanguard of the Renaissance rediscovery of classical learning and secular modes of expression. Descartes was the philosopher of the scientific revolution who sparked an Enlightenment faith in reason as the essential instrument of progress.

There is considerable artificiality in such designations. Greater figures are to be found in each of these eras. There were also earlier figures who anticipated much of what followed. But somehow the zeitgeist seemed literally to pivot around the work of these writers and to head in a new and unexpected—if, in retrospect, seemingly inevitable—direction. That is nowhere truer than of Rousseau.

Rousseau was a child of the Enlightenment. He was friends with the French philosophes who prepared the great *Encyclopedia*, which was intended as a compendium of all secular knowledge and a springboard for further discoveries. He even contributed articles on music. Yet one day he was literally stunned by the thought that reason and progress were

The Wisdom of the Romantics

the enemies of both happiness and morality. Man was born free; he was naturally good in a state of nature. But civilization had corrupted him by bringing wealth and power, for with wealth and power came inequality and the oppression of the many by the few.

Rousseau showed remarkable versatility as a writer. Aside from a highly acclaimed opera and a play for the Comédie-Française, he wrote political tracts, a best-selling epistolary novel, a treatise on education, a memoir that counts among the great books of the Western corpus, and a series of final "reveries" on the elusive search for happiness.

His political writings are understandably famous, though little read today and, even then, only out of a sense of obligation. His advocacy of liberty, equality, and fraternity became the rallying cry of the French Revolution, an event he predicted. More notoriously, he also foresaw and offered an *apologia* for totalitarian socialism. Recognizing that liberty and equality were in substantial tension with each other, he argued that true freedom was to be found in a communal state governed by what he called the "general will," which is empowered to override the individual desires of recalcitrant citizens and, paradoxically, "force men to be free."

But Rousseau quickly lost interest in political advocacy. He recognized that humankind could not return to a condition in which small tribes of hunter-gatherers lived on terms of rough equality and that any new institutions of government would become as corrupt as those currently in existence: "The vices that make social institutions necessary are the same that make their abuses unavoidable."[2] Instead, at a time when scientific advances elevated reason to almost divine status—a status it had not enjoyed since Aristotle—Rousseau focused on the cultivation of individual sensibility. He hoped to recapture the innocent joy and authentic connection with others that humankind had enjoyed in a mythical state of nature, which he posited not as a historical thesis but as a logical etiology of our current feelings of alienation from self and others. In an early book, Rousseau aptly summarizes his fundamental quarrel with the modern world:

> Most of our ills are of our own making, and . . . we could have avoided nearly all of them by keeping the simple, regular, and solitary way of life prescribed by nature.[3]

Each of his major works displays nostalgia for this imagined time of innocence, wholeness, and grace. Despite widely different genres and subject matters, the overriding theme of his works is a reaction against reason and artifice in favor of sensibility. He views civilization and culture not as progress but as a degradation and corruption of man. Man has become unnatural and artificial. His self-love displays itself in ambition for power and wealth. His vanity leads to ostentation and the unequal accumulation of goods far beyond what one person reasonably needs or may properly claim.

It is small wonder that Rousseau was hounded on all sides throughout his life. The philosophes considered him a traitor to their cause of enlightened progress. The aristocrats saw him as an intolerable threat to their entrenched political and economic power. The clergy found his "natural religion"—which shunned doctrinal disputes and organized worship, and which branded Christianity as a tool of authoritarian regimes—more pernicious than atheism insofar as he purported to enlist God himself against the church. Rousseau managed to anger just about everyone. Over time, he grew paranoid, but not without some justification. Villagers, urged on by the clergy, would throw stones at his house. The political authorities would drive him, like the *Flying Dutchman*, from place to place so that he could never find the peace he claimed to seek.

Rousseau considered each of his works a reflection of his life. To understand the books, he believed, readers must understand the man behind them, in all the purity of his intentions and the innocence of his motives. In that sense, all his works are autobiographies, not just the *Confessions*.

Rousseau ushered in a new era of Romantic sensibility. In *The Social Contract*, he stresses the malleability of human nature and its distortion by society. Yet, ultimately, he opts for a politics of individual rather than collective freedom. *La Nouvelle Héloïse* reconstructs the origins of romantic love and its ability to transcend (even if it cannot alter) the hard realities of contemporary society. In *Emile*—the most important book on education since Plato's *Republic*—he offers a vivid example of a Montessori-like upbringing that fosters rather than crushes the innate longings of the spirit. His rejection of revealed religion in the *Profession of Faith of a Savoyard Vicar* ushers in a personal religion of sensibility that dismisses organized worship as just another form of political oppression. His *Reveries of the Solitary Walker*, which treats nature itself as the divinity, will exercise a strong influence on the Romantic poets. Finally, in the *Confessions*, Rousseau seeks to justify himself to the world through an autobiography not so much of events as of the feelings inspired by those events. For better or worse, Rousseau did more than almost any other thinker in making us who and what we are today.

LIFE

Jean-Jacques Rousseau was born in Geneva on June 28, 1712. His mother, Suzanne, died of puerperal fever nine days later. Rousseau bore a burden of guilt for her death throughout his life, a burden his father, Isaac, did little to relieve. "He . . . could never forget that I had robbed him of her," Rousseau would write more than half a century later.[4]

Suzanne, née Bernard, came from a higher social class than Isaac. The Bernards disapproved of her marriage to a lowly watchmaker, despite the fact that her brother married Isaac's sister at the same time. On his wife's death, Isaac's unmarried younger sister, also named Suzanne, kept house for the mercurial Isaac and helped raise Jean-Jacques and his much older brother, François.

Rousseau never attended school. He was largely self-taught once he learned to read. In the evening, he and his father would read to each other from romantic and sentimental novels that Isaac enjoyed as much as his son. Rousseau schooled his emotions on such fare, "giving me the strangest and most romantic notions about human life, which neither experience nor reflection has ever succeeded in curing me of."[5] Plutarch's *Lives of the Noble Grecians and Romans* was also a favorite, along with the Roman historian Tacitus. Rousseau would read them aloud while Isaac worked. Rousseau inherited his father's love of music as well as books, but little else. Isaac spent much of the money from his wife's estate, which was intended for Jean-Jacques and François. Yet Rousseau idealized his father and, throughout his life, would strenuously praise the dignity of artisans who work with their hands to produce useful objects for everyday life.

Rousseau suffered another loss at the age of ten when his father got into a violent quarrel with a nearby landowner and was forced to flee Geneva. Isaac's sister left to tend house for him while Rousseau and his brother were cast on the not-so-good graces of their mother's family. The Bernards promptly apprenticed François to a watchmaker, but after going through several masters, François fled Geneva and disappeared from history. Even the most diligent scholars picking over every aspect of Rousseau's life have failed to find any further news of him.

Rousseau was sent along with one of his cousins, Abraham Bernard, to board with a pastor, Monsieur Lambercier, and his sister Gabrielle, in the nearby town of Bossey. Mostly, the two boys were left to their own devices to play in the countryside and make mischief at home. Rousseau was twice spanked by Gabrielle until she realized the boy found "in the shame and pain of the punishment an admixture of sensuality" that he acknowledged "would determine my tastes and desires, my passions, my very self for the rest of my life. . . . At the moment when my senses were aroused my desires took a false turn and, confining themselves to this early experience, never set about seeking a different one."[6]

Eventually, the country idyll ended, and the two boys were called back to Geneva. They stayed with Abraham's family for a time, another all-too-brief period of freedom. But Rousseau was soon apprenticed to a notary and Abraham to a civil engineer.

Isaac remarried in 1726. Rousseau's new stepmother disliked him, or so Rousseau thought. He accordingly spent little time with them and attempted to visit his father only when she was not present. His apprenticeship as a notary was short lived. The master considered the boy too slow and simple for such a position. Rousseau was duly re-apprenticed to an engraver. Beatings and oppression followed; so, too, in reaction, did lying, stealing, and shirking on the part of Rousseau. The apprenticeship was a stark and bitter contrast to the relative freedom he had enjoyed and made him forever resentful of any hint of tyranny.

Rousseau's sole consolation was rambling in the countryside around Geneva. He had a passion for walking in nature and indulging implausible fantasies of future greatness. Twice he stayed out so late that the gates of Geneva were locked against him. He didn't mind sleeping outside, but both times he was brutally punished by his master. When he found the gates closed a third time, Rousseau turned on his heels and, like his brother before him, fled the city. He was sixteen. "Free and my own master," he would later write, "I supposed that I could do anything, achieve anything."[7]

The Bernards seemed happy to see him go, and Isaac, most cruelly of all, made only a token gesture of going after him. Rousseau always suspected, undoubtedly correctly, that his father (and stepmother) wanted to keep the full income from his mother's inheritance: his own as well as his brother's. It was yet another abandonment for the sensitive youth. Rousseau was alone in the world but young enough to see his aimless flight as a romantic adventure. He even sang under open windows of castles half expecting a beautiful maiden to appear and be captivated by him. And, indeed, something of the sort did happen.

Rousseau at first lodged, a night here and a night there, with friendly farmers in the vicinity of Geneva. Soon, however, he met a Catholic priest eager to gain converts, who sent him to Annecy with a letter of introduction to Françoise Louise Eléonore de La Tour, Baroness de Warens. At twenty-nine, Mme de Warens was more youthful and beautiful than Rousseau had any reason to expect, with the sort of round, full, motherly figure that always appealed to him. Married at fourteen, childless, and long separated from her husband, Mme de Warens clung to a small pension from the king of Sardinia in exchange for promoting Catholicism and apparently acting as a sometime confidential informant and messenger.

Rousseau was immediately smitten. "Let those who deny the affinity of souls explain, if they can," Rousseau insisted, "how from our first meeting, our first word, our first glance, Mme de Warens inspired me not only with the strongest affection, but with a perfect confidence, which has never proved misplaced."[8] Somehow, Rousseau knew that this meeting would reshape his entire life.

Nonetheless, after three days, Mme de Warens sent the boy off to Turin to take instruction in Catholicism at a hospice. "Given into my own keeping while still a child and enticed by caresses, seduced by vanity, lured by hope, forced by necessity, I became a Catholic."[9] His fellow catechumens were by and large a cynical lot. Some traveled from place to place reconverting in exchange for shelter and food. One, a large Muslim boy, traumatized and disgusted Rousseau with his aggressive sexual advances.

Rousseau had no particular interest in religious dogma, but he enjoyed arguing with the priests. The priests enjoyed it less. Rousseau was baptized after only nine days and unceremoniously pushed out of the hospice. He found work as a valet but functioned mostly as secretary to an elderly countess. When she died after five months, he was paid off and dismissed. Her nephew, however, found him employment as a footman to a count. It was again mostly secretarial work, but he showed promise and was tutored in languages and literature by the count's son.

During his time in Turin, Rousseau met the Abbé Gaime, who, thirty-four years later, would provide the inspiration for the Savoyard vicar in *Emile*. Rousseau was impressed with Gaime's deeply felt but nondogmatic form of religion. They took long walks in the countryside, and Rousseau found that the emotions raised in him by nature merged with his religious awakening. Like Spinoza before him, the essence of Rousseau's experience of the divine would always lie in the wonders, the beauties, and the mysteries of nature.

Despite his advantageous position with the count, Rousseau got himself dismissed in September 1729 after being increasingly negligent of his duties. His real desire was to return to Annecy and Mme de Warens. On arrival, he threw himself at her feet and covered her hands with kisses. Rousseau spent most of the next ten years in the home of Mme de Warens, following her from Annecy to Chambéry, and from there to Les Charmettes. She called him her *petit*; he called her his *Mamma*. But they also became lovers at her suggestion, with Rousseau replacing her steward in that position and eventually being displaced in turn by another young man more competent in managing the estate and more ardent in his embraces. "I loved her too much to desire her,"

Rousseau would explain.[10] But Rousseau declined to share his Mamma and finally left for Paris in 1742, at the age of thirty, following stints as a tutor and a self-taught music teacher.

The years with Mme de Warens were critical to Rousseau's intellectual development. In his substantial leisure, he read widely in the classics, both ancient and modern, and taught himself music. He immersed himself even more fully, however, in the development of his sensibility. At Les Charmettes, in particular, Rousseau enjoyed what he called "the short period of my life's happiness . . . those peaceful but transient moments that have given me the right to say I have lived."[11]

> I rose with the sun, and I was happy; I went for walks, and I was happy; I saw Mamma, and I was happy; I left her, and I was happy; I strolled through the woods and over the hills, I wandered in the valleys, I read, I lazed, I worked in the garden, I picked the fruit, I helped in the household, and happiness followed me everywhere; it lay in no definable object, it was entirely within me; it would not leave me for a single moment.[12]

Rousseau would always regard this time with Mme de Warens as a personal golden age, followed by ever-increasing misery and persecution. Both views were exaggerated, but moderation was as foreign to Rousseau's nature as, or so he thought, any form of guile or unkindness. Rousseau considered himself a sensitive heart harried and sullied by civilization. In his most compelling works—*Emile, La Nouvelle Héloïse, Confessions*, and *Reveries of the Solitary Walker*—he would struggle in various ways to recapture that innocence and joy.

Rousseau initially planned to make his name in Paris as a musician. He promoted a new system for musical notation that was considered clever but impractical. His own skills as a composer were still developing, and, as an autodidact, he found few pupils. Instead, he became secretary to le Comte de Montaigu, French ambassador to Venice. There he developed a deep love of Italian music. Montaigu was disorganized and inattentive, and Rousseau gradually took over many of his responsibilities. But Montaigu grew jealous and resentful, and Rousseau was discharged in 1744. He returned to Paris bitter at the injustice, and even more bitter that no one would take the part of the lowly secretary against his aristocratic employer.

On his return to Paris, Rousseau began to associate regularly with Denis Diderot and Jean le Rond d'Alembert, two key Enlightenment figures and coeditors of the famous *Encyclopedia*, a compendium of rational knowledge and progressive ideas.[13] They enlisted Rousseau to write articles for the encyclopedia, mostly focused on music. He began to move in more fashionable circles.

Rousseau was awkward, even tongue-tied, in society and yet prone to enthusiastic outbursts and passionate (if largely suppressed) attachments to unattainable aristocratic women. Aside from Mme de Warens, his sexual encounters were limited and irregular until 1745, when he met Thérèse Levasseur. She was a laundress in her early twenties, pretty and petite. Thérèse was also largely illiterate and couldn't even tell time by a clock. Rousseau's friends looked down on Thérèse and deplored their relationship. But it clearly filled a need for Rousseau, who never had to feel inferior in her presence. Perhaps he was tired of pining after women beyond his reach, even though he continued to do so. Although he eventually married Thérèse in a ceremony with no legal status, his relationship with her was more transactional than otherwise. Indeed, he is quite brutal in the *Confessions* about a woman who stood by him and catered to his needs for some thirty-three years: "What will the reader think when I tell him . . . that from the first moment I saw her till this day I have never felt the least glimmering of love for her; that I no more desired to possess her than I had desired Mme de Warens, and that the sensual needs I satisfied with her were for me purely sexual and had nothing to do with her as an individual?"[14]

The relationship with Thérèse nonetheless lasted until his death in 1778. They had five children, each of whom was duly deposited at Rousseau's insistence in a home for foundlings. Nothing has damaged his posthumous reputation more than this callous abandonment of his children. Rousseau claimed poverty and that he was not suited to raise children—quite an admission from the man who would write the most famous treatise on education since Plato's *Republic*. Indeed, in that very treatise, he obliquely touches on the sore point:

> Whoever cannot fulfill the duties of a father has no right to become one. Neither poverty nor labors nor other people's judgment can exempt him from nourishing his children and bringing them up himself. Readers, you can believe me. I predict that anyone who has a heart and neglects such sacred duties will weep long and bitterly for his error, and will never be consoled.[15]

Whatever his professed regrets, Rousseau never went in search of his children or showed the slightest interest in their individual fates.

In 1749, Rousseau was walking the ten kilometers from Paris to Vincennes, where Diderot was in prison temporarily for one written indiscretion or another. The Académie de Dijon had just published a topic for a prize essay: "Has the progress of the sciences and arts done more to corrupt morals or improve them?" "The moment I read this," Rousseau noted, "I beheld another universe and became another man."[16] The road to Vincennes became his version of Saul's road to Damascus. Suddenly, Rousseau was struck by the fundamental flaws in the entire Enlightenment project. Rousseau argued that man is naturally good but corrupted by civilization and could be saved not by reason but only by the cultivation of sensibility. It was a direct attack on the most firmly held premise of the Enlightenment that art and science bring progress and refinement. Rousseau's *Discourse on the Arts and Sciences* won first prize, and he was suddenly famous.

Rousseau also enjoyed breakthrough success as a composer and librettist with his 1752 opera, *Le Devin du village*. Louis XV loved the opera and had it performed repeatedly. He even invited Rousseau to visit him at court and was apparently prepared to grant Rousseau a lifetime pension. But Rousseau declined the invitation. He was painfully self-conscious in public. He also suffered from the retention of urine—an inability to activate his bladder muscles sufficiently to empty it—coupled with a frequent urgent need to urinate in small amounts. For greater relief, he had to resort to catheters made of glass. Thérèse learned to manipulate these rigid catheters to give him minimal pain. But Rousseau was concerned that a lengthy appearance at court would lead to an accidental discharge that would humiliate him. His friends, and undoubtedly Thérèse as well, deplored the missed opportunity. But Rousseau would later characterize it as a personal declaration of independence.

In fact, Rousseau still made a fair amount of money from the many productions of his opera. Mozart's first opera, written when he was twelve, was an appreciative takeoff on *Le Devin du village*. The pastoral setting and absurd plot lent themselves to parody. But Rousseau's opera is nonetheless lovely and lyrical and still worth listening to.[17] Rousseau would later write a highly regarded *Dictionary of Music* as well as his many articles for the *Encyclopedia*. He made himself controversial, even notorious, with a *Letter on French Music*, in which he argued for the superiority of Italian over French opera.

In 1754, Rousseau returned briefly to Calvinist Geneva, where he renounced Catholicism and reclaimed his citizenship. The former was required for the latter. His father was long since dead, but he stopped off to see Mme de Warens for the first time in more than a decade. Time had not been kind to her. She was now obese, in ill health, and greatly in debt thanks to a series of disastrous schemes to make money. Rousseau had, through the years, helped her with small sums, and he continued to do so, but his charity was tempered by the recognition that most of the money he sent her went to the mountebanks by whom she was always surrounded. He would not visit her again, and she died in 1762.

Rousseau spent the seven years from 1755 to 1762 largely in the countryside outside Paris as the guest of a series of aristocratic patrons who made their houses available to him. He repeatedly refused direct financial gifts, however, and supported himself and Thérèse by copying music, a modest yet useful labor that recalled his artisan origins. Rousseau affected, or felt, a total disregard for polite society. He discarded his watch and dressed like a peasant, often in a flowing Armenian robe, both as a statement and as a convenience in light of his urinary complaint.

Rousseau loved to walk in the countryside and became a passionate botanist. He also continued his lifelong habit of falling in love with inaccessible women and quarreling with his friends and supporters. Rousseau collected grievances, as he gathered plants, each carefully preserved between the leaves of his books. He would go out of his way to find new ones and would even invent them when his resentments required new provocations.

Yet Rousseau entered a remarkably fruitful period as a writer. His *Discourse on Inequality* was published in 1755. An epistolary novel, *La Nouvelle Héloïse*, became a European sensation in 1761. And, in 1762, he published both *Emile* and *The Social Contract*, a double triumph and a double disaster. The two books were banned in Paris and burned in Geneva for their radical politics and natural religion. Church and state alike threw their considerable combined weight at the man who always claimed that his "strongest desire was to be loved by everyone who came near me."[18]

Forewarned of an arrest warrant issued in Paris, Rousseau fled with Thérèse to the village of Môtiers, near Neuchâtel. Rousseau renounced his Genevan citizenship in 1763 and was effectively stateless after that. In 1765, he was driven from his Môtiers retreat when a group of Protestant ministers incited the people to stone the house where he and Thérèse lived. They took refuge in the canton of Bern on a small island in a nearby lake. Rousseau could have happily and quietly lived out his days there. But, under pressure from Geneva, he was soon ordered to leave. Unsurprisingly, his already extreme self-consciousness blossomed into a full-blown persecution complex.

The English philosopher David Hume invited Rousseau and Thérèse to come to England in 1766, but, once there, Rousseau's paranoia led him to accuse Hume of being part of a widespread conspiracy to control and discredit him, a conspiracy joined by his former friends among the philosophes. The delusional man returned to France under an assumed name, where he found protection from the Prince de Conti at the Château de La Trye, a few hundred kilometers from Paris. On his agreement not to publish anything, Rousseau was finally left in whatever peace his troubled soul would allow. He lost himself in nature and resumed the study of botany. He worked on the *Confessions* in the hopes of justifying his life and restoring his reputation.

In 1770, Rousseau moved back to Paris under his real name. No one seemed to care much, and he was unmolested but still paranoid and reclusive. He again copied music to support himself. He botanized with a friend with whom he managed not to quarrel. He gave public readings of the *Confessions* until he was directed by the authorities to stop. And he worked on *Reveries of the Solitary Walker*, which was published posthumously, along with the *Confessions*. In 1778, he moved to the château of the marquis de Girardin, where he died of apoplexy on July 2. The now penniless Thérèse lived another twenty-three years, long enough to see her husband's body carried in triumph and installed at the Panthéon in 1794 as a hero of the Revolution.

LIBERTY AND EQUALITY

It is a basic tenet of classical liberalism of the sort espoused by Adam Smith in his *Wealth of Nations* that economic freedom—freedom of trade, freedom of labor, and freedom of capital—is the surest route to general prosperity. Within a minimalist governmental structure that guarantees property and the fruits of one's labor, each individual can pursue his or her self-interest and, as if guided by an invisible hand, simultaneously act for the benefit of all by creating wealth and driving up the standard of living.

Rousseau will have none of it. He considers economic transactions the worst sort of slavery because they render each person dependent on the actions of others. "Man is born free, and is everywhere in chains," reads his oft-quoted pronouncement. But, as the next sentence makes clear, the manacles are self-fashioned: "This or that man may regard himself as the master of others, but he is more of a slave than they."[19] A laborer is dependent on the one who hires him, but the master is even more dependent on his laborers to maintain his position. Even such simple acts as buying and selling food, clothing, and other articles make the purchaser dependent on the work of the producer and the seller dependent on the money of the buyer. The very division of labor that Adam Smith touted as a key to wealth creation is a relationship of dependence.

Such mutual dependence seems benign, even beneficial, but Rousseau insists that it leads to inequality and a consequent corruption of

THE WISDOM OF THE ROMANTICS

human nature. Each man is born the equal of any other man. True, there are differences in strength and natural talent. But, once society evolved to the point at which each man "needed another's help,"[20] those natural differences were exacerbated by artificial ones. Men began to manipulate and oppress one another. "Some prospered while others were barely able to stay alive. It is thus that natural inequality gradually becomes accentuated by inequalities of exchange, and differences among men, developed by differences in circumstances, become more noticeable and more permanent in their efforts, and begin to influence the fate of individuals in the same proportion."[21] In every society, inequalities in wealth, rank, preferment, and honors are inevitable, thus "making all men competitors, rivals, or rather enemies."[22]

Rousseau compares modern man with man in a state of nature. He does so with a remarkable preface that only a philosopher could write:

> Let us begin, then, by setting aside all the facts, for they are irrelevant to the problem. The investigations that may be made concerning this subject should not be taken as historical truths, but only as hypothetical and conditional reasonings, better suited to casting light on the nature of things than to showing their real origin.[23]

In other words, let us begin with man today and think him back into his likely conditions prior to the formation of complex societies, not as a matter of historical inquiry, but purely as a thought exercise.

Man in a state of nature, Rousseau suggests, was pre-political. The largest social unit was the family or perhaps a small band of hunter-gatherers. There was no private property and thus no disputes over wealth. "The earth produced everything he needed, and instinct prompted him to make use of it."[24] Each man was driven by self-preservation, softened only by what Rousseau calls "the force of natural compassion."[25] His natural desires were for food, sex, and shelter. Anything else was superfluous. Men in a state of nature were not evil because "they d[id] not know what it is to be good."[26] Primitive man had a united soul that pulled in only one direction: self-interest. That made him free and independent. "The only one who does his own will is he who, in order to do it, has no need to put another's arms at the end of his own; from which it follows that the first of all goods is not authority but freedom. The truly free man wants only what he can do and does what he pleases."[27]

All this changed, according to Rousseau, when private property came into being. Property became an object of contention, a marker of inequality that required a social and legal structure to defend it, and that structure inevitably worked to the benefit of the powerful and the oppression of the weak.[28]

> The first man who, having enclosed a piece of land, took it into his head to say, "This is mine," and found people simple enough to believe him, was the true founder of civil society. The human race would have been spared endless crimes, wars, murders, and horrors if someone had pulled up the stakes or filled in the ditch and cried out to his fellow men, "Do not listen to this imposter! You are lost if you forget that the fruits of the earth belong to everyone, and the earth to no one!"[29]

Astonishingly, Rousseau suggests that we could have avoided nearly all the maladies of modern life "by keeping the simple, regular, and solitary way of life."[30] We don't have to accept Thomas Hobbes's dictum that such a way of life was "nasty, brutish, and short" to protest that our collective standard of living has risen dramatically for the better under capitalism. But Rousseau thinks the cost is too great. Man is now divided against himself and necessarily a person of lies and disguises who does his best to compel others to work for his personal benefit. A healthy *amour de soi* (self-love) has been displaced by *amour propre* (vain selfishness), which longs for invidious distinctions of wealth and power. Self-love is entire and complete. Vanity feeds on the degradation of others. In Rousseau's view, inequality and the greed that it provokes are the main drivers of social ills. "If we look upon human society with a calm and disinterested gaze, it seems at first to show us only violence on the part of powerful men and oppression of the weak."[31] It was better for all men to live simple and poor but self-sufficient lives because such men are equal—because equally impoverished—and free—because free from dependence on one another. The law of nature is antithetical to the wealth of the few and the poverty of the many.

Despite his nostalgia for lost innocence and an authentic (if rudimentary) existence, Rousseau does not actually advocate that we return to this imagined state of nature. Nor does he consider it possible to do so. For better or worse, man has become what Aristotle called him: a political animal. But his vision of primitive man leads Rousseau to consider under what circumstances we would be willing to trade such radical freedom and equality for the safety and prosperity of society. Such a transformation can only be pursuant to agreement. Social order, he insists, "does not come from nature" but is "founded on agreements."[32] Hence, he seeks to uncover the ideal "social contract" that can underwrite modern society. Again, Rousseau is not talking about an actual historical contract but an implicit understanding of the terms of our shared commitment to communal living, terms that will—unlike the actual societies that developed—maximize freedom and equality.

As noted, for Rousseau the first imperative of natural man is "to look after his own preservation, his first concerns are those that he owes to himself."[33] That imperative needs to change if we are to join together in a community. In other words, human nature itself must change. Rousseau says that "a man who renounces his freedom renounces his humanity."[34] And yet that is exactly what he proposes. Man's nature, his "humanity," is not something fixed. It is highly malleable and has already evolved in significant ways from the state of nature. Rousseau proposes to complete that transformation. A true community requires nothing less than "changing human nature, . . . transforming each individual . . . into a part of a greater whole from which he, in a sense, receives his life and his being."[35]

We must each of us, then, give up our individual wills in favor of what he calls "the general will" of the community as a whole.[36] That general will is a reflection of popular sovereignty. Rousseau advocates, or at least seems to advocate, a form of radical democracy in which all citizens participate in all decisions. Even representative democracy will not do for Rousseau, who seeks out the extreme in everything: "Once [the representatives] are elected, the people are slaves, they are nothing."[37] Necessarily, then, the city or state must be small enough that the people can participate directly in all important decisions. Ancient Sparta and his contemporary Geneva are Rousseau's favorite examples. Freedom is preserved because the people are sovereign and obey laws of their own making. Equality, too, is preserved because all citizens are equally subject to the "general will" and forgo the luxuries that appease vanity and create envy.

To be successful, any such community requires "the complete surrender of each associate, with all his rights, to the whole community."[38] Resistance cannot be tolerated. "Anyone who refuses to obey the general will shall be compelled to do so by the whole body. This means nothing else than that he shall be forced to be free."[39] For anyone who believes in classical liberalism, no more chilling words have ever been written. The individual counts as nothing. There are no individual rights, for "if individuals retained any rights, each would soon be his own judge on some point or other," and eventually everyone would do the same.[40] All property is held at the sufferance of the state.[41] Even life itself is at the sufferance of the state. "When the government says to [a citizen], 'It is expedient for the state that you die,' he must die, since it is only on that condition that he has so far lived in security, and since his life is no longer merely a gift of nature, but a conditional grant from the state."[42]

Rousseau, accordingly, grants "a universal coercive power" to the state.[43] Nothing less will preserve equality and order. The social contract permits the use of force by the state in the common good. There is no need for constraints on the power granted to the sovereign—such as a bill of rights—because the sovereign has no interest contrary to that of the individuals who compose it.[44] All subunits or "partial societies"—that is to say, all pockets of dissent—must be repressed "to ensure that the general will is always enlightened and the people never mistaken."[45] The general will, by definition, is correct because no other will is tolerated. Personal freedom gives way to collective freedom.

Yet even the general will, Rousseau concedes, must be subtly controlled and manipulated by a higher power. His radical democracy is not so radical after all, for "the people always wills the good, but does not always see it."[46] Indeed, the "blind multitude . . . seldom knows what is good for it" and "must be shown the right path."[47] That is why a perfectly democratic government "is not suited to men."[48]

This reversal is sharp enough to create whiplash in the reader, but Rousseau is unfazed. Since he doesn't trust radical democracy, Rousseau advocates an equally radical form of unquestioned authoritarianism that guides and controls the democracy by establishing laws. The problem inherent in democracy, Rousseau concludes, "is the origin of the need for a lawgiver."[49] But who has the wisdom to function as lawgiver, and why should the democracy follow that lead?

> Anyone who dares to undertake the task of instituting a nation must feel himself capable of changing human nature, so to speak; of transforming each individual, who by himself is a complete and solitary whole, into a part of a greater whole from which he, in a sense, receives his life and his being; of marring man's constitution in order to strengthen it; of substituting a partial and moral existence for the physical and independent existence that we have all received from nature. He must, in short, take away man's resources to give him others that are foreign to him and cannot be used without the help of other men. The more completely these natural resources are annihilated, the greater and more durable are the acquired ones and the stronger and more perfect are the new institutions.[50]

This is where the "noble lie" comes in. Plato needed it for his ideal *Republic*, and so does Rousseau for his very different, but equally totalitarian, version. Lawgivers must "attribute their own wisdom to the gods" so that people will "bear the yoke of public well-being with docility."[51] Through a combination of education, compulsion, and moral/religious suasion, the citizens will learn to love their state above all other things and will freely choose the good of the fraternity ahead of their own private interest. "There is no subjection so perfect as that which keeps the appearance of freedom."[52] The hidden hand of self-interest will be replaced by a new civil religion that is "absolute, sacred, and inviolable."[53] The transformation of humanity will be complete.

The rallying cry of the French Revolution—"liberté, égalité, fraternité"—was thus established, as well as a blueprint for future communitarian systems of government. Surprisingly, though, Rousseau does not believe in revolution. Indeed, however ideal as an intellectual matter—recall his words, "Let us begin, then, by setting aside all the facts, for they are irrelevant to the problem"—Rousseau concludes that his social contract is impossible as a practical matter because "the vices that make social institutions necessary are the same that make their abuses unavoidable." In other words, we can aspire to a new form of freedom, but what we will get is an old form of tyranny and oppression. In that, too, he was prophetic.

Rousseau's analysis of both the problems and the potential of a revised social order has been tremendously influential. Ultimately, however, Rousseau decides that personal freedom is impossible within the context of modern society and is accessible only to the few—mostly artists and philosophers like himself—who retain something of the independence, the self-interest, and the undivided soul of primitive man. As Jean Starobinski, the most original interpreter of Rousseau, explains, "He prefers the absolute of personal salvation to the absolute of community."[54] In *La Nouvelle Héloïse* and *Emile*, Rousseau still clings to the figure of the "lawgiver" as supreme authority necessary to safeguard the illusion of personal freedom. But, in his final two works, the *Confessions* and the *Reveries*, the individual must ultimately stand alone. Rousseau is thus a harbinger not just of the Romantic fascination with communitarian systems of government but also of the Romantic focus on the solitary individual: the person outside society who cultivates his sensibility and seeks to become a "moral and harmonious whole" in his own right.

The Pivot to Sensibility

La Nouvelle Héloïse, published in 1761, went through more than seventeen editions before the end of the century. It swept through a Europe that was primed for a Romantic reaction to the Enlightenment's emphasis on the use of mathematical reasoning to master a purely mechanistic universe. The novel celebrated the primacy of feeling over reason. Voltaire called its success the greatest infamy of the century. In this epistolary novel, passion is the protagonist. The title references the twelfth-century nun Heloise, whose tragic love affair with her one-time tutor, the philosopher Peter Abelard, resulted in a pair of letters from Heloise that have never been surpassed as an expression of romantic love and sexual passion.[55]

The novel revolves around an impecunious philosophy student, Saint-Preux, hired as a tutor for Julie, an impressionable young aristocrat. "What were the parents thinking?" one must wonder, for needless to say the two fall deeply in love. "Our souls touch, so to speak, at all points," Julie writes, "and we feel an entire coherence."[56] This surfeit of emotion must find expression in extravagant language and gestures. "A hundred times a day," Saint-Preux writes, "I am tempted to throw myself at your feet, to bathe them with my tears, to obtain there my death or my pardon."[57] "The cliff is steep, the water is deep, and I am in despair."[58] All the tropes of Romanticism are present: picturesque ruins, moonlit nights, violent storms, and raging torrents. "Meditations," Saint-Preux explains, "take on an indescribably grand and sublime character, in proportion to the grandeur of the surrounding objects."[59]

Jean Starobinski calls *La Nouvelle Héloïse* "a kind of daydream in which Rousseau gives in to his desire for a limpidity he can no longer find in the real world or in human society: his desire for a purer sky, more open hearts, and a world at once more intense and more diaphanous."[60] Such love is, of course, doomed from the outset. Julie and Saint-Preux are kept apart by "the vanity of a cruel father," who insists that his daughter marry a rich man of good family.[61] Saint-Preux laments "this unbearable contrast between the grandeur of my soul and the meanness of my fortune."[62]

For Julie, at least at first, "the heart gives laws only to itself."[63] She succumbs to but then laments, suppresses, and finally transcends her sexual attraction to Saint-Preux. As Julie herself explains, both "innocence and love were equally necessary to me," even though she knew that she could not "preserve them together."[64] Social constraints simply will not allow it. After the death of her mother, she bows to this social reality in obedience to her father and marries the man he has chosen. She becomes a wife and a mother. But, for Saint-Preux, "no other fires shall ever profane the altar at which Julie was adored."[65] He wanders the world. "Without a family and almost without a country, I have no one on this earth but you. Love alone is all I possess."[66]

Abelard was emasculated by Heloise's relatives for seducing her. So, too, is Saint-Preux, though only figuratively. He cannot recover from the loss of Julie's love. Even she chides him to "learn how to bear misfortune, and be a man."[67] But any accommodation to social reality would be a betrayal of his unique passion. He views his suffering as a mark of distinction. "It is one of the miracles of love to make us find pleasure in suffering, and we should regard as the worst of misfortunes a state of indifference and oblivion which would take all the feeling of our misery from us."[68]

Despite her seeming adjustment to married life, Julie is still in love with Saint-Preux. She confesses all to her husband, Wolmar, who—like Emile's fictional tutor—is one of Rousseau's wise lawgivers. He undertakes to guide the two former lovers along the path of sublimated virtue. He announces to Saint-Preux his intention

> to call you into my family, to treat you as a brother, as a friend, to make a sister of her who was your mistress, to give you paternal authority over my children, to entrust you with my rights after having usurped yours— those are the compliments of which I have believed you worthy.[69]

This arrangement works for a time, or at least seems to work. Wolmar guides his expanded family with a gentle hand and manages his estate as "the wisest of mortals."[70] It is a simple life, with its daily, rural routines. The family even joins the workers on the estate in occasional festivals at which they dance, sing, and play games. The idealized feast is an image of our lost innocence and spontaneous joy.[71] It is a true act of communion in which master and peasant meet on terms of equality.

The equality, of course, is an illusion that benefits the master because it reconciles the others to his rule. But the feelings of shared community are genuine, if transient. They all, for a moment, partake in an illusion of freedom and equality created and controlled by Wolmar. Wolmar is a model of authority. He treats even Julie and Saint-Preux, as he treats the workers on his estate, like children who have to be guided by a generous and kindly father.[72] All he asks is that they surrender their passion. The price is ultimately too great.

Julie and Saint-Preux are stifled by Wolmar's "serenity" and the "simple, regulated life" he imposes on all those around him.[73] They are suppressing what gives them their authenticity as individual human beings. They may be like children in the eyes of society, but they have more life in them than the god-like Wolmar. "Everything which was dependent upon my will was devoted to my duty," Julie writes in her last letter to Saint-Preux. "If my heart, which was not dependent upon it, was devoted to you, that was my torment and not my crime."[74] The torment is ultimately too much for her. Julie can find release only in a death that she embraces because she could not embrace Saint-Preux. After all, "it is only to die once more."[75]

In our own, more cynical age, we may find the heightened emotions of *La Nouvelle Héloïse* cloying. Yet much of it is still compelling reading, and it is important to recapture the book's powerful hold on a generation ripe for revolution—socially, politically, and emotionally. The great German poet Goethe was so moved by *La Nouvelle Héloïse* that he visited the locales it portrays with tears in his eyes. His own *Sorrows of Young Werther* will sound similar notes of longing and lost innocence, as will the very different poems of Wordsworth and Pushkin. For Rousseau and other Romantics, feeling, not reason, is the path to truth. Only unvarnished sensibility can reveal the inherent goodness and innocence of man, long stifled by social convention and political oppression. It will take no less than Jane Austen to balance that equation.

CONFESSIONS OF A SENSITIVE HEART

Michel de Montaigne reported on the free flow of his thoughts and experiences, confident that "each man bears the entire form of man's estate."[76] His readers would understand him, he believed, because they shared—for good and for ill—his essential humanity. Rousseau takes the opposite tack in his *Confessions*, confident that he is a man "like no one in the whole world. I may be no better," he disingenuously suggests, "but at least I am different."[77]

These two quotations mark the vast gulf between two writers who made the study of the self the focus of their writings. They also mark the gulf between the Renaissance—which advocated the perfectibility of man according to classical models—and the Romantic period—which promoted the solitary individual nurturing his sensibility apart from the corrupting influence of society.

Both Montaigne and Rousseau sought to give shape and meaning to their experience through the act of writing about it. But Montaigne still followed the echoes, however faint, of Pico della Mirandola's Renaissance rallying cry: "Thou . . . art the molder and maker of thyself."[78] In Montaigne, neither the self that experiences nor the world that is experienced is treated as something fixed and absolute. Both are known, fitfully and imperfectly, through their changing interactions over time. We can still find wisdom, but only in movement and change, not in abstractions or absolutes.

For Rousseau, the self—the true self—is an ever-fixed mark. Each individual is born unique but is shaped and twisted by society. The task Rousseau sets for himself—as Proust would more than 150 years later—is to recapture the self that has been lost in time. Jean-Jacques, like the narrator Marcel, must break through movement and change to rediscover his essential nature. Unlike *The Social Contract*, *Emile*, and *La Nouvelle Héloïse*, moreover, there is no wise lawgiver to form his judgment. His sole guide is "the succession of feelings which have marked the development of my being."[79]

The *Confessions* is accordingly full of Proustian moments fraught with significance, both personal and metaphorical. "These moments," he explains, "would still be present to me if I were to live a hundred thousand years."[80] Rousseau is less concerned with the literal truth of his narrative than with its emotional truth. Details may be (and often are) mistaken, but "I cannot go wrong about what I have felt," he insists, "or about what my feelings have led me to do; and these are the chief subjects of my story."[81] Rousseau's undertaking, which he claims "has no precedent, and . . . will have no imitator," is to allow the reader to "follow me in all the extravagances of my heart and into every least corner of my life."[82] In the process, he intends to recapture and display to the world a portrait of himself "in every way true to nature."[83]

Rousseau began writing the *Confessions* in 1766, when he was fifty-four years old. He was famous and infamous throughout Europe.

He considered himself, with some justification, "a ceaseless wanderer over the face of the earth, expelled from every refuge I might choose, one after another."[84] By then, however, he had found yet another aristocratic patron who offered him protection and allowed him to live unmolested outside Paris, free to botanize in the countryside, to meditate on the course of his life, and to justify himself to a seemingly hostile world.

In defending his criticisms of Shakespeare, Samuel Johnson stresses that "we must confess the faults of our favorite, to gain credit to our praise of his excellencies."[85] Rousseau's "favorite," of course, is himself. He accordingly confesses his faults, but in such a way as to stress the innate goodness of his heart and the purity of his intentions. "I have never put down as true what I knew to be false. I have displayed myself as I was, as vile and despicable when my behaviour was such, as good, generous, and noble when I was so."[86] Indeed, he shows himself far from good on several occasions but blames society, habit, oppression, and inequality for these flaws, which are contrary to his true nature. At his core, he insists, there was only innocence, sincerity, good faith, and fellow feeling. "May any man who dares, say 'I was a better man than he.'"[87]

Part I focuses on the first twenty years of his life. It is not so much a continuous account, however, as a series of vignettes laden with feeling. He had learned from his reading of Plutarch that telling incidents and homely details tell us more about a person's character than his grand successes and failures. He carried that over to writing about his own life. Even in old age, Rousseau is moved to tears by the simple songs that his aunt sang to him when he was a child. One in particular has come back to him: "I strive in vain to account for the strange effect which that song has on my heart, but I cannot explain why I am moved. All I know is that I am quite incapable of singing it to the end without breaking into tears."[88] The *Confessions* is a succession of such memories, only faintly understood in isolation and yet forming a powerful and moving self-portrait. "What he had come to understand, with extraordinary originality," his biographer Leo Damrosch notes, "was that experiences that strangely haunt the memory can be a key to understanding personality."[89] Rousseau offers us a record of a life through its most deeply felt and vividly remembered moments.

Despite the death of his mother, which he was too young to grasp in any event, Rousseau recalls his early childhood as full of kindness and affection from his father, his aunt, his nurse, and everyone else. His will was so rarely thwarted that he wasn't even conscious of having one. "My strongest desire was to be loved by everyone who came near me." That desire was richly fulfilled, but it left him vulnerable. The lovingly enveloped freedom of his childhood would always make Rousseau resent the slightest signs of disaffection or oppression. "Of all the gifts with which Heaven endowed [my parents]," Rousseau explains, "they left me but one, a sensitive heart. It had been the making of their happiness, but for me it has been the cause of all the misfortunes in my life."[90]

That sensitive heart received a serious blow at the home of Mlle Lambercier—she of the spankings that left the young Rousseau so inflamed—and her brother. He was falsely blamed for breaking one of her combs. Appearances were against him, and his repeated denials were treated as stubborn lies. He was severely punished, and by a sterner hand than that of Mlle Lambercier. But the physical punishment was nothing compared to the "indignation, rage, and despair" that he felt at the injustice.[91] "That first meeting with violence and injustice has remained so deeply engraved on my heart that any thought which recalls it summons back this first emotion."[92] Rousseau traces the strength of his hatred of any injustice—political or personal—to this incident.

Yet most of Rousseau's early memories are more sweet than bitter. Mlle Lambercier furnished another when she rushed across a field to see the king of Sardinia, who was passing by. She tumbled over in her hurry, exposing her backside for all to see, including the surprised king.[93] On another occasion, Rousseau and his cousin constructed an underground aqueduct to divert water from M. Lambercier's walnut tree to a willow slip they had planted. Although the ruse was discovered and the aqueduct destroyed, all seemed delighted with the ingenuity. Later he recounts an idyll with two girls on horseback, who invited him to spend the day with them after he came to their rescue and led their horses across a stream. The day passed in all innocence. But, Rousseau insists, "I know that the memory of a day as lovely as that touches me more, charms me more, and recurs to my heart more often than does the thought of any delights I have tasted in all my life."[94]

Rousseau was a great walker, thinking nothing of multiday journeys through the countryside, enjoying the scenery and expecting adventures at every turn. He became one who sings beneath windows that never open,[95] yet it was the anticipation that seemed to matter most to him. He escorted Mme de Warens's maid, Merceret, all the way to her father's house in Fribourg. She was clearly disappointed that Rousseau made no advances, despite their sharing a room at each stop along the way, but Rousseau was too awkward and inexperienced even to know how to begin. On his return, the penniless Rousseau stopped in Lausanne, where he pretended to be a composer from Paris, although he had never been there and "could not score the simplest drinking song."[96] He brashly undertook to compose a piece for an upcoming concert, wrote out all the parts, and distributed them to the musicians as if he actually knew what he was doing. "Throughout all the history of French opera," he admits, "never was there heard such a discordant row."[97] The musicians were choking with laughter, and the audience members were stopping their ears. Yet Rousseau still found pupils and "insensibly . . . learned music by teaching it."[98]

Many of his most memorable moments, of course, were with Mme de Warens, quite apart from the sexual liaison that always made Rousseau uncomfortable. He preferred "those peaceful but transient moments that have given me the right to say I have lived." Picnic dinners in the countryside, suppers in the arbor, picking fruit from the orchards, joining in the grape harvest, and even stripping hemp with the servants in the evening; "all these were for us so many festivals, in which Mamma took as much pleasure as I."[99] Most of all, he cherished their long walks together during which he shared his heart and aspirations with Mamma and never tired of their conversation: "When [I was] brimming over with love of all that was honest and good, my heart could see nothing in the whole of life but innocence and happiness."[100]

Neither the innocence nor the happiness would last. These are confessions, after all, and Rousseau makes three of them in Part I. The first concerns his sexual obsession with being spanked, perhaps not so shocking in our modern, tell-all era. But the second is more disturbing. Following his conversion to Catholicism, Rousseau worked as a valet/secretary for an elderly countess in Turin. On her death, he took a pink and silver ribbon as a memento. The item was missed and discovered among his things. The stammering boy claimed that a servant girl, Marion, had given it to him and then maintained his claim despite her pained denials. "She merely turned to me, and begged me to remember myself and not disgrace an innocent girl who had never done me any harm."[101] But Rousseau simply became more adamant. "I was not much afraid of punishment," he explains; "I was only afraid of disgrace."[102] They were both dismissed. Rousseau found new employment. But Marion faced possible ruin, and the memory of his lie and its likely consequences haunted Rousseau even forty years later.

The third event seems less egregious. Mamma asked him to accompany a local musician, M. le Maître, who had quarreled with his church employer and decided to seek new opportunities in Lyon. They had with them in a box all the music Le Maître had composed in service of the church. There was a potential for dispute over ownership of the music, especially from a church chapter angered by his departure. So Rousseau and Le Maître left the town at night and managed to make it to Lyon unmolested. But Le Maître suffered an epileptic fit, falling insensible in the street and foaming at the mouth. The frightened Rousseau had sufficient possession of himself to call for help and ask that Le Maître be carried to the inn where he was staying. But Rousseau himself fled while the crowd was occupied with Le Maître, so that "the poor man was abandoned by the sole friend upon whom he might have counted."[103] To make matters worse, the box of music was seized at the request of the chapter, and Le Maître lost "the fruit of his talents, the work of his youth, and the resource of his old age."[104] The latter event was hardly Rousseau's fault; he could have done nothing to prevent the seizure. Nor perhaps could he have done much to aid Le Maître's recovery, and the impulsive flight of a youth barely twenty is understandable. Yet the memory of his "cowardly abandonment"[105] never faded.

Of these three "confessions," only the second carries any real sting, and Rousseau was sixteen at the time he impulsively accused poor Marion to spare his own humiliation. Who could in truth say, "I was a better man than he"? Then again, his life did not stop at sixteen or even at twenty, and his claim that he atoned for his crimes "by forty years of honest and upright behavior"[106] can hardly be credited in a man who consigned his five children to the miserable and likely short life of a foundling hospital. That particular "confession" he made only after Voltaire—hardly himself a moral paragon—published an anonymous pamphlet exposing an "abandonment" more inhuman than cowardly. Even then, Rousseau protested that his children were better off as a result and that his enemies "misrepresent me as an unnatural father."[107]

After the incident with Le Maître, Rousseau spent almost a full decade with Mamma. It was a quiet existence, and he would cherish it always as the golden era in his life. But it would not last. He traveled to Geneva to claim his (and his long-disappeared brother's) share of the inheritance from his mother's estate. After that, he went to take the waters in Montpellier for his precarious health and, on the way, had a torrid (if brief) affair with an older woman who was not put off by his backward ways and who herself made the advances poor Merceret waited for in vain.

His health and spirits alike restored, Rousseau returned to Mme de Warens to find "my place filled."[108] Another young man was established there in the twin roles of estate manager and lover, neither of which had been Rousseau's forte. "Suddenly my whole being was thrown completely upside down," Rousseau writes; "that pleasant feeling of joy and hope that enlivens youth left me forever."[109] Mme de Warens reported the change to him in matter-of-fact terms, noting his negligence of the estate and his frequent absences but assuring him that his rights remained unaltered even though he must share them with another. Rousseau responded in words that she likely found more insulting than flattering: "No, Mamma . . . I love you too much to degrade you. Possession of you is too dear to be shared."[110]

Rousseau accordingly resolved, at the age of twenty-nine, to seek fame and fortune elsewhere. "I thought only of going to Paris."[111] He regretted it for the rest of his life, for with that trip, he was convinced, came all the ills that plagued his remaining years. "Nothing suited my character better, nor was more likely to make me happy," Rousseau would always insist, than a "calm and obscure life . . . in the security of my faith, in my own country, among my family and friends."[112] "I was formed to meditate at leisure and in solitude, but not to speak, act, and do business amongst men."[113]

Rousseau's departure for Paris marks the end of Part I (the first six books) of the *Confessions*. It was intended to be the entire work, and it is unfortunate that it was not. Part II chronicles Rousseau's growing paranoia. His "sensitive heart" is replaced by "a heart oppressed by grief," which can offer "nothing but misfortunes, treasons, perfidies, and sad, heart-rending recollections."[114] "The ceiling under which I live has eyes," he complains, "the walls that enclose me have ears. Uneasy and distracted, surrounded by spies and by vigilant and malevolent watchers, I hurriedly put on paper a few disjointed sentences that I have hardly time to re-read, let alone to correct."[115]

Part II has its interest. But too often it is the interest of a case study in which the charming narcissist of Part I falls victim to a full-blown persecution complex and, "forced to speak in spite of myself,"[116] airs his many grievances. That is not to say that Rousseau was not indeed persecuted by authorities (both secular and religious) and betrayed by friends. But, to reverse Lear's remark, he was less sinned against than sinning. As a case in point, while he wrote the words noted above, he was safely and quite comfortably ensconced in a château owned by the Prince de Conti. Even when he moved back to Paris, the authorities left him unmolested, and many people sought his acquaintance and friendship.

Rousseau claims that he acted always from the prompting of his heart; the actions may have been wrong, but the feelings were not. "It is the history of my soul that I have promised to recount, and to write it faithfully I have need of no other memories; it is enough if I enter again into my inner self, as I have done till now."[117] Rousseau at least made good on that promise.

Part I of the *Confessions* stands alone and deserves its place among the greatest works in the Western tradition. It marks a turning inward after the Enlightenment focus on reason, science, and material progress. For Rousseau, our value lies in the purity and intensity of our sensibility;

our feelings transcend rank, wealth, and even education. We must look inward for truth and find there the illumination that gives meaning to experience. The self-taught Jean-Jacques is indeed like no one else. He takes the discordant notes that make up our daily lives and harmonizes them in an opera, both pastoral and passionate. In the ecstasy of each moment, Rousseau finds himself and stands outside time.[118]

DEATH OF A SOLITARY WALKER

Rousseau's last work, *Reveries of the Solitary Walker,* was written sometime between 1776 and his death in 1778. It was found among his papers in two closely written notebooks. Rousseau calls it "a shapeless diary of my reveries" and insists that "I write my reveries only for myself."[119] This protestation does not preclude anticipation of publication, and the work was edited, titled, and shaped by Rousseau. Yet he accurately describes it as "conversing with my soul,"[120] and the intimacy of that conversation is unique among his works. He has, by this time, turned his back on the literary, philosophical, and musical success he had worked so hard to obtain. He is no longer settling scores. He acknowledges no social concerns and no striving for recognition, friendship, or even reconciliation. His "strongest desire" is no longer "to be loved by everyone who came near me." He wants instead to learn to love himself—or at least find "consolation, hope, and peace only in myself."[121] The *Reveries* are both a solitary exploration of the self and a meditation on life and its elusive happiness.

Rousseau's goal is akin to the Epicurean ideal of *ataraxia,* meaning not so much indifference as contentment and peace, a feeling that the world can no longer harm you.[122] Rousseau steps away from those "moments of delirium and passion" that are just "scattered points along the path of life."[123] "In our most intense enjoyments," he writes, "there is hardly an instant when the heart can truly say to us: *I would like this instant to last forever.* And how can we call happiness a fleeting state which leaves our heart still worried and empty, which makes us long for something beforehand or desire something else afterward?"[124]

Goethe will make the phrase *bid the moment stay* the leitmotif and ever-present temptation of his *Faust.* But it no longer tempts Rousseau. Or, rather, he has turned it inside out. Rousseau seeks a "solid enough base" for the soul "to rest itself on entirely," without lamenting the past or striving for the future, a state in which "moments of delirium and passion" are set aside, and existence alone provides not the "imperfect, poor, and relative happiness such as one finds in the pleasures of life, but . . . a sufficient, perfect, and full happiness which leaves in the soul no emptiness it might feel a need to fill."[125] Only when the passions are completely calmed can we learn that we are sufficient unto ourselves and find happiness simply in being alive.

> The sentiment of existence, stripped of any other emotion, is in itself a precious sentiment of contentment and of peace which alone would suffice to make this existence dear and sweet to anyone able to spurn all the sensual and earthly impressions which incessantly come to distract us from it and to trouble its sweetness here below.[126]

Rousseau discovers this sentiment of existence—this pure state of being—in his communion with nature. He walks, he muses, and he botanizes, an "idle occupation" that "transports me to peaceful habitats among simple and good people, such as those with whom I formerly lived."[127] Botany places him in harmony with his natural environment. "The meadows, the waters, the woods, the solitude, above all, the peace and rest to be found in the midst of all that are incessantly retraced in my memory by my imagination."[128] Rousseau's deeply felt religious belief is inextricably linked to this love of nature. He shuns all doctrinal disputes and all attempts to give anthropomorphic traits to God. God, like nature, simply is, and, insofar as we are "sufficient unto ourselves," we can become like God and at one with the natural world.[129] Rousseau's reveries are his own form of worship, and, particularly in his beautiful Fifth Walk, we feel that the troubled heart of Jean-Jacques Rousseau has finally found a measure of peace.

2

Goethe

Poetry and Truth

MARCEL PROUST CALLED GOETHE "THE GREATEST INTELLIGENCE THAT ever existed."[1] Matthew Arnold, the English poet and critic, was equally enthusiastic, if temporally more modest: "In the width, depth, and richness of his criticism of life," Arnold wrote, Goethe is "by far our greatest modern man."[2]

Sages are out of fashion today—at least sages who traffic in anything other than Instagram feeds and TikTok videos. Goethe was the rarest combination of intellect and pragmatism, of creativity and stability, of sensuality and noble ideals, of philosophical understanding and aesthetic sensibility. He was a complete and harmonious individual. His powerful, charismatic personality impressed even Napoleon, who knew a thing or two about personal magnetism coupled with genius.

Goethe was a writer of astonishing fecundity and versatility. He wrote lyric poems, verse plays, novellas, novels, and even a pastoral epic, all of the highest quality. His extensive autobiographical writings reveal a man who embraced experience with passion but on whom no nuance was lost. The most remarkable thing about Goethe is the totality of his vision. His conversations late in life, recorded by his protégé, Johann Eckermann, reveal such wisdom that Friedrich Nietzsche, with pardonable exaggeration, called it the greatest German book.

Ay, there's the rub. Goethe does not translate well. If Goethe had written in English, he would be our greatest writer since Shakespeare and

The Wisdom of the Romantics

Milton. His works would be regularly taught. His poems would be memorized by schoolchildren, assuming schoolchildren still memorize poems. As it is, the college graduate who has read even *Werther* or *Faust, Part I* is all but extinct. That is a shame, because he still has so much to offer us.

Goethe saw Mozart play in Frankfurt in 1763, when Mozart was seven and Goethe was fourteen. The period in which Goethe was raised was comfortably premodern, and a sense of the sacred was still widespread. John Milton would write in 1767, "God is as here and will be found alike / Present and of His presence many a sign."[3] Yet Goethe lived through the French Revolution and the Napoleonic Wars. He watched the Industrial Revolution change the way men and women earned their livings as well as their relationship with nature. He was a contemporary of Isaac Newton, whose clockwork universe—once set in motion—had neither need nor room for divine intervention. Goethe lived in an accelerating and increasingly secular age in which belief in transcendence was fading rapidly. He lived, in other words, in an age much like our own.

Yet Goethe never lost his capacity for awe, which he considered "the finest portion of mankind."[4] All things may be impermanent, but transcendence is not necessary to retain a sense of the sacred. Life has meaning and joy insofar as we strive to capture beauty, show love, and build things of value. Blaise Pascal wrote that "all the unhappiness of men arises from one single fact, that they cannot stay quietly in their own chamber."[5] Goethe had no desire to do so. Embrace your appetites, he tells us. Exercise your power. Foster your love. Above all, "Gedenke zu leben" (Remember to live).

Life

Johann Wolfgang Goethe was born on August 28, 1749, in Frankfurt am Main, a "free" city-state within the remnants of the Holy Roman Empire, which at that time included Habsburg Austria, as well as Prussia and the numerous small principalities and republics that would later become Germany. Goethe's father, Johann Caspar Goethe, was a trained attorney but practiced law only briefly. After his political ambitions sputtered, he purchased an honorific title, imperial councilor, and lived off his inherited properties. He collected paintings and assembled a substantial library.

Johann Caspar was thirty-eight when he married seventeen-year-old Catharina Elisabeth Textor, daughter of the city's lord mayor. Goethe and his sister, Cornelia, who was born in 1750, were the only two children of the marriage to survive infancy. They were very close. Cornelia worshiped her brilliant brother, and Goethe was devastated when she died during childbirth in 1777.

Johann Caspar strictly oversaw his son's education and also arranged for private tutors. The boy had a knack for languages, learning Latin, Greek, French, Italian, English, and even a smattering of Hebrew. Like any gentleman of the time, he also learned to ride, fence, and dance.

When Goethe was ten, the French occupied Frankfurt as part of the Seven Years' War (1756-1763) that enveloped most of Europe. The French forces requisitioned the lower floors of the Goethe family home but otherwise respected the family. A French theater was established, and Goethe regularly attended plays by Molière, Racine, and others. His future character Wilhelm Meister would develop a comparable infatuation with the theater. Both fathers—Goethe's real one and Wilhelm's fictional one—disapproved.

When it came time for college in 1766, Goethe wanted to study classics. But his father sent him to Leipzig to read law. There, at the age of seventeen, he had the first of his many love affairs. After three years of legal studies, however, Goethe suffered a near-fatal hemorrhage and what appeared to be a nervous breakdown. His illness kept him at home in Frankfurt for almost two years. He studied philosophy, beginning a lifelong fascination with Spinoza. He also took drawing lessons and read widely in world literature, especially Shakespeare, as he slowly recovered his physical and mental health.

Goethe resumed and completed his legal studies in Strasbourg in 1771, where he had another love affair. He then worked in a desultory way as a barrister from 1772 until 1774, mostly in Frankfurt but including a short, eventful stay at the Imperial Court in Wetzlar in 1772. There he met Charlotte Buff, a charming and beautiful young woman, with whom Goethe became fascinated, even though (or perhaps because) she was already engaged to another, more successful lawyer, Johann Christian Kestner. The three were close friends, but Goethe's growing passion for

Lotte, as she was called, rendered the situation untenable, which Kestner gently but clearly made known to Goethe. He left Wetzlar abruptly, without taking leave of either Lotte or Kestner, but continued to correspond with Kestner when safely back in Frankfurt. The letters he received from Kestner were the catalyst for Goethe's first novel, *The Sorrows of Young Werther*.

Goethe may have been negligent with his legal career, but he was anything but with his artistic aspirations. His famous dictum, "Ohne Hast, aber ohne Rast" (Without haste, but without rest), is a fair description of the dedication he showed throughout most of his life. His first literary success came in 1773 with the historical drama *Götz von Berlichingen*, about a courageous and free-spirited knight who demands his feudal freedom. Under siege, and his surrender demanded by a captain in the imperial army, Götz responds, "Er kann mich im Arsch lecken!" (He can lick my ass!). Immortal words, to be sure, but more Shakespeare than Racine.

The following year, his epistolary novel, *The Sorrows of Young Werther*, brought him instant fame and a certain notoriety throughout Europe. Both *Götz* and, even more so, *Werther* were the founding exemplars of German Romanticism, the so-called *Sturm und Drang* (storm and stress) movement of the late eighteenth century.[6]

On the rebound from Lotte, Goethe became engaged to Lili Schönemann, daughter of a prominent banking family in Frankfurt. But Goethe had second thoughts, terminated the engagement after only a few months, and abruptly left for Weimar in late 1775 when he was summoned there by the youthful Duke Karl August. Lili managed quite well in her own rebound, marrying a wealthy baron just before her own family went bankrupt.

In Weimar, Goethe was a member of the duke's privy council. Aside from two years in Italy, he passed most of the rest of his life there. He served in various administrative positions, including overseeing roads, the army, and, for a time, the finances. He even led an unsuccessful effort to reopen some defunct silver mines. More successfully and more logically, he helped turn Weimar into a cultural center and home to writers and intellectuals in Weimar proper and at the nearby University of Jena.

Needless to say, Goethe promptly formed yet another romantic attachment, this time to Charlotte von Stein, a married woman who offered only friendship in return. Goethe threw himself into administrative work, determined to make himself a man of practical as well as intellectual wisdom. His father died in 1782, the same year Goethe was ennobled by the duke and added "von" to his name. He continued to write, but not with the concentration he needed. He finished an array of short poems in many genres and began several promising works, including a prose version of his play *Iphigenia in Tauris* and an early draft of what would become part of *Wilhelm Meister's Apprenticeship*. But his writing faltered.

Tired of administrative duties and of his stalled relationship with Charlotte von Stein, Goethe abruptly left for Italy without taking leave of either Charlotte or the duke. He traveled under an assumed name so that he would not everywhere be recognized as the author of *Werther*. Goethe spent the next two years in Italy, mostly in Rome, absorbed by classical art and architecture, sketching constantly, and reclaiming the silver mine of his imagination, a vein that he would never exhaust.

Goethe returned to Weimar in 1788, where he received a retroactive blessing for his trip from the duke, happy to welcome back Weimar's most famous citizen. Goethe still advised the duke in a confidential capacity but largely dropped his official duties. He played a more cultural role as head of Weimar's vibrant theater and overseer of the art institute. In this capacity, he would later be able to provide a much-needed stipend to the young Georg Wilhelm Friedrich Hegel when he was a struggling academic in Jena. Most important, he produced an outpouring of remarkable and remarkably varied works that would not cease until his death in 1832.

In July 1788, shortly after his return to Weimar, Goethe was approached while walking in a park on the river Ilm by the twenty-three-year-old Christiane Vulpius. She was bearing a petition from her brother, who hoped to pursue his education but lacked the finances to do so. Christiane became Goethe's mistress, apparently that same afternoon, and soon thereafter moved into the back rooms of his house. This relationship, like Rousseau's with Thérèse Levasseur, puzzled Goethe's friends and was widely deplored. Charlotte von Stein was prepared to forgive Goethe for his abrupt departure to Italy, but not for his relationship with the uneducated, unsophisticated, and impoverished Christiane. She broke with Goethe completely. The rest of Weimar society simply acted as if Christiane did not exist. Goethe was welcome everywhere, Christiane nowhere.

An early sketch of Christiane reveals pleasant features, an abundance of mussed hair, and a frank sexuality. She clearly fulfilled a need in Goethe, though not solely a sexual one. She was cheerful, efficient, and uncomplicated. They had five children, only one of whom—August, born in 1789—survived infancy. Later in life, perhaps as a result of her isolation and consequent boredom, Christiane drank too much and became corpulent.[7] But Goethe never failed in his devotion to her.

Goethe wrote a series of poems between 1788 and 1790 that were later published under the title *Roman Elegies*. They focus on his relationship in Rome with a mysterious woman known as Faustina, but Faustina gradually morphs into Christiane in the poetry cycle. It is a poetry of sensual fulfilment, not just the sensual longing of *Werther*. It harks back to the love elegies of Tibullus, Propertius, and, above all, Ovid,[8] introducing a classical leavening of Goethe's youthful Romanticism that would transform all his later works. Indeed, in his old age, he was scathing in his assessment of German Romanticism:

> I call the classic *healthy* and the romantic *sick*. . . . Most newer works are romantic, not because they are new, but because they are weak, sickly, and sick, and the works of the Ancients are classical, not because they are ancient, but because they are strong, fresh, happy, and healthy.[9]

Another factor that separated Goethe from the Romantics was his reaction to the French Revolution of 1789. Younger Germans, such as the philosopher Hegel and the poet Friedrich Hölderlin, were enthusiastic celebrants. Goethe called it "the most dreadful of all events."[10] It is not that Goethe did not recognize the egregious abuses of the monarchy and the aristocracy and the miserable conditions of the peasantry. But he was clear-eyed about the consequences of chaos that would manifest themselves in the Terror of 1793/1794. "If a man has freedom enough to live healthily, and to work at his craft," he would later explain to his Boswell, Johann Eckermann, "he has enough; and so much all can easily obtain."[11] Maybe not so easily. But Goethe had a conservative's instinctive regard for stability. He encountered the horrors of war directly while accompanying the duke and the Prussian army at the Battle of Valmy in 1792 and again at the siege of Mainz in 1793.

Goethe formed a deep friendship with the playwright Friedrich Schiller, who wrote *The Robbers*, *Don Carlos*, and other plays epitomizing the *Sturm und Drang* movement. Schiller, like Goethe, was an early proponent of German Romanticism but, under Goethe's influence, became increasingly classical in works he wrote for the Weimar theater.

Yet *Sturm und Drang* came to Weimar regardless in 1806, when French forces under the command of Napoleon defeated the Prussian army at the Battle of Jena. The French occupied the city, and a stray band of soldiers burst into Goethe's house seeking wine. Goethe confronted them dressed only in his nightshirt. The drunken soldiers were intimidated by the great man and left but returned later with bayonets drawn. This time, the redoubtable Christiane sounded the alarm and chased them out. Goethe married her a few days later. Christiane, now Mrs. Goethe, suddenly became socially acceptable. When she died in 1816, Goethe's diary entry read, "My wife nearing her end. Final frightful struggle of her being. She departed toward midday. Emptiness and deathly quiet in and around me."[12] Five years later, however, the evergreen, seventy-two-year-old Goethe would pay court and propose marriage (albeit unsuccessfully) to a seventeen-year-old girl.

Napoleon formally dissolved the Holy Roman Empire, an event that caused hardly a ripple in the loose amalgam of states, principalities, and cities nominally within it. Goethe admired Napoleon for his ability to impose order: "His life was the stride of a demigod, from battle to battle, and from victory to victory."[13] Goethe would even make a suggestion, later seized on by the philosopher Friedrich Nietzsche, that "extraordinary people like Napoleon are outside morality; they operate like physical causes such as fire and water."[14] Napoleon, who claimed to have read *Werther* seven times, was an admirer in turn. He awarded Goethe

the Legion of Honor in 1808, remarking to those assembled, "Voila, un homme!" (Behold a man!).

Grand Duke Karl August, Goethe's longtime patron, died in 1828. Goethe's son died in Rome two years later. Yet he finished *Faust, Part II*, in 1831. It was published after his death, along with his autobiography and a record of his extensive conversations with Johann Peter Eckermann between 1823 and 1832. Nietzsche called *Conversations with Goethe* "the greatest German book," but Goethe himself had broader aspirations, and not just as an aging sage. As he explained to Eckermann, "national literature means little these days; the epoch of world literature is at hand."[15]

Goethe would leave behind, among others works of world literature, five major dramas: *Götz* (1773), *Egmont* (1788), *Iphigenia* (1787), *Torquato Tasso* (1790), and *Faust, Part I* and *Part II* (1808, 1831); four powerful but widely different novels: *Werther* (1774), *Wilhelm Meister's Apprenticeship* (1796), *Elective Affinities* (1809), and *Wilhelm Meister's Travels* (1821); a quasi-epic pastoral: *Hermann and Dorothea* (1797); several autobiographical writings, including *Out of My Life: Poetry and Truth* (1811–1830) and *Italian Journey* (1817); monographs on the metamorphosis of plants, the phenomenology of color, and other scientific issues; volumes of essays and criticism; a book of maxims and reflections; and a wealth of poems in all styles, dozens of which were set to music as lieder, most notably by Franz Schubert, including "Die Erlkönig," which, as sung by the great baritone Dietrich Fischer-Dieskau, is a perfect and compelling fusion of poetry, music, and performance. Goethe also served as an administrator, a minister of state, and a theater director, among other posts.

Goethe died on March 22, 1832. He was eighty-two, his long life bisected by the French Revolution. It would be hard to imagine a richer and more complete life. Goethe was considered Olympian even by his contemporaries, both godlike and remote. We can say of him, echoing Napoleon: here, indeed, was a man.

WERTHER

Goethe claims to have written *Werther* in a mere four weeks. That may be a slight exaggeration, but one compatible with the Romantic vision of genius as an outpouring of passion, uninhibited by traditional forms or social conventions. Goethe, the twenty-five-year-old sometime barrister, did more than anyone else to establish that trope.

His *Werther* burst forth out of Goethe's own emotional turmoil. Indeed, he drew so heavily on his relationship with Charlotte Buff and Johann Kestner that Kestner mildly reproached him for the too obvious parallels: "If . . . you had consulted your heart a bit, then the real persons, from whom you borrowed features, would not have been so exposed to disgrace."[16] Goethe also used specific details and even exact language from Kestner's detailed description of the suicide of their mutual friend, Karl Wilhelm Jerusalem. Today, such direct reliance might lead to a minor literary scandal.[17] But, in 1774, it caused a literary sensation and launched a cult of sensibility to counter the Enlightenment fixation on reason.

There were precursors of Goethe's epistolary novel, most notably Rousseau's *Nouvelle Héloïse* (1761) and Samuel Richardson's *Clarissa* (1748). Those works, too, were extremely popular, though for most modern readers their excessive length detracts from, rather than contributes to, their emotional impact. More significantly, those novels involve letters from multiple sources, and the letters themselves often advance the plot rather than just report on it. In Goethe's novel, all the letters are written by Werther. With few exceptions, we are encased in his consciousness and carried along by the sheer force of his perceptions and the beauty of his prose despite any reservations we might harbor about his character. Not even the respective *Confessions* of Saint Augustine and Rousseau deliver to us so fully the inner life of their subjects. For better and worse, we see the world in real time as Werther sees it. The compact intensity of this psychological study all but compels us to identify with him. Goethe was insistent on this point:

> [*Werther*] belongs to the life of every individual who must accommodate himself and his innate and instinctive sense of freedom to the irksome restrictions of an obsolescent world. Happiness unattained, ambition unfulfilled, desires unsatisfied are the defects not of any particular age, but of every individual human being. It would be a pity indeed if

everyone had not once in his life known a period when it seemed to him as if *Werther* had been written especially for him.[18]

Goethe knew such a period, and it was the writing of *Werther*—the transformation of reality into art—that enabled him to survive it. "It was inevitable, then," he explained, "that I would breathe into the project upon which I had just embarked all the fire that allows for no distinction between what is poetic and what is truthful."[19] Goethe, who conquered his demons through art, once described all his works as "fragments of a great confession."

Although Werther has fire and passion, he cannot channel his turbulent emotions into art, as Goethe was able to do. He is a dilettante, in love with the idea of being an artist, but without the talent or discipline to make that his reality or, rather, as Goethe would put it, to turn his reality into art. "I could not draw a single line at the present moment," he admits, "and yet I feel that I was never a greater painter than I am now."[20] In this, Werther sounds rather like Oscar Wilde's pseudo-eponymous character in *The Importance of Being Earnest*: "I don't play accurately—anyone can play accurately—but I play with wonderful expression. As far as the piano is concerned, sentiment is my forte."[21] Werther has an artist's eye but not an artist's hand. He also lacks the humor and self-recognition of Algernon cum Earnest. Sentiment is his forte, and an aesthetic sensibility unchecked by pragmatism will prove his undoing.

The unnamed editor of Werther's letters addresses the reader in a preamble: "You will not be able to withhold your admiration and love for his spirit and character or your tears for his fate."[22] This is true despite Werther's very great flaws, including a narcissism of stunning proportions. We feel the urgent longing of his soul and the depth of his need for a defining personal narrative that transcends ordinary human existence.

Werther loves children, outcasts, and the impoverished. He has a way with "people of that sort" and is quickly on familiar terms with them.[23] But he is wholly incapable of adjusting himself to the broader world of affairs. At one point, urged by his friend Wilhelm, to whom his letters are directed, he parts from Charlotte and becomes secretary to an ambassador. But Werther's attempt to submerge his passion and to find meaning in work inevitably ends in disaster. Like Rousseau in similar circumstances, Werther has nothing but contempt for a superior whose manner of doing business "is so ridiculous that I often cannot help contradicting him and doing things my own way."[24] The ambassador even requires Werther to rewrite his reports to make them lifeless and bureaucratic. Worse, Werther—to whom distinctions of rank allegedly mean nothing—makes a humiliating social misstep by remaining at an assembly only for aristocrats and, with everyone looking on, is asked to leave. The sensitive Werther is simultaneously mortified by the slight and furious with himself for being mortified. We admire, even as we deplore, his ingenuous and uncompromising personality. "The world runs on from one folly to another," he insists, "and the man who, purely for the sake of others, and without any passion or inner compulsion of his own, toils after wealth or dignity, or any other phantom, is simply a fool."[25]

Werther recognizes that the happy man has simple wants, is content with little, and finds pleasure where he may. "Such a man is at peace, and creates his world out of his own soul—happy, because he is a human being."[26] But Werther cannot embrace such happiness. He can be neither content nor at peace. He is "a wanderer, a pilgrim on this earth!"[27]

Werther follows Rousseau in his love of nature. An early letter, before he even meets Charlotte, is justly famous for its description of a spring morning in a secluded spot which he feels "was created for souls like mine."[28]

> When the lovely valley teems with mist around me, and the high sun strikes the impenetrable foliage of my trees, and but a few rays steal into the inner sanctuary, I lie in the tall grass by the trickling stream and notice a thousand familiar things: when I hear the humming of the little world among the stalks, and am near the countless indescribable forms of the worms and insects, then I feel the presence of the Almighty Who created us in His own image, and the breath of that universal love which sustains us, as we float in an eternity of bliss; and then, my friend, when the world grows dim before my eyes and earth and sky seem to dwell in my soul and absorb its power, like the form of a beloved—then I often think with longing, Oh, would I could express it, could impress upon paper all that is loving, so full and warm within

me, that it might become the mirror of my soul, as my soul is the mirror of the infinite God! O my friend—but it will kill me—I shall perish under the splendor of these visions![29]

Nature, for Werther, is the embodiment of the divine. It penetrates and intermingles with his soul. It is the absolute in which he wants to immerse himself. But this pathetic fallacy—reading into nature one's own exalted feelings—has its dark side. Hegel will soon show that Being and Nothingness are but two false flags of endless becoming. As scholar David Wellbery profoundly notes, Werther seeks "an absolute which—precisely because it exists outside any system of differentiation—appears to the subject both as Being itself, divine presence, and as Nothingness, the radical absence of divinity."[30] Werther, in his attempted embrace of Being, is only a shadow away from the Nothingness into which he will slide.

This elusive contrast between the universe as a divine presence and "an ever devouring, ever ruminating monster"[31] is what Werther brings to his love for Charlotte. For Werther, there can be no compromise. Love, too, must be either "an eternity of bliss" or "the abyss of an ever-open grave."[32]

Charlotte might seem an unlikely surrogate for such extremes. The French theorist Roland Barthes dismisses Charlotte as "quite insipid; she is the paltry character of a powerful, tormented, flamboyant drama staged by the subject Werther."[33] But, of course, part of what Werther loves about Charlotte is that she is not him. She quiets his tortured mind as "she moves in a tranquil happiness within the confined circle of her existence."[34] That is precisely what Werther himself cannot do and even disdains in others. But, in Charlotte, he finds it a balm: "So much simplicity with so much intelligence—so kind, and yet so resolute—a mind so calm, and a life so active."[35] Most of all, Charlotte is vibrantly alive. "She dances with her whole heart and soul: her body is all harmony, elegance, and grace, as if nothing else mattered, as if she had no other thought or feeling; and, doubtless, for the moment, everything else has ceased to exist for her."[36] Charlotte is not plagued by the self-consciousness that separates Werther from others and from himself. He knows neither grace nor harmony and yet longs for both.

In his love for Charlotte, Werther finds his grand narrative.[37] But it is a narrative with only one possible ending. As Charlotte herself notes, her unavailability is part of his attraction to her. In some sense, at least, Werther luxuriates in the misery of his rejected love. It confirms his Romantic self-image as a tragic hero, harboring a passion too great for ordinary life. He will embrace the abyss. "Oh, Wilhelm, how willingly would I have given up my human existence to merge with the wind, or to embrace the torrent!"[38]

How far do Charlotte's own romantic feelings for Werther extend? She clearly has them. There is ample flirtation, as when she has a little bird eat from her lips and then from Werther's. Nor does she discourage his frequent visits and their long walks. But she nonetheless draws a line. She remains within the bounds of proper behavior and respect for her husband. According to Werther, "she would have been happier with me than with him. Albert is not the man to satisfy the wishes of such a heart."[39] But there is no reason to think this is true. Albert is rather bland, but he is also stable, and a peaceful stability is clearly an important component of the ordinary human happiness that Charlotte seeks. Albert does not love Charlotte with the all-consuming passion of Werther, but it is hard to imagine a life with Werther as anything but tempestuous and ultimately unhappy.

The fact is, we don't know Charlotte's true feelings because Werther does not allot Charlotte an inner life. His image of her is all on the surface, and even her external actions are related to us by a subjective narrator eager to see in every mark of preference or affection a shared romantic passion. Only at the end of the book does the neutral narrator, with jarring omniscience, give us deeper insights into Charlotte's own turmoil, when Werther finally presses beyond the bounds she has set by throwing himself at her feet and seizing her hands.

> Her thoughts were confused: she held his hands, pressed them to her bosom; and, turning toward him with the tenderest expression, her burning cheek touched his. They lost sight of everything. The

world vanished before them. He clasped her in his arms tightly, and covered her trembling, stammering lips with furious kisses. "Werther!" she cried with choking voice, turning away. "Werther!" and, with a feeble hand, pushed him from her. And again, more composed and from the depth of her heart, she repeated, "Werther!" He did not resist, released her, and threw himself before her. Charlotte rose, and with confusion and grief, trembling between love and resentment, she exclaimed, "This is the last time, Werther! You shall never see me again!"[40]

Werther will play his self-assigned part to the end. In his farewell letter, he cites the previous night's events as proof that she loves him: "The sacred fire of your lips still burns upon mine. . . . She loves me! . . . She is mine! Yes, Charlotte, you are mine forever!"[41] He calls particular attention to the fact that the pistols he has borrowed from Albert passed through Charlotte's hands: "You, Charlotte, offer me the weapon. You, from whose hands I wished to receive my death. Now—my wish is gratified. I asked my servant. You trembled when you gave him the pistols, but you bade me no farewell."[42] The isolated, unsanctified spot where he asks to be buried, and even the clothes he wears—buff-colored pants tucked into high boots, a yellow waistcoat, and a blue cutaway—are all planned for maximum effect.[43] "The body was carried by workmen. No clergyman attended."[44]

None of this posing detracts from the unfeigned misery suffered by Werther. He is indeed a wanderer on the earth. In a world of endless becoming, we must forge our own meaning. But the absolutes Werther demands—in art, in nature, in religion, and in love—all fail him.[45] He finds no meaning in his life and no home to receive him except the abyss of an ever-open grave. His "heart is now dead; no delight will flow from it."[46]

Werther's end is wrenching. And yet it is also a monstrous act of revenge against the quotidian contentment of Charlotte and Albert. Incredibly, Werther expresses a hope that his death will free them both to be happy, as if he were making a supreme sacrifice for their sake. His ego is a black hole that drags Charlotte and Albert into the depths of his own unfathomable darkness. Three lives are destroyed.

Werther resonated deeply throughout Europe. Happiness unattained, ambition unfulfilled, and desires unsatisfied are indeed known to every individual human being. But, as Goethe later put it, "everyone now burst out with his exaggerated demands, ungratified passions, and imagined suffering."[47] There were even rumors of copycat suicides, right down to the clothes Werther wore, committed by readers carrying the slender volume as if it were a passport to romantic apotheosis.

Goethe disclaimed responsibility for such extravagance, noting that Werther was a warning, not a model: "From the outset Werther's youthful bloom is shown as blighted by a fatal worm."[48] True, perhaps, but not completely convincing. Goethe himself had solicited admiration for Werther's character and tears for his fate. But the book's reception was undoubtedly pivotal in Goethe's own turn away from the German Romanticism he created. In an echo of Hamlet, Werther had asked, "What is man—that much praised demigod?"[49] In *Faust*, Goethe will provide a more classical answer to that question.

FAUST

The legend of Dr. Johann Georg Faust, who sold his soul to the devil for pleasure and power, was in circulation for centuries before the British playwright Christopher Marlowe wrote his *Tragical History of the Life and Death of Doctor Faustus* in 1592. Goethe himself knew the story from a young age through puppet shows and chapbooks (an early incarnation of inexpensive, illustrated paperbacks). Faust was already what the critic Ian Watt has labeled one of the "myths of modern individualism,"[50] joining Don Juan, Don Quixote, and Robinson Crusoe as an archetype of human consciousness, before Goethe turned the story to his own purposes to grapple with the dramatic changes in philosophy, science, politics, economics, and technology that marked the Enlightenment and its aftermath.

Goethe started on *Faust* in 1772, at the age of twenty-three. Progress was slow and sporadic. An early manuscript version, known as the *Urfaust*, was developed between 1772 and 1775. *Faust: Ein Fragment* was published in 1790, but Part I of the drama was not completed until 1806 and was published only in 1808. Goethe returned to it in the mid-1820s, finishing Part II in July 1831 but sealing the manuscript with instructions that it not be published until after his death, which came the following year.

Goethe thus labored on *Faust* on and off for sixty years. During that time, the American and French Revolutions exploded, followed by the Napoleonic Wars, the dissolution of the Holy Roman Empire, two Restorations, and the July Revolution of 1830, all against the background of an Industrial Revolution that shifted power from landowners to capitalists and diverted workers from agriculture to factories.

Goethe was remarkably productive during this sixty-year period. An enormous literary output flowed readily from his pen. But *Faust* was a struggle from the beginning. It was Goethe's attempt to answer the question of what it is to be a human being in the face of such changes. Classical, medieval, and Renaissance cultures provided a coherent framework for life and society, but where are meaning and purpose to be found in our secular, fragmented world? Some say *Faust* marked the end of the Western literary tradition that began with Homer. I would suggest, rather, that it deliberately splintered that established path in a thousand directions. The countless allusions to Homer, Dante, Milton, and Shakespeare—to name just a few—are a calculated literary overload, in which parody becomes both tribute and pitiless measuring stick. What worked in the past does not necessarily work in the present.

The resulting "play" is as fragmented and incoherent (as that term is used in physics, to indicate light waves that are of different lengths and out of sync with one another) as the world it purports to be portray. Harold Bloom, though a great admirer of Goethe, called *Faust* "the most grotesque and unassimilable of major Western poems in dramatic form."[51] Goethe's protégé, Friedrich Schelling, was more polite but still equivocal in calling it "a work comparable only to itself and completely self-contained."[52] The German poet Heinrich Heine argued to the contrary that "it is really as spacious as the Bible and, like it, embraces heaven and earth, together with man and his exegesis."[53] Small wonder that readers, particularly of Part II, have been alternately dazzled and bemused by the array of genres and voices.

Marlowe's *Doctor Faustus* was a relatively straightforward morality play. Having mastered the standard faculties—logic, medicine, law, and divinity—Faustus is "glutted now with learning's golden gifts."[54] In his midlife crisis, he meddles in magic and necromancy and summons up Mephistopheles, the servant of Lucifer. Faustus bids Mephistopheles to strike a deal for him with his master:

Say [Faustus] surrenders up to him his soul,
So he will spare him four and twenty years,
Letting him live in all voluptuousness,
Having thee ever to attend on me,
To give me whatsoever I shall ask,
To tell me whatsoever I demand.[55]

It is a simple bargain. Faustus writes the deed of gift with his own blood as Mephistopheles mutters, "He will buy my service with his soul."[56]

Needless to say, the twenty-four years quickly pass. After them looms an eternity. Not even a reincarnation of Helen of Troy—"the face that launched a thousand ships / And burnt the topless towers of Ilium"[57]—is sufficient to make the bargain anything but one-sided. Faustus would bid time stop:

Stand still, you ever-moving sphere of heaven,

. . .

That Faustus may repent and save his soul.

. . .

Ugly hell, gape not! Come not, Lucifer!
I'll burn my books! Ah, Mephistopheles![58]

Alas, repentance is in vain. Faustus's body is torn apart by demons and his soul consigned to hell. Nothing in earth's ephemera is worth a man's immortal soul.

But suppose there is no immortal soul. Suppose ephemera are all we have. No heaven to reward; no hell to punish. Can we find any satisfaction or meaning in our lives? In such a light, Faust's wager with Mephistopheles casts a very different shadow.

We meet Goethe's Faust on the brink of suicide. Like his British precursor, he has studied everything and learned nothing. "The very thing one needs one does not know, / And what one knows is needless information."[59] Using magic, he summons the Earth Spirit "to grant me a vision of Nature's forces / That bind the world, all its seeds and sources / And innermost life—all this I shall see."[60] But the Earth Spirit—a clear reference to Spinoza's equation of God with Nature—rejects his request.

> In life like a flood, in deeds like a storm
> I surge to and fro,
> Up and down I flow!
> Birth and the grave
> An eternal wave,
> Turning, returning,
> A life ever burning:
> At Time's whirring loom I work and play
> God's living garment I weave and display.[61]

Faust can never obtain that vision. He can observe the external garment, but he cannot comprehend the innermost life of the world.

> I am not like a god! Too deeply now I feel
> This truth. I am a worm stuck in the dust,
> Burrowing and feeding, where at last I must
> Be crushed and buried by some rambler's heel.[62]

Faust longs "to soar beyond the dust / Into the realm of high ancestral minds."[63] He knows that is impossible. Yet he stops short of taking the dark, brown potion he has prepared. His hand is stayed by beauty and by childhood memory. It is Easter morning, and he hears a chorus singing and bells chiming: "These strains, so long familiar, still / They call me back to life."[64] He no longer believes the message of salvation, but the echoes of that belief bring before him a long-forgotten day "when a bell's chime / Was deep mysterious music, and to pray / Was fervent ecstasy."[65]

This ancient enchantment is enough to keep Faust alive, though he knows that he is deceived by his own homesick heart. In a remarkable passage, he curses everything that men strive for on earth: high pretense, intellectual pride, surface beauty, honor, fame, property, even wife and child.

> I curse love's sweet transcendent call,
> My curse on faith! My curse on hope!
> My curse on patience above all![66]

Yet even in this despair, or, rather, especially in this despair, Faust is susceptible to Mephistopheles. The mere memory of belief is enough to give him a phantom flicker of hope. Only the faintest line separates what he curses and what he cherishes.

Goethe's Faust does not barter his immortal soul. He has none to trade away. Instead, he makes a bet with Mephistopheles that Mephistopheles can show him nothing in human life so wonderful, so fair, so compelling that he would to the moment say, "Verweile doch! Du bist so schön!" (Beautiful moment, do not pass away!). Mephistopheles, like Milton's Satan, is a nihilist: "I am the spirit of perpetual negation."[67] He sees no value in any aspect of human life. All things deserve to perish. But Mephistopheles thinks that he can instill in Faust an illusion of value. Either way, Mephistopheles wins: either Faust finds nothing worth retaining and lapses back into his own nihilism or he falls under the sway of an illusion that will inevitably disappoint and condemn him.

Yet, either way, Faust wins as well. Faust's goal is experience, not pleasure. He wants, through constant striving, to learn firsthand all that life has to offer.

> I tell you, the mere pleasure's not the point!
> To dizzying, painful joy I dedicate
> Myself, to refreshing frustration, loving hate!
> I've purged the lust for knowledge from my soul;

Now the full range of suffering it shall face,
And in my inner self I will embrace
The experience allotted to the whole
Race of mankind; my mind shall grasp the heights
And depths, my heart know all their sorrows and delights.
Thus I'll expand myself, and their self I shall be,
And perish in the end, like all humanity.[68]

"Thus I'll expand myself, and their self I shall be" (Und so mein eigen Selbst zu ihrem Selbst erweitern—literally, "And so mine own self in their selves enlarge"). Faust wants to know the full scope, including the heights and depths, of human existence, to view it whole and sound, and judge what it is worth.

Mephistopheles scoffs at this pretension. No one can view life whole and sound except God (or, we might add, an artist of genius). Even extraordinary men like Faust must be satisfied with their limited perspective.

We do assure you, such totality
Is only for a god; perpetual light
Is God's alone, me and my kind
He has banished to darkness, and you'll find
You men must live with day and night.[69]

Faust accepts the challenge: "Yet I swear I'll achieve it!"[70] If ever he grows so tired as to forfeit his will and cease his striving for "totality" and "perpetual light," he will be ready to die.

Faust's wager warrants comparison with Pascal's, generally misunderstood as a throw of the dice in which Pascal chooses to believe in God and lead a pious life in the hope of infinite happiness after death. The potential long-run payoff supposedly dwarfs the sacrifice, however small the odds, that the faithful are indeed rewarded in an afterlife.[71] By contrast, Faust seeks to experience this life as fully as possible. The immediate payoff supposedly outweighs the infinitesimal risk of a life after death in which he will have to become the servant of Mephistopheles. Pascal chooses death; Faust chooses life.

In fact, Pascal and Faust are closer than one might expect. Both seek glimmers of the perpetual light of the divine. Pascal believes the light is real and that someday he will see its totality. That is the only way he can make sense of the world as he experiences it. Faust believes it is an ancestral illusion, but he dares, and perhaps even wants, Mephistopheles to prove him wrong. Pascal and Faust share the same longing for the absolute and the same doubts. God has disappeared behind the mechanical universe of Descartes and Newton. So where are we to find anything of true value? Pascal's answer is to sit quietly in a room and wait for illumination. Faust's answer is to scour human life from top to bottom in search of what he does not expect but secretly hopes to find. The Faust of Part I is a quintessential Romantic in contrast to the world-weary realism of Mephistopheles.

Faust certainly does not find meaning in the first place Mephistopheles takes him, which is Auerbach's Tavern, a pale counterpart to Shakespeare's Boar's Head Inn, frequented by Falstaff and Prince Hal. The merrymakers at Auerbach's are a sorry crew in comparison, though Mephistopheles insists otherwise:

> Life can so easily be fun! These folk
> Have made it one long feast and one long joke.
> With little wit but with much pleasure
> Round in this narrow ring they dance their measure,
> Like kittens chasing their own tails.
> So long as their headache's not too bad
> And drinks on credit can be had,
> This carefree idyll never fails![72]

Faust unsurprisingly considers the tavern regulars stupid and vulgar and insists on leaving. Frosch is no Falstaff. This is the first, but certainly not the last, experience that fails to live up to the expectations created by literature. Indeed, that is a recurring theme of the drama, especially in Part II. The scholarly Faust, though ostensibly having left his vast library behind, still sees everything through the prism of books. He wants to know the world but is trapped within the Western canon, next to which the world seems shabby and shallow.

Mephistopheles decides to lighten Faust up by shedding thirty years with the help of a witch's brew. Asked if there is not a better way to stay youthful, Mephistopheles offers some surprisingly good advice. Work the land, he tells Faust. Live frugally, eat simple food, and be as humble and accepting as a beast. Defecate outdoors, and "be primitive / In body and mind."[73] Of course, Faust can no more follow such advice than he can take pleasure in the low life at Auerbach's Tavern. He is too proud of his intelligence and sophistication. Faust is already failing in his pledge to "mine own self in their selves enlarge." The lower half (or more) of humankind simply does not interest him, and he will share nothing of their lot. So the witch's brew it is, and Mephistopheles decides on Faust's next temptation, again drawn from literature: "With that elixir coursing through him, / Soon any woman will be Helen to him."[74]

Margareta, known familiarly as Gretchen, is no illusion. But neither is she Helen of Troy, the poetic embodiment of absolute beauty. Gretchen is a simple girl—devout, demure, and poor. She is very pretty but too easily dazzled by the noble-looking Faust and the box of jewels provided to him by Mephistopheles. Her very innocence and trust, and the return of his youthful vigor, combine to ignite Faust's lust. There follows an episode of conquest and destruction that Faust himself recognizes is more suitable for Don Juan than for himself. He expresses scruples, but Mephistopheles brushes them away and assures Faust that when the time comes, he will, like all others, make false "vows of love, and nonsense of that kind."[75] When Faust responds—"It will come from my heart"[76]—we know that Gretchen's downfall and Faust's hypocrisy are assured. "Don't be afraid!" he later tells her:

> Oh, let my eyes,
> My hands on your hands tell you what
> No words can say:
> To give oneself entirely and to feel
> Ecstasy that must last for ever!

For ever!—For its end would be despair.
No, never-ending! Never ending![77]

Gretchen's story unfolds as expected. She is seduced and abandoned. So much for "never-ending! Never ending!" Worse, to enable their tryst, she gives her mother a sleeping draft provided by Faust from which she never awakes. Still worse, her soldier brother, Valentine, seeks to avenge her honor but is parried by Mephistopheles, who then paralyzes Valentine's arm while Faust, who is no soldier, delivers a killing thrust. Valentine dies cursing his sister in the most vulgar terms. Gretchen goes mad (like Hamlet's Ophelia) and drowns her newborn baby. She is imprisoned and condemned to die.

Meanwhile, Faust is off with Mephistopheles at a Walpurgis Night gathering of spirits on the highest summit in the Harz Mountains. There are deliberate echoes of Shakespeare's *Midsummer Night's Dream* in the confusion of voices and the puckish will-o'-the-wisp, who serves as their guide, but none of the lyrical magic of that play. The spirits are caustic and bitter, and their tedious epigrams lack the saving grace of love. They diminish rather than expand. In an enlightened world, of course, they should not even exist. Yet they decline to disappear on that account. One even takes on the form of Gretchen—pale, imprisoned, and facing imminent execution.

Faust blames Mephistopheles for hiding Gretchen's plight from him and "lull[ing] [him] with vulgar diversions."[78] Mephistopheles understandably takes issue with that accusation: "Who was it who ruined her? I, or you?"[79] Faust is furious—presumably with himself as much as Mephistopheles—and insists on rescuing Gretchen. But she will have none of it. Faust, like Macbeth, has blood on his hands that will not wash off. And she herself is prepared to face the righteous judgment of her God:

Oh Father, save me, do not reject me,
I am yours! Oh holy angels, receive
Me under your wings, surround me, protect me![80]

In a deliberately lame bit of stage business, Gretchen's penitence is enough to summon a voice from above to counter Mephistopheles's condemnation: "She is redeemed!"[81] The *deus ex machina* of classical Greek drama has been reduced to this. Despite a renewed promise to stay with her always, Faust disappears with Mephistopheles, and Part I ends with the faint voice of Gretchen calling after him in vain.

If that sounds like the plot of an opera, it is. It shares elements with Mozart's roughly contemporaneous *Don Giovanni*. The self-contained tragedy of Gretchen will itself be turned into an affecting, if somewhat cloying, opera (named for Faust, of course, not Gretchen) by the French composer Charles Gounod.

So far, Faust has utterly failed to enter into the lives of others and his "own self in their selves enlarge." He displays the same relentless subjectivity as Werther; Gretchen, like Charlotte, exists only in relation to himself. Faust cannot escape the shaping power of an imagination saturated in literature and driven by his own ego. It is not Faust who vanishes but the world he purports to experience.

Even that modicum of experience, moreover, is washed away in the prologue of Part II. Faust is responsible for four deaths: Gretchen, their child, her mother, and her brother. Yet we find him in a sort of earthly paradise, where spirits sing him to sleep and bathe him in the waters of Lethe.

> Heal now his heart, in noble elfin fashion:
> Soothe its fierce conflict and the bitter passion
> Of self-reproach's burning darts, make clean
> His soul of all the horrors it has seen.[82]

Those "horrors" are of Faust's own devising, with the help of Mephistopheles. Yet he awakes with the "pulse of life" breaking strong and pure and "new resolution taken / To strive on still towards supreme existence."[83] That dream-enhanced state will persist throughout Part II.

In the refracted rainbow of a waterfall, Faust has a vision:

I watch a mirror here of man's whole story,
And plain it speaks, ponder it as you will:
Our life's a spectrum-sheen of borrowed glory.[84]

Am farbigen Abglanz haben wir das Leben (literally, "In the reflection of color we have our life"). David Luke's translation is excellent in capturing the new German idealism inspired by such diverse figures as Johann Fichte (whom Goethe helped to a professorship at Jena), Hegel (to whom Goethe directed a much-needed subsidy), and Arthur Schopenhauer (whose overinvolved mother was one of the few Weimar residents to visit Christiane Vulpius before she became Mrs. Goethe). Goethe and Schopenhauer in particular shared a fascination with color, and, although their anti-Newtonian accounts diverged from each other, both believed that color is not an objective phenomenon but is shaped by our perceptions. In *The World as Will and Representation*, published in 1818, Schopenhauer argues that the entire phenomenal world—what we perceive—is merely a representation of our own making and that the underlying reality of the world—in Kantian terms, the "noumenal realm"—is nothing but ceaselessly churning will, a font of primal energy that exists outside of, but underwrites, the world of space and time.

Goethe was not following Schopenhauer in this regard, any more than he was following the only slightly less extravagant views of Hegel discussed in the next chapter. Goethe was not a philosopher and had little regard for abstract theories. But all of *Faust, Part II* is built around this basic dichotomy between "the ever-stirring, wholesome energy / Of life"[85] and the "spectrum-sheen of borrowed glory." The former gives rise to the latter, particularly in works of art, but also in our political structures and social institutions. Such cultural artifacts must always be renewed by the pulse of life lest they become dead things rather than outlets for creative power.

This point is illustrated—quite subtly—in Faust's encounter with the emperor, which immediately follows the prologue. The empire is all-but bankrupt. Many are the demands, but few are the sources of revenue. Mephistopheles offers a solution: "There is gold in the earth, coined and uncoined, / Hoards hidden under walls, rocks precious-veined."[86] The only problem is to find and extract it. Mephistopheles brushes that issue aside. We know it is there, and the emperor owns the land; therefore, the emperor owns the treasure and need simply issue letters of credit (paper currency) secured by the treasure. It is all a conjuring trick, an illusion, but as long as everyone goes along and "treat[s] this as sound money,"[87] it will become just that. And so it does. The emperor is suddenly rich and the empire on a sound fiscal footing. But, to maintain the illusion, to retain trust in the financial system, the emperor will occasionally have to dig into the primal hoard and "sell a golden chain or cup."[88] Without such replenishment, the illusion eventually ends in rampant inflation and bankruptcy. So, too, our cultural institutions must be constantly replenished by the ever-stirring, wholesome energy of life lest they become moribund and lose their meaning.

Mephistopheles's next conjuring trick is far more complicated. The emperor wants to see Helen and Paris, the ideal woman and man of Homer's *Iliad*. But, as Mephistopheles explains to Faust, "conjuring Helen out of time / Like phantom paper-money from the air,"[89] is a far more difficult task. He can produce only pale imitations, "Satan-sweethearts,"[90] that will remain lifeless and unconvincing. If Faust wants his re-creations to have the genuine pulse of life, he must dig into the primal sources of great art, as Homer himself did. Mephistopheles explains:

> Enthroned in solitude are goddesses—
> No place, no space around them, time still less [that is, they
> exist outside space and time];
> I mention them with some uneasiness.
> They are *the Mothers*.[91]

It is a comical moment, particularly for post-Freudian readers, but that does not detract from the seriousness of the allegory. There is no path to these ancient forces of creativity and fecundity. Anyone who seeks them will know solitude and desolation. Faust himself is only partly successful in re-creating the most famous couple of antiquity and making them his own: "What once has been, what once shone gloriously, / Still stirs there, seeking evermore to be."[92] But, as a medieval figure, Faust cannot truly enter into the classical experience. He can only present Helen and Paris as in a dumb show, while the guests of the emperor idly critique their looks and deportment. Faust desperately wants these classical figures to be a living presence: "Here are realities."[93] But, when he tries to intervene to prevent Paris's rape of Helen, the spirits dissolve into mist, and Faust is stunned by an explosion from the collision of the classical and the medieval worlds.

He awakes back in his former study, as if he must start anew. Part II begins in earnest on a different footing from Part I. As Goethe explained to Eckermann:

> The first part is almost entirely subjective; it proceeded entirely from a perplexed impassioned individual, and his semi-darkness is probably highly pleasing to mankind. But in the second part there is scarcely anything of the subjective; here is seen a higher, broader, clearer, more passionless world, and he who has not looked about him and had some experience will not know what to make of it.[94]

We can quibble with Goethe's explanation. Faust himself is far from passionless in Part II. But his passion is directed toward the "spectrum-sheen of borrowed glory," the worlds of culture, science, and government, each of which is treated with mock seriousness in Part II, though, again, the parody does not detract from the power of the allegory. Modern science is represented by the Homunculus—a little man in a test tube created by Faust's former student Wagner and clearly inspired by Mary Shelley's *Frankenstein*, published in 1818. Government is represented by the crumbling empire but also by the great reclamation project that occupies Faust's last years. Beauty and art are represented by Helen, and from the union of the classical Helen and the medieval Faust will be born Euphorion, the embodiment of modern poetry. *Faust, Part II* roams freely between these three cultural periods: ancient, medieval, and modern. History may be chronological, but all times will intermingle in Faust's consciousness. As Chiron, wisest of the centaurs, explains to Faust, "the bard's not bound by time—he makes his own."[95]

Faust is a man "steeped in medieval mist," who must escape "that mad world of monks and armor-plated / Knights."[96] In a classical Walpurgis Night, set as a counterpoint to the medieval Walpurgis Night of Part I, Faust encounters numerous figures from ancient Greece, including the Sphinx, the Sirens, Chiron, Oedipus, Ulysses, the Argonauts, Hercules, and even great Achilles. Like Goethe in Italy, Faust can regain the classical world only by leaving his study and cleaving to the earth of Greece.

> The soil her feet have trod, the sea
> That lapped against them; even enough for me
> This very air whose language was her own!
> Here, by a miracle, here I am in Greece!
> At once I sensed the ground; what could release
> Me from my sleep but this fresh spirit's glow!
> And thus I stand: Antaeus was strengthened so.[97]

Antaeus, son of the earth goddess, Gaia, had his strength renewed whenever he touched the earth. Hercules, realizing this, lifted him off the ground and crushed him. Faust will try to avoid a similar fate.

Having made his connection with the soil and air of Greece, Faust is ready to encounter a resurrected Helen. "She rules me now, my fixed, my guiding star: / I cannot live till I find Helena!"[98] In the event, it is Helena who comes to Faust. Home at last in Sparta, she learns that her husband, Menelaus, plans to sacrifice her in revenge for her elopement with Paris. Or so, at least, Mephistopheles tells her in the guise of the old hag Phorcyas. Helen's only escape from the rage of Menelaus is to become yet another man's mistress. Through "trails of mist," Helen escapes the classical world and finds refuge in the gothic castle of armor-plated Faust.

There follows an idyllic interlude in pastoral Arcadia, yet another chronological and geographical incongruity available to poetry. How long it lasts is unclear, but Faust and Helen give birth to Euphorion, "the future / Master-maker of all beauty."[99] Alas, "beauty weds not long with happiness."[100] Euphorion, like Antaeus, loses his connection with the earth, source of all poetry, when he tries to fly. On his death, Helen returns to the underworld, telling Faust:

The bond of love is severed now, and so of life;
Bewailing both, I bid a sorrowful farewell
To you, and cast myself once more into your arms.
Persephone, receive us both, the boy and me![101]

After failing yet again to hold on to evanescent beauty, Faust will opt for power. He rejoins forces with the emperor and resolves to reclaim land currently rendered useless by the rise and fall of the tide. He takes personal offense at the sea "venting its rage upon the flat, wide shore"[102] and resolves that "from our coast / I'll ban the lordly sea, I'll curb its force, / I'll set new limits to that watery plain / And drive it back into itself again."[103] It is an insane boast, akin to King Canute commanding the waves to recede or Xerxes ordering the waters of the Hellespont to be whipped in punishment after a storm destroys the pontoon bridges needed for his invasion of Greece. Faust's desire to control the elements smacks of the hubris of Greek tragedy. Yet he very nearly succeeds.

Faust becomes "feudal lord of all the coast"[104] and sends his slaves to tame the sea.

Dams and dikes built in a day
Stole the birthright of the waves
And usurped the ocean's sway.
Now green fields and gardens lie,
Woods and villages have grown
Up all round.[105]

But Faust's control is not complete. Worldly power always falls short. Adjacent to the reclaimed land, an old married couple, Baucis and Philemon, owns a small house amid some linden trees with an adjacent chapel. In Greek mythology, as told by Ovid,[106] Baucis and Philemon, despite their poverty, provided hospitality to two travelers spurned by all others in their village. The travelers were the gods Zeus and Hermes in disguise. Zeus destroyed the entire village except for the couple's cottage, which he turned into a temple where Baucis and Philemon served as guardians. He also granted them one wish, which, as requested by Baucis, was that "the same hour take us both together, / and that I should not live to see her tomb / nor she survive to bury me in mine."[107] They spent their remaining years quietly together until, on the verge of death, they were transformed into linden trees, standing side by side, sharing a single trunk, with their limbs intertwined.

It is a beautiful story, easily the loveliest in all of Ovid. The elderly couple finds happiness in a simple life of piety, hospitality, and devotion to each other. No ceaseless and therefore senseless striving—just a quiet, contented existence, marked by the tolling of the chapel bell. Faust cannot bear it. The unstoppable developer is stymied by a couple to whom money and power are as nothing. Each tolling of the bell is a reproach. He orders Mephistopheles to make them leave. "The old couple must give way! / I chose that linden clump as my / Retreat: those few trees not my own / Spoil the whole world that is my throne."[108]

It is "a rash command, too soon obeyed!"[109] When Mephistopheles and his henchmen manhandle the elderly couple, they drop dead of terror. A wanderer whom Baucis and Philemon once rescued from the sea, and who has returned to thank them, draws his sword in their defense and is also killed. In the struggle, live coals are scattered, and the house and chapel burn down. Faust's goal is achieved. He tries to disclaim the means—"I said exchange, not robbery! / Deaf savages! I curse this deed"[110]—but he can no more shift blame to his intermediaries than Henry II, who once asked, "Who will rid me of this troublesome priest?"

Though he does not know it, Faust's reclamation project is now doomed, as Baucis himself had predicted: "I'd not trust that soil for long."[111] The land that Faust thought would be the source of his strength will once again be mastered by the sea. Faust has lost his capacity for awe at the natural world, which he treats as something only to be controlled and shaped by his will. All sense of the sacred—which governed the premodern world—is gone. That loss is symbolized by his sudden blindness. Faust once recognized that "our sense of awe's what keeps us most alive. / The world chokes human feeling more and more, / But deep dread still can move us to the core."[112] Faust can no longer be moved even by the deepest dread or the most solemn of moral obligations. In his blindness, he believes the digging he hears is the completion of his project. In fact, the ghosts of the dead are digging his grave.

And yet Faust is saved. He has spent a lifetime in service of the devil (even though the devil is supposedly in service to him). He has compassed the death of seven people (not counting those killed in war). He has indulged his every desire. Sex and power have been the driving forces of his life. He is unrepentant. And yet Faust is saved. Why?

There are as many answers as there are Goethe scholars. Two competing themes predominate, marked by two magnificent speeches from Faust. One explanation is that Faust has laid the foundation for a modern paradise on earth. It is precisely his rejection of the premodern world, with its oppressive religion, rigid class structure, rampant inequality, and hapless "divine" monarchs, that redeems Faust. He has a vision for the future that he is striving to realize:

> Youth, manhood, age, their brave new world have founded.
> I long to see that multitude, and stand
> With a free people on free land!
> Then to the moment I might say:
> Beautiful moment, do not pass away![113]

Even the deaths of Baucis and Philemon may be justified as necessary to our progress toward utopia. As Rousseau explained, we must force men to be free, even if we kill them in the process. On this view, Faust is saved because his conditional ("Then to the moment I might say") has not yet been realized and will be realized only when "many ages shall have passed."[114]

A second account suggests that Faust is saved precisely because his restless spirit finds no resting place and rejects all transcendent consolation. His speech—which warrants comparison with Dante's Ulysses and Milton's Satan—should be quoted in its entirety:

> I merely raced across the earth,
> Seized by the hair each passing joy,
> Discarded all that did not satisfy;

THE WISDOM OF THE ROMANTICS

What slipped my grasp, I let it go again.
I have merely desired, achieved, and then
Desired some other thing. Thus I have stormed
Though life; at first with pride and violence,
But now less rashly, with more sober sense.
I've seen enough of this terrestrial sphere.
There is no view to the Beyond from here:
A fool will seek it, peer with mortal eyes
And dream of human life above the skies!
Let him stand fast in this world, and look round
With courage: here so much is to be found!
Why must he wander into timelessness?
What his mind grasps, he may possess.
Thus let him travel all his earthly day:
Though spirits haunt him, let him walk his way,
Let both his pain and joy be in his forward stride—
Each moment leave him still unsatisfied![115]

A third account, less popular with scholars, is also possible. Just as Dante is saved by the intercession of Beatrice, so Faust is saved by the love and prayers of Gretchen to the Virgin Mother, whom he joins in paradise: "Love itself looks down / To favor him with grace."[116]

Yet Mephistopheles, too, must have his say. Faust's striving is meaningless. So, too, is his alleged salvation. His life is over and done. Mephistopheles scoffs at the thought that Faust is better off "there" than in hell:

It's all the same to me!
Why bother to go on creating?
Making, then endlessly annihilating!
"Over and past!" What's that supposed to mean?
It's no more than if it had never been,
Yet it goes bumbling round as if it were.
The Eternal Void is what I'd much prefer.[117]

Mephistopheles's account of human life follows Macbeth, a similarly Faustian figure: "It is a tale / Told by an idiot, full of sound and fury, / Signifying nothing."[118] This is the ultimate nihilism, but one to which Faust himself never quite succumbs: "Let both his pain and joy be in his forward stride."

There is also the farcical opera buffa ending in which Mephistopheles is so obsessed with the naked bottoms of the swarming cherubim that he fails to notice when they spirit Faust's soul away.

Goethe leaves us with no directions to guide our reading. Harold Bloom claims that "Goethe is delightedly content to abandon us to ultimate contradiction and confusion."[119] I would question the words *delightedly content*. Goethe does abandon us to contradiction and confusion. But he feels that same contradiction and confusion when faced with the modern world. It is in that sense that the Western literary tradition begun by Homer ends with Goethe's *Faust*. We can trace a fairly clear arc of poetic development from Homer though Virgil, Horace, Dante, Petrarch, Shakespeare, and Milton. The vast array and variety of literary allusions in *Faust*, which make it an annotator's dream, demonstrate that Goethe had fully incorporated that tradition. And his constant resort to parody demonstrates that he was at a loss on where to take that tradition next. Encounters with art had become a substitute for tapping the "the ever-stirring, wholesome energy / Of life." The literary empire he cherished seemed on the brink of bankruptcy. Goethe, so much a product of eighteenth century, found himself adrift in the third decade of the nineteenth.

The French Revolution proclaimed a dramatic break with the past relationship of citizens to their governments. So, too, the Industrial Revolution fundamentally remodeled society and changed the relationship of men and women with the circumstances of their employment. Technology changed our relationship with nature. It is not surprising that poetry would need to undergo a similar break with its past. Nor is it surprising that even a poet of Goethe's genius would see only contradiction and confusion ahead of him. That is always the state of "modern" man, whether in the first century or the nineteenth.

On finally finishing *Faust*, Goethe told Eckermann, "My remaining days I may now consider a free gift; and it is now, in fact, of little consequence what I now do, or whether I do anything."[120] Goethe's massive contribution to Western thought and our increasingly fragmented sense of self was at an end. For a time, he thought Byron might take up the torch. But that was left for others. Goethe could hold on to only one truth: "What can we in fact call our own except the energy, the force, the will!"[121]

3

Hegel

The World Spirit Realizing Itself

Even the most enthusiastic student of philosophy is likely to reconsider her major when required to read Hegel. His labored Teutonic style, numerous neologisms, and maze-like sentence structure recall Mark Twain's quip: "Whenever the literary German dives into a sentence, this is the last you are going to see of him till he emerges on the other side of his Atlantic with his verb in his mouth."[1] Hegel's predecessor, Immanuel Kant, was notoriously hard to read. But Kant's prose was pellucid in comparison. Even one of Hegel's clearest expositors concedes that reading him is "the intellectual equivalent of chewing gravel."[2]

And yet Hegel is arguably the most important philosopher of the nineteenth century and understanding him is key to the history of Western thought, not just in philosophy but also in general culture and political theory. Indeed, the fact that we conceive of Western thought as having a history is itself largely due to Hegel, who believed that our concepts—our ways of dividing and understanding reality—can be fully understood only in the context of their historical development and their increasing capacity to capture simultaneously the richness and the unity of all that exists.

Every concept implies others, particularly those that stand in contrast to it. Universal and Particular, Mind and Body, Appearance and Reality, Freedom and Determinism: these opposing concepts are in a dialogue with one another and, through a process of dialectic, reveal not only their differences but also their identity at a higher level of understanding. Dialectic is not a refutation but an outgrowing, a succession of ideas each more complete than the last.

Hegel had an unswerving faith in providence, purpose, and system that is largely foreign to us today. But he also believed that understanding the limitations in our concepts, and striving to overcome those limitations, leads to a greater and more unified understanding of human life and the natural world and hence a new form of enlightenment. Philosophy is not a succession of unsatisfactory systems; rather, it is a self-correcting process that increasingly comes to know itself and approach the truth. There are no limitations on the subject matter of philosophy; the conceptual bases of religion, history, morality, politics, art, and science must all be explored to gain a full appreciation of the reality in which we live and think. The content of those fields is left to their practitioners, but their concepts are all fodder for Logic—Hegel's term for the exploration of the concepts in which we think about and know the world.

Hegel's rhetoric is extravagant; his claims are equally so. Logic, he tells us, will ultimately embrace Nature and Spirit, absorbing them in the Absolute. The realms of thought, the empirical world, and spirit will all coalesce in what he calls "the fullest, most comprehensive, and most adequate system of all."[3] Hegel's philosophy is the world spirit coming to understand itself.

LIFE

Georg Wilhelm Friedrich Hegel—known to his family as Wilhelm—was born in Stuttgart, in the duchy of Württemberg, on August 27, 1770. Ludwig van Beethoven and William Wordsworth were born in the same auspicious year.

Wilhelm was one of six children, but only two others survived to adulthood: his adoring sister, Christiane, to whom he remained close, and his brother Georg Ludwig, who became a captain in Napoleon's army and died, or at least disappeared, during the Russian campaign.

Wilhelm came from a family of teachers, preachers, and civil servants. His father, Georg Ludwig, studied law and ended up as a senior official. His mother, née Maria Fromm, daughter of another lawyer, was educated enough to teach him Latin at an early age and wanted him to become a theologian.

Maria died when Wilhelm was only thirteen. The devastated boy had several serious illnesses and developed a speech impediment following his mother's death. He continued his studies but stayed close to home, first at the *Untergymnasium*, which he attended from age six to fourteen, and then at a full *Gymnasium* from fourteen to eighteen. It was a typical Enlightenment education, with classics, science, and mathematics joined by a heavy helping of Lutheran religion. Hegel was brilliant, hardworking, and always at the top of his class. He was also tutored in geometry and French and was an avid reader of Rousseau.

In 1788, Hegel earned a scholarship to study theology at a Lutheran seminary attached to the University of Tübingen. Though called "the old man" by his fellow students, Hegel was by no means a bookish recluse or a somber seminarian. He was friendly and outgoing, played cards, and joined in college drinking bouts. Among his closest friends were the future poet Friedrich Hölderlin and the future philosopher Friedrich Schelling. They shared a room and a disdain for seminary studies.

They also shared an unbridled enthusiasm for the French Revolution, marked by the Storming of the Bastille in 1789. Hegel called it a "glorious dawn" and celebrated the occasion by planting a liberty tree with his fellow students. Despite the Reign of Terror of 1793/1794, the anticlericalism of the Committee of Public Safety, and the rise of Napoleon, every July 14 Hegel would drink a toast to the original spirit of liberty, equality, and fraternity that powered the Revolution, a spirit he thought would renew itself in Germany and find its philosophical voice in his works.

Unsurprisingly, Hegel decided he did not want to become a Lutheran minister. He wanted to switch to studying law, but his father would not let him. He had to finish his theological training, even though Hegel had by then lost interest in his formal studies. His reading outside the coursework—in history, science, and, above all, philosophy—became his focus. He even joined a club devoted to the works of Immanuel Kant, whose three *Critiques* (of *Pure Reason*, *Practical Reason*, and *Judgment*) dominated German philosophy.[4] Hegel graduated in 1792 and (much to his relief) was not assigned work as a pastor, which the scholarship he had received would have required him to accept. Instead, he found successive positions as a private tutor for two different families, first in Bern and then in Frankfurt. It was a standard (if not particularly distinguished) path for a would-be man of letters. During this period, Hegel wrote several pieces on religious topics, including the life of Jesus.

Hegel received a small inheritance on the death of his father in 1799. This money allowed him to give up tutoring, and in 1801 he moved to Jena, which was at that time the center of the Romantic movement in Germany. Invited by Schelling, who had already established himself there, Hegel became a *privatdozent* at the University of Jena, a position Kant had held in Königsberg for many years. As a *privatdozent*, Hegel was allowed to give lectures and charge fees for attendance. Unlike Kant, however, Hegel had few students. Schelling and Johann Fichte were the most celebrated philosophers in Jena, and they were gradually leading a revolution of their own.

Kant had famously argued that experience is shaped by the categories of our own understanding, and, hence, we can know only the appearance of things, not things-in-themselves. In Kant, speculative metaphysics (what exists) was replaced by epistemology (what we can know). This approach made speculative philosophy seem like a dead end. Fichte reacted to the challenge with an extreme form of idealism, arguing that since we cannot know anything about the thing-in-itself, it is as if it doesn't exist. Only what is shaped and known by our own minds exists. Human knowledge is thus inherently subjective. Schelling built on this subjectivity of experience to overcome the Kantian division between reason and passion by stressing the importance of art and a direct encounter with nature to ensure the harmony of the human spirit. Subjectivity, passion, imagination, and the healing powers of art and nature became the main tropes of the Romantic movement spawned in Jena.[5] Reason was toppled from its Enlightenment throne.

Hegel stood largely aloof from these developments while he slowly formulated his own thoughts. In 1805, he was promoted to extraordinary professor, but the "extraordinary" designation simply meant that he still received no salary. Salaries were reserved for ordinary professors. Hegel completed his first major work, *The Phenomenology of Spirit*, in October

1806. He managed to smuggle the last chapter out to his publisher as French forces under Napoleon were surrounding the city.

Napoleon routed the Prussian army at the battle of Jena on October 14, 1806. Despite Napoleon's 1804 proclamation of himself as emperor, Hegel was sufficiently impressed to call him *die Weltseele zu Pferde* (the world soul on horseback):

> The Emperor—this world soul—I saw riding through the city to review his troops; it is indeed a wonderful feeling to see such an individual who, here concentrated into a single point, sitting on a horse, reaches out over the world and dominates it.[6]

Hegel's *Phenomenology* came out in 1807 to only modest success and even more limited comprehension. It is easily one of the most difficult texts in the history of philosophy, rivaled in that respect only by Hegel's later works. Still, it caused a rift with Schelling, whose views Hegel attacked by implication, if not by name. Fichte, too, broke with Hegel, who was now largely frozen out by the German philosophical establishment. Yet it was Hegel who would answer Kant's challenge, restore metaphysics to the center of philosophy, and then rethink Morality, Aesthetics, Politics, History, and Religion on that basis. He was the last of the great systematizers.

The French occupation, however, had driven away the few students Hegel had in Jena. He received a small salary from the university through the intervention of the poet and then-minister of culture Johann Wolfgang von Goethe. But it was not enough to live on, so he left Jena and academics in 1807 and moved to Bamberg to become the editor of the *Bamberger Zeitung*. He also left behind an illegitimate son, Ludwig, whom he had fathered with his landlady, who had been abandoned by her husband. Hegel moved from Bamberg to Nuremberg the following year to become the rector of a *Gymnasium*.

His oldest students were only seventeen or eighteen, but he lectured to them on his philosophical theories. One can only imagine their befuddlement. In 1811, Hegel, then forty-one, married a much younger woman from an established family in Nuremburg. They had two sons together, one of whom, Karl Friedrich Wilhelm, lived to see the twentieth century. Hegel's reputation was growing along with his family.

In 1816, Hegel was named a professor of philosophy in Heidelberg. His former landlady having died, Hegel retrieved the ten-year-old Ludwig and brought him to live with the family in Heidelberg. In 1818, Hegel was named to the prestigious chair of philosophy at the University of Berlin, where he remained until his death in 1831. His massive output of writings continued throughout this period. He published his *Science of Logic* in three volumes in 1812, 1813, and 1816, followed by the *Encyclopedia of the Philosophical Sciences* in 1817, and the *Philosophy of Right* in 1821. His extensive lectures on aesthetics, the philosophy of history, and the history of philosophy, among other topics, were published posthumously, edited from a combination of Hegel's own lecture notes and student notes.

Hegel grew increasingly conservative as he aged, embracing a political and religious orthodoxy seemingly at odds with his revolutionary philosophical ideas. In 1830, he was named rector of the University of Berlin. He died the following year during a cholera epidemic. Hegel's final words were reported to be "Only one man ever understood me. And he didn't understand me."[7] The anecdote is likely apocryphal but too good not to quote.

What Is Philosophy?

The first thing to understand about Hegel's philosophy is that it is uncompromising. Philosophy is a search for Truth—not truth with a small *t*, but rather Truth about the fundamental nature of Reality, which he calls the Absolute. In German, all nouns are capitalized, but the one thing not hard to grasp in reading Hegel is the special emphasis he gives to certain talismanic words and phrases.

The word *philosophy* is a cognate of two Greek words: *philo-sophia*, the love of wisdom. The oracle at Delphi proclaimed Socrates to be the wisest man in the world. Socrates, displaying his famous irony, agreed with the oracle but only in a negative sense: Socrates is wise insofar as he knows he is not. Others, by contrast, believe they are wise but are not.

That makes Socrates wiser than those who think they know what they do not know.

With few exceptions, philosophers since Socrates, including Plato and Aristotle, are in the latter camp. They believe that philosophy can give them a special kind of knowledge about the nature of reality, our place in the world, and our moral and political obligations. But they constantly disagree with one another on all those points, which many think casts shameful discredit on the entire enterprise. Not Hegel.

For Hegel, philosophy is the broadest form of *Wissenschaft*, which is generally translated as science but is broader in scope and embraces all knowledge. The empirical sciences are just a subset of *Wissenschaft*, and the philosopher's job is to understand the unified structure of all human knowledge: scientific, moral, aesthetic, and religious. But Hegel views metaphysics as the necessary starting point for all philosophy. What is real? What are the ultimate constituents of reality? Such questions cannot be answered by the empirical sciences alone because the empirical sciences themselves are dependent on and embedded within the broader conceptual scheme that philosophy must explore. Metaphysics seeks to go "beyond physics"—beyond what we can learn through everyday experience and scientific experiments—to a knowledge of reality acquired by reason and thought.

The second thing to understand is that, in Hegel's view, past philosophies are not errors but partial truths that fall short of complete understanding. Philosophical disagreements are not to be resolved by declaring one system true and another false. They are all part of "the progressive unfolding of truth."

> The more conventional opinion gets fixated on the antithesis of truth and falsity, the more it tends to expect a given philosophical system to be either accepted or contradicted; and hence it finds only acceptance or rejection. It does not comprehend the diversity of philosophical systems as the progressive unfolding of truth, but rather sees in it simple disagreements.[8]

THE WISDOM OF THE ROMANTICS

Heraclitus contended that all things are in flux and that nothing abides. Parmenides argued that everything is permanent, and that change is an illusion. Each marks a significant development in the history of thought, but each offers only a partial perspective, a partial truth to be corrected by later philosophers. Plato, Aristotle, the Stoics, the Skeptics, Augustine, Descartes, Locke, Hume, Kant—all of whom are discussed in earlier books in this series—provide us with an increasingly rich but still partial view of what Hegel calls "the earnestness of life in its concrete richness."[9] Hegel essentially created the history of philosophy as a proper subject of study in its own right that seeks to understand what each new philosopher has to offer us, what each contributes to the growth of knowledge. We do not so much agree or disagree as we absorb what is valuable, while recognizing where each fall short.

Hegel waxes eloquent on this process using the metaphor of a tree passing through successive phases of growth:

> The bud disappears in the bursting-forth of the blossom, and one might say that the former is refuted by the latter; similarly, when the fruit appears, the blossom is shown up in its turn as a false manifestation of the plant, and the fruit now emerges as the truth of it instead. These forms are not just distinguished from one another, they also supplant one another as mutually incompatible. Yet at the same time their fluid nature makes them moments of an organic unity in which they not only do not conflict, but in which each is as necessary as the other; and this mutual necessity alone constitutes the life of the whole.[10]

Hegel's quarry is nothing less than "the life of the whole," and he offers his philosophy as the culmination of this process. Only Hegel's system will grasp the unity of the whole, the organic unity of the Absolute of which all past thinkers have provided merely a glimpse. The audacity is breathtaking. But the undertaking is a serious one, and each reader of Hegel must judge for herself how well he delivers.

AFTER KANT

Immanuel Kant is one of those thinkers who considered the current state of philosophy scandalous. Its unresolvedly conflicting claims are due, Kant concluded, to the fact that philosophers purport to opine on the nature of reality without first examining the tools at hand. How can we determine *what* we know, he asked, before determining *how* we know it? I have discussed Kant in detail elsewhere,[11] so I will summarize his answer only briefly here.

Kant argued that neither experience (as empiricists such as John Locke contended) nor reason (as rationalists such as Gottfried Leibniz contended) alone provides knowledge. Both are necessary, and both make a critical contribution. "Without sensibility," he explains, "no object would be given to us, without understanding no object would be thought."[12] There are conditions necessary to experience, and we can know those conditions with certainty prior to and apart from experience. These conditions for possible experience include a self that has the experience, an external world that is experienced, and the strict succession of events governed by cause and effect. But all knowledge, other than our formal knowledge of what he calls the "categories of our understanding," must come from experience itself.

It follows, Kant believes, that we can have no knowledge of things as they are in themselves. We know objects as they appear to us, as they are shaped by the combined forces of our sensibility and understanding. But those forces are subjective rather than objective. They are essential to our experience, not because they inhere in the objects of our understanding, but rather because they are inseparable from our understanding itself. If experience *has to be* a certain way for it to be intelligible to us, then those critical features of experience are something that we impose on it rather than derive from it. "We can know *a priori* of things only what we ourselves put into them."[13]

Kant insists that the objects of experience are empirically real. They are not just constructs out of our sense perceptions, because their persistent reality is necessary to our sense of our own existence through time. But we can still know them only as objects of possible experience. We have no idea what they are in themselves, apart from our experience of them. Indeed, the whole concept of an "object" has only empirical content and hence no legitimate application outside of experience. The same is true of the "I" that has this experience. We know only the formal qualities of the "I" that persists in experience, not its underlying reality. We don't know whether the "I" is material or immaterial, temporal or immortal. Such concepts have no application to "objects" beyond our direct experience.

Thus, the concept of things-in-themselves—or "noumena," as Kant sometimes calls them in opposition to phenomena—is a purely negative one. It is empty of content. Speculative metaphysics is therefore impossible. Kant traces the boundaries of human reason from the inside. Anything outside those boundaries—God, the immortal soul, even freedom of action undetermined by laws of cause and effect—is not a legitimate object of knowledge. The true nature of reality—a reality that transcends everyday life—is inherently unknowable and ineffable.

In short, Kant pretty much took the fun out of philosophy. It is a dead end because we quickly bump up against *The Bounds of Sense*, as P. F. Strawson titled his seminal book on Kant.[14] We cannot obtain truly objective knowledge of things as they are in themselves; all knowledge is "subjective" in the sense that we filter that knowledge through the categories of our sensibility and understanding.

In Hegel's day, German philosophy was struggling under the weight of Kant's three *Critiques*. It responded in two main ways. Fichte and his followers adopted a radical form of idealism. If we cannot have objective knowledge of things-in-themselves, then things-in-themselves have no objective existence. Our subjective thoughts are all that exist. By contrast, Romantic thinkers, such as Schelling, seized on Kant's suggestion that God, freedom, and immortality could be objects of belief even if not of knowledge. They cited intuition and faith as means of escaping the bounds of sense, thereby slipping into mysticism.

Hegel rejects both tacks. "It is the sickness of our time," he writes, "to despair of ever knowing more than something subjective."[15] Hegel challenges the whole premise of Kant's enterprise: that one must examine the tools of knowledge before employing those tools in the search for knowledge.

> It is one of the main viewpoints of the Critical philosophy [i.e., of Kant and his followers] that, prior to setting about to acquire knowledge of

God, the essence of things, etc., the faculty of knowing itself would have to be examined first in order to see whether it is capable of achieving this; that one must first come to know the instrument, before one undertakes the work that is to be produced by means of it.[16]

This is nonsense, Hegel contends. Knowledge itself must be used to evaluate knowledge. "The examination of knowing cannot take place other than by way of knowing. With this so-called instrument, examining it means nothing other than acquiring knowledge of it."[17] Trying to know how we know is itself a form of knowing; it cannot be bracketed off as a methodology without assumptions. "To want to know before one knows is as incoherent as the Scholastic's wise resolution to learn to swim, before he ventured into the water."[18]

We are cast into the world *in medias res* (in the middle of things). A later philosopher, Otto Neurath, would extend Hegel's water metaphor: our knowledge is a boat in the middle of the sea. We cannot reconstruct that boat from scratch but must make such improvements as we can while continuing to float in it. There is no metaphysical dry dock in which we can start from scratch and examine our claims separate and apart from what we already accept as knowledge. We must know in order to know.

It is a matter of common belief that we perceive objects and that those objects are separate from ourselves. That is our starting point. We don't just perceive the appearance of those objects; we perceive the objects themselves. That is not to say that additional or different modes of perception are not possible. And it certainly doesn't mean that science cannot provide knowledge of the nature of objects beyond what our senses supply. What it does mean is that the world as it appears to us and the world as it is are not two separate things. We know things as they are in themselves because that is what knowing is. There is nothing subjective about our everyday knowledge: "the truth is what is objective."[19] We can all think of instances in which appearances are deceiving, such as a spoon looking bent when placed in water. But that sort of exception merely reinforces the fact that in almost all other cases appearance and reality are united. The concepts coalesce and overlap, as in a Venn diagram. Or, rather, the concept of appearance as opposed to reality is a special case, and vice versa. The limitations of each give meaning to the other.

What this means for Hegel is that reality is given to us directly in experience. Reality is immanent, not transcendent as it is for Kant. We are literally awash in it. Things as they are in themselves are known to us directly, and our knowledge is deepened and increased by empirical science and also by philosophical thought that overcomes the apparent opposition of appearance and reality, subject and object, and even matter and mind, through a greater understanding of the concepts involved. This process, which Hegel calls "dialectic," restores metaphysics to its proper place in philosophy. But it is metaphysics grounded in logic.

Logic and Metaphysics

The idea that metaphysics is grounded in logic goes back to Plato's doctrine of the forms, which has bedeviled readers for 2,400 years, starting with Plato's own pupil, Aristotle. The forms are eternal, immutable, and immaterial, but they underlie and give structure to the visible world. The forms are apprehended by thought alone. They are what makes discourse possible by providing a shared meaning to everyday words. Plato believes that there is a solid, irreducible core to each universal concept that is intelligible to us. Through the application of *logos* (reason; what can be understood and expressed in speech), we can proceed from particular instances to a direct apprehension of that form. Plato calls the process dialectic. It entails an intellectual slicing and dicing of concepts—or, to change the simile, the cutting and polishing of a perfect, translucent diamond—so that the exact contours and full brilliance of each form are directly apparent to our reason. Having grasped this "unhypothetical first principle," reason "reverses itself and, keeping hold of what follows from it, comes down" to understand for the first time and with a clarity hitherto impossible the particular instances of that form in the world.[20]

Aristotle famously rejected Plato's theory. He thought it was nonsense to suggest that universal terms have an existence separate from the particulars to which they are applied. To take a homely example, consider the chair in which you are sitting. We apply the universal term *chair* to many different pieces of furniture. Despite differences, they are all chairs.

But there is no concept of "chairness" that exists independently of these examples (or at least not as a metaphysical entity). A universal concept is not a metaphysical particular. So, too, with more amorphous concepts such as justice and piety. We can abstract these concepts from experience, but the concepts do not have some independent, metaphysical existence separate and apart from the particular instances to which they are applied.

In traditional terms, Plato was a realist—the forms have an objective existence independent of our grasp of them—whereas Aristotle was a nominalist—only individual "things" are real, and, while universals can be ascribed to things, they have no existence separate from them. Nominalism and realism are conflicting metaphysical theories. But they take their meaning from each other. We cannot understand one except in terms of how it limits the other, and vice versa. Universals and particulars are, in that sense, codependent. Hegel's fundamental insight—really, the core of his philosophy—is that such conflicting terms can and must be reconciled to each other in a higher synthesis if our thought is to advance in scope and clarity. Universals don't exist apart from particulars, but particulars don't exist except in terms of the universals that apply to them. From a phenomenological perspective, we perceive particulars as a collection of universals and universals as embodied in particulars. Both are given to us in experience. Assigning one metaphysical priority over the other (as both realism and nominalism do) is a mistake; indeed, it is the foundational philosophical mistake.

Hegel recognizes that Aristotle is not really as far from Plato as he first appears. According to Aristotle, we use universal words by applying them to particulars. But we know which things to apply them to (a chair versus a table) because universals embody the formal and final causes of the things to which they apply. The formal cause is the essence of the thing—"the account of what-it-is-to-be"—for example, a chair. It is "the form or the archetype, i.e., the definition of the essence."[21] The final cause is "the purpose of the thing" (in the case of a chair, to sit in). It is "that for the sake of which a thing is done, e.g., health is the cause of walking about."[22] The formal and final causes are related because the purpose of each thing is to fulfill its essence. If we understand both the formal and the final causes of things, then we understand how universals apply to them. The formal and final causes are, for Aristotle, what make discourse possible by providing a shared meaning to everyday words.

The main difference between Plato and Aristotle, then, is that Plato's metaphysics is static, whereas Aristotle's is dynamic. Plato's forms are immutable and must be understood as such. In that respect, he agrees with Parmenides. What is truly important is permanent; change is an illusion. Aristotle's causes are fluid and must be understood as such. In that respect, he agrees with Heraclitus that all things are in flux and that nothing abides.[23] In terms of the metaphysical status of universals, Plato sees Being and Aristotle sees Nothingness.

We thus have an opposition between Being and Nothingness to match the opposition between universals and particulars. But, again, the two concepts don't just conflict; they also overlap in important respects. As Hegel explains, "this pure being is a pure abstraction and thus the absolutely negative which, when likewise taken immediately, is nothing."[24] "But as correct as the unity of being and nothing is, so it is also correct that they are absolutely different, i.e., that the one is *not* what the other is."[25] Both concepts are simultaneously retained and reach a higher synthesis in the concept of Becoming. "The truth of being as well as of nothing is therefore the unity of both; this unity is becoming."[26]

Being and Nothingness are not separate metaphysical realms with an unbridgeable gulf between them; rather, they come together in a single realm of Becoming that we capture in our concepts. Hegel uses the term *Begriff*, which is broader than our term *concept*, because it refers to the purpose or essence of the thing; in Aristotelian terminology, *Begriff* refers to the formal cause (the essential nature) and the final cause (how it fulfills that essence). The "form or the archetype" is not something that abides apart from particulars (any more than particulars can be separated from the universals they embody); it is the way we capture in words what is constantly changing.

Hegel's core premise—which, however radically different in development, would later form the impetus for Ludwig Wittgenstein's *Philosophical Investigations*—is that philosophical problems arise from the one-sided application of oppositional concepts. Those problems are resolved by a higher synthesis or, in Wittgenstein's terminology, by an *übersicht* (overview) of the area of language in question. Hegel describes this process as *aufheben*, a verb that combines a sense of abolishing and yet preserving and transcending the more limited concept. The term *aufheben* is frequently translated as "sublation," which is a nineteenth-century neologism created precisely for the purpose of having an English-language counterpart to *aufheben*.

Hegel broadens the perspective on two oppositional concepts in order to dissolve the conflict between them in a three-step process. First, he identifies the philosophical tension between two opposing concepts—such as particular and universal, being and nothingness, mind and body, subject and object, and freedom and determinism. Second, he focuses on how the two concepts limit each other and therefore depend on one another for their meaning—the subject "I" exists in opposition to the objects that are experienced: the object is the "not I," and the "I" is the "not other." Third, he finds a broader perspective in which the tension caused by prioritizing one concept over the other disappears.

Hegel thus seeks to overcome the subject/object distinction embodied in ordinary language and thought. Subject and object are not the same: "the one is *not* what the other is." But both concepts can be simultaneously retained and coalesce in the higher synthesis of intersubjectivity. The truth of subject and object "is therefore the unity of both." We are not talking about separate metaphysical entities; rather, we are dealing with one substance that can both think and be thought. In Hegel, the classic dualism of mind and body gives way to the monism of Spinoza, Hume, and other post-Cartesian philosophers:

> If we say, for instance, "the absolute is the unity of the subjective and the objective," this is, to be sure, correct but one-sided insofar as only the *unity* is expressed here and emphasis is placed on it alone, whereas in fact the subjective and the objective are indeed not only identical but also distinct.[27]

The same applies to the apparent gap between self and other. In intersubjectivity, we find an "'I' that is 'We' and 'We' that is 'I.'"[28] The so-called problem of "other minds" dissolves in the recognition that our concepts are necessarily shared. They necessarily embrace both self and other.

This process is pretty much the opposite of what Plato thinks of as dialectic, which involves clarifying each concept in isolation. As Hegel explains, "the dialectical moment is the self-sublation of such finite determinations by themselves and their transition into their opposites."[29] "The speculative or the positively rational grasps the unity of the determinations in their opposition, the affirmative that is contained in their dissolution and their passing over into something else."[30] In other words, we broaden our perspective to embrace both of the prior, opposing concepts, dissolving, uniting, and transforming them into knowledge at a higher level of generality. The last step is, of course, the tricky one and warrants further exploration. But, first, we have to be clear on Hegel's objective.

Kant attacks metaphysics insofar as it seeks knowledge of things that transcend experience. The pursuit of such knowledge leads us into contradictions—Kant calls them antinomies—because nothing transcends experience. Outside experience, broadly understood, our concepts have nothing to which they can attach themselves in a sensible way. Neither a proposition that transcends experience nor its opposite can be either defended or refuted. Knowledge of nothingness—like knowledge of indeterminate being, conceived as something beyond all possible experience—is empty and incoherent. As Hegel explains, being is "pure indeterminateness and emptiness. There is nothing to be intuited in it. . . . Being, the indeterminate immediate, is in fact *nothing*."[31] As noted above, thinking about being and thinking about nothingness are indistinguishable.

It is the experience of becoming—which Hegel calls "phenomenology"—that constitutes our reality, and that experience must be capturable in concepts to be actual for us. "What is rational, is actual, and what is actual, is rational."[32] In other words, in its essence, reality is conceptual as well as actual; that is, reality is amenable to concepts, and our concepts can capture what exists.[33] For Hegel, it is the rationality of the actual and the actuality of the rational that make discourse possible by providing a shared meaning to everyday words.

Wittgenstein famously, or infamously, suggests that philosophical problems arise when language goes on holiday. What he means is that philosophers use terms outside their context in ordinary language and thus trap themselves in apparent philosophical conundrums. The philosopher is like a fly banging hopelessly against the clear sides of a bottle. But when words are returned to their proper context, the philosophical problems disappear. We "show the fly the way out of the fly-bottle."[34] We don't learn anything new by this process. Rather, we seek "to understand something that is already in plain view."[35]

Hegel has a very different vision of philosophy, even if his methodology is in some respects similar. Hegel's quarry is nothing short of absolute truth about the world, a perfect alignment of concepts and reality. Logic and metaphysics coalesce in his phenomenology. That is, to experience reality, we must have an adequate system of concepts, and to have an adequate system of concepts, reality must conform to the conditions necessary for such a system. This seems, of course, like an expansion of Kant's epistemological point. For Hegel, the point is metaphysical, but it is an immanent metaphysics. The world is given to us directly in experience and is captured in our concepts. There is no epistemological and, hence, no metaphysical gap between thought and thing, between subject and object, or even between self and other. "Logic thus coincides with metaphysics, i.e., the science of things captured in thoughts that have counted as expressing the essentialities of things."[36]

Philosophy seeks the broadest and most all-encompassing truth about reality. For Hegel, the dialectical process ends in an intellectual vision of the Absolute, in which Thought, Nature, and Spirit all overcome their dichotomies and coalesce in a single system. The language is obscure and overwrought. But the basic idea is compelling and not at all crazy. The goal of philosophy is to become fully aware of the rationality of the world. Everything in the world is comprehensible to us with the right concepts. Indeed, as Einstein puts it, "the most incomprehensible thing about the universe is that it is comprehensible." What Hegel is trying to do is to explain why that is the case, why the actual is rational and the rational actual. In a sense, Hegel is offering a foundation for science, broadly understood, even while recognizing that science, as a body of empirical knowledge, needs no such foundation.

We go astray in doing philosophy because our everyday thinking is too binary. Everything is either/or, one-sided, and oppositional.[37] "Reason's battle," Hegel tells us, "consists in overcoming what the understanding has rendered rigid."[38] We must overcome the false dichotomies of understanding. Once we do so, we are confronted—come face to face, so to speak—with the Absolute. "The idealism of the speculative philosophy . . . has the principle of totality and shows itself to reach beyond the one-sidedness of the abstract determinations of the understanding."[39]

The Absolute is the purely logical idea of the one universal, dynamic substance (both being and nothingness) that manifests itself in subject and object, mind and body, nature and spirit, all modes of becoming that are given directly to us in experience. It is the pure unity behind the diversity and contradictions where oppositions are overcome. We might, following Spinoza, call this conceptual union of Being and Nothingness God or, following Hegel, the Absolute. Either way, there are no predicates to further characterize this starting point. God, or the Absolute, is "pure indeterminateness." The concept is empty of content. It finds reality only in becoming.

Hegel's position is generally considered a form of Idealism, but the Idealism is not one-sided, turning all of reality into a subjective projection. It is fully compatible with empirical science and common understanding. Hegel's phenomenology is a synthesis of Idealism and Realism. Concept is not superior to Object. They exist on the same level. One is not reduced to the other; both are incorporated in a higher idea. What the object is in and for itself is brought to consciousness in concepts. That is truth. That is knowledge, and it is incoherent to suggest otherwise. There is no gap between thought and thing such that we cannot think about things as they are in themselves.

THE MANIFOLD SELF-DIFFERENTIATING EXPANSE OF LIFE

For Hegel, the actual is not only rational but also organic. Being and Nothingness meet in Becoming. The *aufheben* of the dialectical process is mimicked in the history of humankind. Earlier, more limited stages of development are overcome, yet preserved and transcended, as the Absolute becomes conscious and separates the world into objects before reaching stages of self-consciousness that enable it to overcome some of the very divisions it has created. All humans pass through the same stages of development, which recapitulate the development of the species. Even more broadly phrased, the division between organic and inorganic matter is itself overcome in the union of Logic, Nature, and Spirit, as inert matter becomes living matter, becomes conscious matter, and becomes self-consciously aware of itself, its history, and its inherent rationality.

Again, this is not a crazy idea, despite the obscure language in which it is couched. It is commonly accepted in broad terms as a matter of natural science that life evolved out of nonlife, developed consciousness, and ultimately, in humankind, became self-conscious and aware of its own development. There is nothing mystical about that process, despite the fact that we are still, even today, unable fully to account empirically for the transition from inorganic to organic matter, from vegetative life to consciousness, and from consciousness to the peak of self-consciousness found in ethics, art, and religion. All that is a matter for science to understand. What Hegel offers is a philosophical account of the same process of development in his phenomenology of the spirit.

What is harder to accept, though, is that Hegel believes, with Aristotle, that the entire process is teleological. That is, all things have a purpose and a natural development that is realized in history. That is what Aristotle means when he says that formal and final causes are related because the purpose of each thing is to fulfill its essence. It is what Hegel means when he says that the actual is rational and that the rational is actual. Hegel's idealism and realism meet in the *aufheben* of logic, nature, and spirit. History has an inherent arc. It develops not by chance, or by external design, but its development is inherently rational. History has a purpose, and that purpose is for Absolute Spirit to realize its immanent essence.

The Roman emperor and Stoic philosopher, Marcus Aurelius, poses a powerful dichotomy: either the world is a result of the chance interaction of atoms in the void or it is a unity of order and providence.[40] Ultimately, he concludes, we can't know, and it doesn't matter. Our moral obligations remain the same either way. Hegel opts for the unity of order, but it is an immanent order, an order built into our understanding and experience of the world. It is contained within the phenomenology of the spirit.

Consciousness must be explored from within. The ascending order of consciousness does not leave prior states behind; rather, it incorporates them in something richer and deeper. "The moments which the spirit seems to have left behind," Hegel explains, "it also possesses in its present depth. As it has run through its moments in history, it has to run through them in the present—in the Concept of itself."[41] In order to understand where we are today, we have to recapitulate the entire history of thought. That is true generally, as well as in specific areas such as the empirical sciences, literature, art, and music. We must, with Rousseau, own the faltering steps of our past in order to ensure the bold strides necessary to our future.

Hegel accordingly traces the progress of spirit from the most basic form of sense experience to scientific philosophy. The different forms of consciousness, along with the philosophical systems that fixate on them, provide a limited perspective on truth that is overcome in subsequent stages and is then overcome in turn. It is a journey both historical and logical, personal and general. Each of us participates in and contributes to the teleology of the world spirit.

Hegel begins his discussion with three phases of consciousness: sense-certainty, perception, and understanding.

Sense-Certainty. When philosophers think about the foundations of knowledge, they often turn to what Hegel calls "sense-certainty." "Sense-certainty appears to be the truest knowledge" because it is unmediated by the presuppositions of thought.[42] It is a pure experience of an individual object given to us directly through the senses. It is the raw data of knowledge to which we can refer only in ostensive terms such as *this*, *here*, and *now*, accompanied perhaps by a pointing gesture. "Our approach to the object must also be *immediate* or *receptive*; we must alter nothing in the object as it presents itself. In *ap*prehending it, we must refrain from trying to *com*prehend it."[43] That is, we must not reduce sense-certainty to concepts, which deal in universality rather than particularity. Sense-certainty is our most fundamental ontological connection with the world and hence the foundation of all knowledge. We experience the pure individual "this" with no admixture of the universal.

Except that we don't, as Hegel convincingly shows. There is no such thing as unmediated experience. So-called sense-certainty is already complex, because it requires both an "I" that experiences and a "that" which is experienced.

> In sense-certainty, pure being at once splits up into what we have called the two "Thises," one "This" as "I," and the other "This" as object. When we reflect on this difference, we find that neither one nor the other is only immediately present in sense-certainty, but each is at the same time mediated: I have this certainty *through* something else, viz. the thing; and it, similarly, is in sense-certainty *through* something else, viz. through the "I."[44]

Suppose I look at a house and direct the attention of my senses "here." But then I turn to look at a tree. The house vanishes but not the "here." "'Here' itself does not vanish; on the contrary, it abides constant in the vanishing of the house, the tree, etc., and is indifferently house or tree."[45] That is, "the 'This' shows itself to be a mediated simplicity, or a universality."[46]

Philosophers have objected that the "this" is used to indicate not a universal but a determinant particular. When I say "this," I mean a particular "this," not a universal "this." But Hegel's response is that my private meaning cannot limit the universality of the concept "this." "This that is meant cannot be reached by language, which belongs to consciousness, i.e., to that which is inherently universal."[47] Our private meaning has no part to play and yet "is all that is left over in the face of this empty or indifferent Now and Here." So, too, the "I" "is merely universal like 'Now,' 'Here,' or 'This' in general."[48] "I can no more say what I mean in the case of 'I' than I can in the case of 'Now and 'Here.'"[49]

This is a remarkable anticipation of Wittgenstein's argument against the possibility of a purely private language.[50] Language is shared; we can only gain knowledge of something shared. Apprehension without conception has no role to play in that language. What is shared is not unique

THE WISDOM OF THE ROMANTICS

to the individual having the experience. Universals such as "this" and "here" and "now" cannot provide the unique designation of individuality required for the theory of sense-certainty as unmediated.[51] It is the mediated universal that is given in experience, not the unmediated individual. "So it is in fact the universal that is the true content of sense-certainty."[52]

Perception. Given the failure of sense-certainty to establish a preconceptual form of knowledge of individual objects, Hegel turns to universals, the characteristics that objects share with other objects. "Experience teaches me what the truth of sense-certainty in fact is . . . i.e., it is a universal."[53] We gain knowledge only by conceptualizing experience: "Instead of knowing something immediate I take the truth of it, or *perceive* it."[54] Unlike sense-certainty, perception is not "something that just happens to us."[55] It is an active process. The act of perceiving "takes what is present to it [i.e., the object perceived] as a universal,"[56] or, more precisely, a bundle of properties. The object of perception is just "the thing with many properties."[57]

Yet this treatment of universals raises its own problems because there is no unique determinant essence, no "thinghood" given in perception that holds these properties together. Take, for example, a grain of salt.

> This salt is a simple Here, and at the same time manifold; it is white and also tart, also cubical in shape, of a specific gravity, etc. All these many properties are in a single simple "Here," in which, therefore, they interpenetrate; none has a different Here from the others, but each is everywhere, in the same Here in which the others are. And, at the same time, without being separated by different Heres, they do not affect each other in this interpenetration. The whiteness does not affect the cubical shape, and neither affects the tart taste, etc.; on the contrary, since each is itself a simple relating of self to self it leaves the others alone, and is connected with them only by the indifferent Also. This Also is thus the pure universal itself, or the medium, the "thinghood," which holds them together in this way.[58]

On this theory we have a One—the salt—and an Also, the collection of interpenetrating properties. But the One is not equal to the Also—a thing is not identical to its properties—and thus we toggle back and forth before viewing the salt as an objective essence with properties and as a simple plurality of properties. "Consciousness alternately makes itself, as well as the Thing, into both a pure, many-less One, and into an Also that resolves itself into independent 'matters.'"[59] In the former case, the properties are inessential predicates; in the latter case, the properties are essential: "The unessential, which is nonetheless supposed to be necessary, cancels itself out."[60] Is the "One" an invisible coat hanger on which inessential properties are draped, or is it reduced to the Also, the interpenetrating collection of properties? As discussed above, Hegel works out a solution to the "problem" of universals and particulars in his works on logic. But, here, he presses the dilemma to show how the transition from particulars (sense-certainty) to universals (perception) does not resolve the metaphysical and epistemological issues concerning our knowledge of the world.

> Thus the object in its pure determinatenesses, or in the determinatenesses which were supposed to constitute its essential being, is overcome just as surely as it was in its sensuous being. From a sensuous being it turned into a universal; but this universal, since it originates in the sensuous, is essentially conditioned by it, and hence is not truly a self-identical universality at all, but one afflicted with an opposition; for this reason the universality splits into the extremes of singular individuality and universality, into the One of the properties, and the Also of the "free matters."[61]

Understanding. As an ontological foundation for our knowledge of the world, Hegel has found both pure sense-certainty and the perception of properties to be unsatisfying. The final phase of consciousness explored by Hegel is understanding, by which he means a scientific, empirical grasp of the laws of nature. He accordingly looks to the concept of force, which underlaid much of scientific thought at that time, particularly in physics. In other words, Hegel explores something like an "interaction of atoms in the void" approach. I won't belabor his discussion, because Hegel quickly concludes that, however useful, there is too great a gap between the account of reality given by science and our commonsense experience of the world for us to reduce the latter to the "super-sensible" realm of the former. The world as it appears to us in perception must be the starting point of the phenomenological inquiry.

Hegel now shifts from consciousness to self-consciousness, from focusing on the objects of experience to the subject having the experience. Self-consciousness "has itself as pure 'I' for object."[62] The subject regards objects external to itself as something for use, something to be not just understood intellectually but also mastered practically. In self-consciousness, objects other than the "I" are reduced to objects of desire to be used up and absorbed by the subject. But that approach inevitably creates tensions, for, in the case of people, "the 'other' is also a self-consciousness; one individual is confronted by another individual."[63] Hegel thus makes a whiplash-inducing pivot from theoretical reason (based on metaphysics and epistemology) to practical reason (based on action) in order to explore how the "self" interacts with the "other."

At first, each self wants to destroy the other in order to assert its own untrammeled will and fulfill its own desires without restraint. Assuming "self" and "other" survive this initial "life and death struggle," however, each will eventually realize that, just as the subject and the object only have determinant meaning in relation to each other, so, too, self-consciousness exists only in being acknowledged by another self-consciousness. "Self-consciousness exists in and for itself when, and by the fact that, it so exists for another; that is, it exists only in being acknowledged."[64] This is a fairly straightforward point: we are conscious of our own consciousness only to the extent that we are distinguished from and conscious of others. "Self-consciousness is faced by another self-consciousness; it has come out of itself."[65] This "process of recognition" is essential to the development of self-consciousness in both parties.

The dominant self, however, will still insist on imposing its will on the subordinate other. They will accordingly settle into a relationship of master and slave. The slave is put to work, providing the master with the objects of his desire. "The outcome is a recognition that is one-sided and unequal."[66] The slave works and provides objects for consumption by, and to fulfill the desires of, the master. Eventually, however, the tables will be turned because the slave, through work, "becomes conscious of what he truly is" and thus will "be transformed into a truly independent consciousness," whereas the master's consciousness remains dependent on the servant.[67] Both master and worker will achieve true freedom only when they recognize themselves as mutually recognizing each other and thus coexist on terms of equality.

This handful of sections on the master/slave dynamic[68] were heavily influenced by Rousseau. Despite their contentious obscurity, they are among the most famous in all of Hegel, largely because Marx and other "Young Hegelians" founded their workers' paradise on the dialectical process of history that Hegel seemed to promise would lead to the abolition of the master/slave relationship. Whether that is an accurate reading of Hegel remains controversial. What should not be controversial is Hegel's emphasis on the freedom and independence of both self and other as mutually reinforcing. Self-consciousness is simultaneously collective and individual. Recognition of the free and independent consciousness of the other is a precondition of the freedom and independence of the self's own consciousness.

> This absolute substance which is the unity of the different independent self-consciousnesses which, in their opposition, enjoy perfect freedom and independence: "I" that is "We" and "We" that is "I."[69]

Hegel walks quickly through various historical attempts to liberate self-consciousness from external constraints and the "bustle of existence."[70] The Stoic denies importance to the world; the Skeptic denies existence to the world. And what Hegel calls the Unhappy Consciousness seeks to transcend the world with a mystic leap into the beyond. None of these accounts are satisfactory. Each in its own way ignores what Hegel beautifully calls "the manifold self-differentiating expanse of life."[71] The external world loses its "otherness" not through indifference or denial or some transcendent leap into the ineffable but only when the world itself becomes a recognized aspect of self-consciousness through the dialectical process.

THE WORLD SPIRIT REALIZING ITSELF

We have explored the two major strands of Hegel's thought: the logical dialectic that resolves and transcends the apparent dichotomies in our concepts, and the phenomenology that traces the growth and increasing awareness of the Spirit through levels of consciousness and self-consciousness. Eventually, these two strands will come together. But, at the end of the last section, we left the Spirit alienated from the world it inhabits and desperate to overcome the sense of "otherness" that keeps it from fully embracing the manifold self-differentiating expanse of life. For that, we need absolute knowledge or, as Hegel sometimes puts it, knowledge of the Absolute, also known as God, the infinite, or the unconditioned.

> Everything else is error and gloom, opinion, striving, caprice and transitoriness; the absolute idea alone is being, imperishable life, self-knowing truth, and the whole of truth.[72]

Reason is our greatest tool for controlling the world and promoting utility and progress. But reason also separates and divides. Reason seeks to understand determinant conceptual oppositions, particularly subject/object, mind/body, and universal/particular. Those dichotomies must be sublated, with differences in the conceptual pairs simultaneously negated, preserved, and overcome by recognizing the dependence of each concept on its counterpart and their potential merger in one substance that forms a unity even as difference is retained. Enlightenment science—which focused on the mechanical interaction of natural forces—followed such a path. But Enlightenment science, strictly understood, left out the Spirit, which is the highest stage in human development, coming after consciousness, self-consciousness, and reason. Spirit must come to terms with being and nothingness in order to find meaning in life. For that task, understanding is not enough. Spirit must overcome the shortcomings of Enlightenment rationalism.

> From the standpoint of the understanding, life is usually regarded as a mystery and generally as incomprehensible. . . . Life is, in fact, so little

something incomprehensible that in it we are confronted with the concept itself and, more precisely, the immediate idea existing concretely as a concept. With this, then, the deficiency of life is also at once articulated. This deficiency consists in the fact that here concept and reality do not truly correspond to one another. The concept of life is the soul and this concept has the body for its reality.[73]

To overcome the deficiency of life wrought by pure rationalism, Absolute Spirit is needed. "Reason is Spirit when its certainty of being all reality has been raised to truth, and it is conscious of itself as its own world, and of the world as itself."[74] Absolute Spirit is not the transcendent or the ineffable, which Hegel calls "nothing else than the untrue, the irrational, what is merely meant."[75] Absolute Spirit is given to us in the world. God manifests itself in the world. The infinite is contained within the finite. Martin Heidegger famously asked, "Why is there something rather than nothing?" But Heidegger's question is, in the end, incoherent because being and nothingness are defined in terms of each other; they negate each other, in their determinant difference, and their sublation is found in becoming. The world is endless becoming. It is "eternal creation, eternally alive, and eternal spirit."[76]

Yet that world still has a rational structure that is captured in our shared concepts and is therefore accessible to us in thought. That rational structure is inherent in reality not imposed on reality by the subject. There is no metaphysical gap between subjective appearance and objective reality. In that sense, the rational is actual, and the actual is rational. We can know the world, but it is only through Spirit that we can find ourselves at home in the world. God, or the Absolute Spirit, simply is the manifold self-differentiating expanse of life in which our lives unfold.

Spirit, too, confronts and ultimately overcomes determinant concepts of the understanding. Morality deals with the tension between inclination and duty, between individualism and community. These determinant differences are sublated in the recognition that each consciousness is part of a shared universal consciousness that guarantees the value and respect due to others. "This distinction between the universal consciousness and the individual self is just what has been superseded,

The Wisdom of the Romantics

and the supersession of it is conscience. The self's immediate knowing that is certain of itself is law and duty."[77] Art likewise grapples with the inherent tension of beauty and truth that is sublated in works of genius. Most important, religion, properly understood, sublates the finite and the infinite, the temporal and the eternal, in an immanent God who is everywhere and everything. "The divine nature is the same as the human, and it is this unity that is beheld."[78]

Moral exemplars, works of art, and religious allegories are all partial forms of Absolute Spirit realizing itself and seeking meaning in life. Their "picture-thinking" gives us shining moments of the reality that lies beyond a narrow rationalism.

> The subjective dimension that is supposed to be merely subjective lacks any truth, contradicts itself, and passes over into its opposite [the objective dimension], as does the finite that is supposed to be merely finite, the infinite that is supposed to be merely infinite, and so on. By this means, the process of passing over into its opposite and the unity in which the extremes are as something sublated, as a shining or as moments, reveals itself as their truth.[79]

Only philosophy, however, can give us absolute truth, understood as "the truth of all modes of consciousness, because, as that development [in the *Phenomenology of Spirit*] made clear, only in absolute knowledge has the separation of the object and the certainty of oneself completely resolved itself."[80] This truth is absolute in that it is not limited by our cognitive capacities. We know reality, not just some appearance of reality. The world remains determinant in all its "manifold self-differentiating expanse of life." But the world and self-consciousness come together, preserved and destroyed, in the higher unity of the Absolute.

Another way of putting what is essentially the same point is that we exist in and through our shared concepts. We recognize the same universals. Our thoughts mirror our concepts, which in turn mirror reality. Nature and Spirit both must be susceptible to capture in our concepts. "Nothing . . . can subsist utterly without the identity of the concept and reality."[81] Language is a shared medium. Logic, nature, and spirit coalesce in the intersubjectivity of our concepts. "The idea is the true in and for itself, the absolute unity of the concept and objectivity. Its ideal content is none other than the concept in its determinations."[82]

Hegel thus seeks to restore philosophy to its rightful place as the queen of the sciences and the most important human endeavor. He provides a comprehensive framework in which all knowledge exists. Reason seeks understanding in science. The Spirit seeks meaning in morality, art, and religion. But, ultimately, only philosophy provides what Hegel calls "the fullest, most comprehensive, and most adequate system of all."[83] The history of philosophy is the history of thought about Absolute Spirit; put differently, it is the history of the Absolute Spirit recognizing itself and its completion in Hegel's work.

As J. N. Findlay explains in his foreword to the *Phenomenology*, our consciousness "must see the world, in all its natural and social arrangements, as something to be known, enjoyed, and improved by all, since it embodies the same universality that is active in each subject."[84] Logic, Nature, and Spirit coalesce in a single comprehensive and comprehensible system. The world is familiar to us in all its aspects. We are at home.

> We shall not cease from exploration
> And the end of all our exploring
> Will be to arrive where we started
> And know the place for the first time.[85]

4

Wordsworth

Meaning and Memory

What is a Poet? . . . He is a man speaking to men: a man, it is true, endued with more lively sensibility, more enthusiasm and tenderness, who has a greater knowledge of human nature, and a more comprehensive soul, than are supposed to be common among mankind; a man pleased with his own passions and volitions, and who rejoices more than other men in the spirit of life that is in him; delighting to contemplate similar volitions and passions as manifested in the goings-on of the Universe, and habitually impelled to create them where he does not find them.[1]

WILLIAM WORDSWORTH IS COMMONLY AND JUSTLY REGARDED AS the greatest English poet after Shakespeare and Milton. Yet he was neglected, even ridiculed, in his early years for writing about unpoetic matters—the tribulations of ordinary men and women—in the unpoetic language of common speech. And he was neglected, even ridiculed, in his later years for having outlived his poetic powers, overshadowed by that trio of Romantic shooting stars—Byron, Shelley, and Keats (of whom only Byron made it past his thirtieth year).

Wordsworth fully expected and even invited a negative reaction to his first volume of poems, *Lyrical Ballads*, which he published jointly and anonymously with Samuel Taylor Coleridge in 1798. It contains an advertisement that effectively dares readers to appreciate the poems and chides them in advance for failing to do so. His central premise is that every subject can furnish material for poetry if approached in the right way. He wants his verse to contain "a natural delineation of human passions, human characters, and human incidents," and he offers his poems, somewhat archly, as "experiments . . . written chiefly with a view to ascertain how far the language of conversation in the middle and lower classes of society is adapted to the purposes of poetic pleasure."[2]

Wordsworth did not want to muddy our reactions to the characters and incidents in his poems with the high poetic diction and artificial phrases of his day. Nor did he want to celebrate epic deeds of famous men and women. He taught us that familiar expressions of everyday usage can invest even the most humble condition with a sort of incandescence conjured by close attention and loving concern. Wordsworth is sometimes sentimental—at his worst, even saccharine. But his best poetry is remarkably evocative and moving. Indeed, no poet has written better about nature as a reflection of, and balm to, spirit; about the deep emotions of men and women otherwise of no account to the world; and about the pervading sense of loss that can overwhelm our lives unless we somehow recapture that "aspect more sublime" which gives them meaning.

Wordsworth's greatest work, *The Prelude*, tracks the growth of his aesthetic sensibility. It is a portrait of the poet as a young man, an epic narrative focused not on actions but on intellectual, spiritual, and emotional growth. Like Rousseau's *Confessions* or Goethe's *Poetry and Truth*, Wordsworth zeroes in on the singular incidents, the "spots of time," that shaped his character and now inform his memory. But he does so in sustained verse of a power and compression that renders his experience a parable of deeper meaning. Wordsworth fundamentally changed what we expect from poetry and, in the process, what we expect from life. Without him, Byron, Shelley, and Keats could not have become what they were. He is the father of modern poetry.

Life

William Wordsworth was born on April 7, 1770, near the northern edge of the Lake District of England, with which his name and reputation will forever be linked. Like Antaeus, he drew his poetic strength from his native soil.

William was the second of five children. His three brothers, Richard, John, and Christopher, became, respectively, a lawyer, a sea captain, and the master of Trinity College, Cambridge. William was closest to his sister, Dorothy, herself a noted poet and diarist, who was born on Christmas Day 1771.

The children's mother died just before William's eighth birthday. The boys were sent to boarding school. Dorothy went to live with cousins in Halifax. She was separated from her brothers for ten years, not even returning to visit during summer vacations or the Christmas holidays, as the boys did from their grammar schools. The pain of that separation never left her.

Their father, who served as a legal agent for a nobleman, died in 1783. A cousin and uncle took responsibility for the now-orphaned children. William learned Latin and was an enthusiastic reader of Ovid and the budding genre of novels. First encouraged by his father, he also memorized large passages from Shakespeare, Milton, and Edmund Spenser, author of the allegorical fantasy *The Faerie Queene*. But most important were his long walks in the countryside. From his earliest years, he felt a spiritual union with nature to which he was inclined to give poetic, philosophical, and religious expression.

Wordsworth entered St. John's College, Cambridge, in 1787. His college years were marked by neither incident nor industry. He went on walking tours with college friends during the holidays, including an extended trip with Robert Jones to France, Switzerland, and Germany in the summer and fall of 1790. He even met the German poet Goethe. But the main excitement was in France. The Storming of the Bastille on July 14, 1789, had marked the opening of the French Revolution, and Wordsworth was swept up in its spirit. As he later wrote in *The Prelude*, "Bliss was it in that dawn to be alive, / But to be young was very heaven."[3]

The revolution continued at a low boil for several years. A constitutional monarchy was imposed on the king, but it would not last. Even in its early, relatively benign stages, the French Revolution invoked mixed reactions in England. Edmund Burke's 1790 pamphlet, *Reflections on the*

Revolution in France, made the conservative case for monarchy, aristocracy, and property. Thomas Paine's 1791 response, *Rights of Man*, stressed the right of the people to revolt against a government that did not serve their interests. The dueling pamphlets have pretty much staked out the intellectual grounds on both sides—conservative tradition and radical reform—ever since.

Wordsworth, who at that point was firmly in Paine's camp, returned to France in 1792 after graduation. There he had an affair with Annette Vallon, a French woman of whom little is known other than that she was a Catholic and a staunch royalist. A daughter, Caroline, was born in December 1792, when Wordsworth was twenty-two. But Wordsworth had prudently retreated to England by then. The French Revolution was taking a decidedly darker turn, and it would soon be unsafe for an Englishman to remain in France. That was particularly true for Wordsworth, who favored (and was friends with) the so-called Girondins, who were the moderate faction of the Jacobin party. The radical faction, known as the Montagnards, forced Louis XVI to abdicate in August 1792 and executed him in January 1793. Marie Antoinette followed in October of the same year. The Montagnards declared a republic and, under the leadership of Maximilien Robespierre, began a Reign of Terror not only against aristocrats, the clergy, and other perceived counterrevolutionaries but also against the more moderate Girondins. Citizens of hostile foreign powers faced arrest and fled the country. The so-called Committee of Public Safety executed more than ten thousand people before Robespierre himself fell to the guillotine in 1794. Many more died in prison.

France declared war on England in 1793. The intermittent conflict between the two countries would prevent Wordsworth from returning to France until 1802, when he and Dorothy went to Calais together to meet with Annette and to see his nine-year-old daughter, Caroline, for the first time. Wordsworth was then on the verge of marrying his childhood family friend Mary Hutchinson. Caroline remained in France with her mother. It is unknown what financial arrangements were made for Caroline, but Wordsworth later wrote one of his greatest sonnets to commemorate his walk on the beach with her, using the Christian imagery of her mother largely absent from his other poems.

It is a beauteous Evening, calm and free;
The holy time is quiet as a Nun
Breathless with adoration; the broad sun
Is sinking down in its tranquility;
The gentleness of heaven is on the Sea:
Listen! the mighty Being is awake
And doth with his eternal motion make
A sound like thunder—everlastingly.
Dear Child! dear Girl! that walkest with me here,
If thou appear'st untouch'd by solemn thought,
Thy nature is not therefore less divine:
Thou liest in Abraham's bosom all the year;
And worshipp'st at the Temple's inner shrine,
God being with thee when we know it not.[4]

It is a lovely sonnet but rather abstract, and hardly a substitute for a father as an active presence in his daughter's life.

Wordsworth, however, was focused on pursuing his career as a poet and on building the support structure—sister, wife, friends—that would encourage and sustain him in that work. He and Dorothy had begun living together in 1795; they would never again part. Wordsworth received a small legacy from a friend that enabled him to devote himself to poetry.

Also in 1795, Wordsworth began an intense friendship with Samuel Taylor Coleridge, and they made plans to conquer the poetic world together. Coleridge had a unique, instinctive talent that arguably exceeded even that of Wordsworth. His "Frost at Midnight" is perhaps the finest, most heartfelt poem ever written about fatherhood and a vibrant reproach to Wordsworth's somewhat chilly sonnet to Caroline.

Dear Babe, that sleepest cradled by my side,
Whose gentle breathings, heard in this deep calm,
Fill up the interspersèd vacancies
And momentary pauses of the thought!
My babe so beautiful! it thrills my heart
With tender gladness, thus to look at thee.[5]

Coleridge wrote other achingly beautiful poems, such as "The Eolian Harp" and "This Lime-Tree Bower My Prison." His more symbolic, mystical poems, "The Rime of the Ancient Mariner" and "Kubla Khan," have ensured his fame and his place in all anthologies. But he suffered from a depression poignantly described in "Dejection: An Ode":

A grief without a pang, void, dark, and drear,
A stifled, drowsy, unimpassioned grief,
Which finds no natural outlet, no relief,
In word, or sigh, or tear.[6]

Wordsworth found his own poetic voice in the 1797 version of "The Ruined Cottage."[7]

The poem, discussed below, is a herald of English Romantic poetry. The following year, he wrote what many consider his finest poem, "Lines Written a Few Miles above Tintern Abbey." The year 1798 is often referred to as Wordsworth's *annus mirabilis* for the quantity and quality of his output. The same could be said of Coleridge.

Depression, an unhappy marriage, and addiction to opium would ultimately destroy Coleridge and shatter his friendship with Wordsworth. But, in 1798, the two collaborated on *Lyrical Ballads*, a book that would radically change the writing and reading of poetry. All but four of the poems were written by Wordsworth, but Coleridge's contributions included "The Rime of the Ancient Mariner" as well as "The Nightingale," which would inspire John Keats's famous "Ode." A manifesto—in the form of an advertisement for the book—called for a new form of poetic language and subject matter. Though published anonymously, the volume's authorship was an open secret.

In 1799, Wordsworth, Coleridge, and Dorothy traveled to Germany to learn German and, at least in Coleridge's case, to study the idealist philosophy prevalent there. Coleridge, despite his concrete talents as a poet, had a passion for abstract philosophy and literary theory. He urged Wordsworth to write a lengthy philosophical poem to be called *The Recluse*. It would be a theory of everything, in the spirit of the German idealists. But Wordsworth's mind and talents did not run in a theoretical or systematic direction. He had a powerful, self-preserving sense of his strengths as a poet, and, though he never formally abandoned the project, he let it languish. Wordsworth did, however, absorb some aspects of German idealism that would find their way into his poems in inchoate but haunting ways.

Wordsworth and Dorothy moved back to England in 1799, staying briefly with the Hutchinsons before settling in Grasmere in what would become known as Dove Cottage, still a Lake District shrine for all lovers of Romantic poetry. They walked everywhere. Wordsworth composed poetry on his walks, holding hundreds of verses in his mind before he transferred them to paper.

He published a second edition of *Lyrical Ballads* in 1800, with some changes in the poems chosen for the first volume along with a second volume of new poems written entirely by Wordsworth. He also wrote a lengthy preface explaining his theory of poetry as "emotion recollected in tranquility."[8]

Neither edition of *Lyrical Ballads* was particularly well received. Indeed, some reviews were actively hostile. Yet Wordsworth persevered, determined to create his own audience for his poetry. Over the next five years, he continued to write many shorter poems, even as he embarked on his greatest sustained effort. This epic poem—addressed to Coleridge and published only after Wordsworth's death as *The Prelude*—was loosely autobiographical. It traced the growth of the poet's mind and sensibility. His wife's choice of title was apt because Wordsworth considered this project of self-exploration and self-revelation to be a necessary prelude to *The Recluse.* He referred to it as the antechapel of the planned cathedral. In reality, it served at least in part as an excuse for deferring work on *The Recluse.*

The year 1802 was eventful for Wordsworth. After collecting a long-standing debt owed to his father, which provided him with a further measure of independence, he visited France to settle his affairs with Annette and Caroline. Shortly thereafter, he married Mary Hutchinson.

Mary joined Wordsworth and Dorothy at Dove Cottage. She would bear five children. The growing family moved briefly to Hall Farm, in Leicestershire, in 1806. Mary's sister Sara joined them there. So, too, would Coleridge, recently separated from his wife. Coleridge promptly fell passionately in love with Sara and became convinced that she and Wordsworth were having an affair. That suspicion exacerbated tensions between the two men, though a clean break did not come until 1810. They reconciled two years later, but the friendship was never the same.

Wordsworth finished a complete draft of *The Prelude* in 1805. Although he continued to tinker with the poem until his death, it is the 1805 version that is commonly read today. Wordsworth himself never published his most important work. Despite a massive ego, even Wordsworth seemed embarrassed to have written an extended poem about himself and the growth of his poetic sensibility. That is also partly why he claimed that it was merely the antechapel to a more extensive project. He had prose models for the autobiography of a creative genius in both Rousseau and Goethe. But Wordsworth wanted to write an epic poem about himself that would rival Milton's *Paradise Lost*. "The world was all before them," Milton wrote, as Adam and Eve "took their solitary way" out of paradise.[9] That is Wordsworth's theme as well—"the earth is all before me"[10]—as he explores the mixture of loss, memory, and hope that makes up human life this side of paradise.

His shorter poems, too, were often focused on rediscovering a sense of the sacred in everyday life.

The Child is Father of the Man;
And I could wish my days to be
Bound each to each by natural piety.[11]

By 1805, Wordsworth had completed most of his best work as a poet. With notable exceptions, including the poem just quoted and the one below, his later fame depended on a remarkably fruitful eight-year period starting in 1797, when he was twenty-seven. Wordsworth had more than his own share of losses, even aside from the early deaths of his parents. His brother John, who often stayed with them when on shore, was lost at sea in 1805. In 1812, two of his children, first Catherine (age four) and then Thomas (six), died. He wrote his most moving sonnet a year or two after Catherine's death:

Surprised by joy—impatient as the Wind
I wished to share the transport—Oh! with whom
But Thee, long buried in the silent Tomb,
That spot which no vicissitude can find?
Love, faithful love recalled thee to my mind—
But how could I forget thee?—Through what power,
Even for the least division of an hour,
Have I been so beguiled as to be blind
To my most grievous loss?—That thought's return
Was the worst pang that sorrow ever bore,
Save one, one only, when I stood forlorn,
Knowing my heart's best treasure was no more;
That neither present time, nor years unborn
Could to my sight that heavenly face restore.[12]

Despite such stunning counterexamples, Wordsworth outlived his talent, even as his fame steadily grew. More painfully, he outlived those who were dear to him. Coleridge died in 1834; Sara Hutchinson in 1835. His sister, Dorothy, suffered increasing dementia starting in 1835 and finally died in 1847, the same year his cherished daughter Dora (named after his sister) died of tuberculosis. Dora was a talented poet in her own right but, like all the other women in his life, devoted herself to Wordsworth. He and his wife planted hundreds of daffodils in her memory. "Dora's Field," as it is still known, is now a National Trust property.

Disillusioned by the changes in France and, in particular, by the crowning of Napoleon as emperor, Wordsworth grew increasingly conservative. He took a government post as Distributor of Stamps in 1813, which finally put him on a reasonably solid financial footing. In 1813, he moved the family to Rydal Mount, his last home. Later, he campaigned for the Tory party. A revolutionary at nineteen, he was a Tory at forty-eight and finally poet laureate in 1843 at the age of seventy-three. Wordsworth was still vigorous, climbing the three-thousand-foot Mount Helvellyn at the age of seventy, a seven-plus-hour hike, demanding even for a much younger man. Wordsworth died on April 23, 1850, at the age of eighty.

The Wisdom of the Romantics

Attention Must Be Paid:[13] A Poetry of Everyday Life

In a lengthy preface to the 1800 two-volume edition of *Lyrical Ballads,* Wordsworth expands on the poetic manifesto announced in the earlier advertisement. He makes four points.

First, he famously characterizes poetry as "emotion recollected in tranquility." It is a catchy phrase but seems extremely limiting. In fact, though, Wordsworth is not saying that poetry is *about* emotion. Rather, it takes its *origin* from emotion. Poetry can and should be about anything and everything that matters to us—characters, incidents, places, and circumstances that lead to a "spontaneous overflow of powerful feelings."[14] These things engage our attention precisely because we feel strongly about them, and so, when they are given poetic expression, "an emotion, similar to that which was before the subject of contemplation, is gradually produced, and does itself actually exist in the mind."[15] A mountain lake can give us a tranquil joy; so, too, can a poem describing such a place. Wordsworth in his poetry often seems to indulge in the "pathetic fallacy"—that is, the attribution of human emotions to inanimate things. Here he is saying that poetry can and should distill the same emotions evoked by the things themselves. To be sure, reading a poem about a mountain lake and sitting by a lake are completely different experiences. The former is not just an echo of the latter. Indeed, the former can actually change and enhance our reactions to the latter. We can be affected more by the lake in the poem than we ever were by the lake itself. Wordsworth himself would agree with that last statement. He considers the point of poetry to develop our sensibility so that we feel more and see more. But he also finds a necessary connection between our poetry of things and the things themselves.

Second, as the subjects of his poems, Wordsworth seeks out common men and women, particularly those on the fringes of communal life, because their emotions are simpler and more readily communicated.

> Low and rustic life was generally chosen because in that situation the essential passions of the heart find a better soil in which they can attain their maturity, are less under restraint, and speak a plainer and more emphatic language; because in that situation our elementary feelings

> exist in a state of greater simplicity and consequently may be more accurately contemplated and more forcibly communicated; because the manners of rural life germinate from those elementary feelings.[16]

It is not clearly correct that the rural poor and the outcast have either simpler or more transparent emotional lives. There is a certain condescension in such a view. But no one can doubt that it was time, if only as a corrective, for poetry to concern itself with the full range of human types and circumstances. And it may well be true that those without education or experience in society have less tendency to disguise or distort their condition in artificial language. "Being less under the action of social vanity they convey their feelings and notions in simple and unelaborated expressions."[17] This directness makes empathy easier. We can enter into their lives. We can feel their emotions.

This leads to Wordsworth's third point. He wants not only "to choose incidents and situations from common life" but also "to relate or describe them, throughout, as far as . . . possible, in a selection of language really used by men."[18] He therefore shuns what is usually called "poetic diction," because no living human being would ever use it in daily life. For Wordsworth, there is no essential difference between poetry and good prose other than its metrical composition.

Wordsworth recognizes that readers may find the language of his poems too familiar and without sufficient dignity. "They will look around for poetry, and will be induced to inquire by what species of courtesy these attempts can be permitted to assume that title."[19] In one sense, Wordsworth wants to democratize poetry by using the "language of conversation in the middle and lower classes of society." He adapts to literature the egalitarianism of the French Revolution. In a deeper sense, though, Wordsworth seeks "a more permanent and a far more philosophical language than that which is frequently substituted for it by Poets."[20] He rejects the personification of abstract ideas—so common in eighteenth-century poetry—in favor of concrete images that reveal the moral and spiritual aspects of human life.

That leads to Wordsworth's fourth, and most important, point. He wants to retain or recapture a sense of the sacred in all things. "The human mind," he writes, "is capable of excitement without the application of gross and violent stimulants."[21] Poetry need not search out obscure dramatic incidents. It is sufficient to illuminate the ordinary. The world is all before us. All that we need do is pay attention, giving people and objects their due. "I have at all times endeavored to look steadily at my subject."[22] This sort of careful attention illuminates the general in the particular. "Poetry is the image of man and nature."[23] Its object "is truth, not individual and local, but general, and operative; not standing upon external testimony, but carried alive into the heart by passion."[24]

These are the four principles that guided at least his early writing and by which Wordsworth would have us judge his poetry. They are the means by which Wordsworth deeded to us what the essayist and critic William Hazlitt calls "a new style and spirit in poetry." But they also created a narrative problem for Wordsworth, at least when he moved away from the simpler, ballad form. He was a gentleman and a well-traveled graduate of Trinity College. Wordsworth himself was far from "low and rustic life." So how could he speak in "the very language" of such men and women, and why would he so restrict his vocabulary and syntax?

That question is confronted directly in the 1798 version of "The Ruined Cottage." There are two narrators of this poem. The first (to whom we can safely refer as Wordsworth) provides a framing narrative for the second, an old peddler who knew Margaret and her husband, the principal characters in the poem. Wordsworth encounters the peddler sitting in the shade of a dilapidated cottage with an overgrown garden. But the peddler does not speak in the language of the lower classes. Instead, he launches into a moving elegy:

> We die, my Friend,
> Nor we alone, but that which each man loved
> And prized in his peculiar nook of earth
> Dies with him, or is changed, and very soon
> Even of the good is no memorial left.
> The Poets, in their elegies and songs
> Lamenting the departed, call the groves,
> They call upon the hills and streams to mourn,

And senseless rocks—nor idly, for they speak
In these their invocations with a voice
Obedient to the strong creative power
Of human passion.[25]

All the elements Wordsworth values are present in this poem, which heralds the unheralded and elicits emotions in the listener (Wordsworth) and, by extension, the reader, comparable to those experienced by the peddler himself. Indeed, once the landscape is infused with the tale he has to tell, even the hills, streams, and "senseless rocks" of that "peculiar nook of earth" seem to mourn with him. Despite the sophisticated language and syntax, the images are so direct and concrete and deeply felt that "the things of which he spake / Seemed present."[26]

The peddler tells of his long, if intermittent, friendship with Margaret and her husband, who "passed their days / In peace and comfort, and two pretty babes / Were their best hope next to the God in Heaven."[27] He was steady and industrious. She welcomed all passersby, especially the peddler: "A daughter's welcome gave me, and I loved her / As my own child."[28]

Yet, after "two blighting seasons when the fields were left / With half a harvest, it pleased heaven to add / A worse affliction in the plague of war, / A happy land was stricken to the heart."[29] By the time her husband recovered from a debilitating illness, "the little he had stored to meet / The hour of accident, or crippling age, / Was all consumed."[30] With no work to be found and two small children to feed, he grew increasingly agitated, walking from home to town without an errand or wandering among the barren fields. Eventually, he enlisted as a soldier, leaving for war in a distant land with no farewell but a purse of gold, the price of his enlistment, left on the casement.

> "I trembled at the sight,"
> Said Margaret, "for I knew it was his hand
> That placed it there.
>
> . . .
>
> He left me thus. Poor Man, he had not heart

THE WISDOM OF THE ROMANTICS

To take farewell of me, and he feared
That I should follow with my babes, and sink
Beneath the misery of a soldier's life."[31]

The poem tells of the heartache and withering loss of Margaret, as she sinks beneath the misery of her memory, her hope, and her love. She is ruined by what is best in her.[32] The state of the cottage and garden mirror that decline. One child was apprenticed by the parish and left home. Her baby "from its mother caught the trick of grief"[33] and ultimately died. For five tedious years of "unquiet widowhood,"[34] Margaret would sit on the bench by the road asking each person passing whether he had seen her husband or knew of his fate. "And here, my friend, / In sickness she remained; and here she died, / Last human tenant of these ruined walls."[35]

Margaret's story brings Wordsworth to tears of compassion. But the peddler demands more of poetry.

It were a wantonness, and would demand
Severe reproof, if we were men whose hearts
Could hold vain dalliance with the misery
Even of the dead, contented thence to draw
A momentary pleasure, never marked
By reason, barren of all future good.[36]

Margaret's story is not an entertainment that brings the self-indulgent relief of tears. There must be a higher moral purpose to any poem, and the peddler finds it in "a power to virtue friendly."

There is often found
In mournful thoughts, and always might be found,
A power to virtue friendly; were't not so
I am a dreamer among men, indeed
An idle dreamer.[37]

The poet is not to be an idle dreamer or an entertainer providing excitement by gross and violent stimulants. His poem has a moral purpose; it can teach us to see and to empathize and thereby lead to virtue and true compassion.

This moral dimension is even starker in "The Old Cumberland Beggar." There is only a single narrative voice, but that narrator is again part of the scene. We see what he sees and are meant to feel what he feels. On his walk, the narrator encounters the aged beggar sitting on some rude masonry by the road. The beggar draws from his bag the scraps of food he has been given. It is an indelible image, beautiful and moving in its vividness.

> In the sun,
> Upon the second step of that small pile,
> Surrounded by those wild unpeopled hills,
> He sat, and ate his food in solitude:
> And ever, scattered from his palsied hand,
> That, still attempting to prevent the waste,
> Was baffled still, the crumbs in little showers
> Fell on the ground; and the small mountain birds,
> Not venturing yet to peck their destined meal,
> Approached within the length of half his staff.[38]

The beggar is a familiar sight, known to all; even the narrator has seen him since childhood, when he already seemed as old as he is now, bent double as he walks, eyes fixed on the ground around his feet, and his pace so slow that he barely disturbs the dust, and the dogs in nearby cottages tire of barking at him before he has even passed their doors. He is one with his surroundings but so "helpless in appearance" that travelers on horseback dismount and hand him alms rather than casting them on the ground, and the postboys pass him carefully on the road.

"Deem not this Man useless," the narrator enjoins, "deem him not / A burden of the earth!"[39]

> 'Tis Nature's law
> That none, the meanest of created things,
> . . .
> should exist
> Divorced from good—a spirit and pulse of good,
> A life and soul, to every mode of being
> Inseparably linked.[40]

The Cumberland beggar is a living man, and no man can sink "so low as to be scorned without a sin."[41] He inspires charity in others and thus links them with their own best selves and with one another, learning sympathy and thought in a world filled with "want and sorrow."[42]

> [Even] the poorest poor
> Long for some moments in a weary life
> When they can know and feel that they have been,
> Themselves, the fathers and the dealers-out
> Of some small blessings; have been kind to such
> As needed kindness, for this single cause,
> That we have all of us one human heart.[43]

Harold Bloom calls the Cumberland beggar "Wordsworth's finest vision of the irreducible natural man, the human stripped to the nakedness of primordial condition and exposed as still powerful in dignity, still infinite in value."[44] The beggar is not an economic statistic or a nuisance to be confined in a poorhouse. He is a living man, a part of the natural world he inhabits, and he projects and bestows dignity on those who encounter him on a humane level. Like the leech gatherer in "Resolution and Independence" who, despite many hardships, gains an "honest maintenance" in his "employment hazardous and wearisome,"[45] the Cumberland beggar is radiant in the light of the attention cast on him by the poem. They are both sacred beings and to be attended to as such.

Wordsworth's 1800 poem "Michael" is the culmination of his poetic promise to develop our emotional sensibilities by portraying common men and women in the harsh circumstances of everyday life using plain and simple language that finds the sacred in the profane.

Michael is a shepherd with a modest holding in a valley amid barren mountains, far from any town. He inherited it, burdened with debt, and he and his wife, Isabel, worked for years to own the land free and clear. Michael's spirit is infused by that land. His proud identity is one with his sense of place.

> So liv'd he till his eightieth year was pass'd.
> And grossly that man errs, who should suppose
> That the green Valleys, and the Streams and Rocks
> Were things indifferent to the Shepherd's thoughts.
> Fields, where with cheerful spirits he had breath'd
> The common air; the hills, which he so oft
> Had climb'd with vigorous steps; which had impress'd
> So many incidents upon his mind
> Of hardship, skill or courage, joy or fear;
> Which like a book preserv'd the memory
> Of the dumb animals, whom he had sav'd,
> Had fed or shelter'd, linking to such acts,
> So grateful in themselves, the certainty
> Of honorable gains; these fields, these hills
> Which were his living Being, even more
> Than his own Blood—what could they less? had laid
> Strong hold on his affections, were to him
> A pleasurable feeling of blind love,
> The pleasure which there is in life itself.[46]

They have one child, Luke, the son of Michael's old age but all the dearer to him for that. For "a child, more than all other gifts, / Brings hope with it, and forward-looking thoughts, / And stirrings of inquietude, when they / By tendency of nature needs must fail."[47]

Michael "rock[s] / His cradle with a woman's gentle hand"[48] and, as soon as the boy is old enough, brings him into the fields. They are constant companions, almost playmates, the boy always in Michael's

THE WISDOM OF THE ROMANTICS

sight, and Luke, through his eighteenth year, grows healthy and strong. Michael's sense of connection with the land is reinforced by the prospect that he will bequeath his freehold—modest but unburdened—to his own child: "the Old Man's heart seem'd born again."[49]

But the broader world—a world of finance and legal entanglements that Michael does not fully understand—intervenes. Many years earlier, he had pledged surety to a brother's son who seemed industrious and successful but on whom "unforeseen misfortunes suddenly / Had press'd."[50] The forfeiture is almost half the value of the land. But Michael will not sell his patrimony. Instead, he resolves to send Luke to town, where another kinsman will find work for him, and he can earn the money needed to repair the loss.

It is a wrenching decision for Michael and his wife alike. The physical hardship is nothing—Michael, despite his advanced age, will again take on all the tasks hitherto resigned to Luke. But the emotional separation is far harder. Luke will leave with a heavy heart but also many hopes of life in the town, and Michael does not begrudge him those hopes, though he fears them. Michael and his son are bound together "only by links of love,"[51] and Michael hides his fears that those links will prove insufficient among the distractions of life in town. He seeks a solid covenant between them in the form of a planned sheepfold to which Luke will lay the cornerstone.

> Let this Sheep-fold be
> Thy anchor and thy shield; amid all fear
> And all temptation, let it be to thee
> An emblem of the life thy Fathers liv'd,
>
> . . .
>
> a covenant
> 'Twill be between us—but whatever fate
> Befall thee, I shall love thee to the last,
> And bear thy memory with me to the grave.[52]

Michael understands that a lifetime of toil for "so little gain" is not an attractive prospect for a boy of eighteen. Luke loves him. He knows that.

But "domestic affections" and the land of his forebears will not be enough to hold him. Michael sends Luke off so as not to condemn the boy to a burdened homestead in a harsh, unyielding land.[53] He holds steadfast to hope, but it is an act of will rather than faith. Even as Luke laid the cornerstone, "the Old Man's grief broke from him."[54]

The first reports from the kinsman are positive, and Luke writes loving letters home, which his parents read with joy. Michael allows himself to hope in earnest and works at the sheepfold when he can find a leisure hour. But it does not last. "Luke began / To slacken in his duty, and at length / He in the dissolute city gave himself / To evil courses: ignominy and shame / Fell on him, so that he was driven at last / To seek a hiding-place beyond the seas."[55]

The narrator does not tell us about Michael's emotions on hearing this news. He does not tell of tears or rants or cries of despair. The narrative is all the more powerful and moving for its restraint, mirroring Michael's own restraint.

> There is a comfort in the strength of love;
> 'Twill make a thing endurable, which else
> Would break the heart:—Old Michael found it so.
> I have convers'd with more than one who well
> Remember the Old Man, and what he was
> Years after he had heard this heavy news.
> His bodily frame had been from youth to age
> Of an unusual strength. Among the rocks
> He went, and still look'd up upon the sun,
> And listen'd to the wind; and as before
> Perform'd all kinds of labor for his Sheep,
> And for the land his small inheritance.
> And to that hollow Dell from time to time
> Did he repair, to build the Fold of which
> His flock had need. 'Tis not forgotten yet
> The pity which was then in every heart
> For the Old Man—and 'tis believ'd by all

That many and many a day he thither went,
And never lifted up a single stone.[56]

That last line has such power that it cannot fail to move the reader to the tears that Michael himself cannot shed. As Wordsworth will later write, there are some "thoughts . . . too deep for tears."[57]

Had he written nothing more than "The Ruined Cottage," "The Old Cumberland Beggar," "Resolution and Independence," and "Michael," Wordsworth would have forged his place in the history of English-language poetry between Milton and the present day. Add in the greatest of his sonnets and short poems—"We Are Seven"; "My heart leaps up"; "It is a beauteous Evening, calm and free"; "I wandered lonely as a Cloud"; "The world is too much with us"; and "Surprised by joy," among others—and he lays claim to a prominent place in that history. But Wordsworth was hardly done. He explored an entirely new dimension in two longer poems: "Lines Written a Few Miles above Tintern Abbey, on Revisiting the Banks of the Wye during a Tour," and "Ode: Intimations of Immortality." And *The Prelude* became both the cornerstone and the capstone of his career. It is Wordsworth's covenant with his readers.

TINTERN ABBEY

"Tintern Abbey" is strikingly different from the other poems Wordsworth contributed to *Lyrical Ballads*. It marks a sharp shift in focus and tone from his sympathetic portraits of common men and women enduring hardship with dignity. Attention must still be paid, but now to the thoughts and feelings of the poet himself. He becomes the narrator of his own emotional, spiritual, and intellectual life. John Keats, though an admirer, called this new mode "the wordsworthian or egotistical sublime."[58] It is definitely both egotistical (though no more so than Rousseau or Goethe) and sublime (perhaps more than either). Wordsworth is paving the way for the full-scale treatment of the growth of his sensibility in *The Prelude*.

The conceit of the poem is the poet's return, after a substantial stay in towns and cities, to the countryside of his youthful rambles and how his passionate love of nature has been transmuted into other gifts.

> Though absent long,
> These forms of beauty have not been to me,
> As is a landscape to a blind man's eye:
> But oft, in lonely rooms, and mid the din
> Of towns and cities, I have owed to them,
> In hours of weariness, sensations sweet,
> Felt in the blood, and felt along the heart,
> And passing even into my purer mind
> With tranquil restoration:—feelings too
> Of unremembered pleasure; such, perhaps,
> As may have had no trivial influence
> On that best portion of a good man's life;
> His little, nameless, unremembered acts
> Of kindness and of love. Nor less, I trust,
> To them I may have owed another gift,
> Of aspect more sublime; that blessed mood,
> In which the burden of the mystery,
> In which the heavy and the weary weight
> Of all this unintelligible world,
> Is lighten'd:—that serene and blessed mood,
> In which the affections gently lead us on,
> Until, the breath of this corporeal frame,
> And even the motion of our human blood
> Almost suspended, we are laid asleep
> In body, and become a living soul:
> While with an eye made quiet by the power
> Of harmony, and the deep power of joy,
> We see into the life of things.[59]

This remarkable passage focuses not on the poet's current encounter with nature but on the effects of past encounters even when he is far from the scenes that made such an overwhelming impression on him. Those effects are threefold. First, memory provides him with "sensations sweet," a "tranquil restoration" or echo of what he once felt that eases the "hours of weariness." Second, even "unremembered pleasure[s]" can educate our feelings and pass into our moral beings to inspire acts of kindness and of love. Third, the forms of beauty themselves instill in him a "blessed mood, / In which the burden of the mystery, / . . . Of all this unintelligible world / Is lighten'd."

Wordsworth is tentative on both the second and the third points: "may have had no trivial influence"; "I may have owed another gift." It is also worth noting that, on the second point, he shifts to the third person ("a good man's life") so as not to be claiming such credit for himself. But both the second and the third points are part of Wordsworth's "cheerful faith that all which we behold / Is full of blessings."[60] In his heedless youth, he bounded over mountains with "glad animal movements" and "had no need of a remoter charm, / By thought supplied."[61] The vivid colors and forms of nature no longer inspire "aching joys" and "dizzy raptures."[62] But he finds "abundant recompense" in the power of nature "to chasten and subdue."[63] He often hears in it "the still, sad music of humanity."[64] It is a beautiful image, developed by poets from Shakespeare to Goethe and by philosophers from Pythagoras to Schopenhauer, suggesting that music and nature are emanations of the same spirit and can instill in us a sense of connection with others and inspire acts of kindness and love. In the quiet "power / Of harmony," he finds "the anchor of my purest thoughts, the nurse, / The guide, the guardian of my heart, and soul / Of all my moral being."[65]

These reflections also lead Wordsworth to more "elevated thoughts; a sense sublime / Of something far more deeply interfused."[66] The images he uses are religious but by no means Christian. Tintern Abbey itself lies in ruins. The locus of the poem is several miles above it. Religion gives way to nature as the source of spiritual well-being and harmony. Wordsworth is closer here to Spinozian pantheism or German idealism than any doctrinal religion. The "felt / . . . presence" that disturbs him has its "dwelling i[n] the light of setting suns, / And the round ocean, and the living air, / And the blue sky, and in the mind of man."[67] It is a "motion and a spirit, that impels / All thinking things, all objects of all thought, / And rolls through all things."[68] Wordsworth is careful not to say that this felt presence solves "the mystery, / . . . Of all this unintelligible world." At most, it lightens the burden of that mystery by allowing us to "see into the life of things." The emphasis here should be on "life," not "things." There is no metaphysical riddle to be answered—only a deeper appreciation and love of all that exists. In such a mood, we "become a living soul." Hegel would describe this felt presence as Absolute Spirit realizing itself. In Wordsworth, it is a powerful feeling and a source of joy, but not a doctrine.[69]

Accordingly, Wordsworth does not end on these elevated thoughts. They provide no answer. The world is still unintelligible, but no less a source of joy. Despite the diminished intensity of his physical experience, he nurtures the "pleasing thoughts / That in this moment there is life and food / For future years."[70] He is creating new memories to be stored and infused with future meaning. Even more important is the fact that he is sharing this "present pleasure"[71] with his sister, Dorothy, in whose voice "I catch / The language of my former heart, and read / My former pleasures in the shooting lights / Of thy wild eyes."[72] It is in the physical presence of Dorothy, not in the abstractions of humanity and spirit, that Wordsworth finds his greatest recompense. Consciously echoing the magnificent last stanza of Coleridge's "Frost at Midnight,"[73] Wordsworth says a prayer for his sister:

> Therefore let the moon
> Shine on thee in thy solitary walk;
> And let the misty mountain winds be free
> To blow against thee: and in after years,
> When these wild ecstasies shall be matured
> Into a sober pleasure, when thy mind
> Shall be a mansion for all lovely forms,
> Thy memory be as a dwelling-place
> For all sweet sounds and harmonies.[74]

Such memories will be a balm against misfortune as well as a source of "tender joy."[75] That is the final recompense for Wordsworth. He returns to nature "with far deeper zeal / Of holier love,"[76] knowing that Dorothy will always remember them standing together on the banks of the River Wye.

> Nor wilt thou then forget,
> That after many wanderings, many years
> Of absence, these steep woods and lofty cliffs,
> And this green pastoral landscape, were to me
> More dear, both for themselves, and for thy sake.[77]

THE IMMORTALITY ODE

Wordsworth's transition from chronicler of the common man to chronicler of his own sensibility continues in his "Ode," commonly subtitled "Intimations of Immortality." The poem, begun four years after "Tintern Abbey," registers an even more acute sense of loss in Wordsworth's inability to recapture his youthful ravishment by nature.

> There was a time when meadow, grove, and stream,
> The earth, and every common sight,
> To me did seem
> Appareled in celestial light,
> The glory and the freshness of a dream.
> It is not now as it hath been of yore—
> Turn wheresoe'er I may,
> By night or day,
> The things which I have seen I now can see no more.[78]

It will also be less clear than in "Tintern Abbey" that there is "abundant recompense" for this loss. That is, in part, what the poem seeks to measure.

Wordsworth still gazes with delight on the rainbow, the rose, the moon, and the rising and setting of the sun. "But yet I know, where'er I go," he laments, "that there hath passed away a glory from the earth."[79] Wordsworth's disappointment is banished only by recalling "a timely utterance,"[80] which is generally thought to refer to his conversation with the leech gatherer in "Resolution and Independence," also written in 1802.[81] The old man, though bent double, with "a more than human weight upon his frame," "cheerfully uttered" his courteous words with "so firm a mind" and such innate dignity as to put the dejected poet to shame: "God," Wordsworth implored, "be my help and stay secure; / I'll think of the Leech-gatherer on the lonely moor."[82]

Wordsworth now recalls that resolution and sets aside his sense of personal loss—"No more shall grief of mine the season wrong"[83]—in favor of a more accepting attitude. He listens with true delight to the sounds of the sheep, the cry of the shepherd boy, and the joyful shouts of children who "keep holiday" with "the heart of May."[84] "Ye blesséd Creatures," Wordsworth notes, "I have heard the call / Ye to each other make."[85] T. S. Eliot will adapt the line for his timorous and disappointed Prufrock: "I have heard the mermaids singing, each to each. / I do not think that they will sing to me."[86] But Wordsworth rejoices in the spontaneous overflow of young lives even though, at the age of thirty-two, he no longer feels part of their jubilee. He poses the question that will guide the rest of the "Ode":

> Whither is fled the visionary gleam?
> Where is it now, the glory and the dream?[87]

As of 1802, the poem ended after four stanzas with that alternatively stated question. There was a two-year gap before Wordsworth added seven more stanzas in an apparent attempt to provide an answer.

Wordsworth toys at first with the idea that the soul exists prior to birth:

> The Soul that rises with us, our life's Star,
>   Hath had elsewhere its setting,
>   And cometh from afar:
>   Not in entire forgetfulness,
>   And not in utter nakedness,
> But trailing clouds of glory do we come

THE WISDOM OF THE ROMANTICS

> From God, who is our home:
> Heaven lies about us in our infancy![88]

But these clouds of glory disperse; the celestial light fades as we age. "Shades of the prison-house begin to close / Upon the growing boy"; the "vision splendid" no longer attends the youth; and "at length the Man perceives it die away, / And fade into the light of common day."[89] The world and "dialogues of business, love, or strife" conspire to make us forget.[90]

> Full soon thy Soul shall have her earthly freight,
> And custom lie upon thee with a weight,
> Heavy as frost, and deep almost as life![91]

Wordsworth is surely recalling the beautiful lines from *The Merchant of Venice*, spoken by Lorenzo to Shylock's daughter:

> How sweet the moonlight sleeps upon this bank.
> Here will we sit and let the sounds of music
> Creep in our ears; soft stillness and the night
> Become the touches of sweet harmony.
> Sit, Jessica. Look how the floor heaven
> Is thick inlaid with patens of bright gold.
> There's not the smallest orb which thou behold'st
> But in his motion like an angel sings,
> Still choiring to the young-eyed cherubins.
> Such harmony is in immortal souls,
> But whilst this muddy vesture of decay
> Doth grossly close it in, we cannot hear it.[92]

This earthly freight, this muddy vesture, heavy as frost, dulls our senses and obscures for us not only the celestial light and sweet harmony but also our "primal sympathy"[93] for one another. Yet embers remain, Wordsworth insists, and can be kindled through memory into something like "perpetual benediction."[94] The key is to recognize that "our noisy years"

130

are just "moments in the being / Of the eternal Silence: truths that wake, / To perish never."[95]

What are these truths that wake, to perish never? Wordsworth seems to flirt with Plato's doctrine of recollection or anamnesis: the remembering of something our souls knew before birth and can still glimpse—the eternal forms that underlie our transitory existence. But Wordsworth is not seeking metaphysical or religious truth. His truth is not in "the being / Of the eternal Silence" but in the "noisy years" that interrupt that silence, however briefly. His truth that will never perish is found not in the eternal but in the transitory. What Wordsworth is seeking is meaning in memory through the power of poetry.

> Though nothing can bring back the hour
> Of splendor in the grass, of glory in the flower;
> We will grieve not, rather find
> Strength in what remains behind;
> In the primal sympathy
> Which having been must ever be;
> In the soothing thoughts that spring
> Out of human suffering;
> In the faith that looks through death,
> In years that bring the philosophic mind.[96]

"The philosophic mind" is not measured by its capacity for abstract ideas. "Faith" is not measured by a belief in immortality, which Wordsworth has elsewhere called "too shadowy a notion."[97] It is in the poetry of our brief noisy years that imperishable truths can be found. Poetry is his religion and his philosophy. Wordsworth is a man who has "kept watch o'er man's mortality."[98] No more but no less, and that is paradise enough.

> Thanks to the human heart by which we live,
> Thanks to its tenderness, its joys, and fears,
> To me the meanest flower that blows can give
> Thoughts that do often lie too deep for tears.[99]

The Prelude

The Prelude is no "antechapel." It is a stand-alone house of worship, in which the poet, his spirit "clothed in priestly robes," performs his "holy services."[100] For Wordsworth, poetry is a sacred vocation superior to both religion and philosophy in its ability to see into the heart of things and find meaning and purpose in life.

The poem begins with Wordsworth in crisis. Urged on by Coleridge, he longs to write "some work / Of glory"[101] and yet feels inadequate to the task.

> For either still I find
> Some imperfection in the chosen theme,
> Or see of absolute accomplishment
> Much wanting, so much wanting in myself,
> That I recoil and droop, and seek repose
> In indolence from vain perplexity,
> Unprofitably traveling towards the grave,
> Like a false Steward who hath much received
> And renders nothing back.[102]

"Was it for this," he asks himself, that he was bathed from his first hours in the "ceaseless music" of a nearby stream and grew up coursing through groves and over hills, "fostered alike by beauty and by fear"?[103] The questions Wordsworth confronts in *The Prelude* are: What was he born to do and how should he understand the "filial bond / Of nature, that connect[s] him with the world"?[104] And, most important, how can he bring order to the confusion of thoughts and memories that makes up his conscious mind? "To analyze a soul" seems an impossible task.[105] There are too many "discordant elements": terrors, early miseries, regrets, and vexations.[106]

Yet Wordsworth is convinced that, however hidden, there is an order to be found in the human soul and finding that order is essential to his task as a poet.

The mind of man is framed even like the breath
And harmony of music. There is a dark
Invisible workmanship that reconciles
Discordant elements, and makes them move
In one society.[107]

This "dark / Invisible workmanship"—clearly a pre-Freudian reference to the subconscious mind—can provide unity and meaning to our experience. But how we can attain that level of insight is unclear. A man cannot "parcel out / His intellect by geometric rules" or "know[] the individual hour in which / His habits were first sown."[108] Abstract thought will take us no closer to the understanding we crave. The key, rather, is to focus on "spots of time," luminous moments that take on a significance in memory out of proportion to their impact at the time.

There are in our existence spots of time,
Which with distinct preeminence retain
A renovating Virtue, whence, depressed
By false opinion and contentious thought,
Or aught of heavier or more deadly weight,
In trivial occupations and the round
Of ordinary intercourse, our minds
Are nourished and invisibly repaired.[109]

James Joyce will call these spots of time epiphanies, which captures their quasi-religious, quasi-mystical significance. Martin Heidegger, the heir of German idealism, will use the term *lichtung*—literally, a glade or clearing in a forest—in which Being stands out in full relief before returning into shadows.[110] These are moments—"gleams like the flashing of a shield"[111]—that shine in our memories with a profound, transfiguring light. It is the ability to capture such moments, whether in poetry or prose, that moves a work of art from the banal to the transcendent.[112]

In *The Prelude*, these spots of time serve three functions. First, they account for some of the most beautiful passages of poetry that Wordsworth ever wrote. Their surface sheen summons deeper resonances.

The Wisdom of the Romantics

Second, these carefully chosen spots of time ground and propel the narrative, just as they did in Rousseau's *Confessions*. "These moments," Rousseau explains, "would still be present to me if I were to live a hundred thousand years."[113] As Wordsworth notes:

> Such moments worthy of all gratitude
> Are scattered everywhere, taking their date
> From our first childhood; in our childhood even
> Perhaps are most conspicuous. Life with me,
> As far as memory can look back, is full
> Of this beneficent influence.[114]

Readers of *The Prelude* will have their favorites. Some of these spots of time may be more metaphorical than biographical, but that has—as it had in Rousseau—little bearing on their emotional and literary value. Life is transmuted into poetry through the creative offices of memory.

One night, when on a schoolboy holiday, Wordsworth (or at least the narrative "I") came across a shepherd's boat tethered in a cove and spontaneously embarked, rowing steadily across the moonlit lake toward a distant ridge on the horizon. But nature intervened in his "act of stealth" and its "troubled pleasure."[115] Behind the ridge appeared a huge cliff, which "rose up between me and the stars, and still, / With measured motion, like a living thing, / Strode after me."[116] The terrified boy turns and, with trembling hands, retreats to the cove where the boat was moored. For many days he is plagued by "a dim and undetermined sense / Of unknown modes of being."[117] His mental state assumes a palpable form in nature—a pathetic fallacy, to be sure, but of the sort we have all experienced, as nature seems to take on an intentional and sometimes frightening aspect.

Another night—so many of these spots of time occur against a darkened landscape—Wordsworth goes skating with a group of boys. "All shod with steel / We hissed along the polished ice, in games / Confederate," imitating a pack of hounds chasing a hare.[118] It is an indelible image of lively fellowship, but not without its darker undertones. Wordsworth is compelled to seek his own solitary communion, in a passage of stunning beauty and profound meditation:

Not seldom from the uproar I retired
Into a silent bay, or sportively
Glanced sideway, leaving the tumultuous throng,
To cut across the image of a star
That gleamed upon the ice; and oftentimes,
When we had given our bodies to the wind,
And all the shadowy banks on either side,
Came sweeping through the darkness, spinning still,
The rapid line of motion; then at once
Have I, reclining back upon my heels,
Stopped short, yet still the solitary Cliffs
Wheeled by me, even as if the earth had rolled
With visible motion her diurnal round;
Behind me did they stretch in solemn train
Feebler and feebler, and I stood and watched
Till all was tranquil as a summer sea.[119]

In another passage, at the start of the Christmas holidays, he goes into the fields, "impatient for the sight / Of those two Horses which should bear us home, / My Brothers and myself."[120] His mind is all on pleasure. But he is not home even ten days before his father dies, "and I and my two Brothers, Orphans then, / Followed his Body to the Grave."[121] The memory of that scene of waiting haunts his mind as if, in "such anxiety of hope,"[122] he had missed the signs of mortality: the rain, a single sheep, a blasted tree, the bleak music the wind made on an old stone wall, and the dim outline of shapes approaching through the mist. It is only in retrospect that the scene acquires such ominous significance.

Indeed, one of the most famous moments in the poem is a moment memorably missed. Wordsworth and his companion are crossing the Alps, from Switzerland into Italy, with a larger group from which they have separated. They follow the path for some time and, at a junction, turn uphill to finish their climb, only to be told by a peasant that they must descend. After all the "effort, and expectation, and desire,"[123] they had crossed the Alps without ever knowing it. The moment, though missed and unmarked at the time, is recovered and given transformative meaning in memory.

That brings us to the third purpose of "spots in time" in *The Prelude*. They are portals to a realm of spirit every bit as vast and varied as nature itself. In these spots of time, there is a poetic melding of mind and nature.

> With bliss ineffable
> I felt the sentiment of Being spread
> O'er all that moves, and all that seemeth still,
> O'er all that, lost beyond the reach of thought
> And human knowledge, to the human eye
> Invisible, yet liveth to the heart.[124]

Each such experience triggers reflections on nature and being; these reflections are repeated throughout *The Prelude* but gain power in their repetition. They are a constant reminder of the sacred that infuses all things.

This is not to say that Wordsworth is expressing traditional religious sentiments. He does talk about "that spirit of religious love in which / I walked with Nature,"[125] but without committing to anything more than "an under-presence, / The sense of God, or whatsoe'er is dim / Or vast in its own being."[126] His devotion is secularized and yet transcendent.[127] He will use the tropes of both religion and philosophy without either falling into the abyss of idealism or surrendering to the straitjacket of sectarian dogma. Wordsworth is just as likely to use the language of pagan worship to capture what Freud will call the "oceanic feeling" of the spiritual unity of all things.

> Wisdom and Spirit of the Universe!
> Thou Soul that art the Eternity of Thought!
> And giv'st to forms and images a breath
> And everlasting motion![128]

For Wordsworth, the interior world mirrors the exterior: "all objects, being / Themselves capacious, also found in me / Capaciousness and amplitude of mind."[129] The mind is just as vast and sublime as the universe. "Gone, we are as dust,"[130] but our hope lies here in the world, in the transience of beauty and the permanence of poetry.

> With life and nature, purifying thus
> The elements of feeling and of thought,
> And sanctifying by such discipline
> Both pain and fear, until we recognize
> A grandeur in the beatings of the heart.[131]

5

Jane Austen's Heroines

IN 1817, FOUR MONTHS BEFORE HER DEATH, JANE AUSTEN WROTE TO her twenty-four-year-old niece, Fanny Knight, whose suitor had criticized the behavior of Austen's female characters.

> Do not oblige him to read any more. Have mercy on him, tell him the truth, and make him an apology. He and I should not in the least agree, of course, in our ideas of novels and heroines. Pictures of perfection, as you know, make me sick and wicked.[1]

The unnamed suitor should indeed have been spared any further reading. Precisely what makes the novels of Jane Austen so compelling is that her heroines are not models of insipid perfection. They are living, breathing women with virtues that can look very much like flaws, flaws that can look very much like virtues, and a penchant for errors that they struggle to recognize and correct over the course of their histories.

Jane Austen's novels are firmly grounded in the extended Regency period in which she passed all her adulthood. They call into being an agrarian, preindustrial England that was rapidly disappearing even as her prose both rendered it immortal and transcended it. Jane Austen brought the novel into the modern world. As Sir Walter Scott explains in lamenting her early death:

> That young lady had a talent for describing the involvements and feelings and characters of ordinary life, which is to me the most wonderful

I ever met with. The Big Bow-wow strain I can do myself like any now going; but the exquisite touch, which renders ordinary commonplace things and characters interesting, from the truth of the description and the sentiment, is denied to me.[2]

Six different heroines (seven, if you count both Miss Dashwoods) navigate their way through an increasingly complex world without much help (and often positive hindrance) from their parents. There are false flags to mislead them: the boorish (John Thorpe), the deviously charming (Willoughby, George Wickham, Henry Crawford), and the guarded and mysterious (Frank Churchill, William Elliot). But moral concerns firmly anchor each of the heroines. Each preserves her own integrity and finds happiness in her own way. The richness of the six completed novels that Jane Austen left us is inexhaustible.

LIFE

Jane Austen was born on December 16, 1775. She was the seventh of eight children and the second daughter of George Austen and Cassandra Leigh. George and Cassandra met in Oxford, where he attended St. John's College, and she was the niece of the master of Balliol. He became a clergyman, and they married in 1764 after he obtained the living at the Steventon parish in Hampshire.

George had been an orphan who worked hard to earn a fellowship at Oxford. He was from an impoverished branch of an old and well-off family, the Austens, who earned their money in trade as wool merchants. Their children would benefit, albeit unevenly, from numerous family connections. Jane could still, though just barely, have echoed Elizabeth Bennet, who insisted to Lady Catherine de Bourgh, "[My father] is a gentleman; I am a gentleman's daughter."[3]

Cassandra was twenty-six when her first child was born. She was forty when the last arrived in 1779. She followed the same routine with each of her children. She breastfed and cared for them at home for about fourteen weeks before handing them off to a village woman, Elizabeth Littlewood, to be tended for the next twelve to eighteen months. They returned when they were old enough to walk and to speak. Cassandra wanted them to be independent and hearty; mother–child bonding was not the desideratum it is considered today. Her husband, however, the one-time orphan, would visit whichever child was away from home on an almost daily basis. He was by all accounts a kind and gentle man. His brother-in-law, Tysoe Saul Hancock, unkindly quipped, "I fear George will find it easier to get a family than to provide for them."[4] But George supplemented his modest income as a country cleric by farming and taking in three or four boys at a time as student boarders.

The growing family moved into a newly renovated Steventon Rectory in 1768. They were a close-knit, noisy bunch, despite the fourteen-year range of ages. Home theatricals, games, sports, poems, and literary sketches were fixtures of daily life. Two of Jane's brothers, James and Henry, attended Oxford and even started a short-lived literary magazine, *The Loiterer*. Their mother would frequently grace family occasions with a poem.

The second child, George, had severe developmental difficulties. Eventually, he was sent to live with a couple already caring for his equally disabled uncle, Tom Leigh. The third child, Edward, known affectionately as Neddy, was adopted by wealthy, childless cousins, the Knights, in 1783. Austen is writing from experience when, with respect to Frank Weston's transformation into Frank Churchill, she has Emma remark, "There is something so shocking in a child's being taken away from his parents and natural home!"[5]

Jane's brother Frank went to sea at the age of fourteen and eventually became admiral of the fleet. The baby, Charles, also joined the navy, rising through numerous military engagements to the rank of rear admiral. He always remained close to his sister and was a devoted reader of her novels, even advising on the proper naval vocabulary in *Mansfield Park* and *Persuasion*.

In 1783, Jane Austen, along with her sister, Cassandra, and a cousin, Jane Cooper, were sent to Oxford to be educated by one Mrs. Ann Cawley, who, like Mr. Austen, boarded students. Mrs. Cawley took the girls with her when she moved to Southampton later in the year, but they were quickly engulfed in a typhoid pandemic. Jane Cooper's mother, who rushed to remove the girls from school, contracted the disease and died.

THE WISDOM OF THE ROMANTICS

Jane Austen herself was gravely ill, and she and Cassandra returned and were educated at home for the next two years before attending the Abbey House School in nearby Reading in 1785. The headmistress, Mrs. La Tournelle, had a cork leg and a fondness for theater. But the education was indifferent at best. Presumably, the girls learned French, needlework, dancing, and music. But the fees for such an education proved too expensive for the Austen family. After 1786, the eleven-year-old Jane Austen returned home to Steventon. As one of her biographers notes, the school at Reading "was to be her last independent adventure in the outside world. Thereafter, for the rest of her life, she never strayed outside the enclosure of her family circle."[6] Except, of course, in her imagination.

Jane had access to her father's library and the texts he used in teaching his boarders. She was widely read in poetry, history, sermons, and essays. Her favorite moralists were Samuel Johnson and William Cowper, the poet of the English countryside who was likewise a favorite of Wordsworth and Coleridge. But novels, of course, proved her true love. She was thoroughly conversant with the emerging tradition of English novelists, starting with Defoe and Swift and extending to Richardson, Sterne, Fielding, and Goldsmith. She was also a fan of the popular Gothic thrillers penned by Ann Radcliffe and knew the works of other contemporary women writers such as Fanny Burney and Maria Edgeworth.

Novels at that time were frequently disparaged as light entertainment for ladies, without the more serious educational and moral purposes of history and essays. Indeed, it was considered embarrassing to acknowledge reading such frivolous fare. Jane Austen would have none of this. In *Northanger Abbey*, she launches a powerful defense of novels—"performances which have only genius, wit, and taste to recommend them"[7]—that has never been improved on. She literally halts her narrative—a narrative making sport of the excesses of gothic novels—to take apologetic readers to task:

> "And what are you reading, Miss——?" "Oh! it is only a novel!" replies the young lady; while she lays down her book with affected indifference, or momentary shame. . . . In short, only some work in which the greatest powers of the mind are displayed, in which the most thorough

142

knowledge of human nature, the happiest delineation of its varieties, the liveliest effusions of wit and humor are conveyed to the world in the best chosen language.[8]

It is a new manifesto worthy of Wordsworth and much more compact. But whereas Wordsworth defends poetry that gives voice to society's outcasts, Jane Austen defends a genre that illuminates our daily interactions in morally charged language of great penetration and elegance.

Jane Austen's life at Steventon was quiet; those of her cousins were rather less so. Her father's sister, Philadelphia Austen, fearful of becoming an old maid, had decamped to India, where she married the much older Tysoe Hancock. She also reputedly had an affair with—and a child by—Warren Hastings, a high-level official in the East India Company who was later the governor general of India. The daughter, whoever her father might have been, was raised as Eliza Hancock, but Hastings made sure that she was well provided for.

Eliza was worldly and a bit wild. In 1781, she married a French nobleman and became the Countess de Feuillide, much to her mother's delight. She visited the Austen family with her child, the impressively named Hastings François Louis Eugène Capot de Feuillide. She dazzled her provincial cousins, especially the much younger Jane, and joined in their theatricals, always, of course, in the starring role. Her husband unwisely remained in revolutionary France, where he was guillotined, and his property seized in 1794. Fortunately, Eliza still had substantial funds put in trust for her by Warren Hastings. She married her first cousin, Jane's brother Henry, in 1797.

To add to the family drama, Lord Hastings had been impeached and charged with high crimes and misdemeanors in 1786. The proceedings dragged on for nine years before he was finally found not guilty, and all charges were dropped. Even closer to home, rich aunt Jane Leigh-Perrot—who had adopted James Austen—was accused of shoplifting a piece of lace and jailed in 1799. The charges appeared to be a setup for an extortion plot, or so Leigh-Perrot claimed. Her husband was loyal enough to share her pretrial imprisonment. Though faced with possible transportation to Australia, Leigh-Perrot went to trial, spoke out

THE WISDOM OF THE ROMANTICS

against the charges, and received numerous character testimonials. After the briefest deliberation, she was found not guilty.

Jane and her sister, Cassandra, each had her own flirtation with romance. In 1795, Jane was introduced to Tom Lefroy, a relative of neighbors in Steventon. They were immediately smitten with each other. In a letter to Cassandra, Jane is flippant: "I mean to confine myself in future to Mr. Tom Lefroy, for whom I do not care sixpence."[9] But Jane and Tom were sufficiently demonstrative in their affections that Lefroy's family grew alarmed, for Jane had no fortune to bestow on a husband who needed to make his way in the world. Tom was promptly ordered to decamp from Steventon, and the relationship ended before it fully began. Jane sent a second letter to Cassandra, whose light tone seems to conceal genuine disappointment: "At length the day is come," she writes, "on which I am to flirt my last with Tom Lefroy, and when you receive this it will be over. My tears flow as I write at the melancholy idea."[10] Tom Lefroy went on to marry an heiress and eventually became the chief justice of Ireland.

Cassandra, meanwhile, was engaged to Tom Fowle, a former student of her father and a close friend of her brother James. But Tom was a penniless clergyman, and they could not marry without money. He accepted a position in 1795 as chaplain to a regiment assembled to fight the French in the West Indies. Tom was determined to make enough of a fortune to marry Cassandra. But shortly before his expected return in 1797, he contracted a fever and died. Cassandra, though only twenty-four, largely withdrew from society, and she and Jane became inseparable. Tom left Cassandra a generous bequest of one thousand pounds.

In the summer of 1795, Mr. Austen gave up taking in pupils, which freed Jane from laundry and meal preparation and left her time to devote to her writing. She was remarkably productive. That same year she completely rewrote an earlier epistolary novel about two sisters, called *Eleanor and Marianne*. It would later be published as *Sense and Sensibility*. In 1797, she wrote a draft of *First Impressions*, which became *Pride and Prejudice*. And in 1799, she finished a draft of *Susan*, which became *Northanger Abbey*. She had completed three novels before her twenty-fifth birthday.

Unfortunately, Jane's spurt of productivity was cut short in 1800 when her father retired and moved to Bath with his wife and two daughters. The change disrupted her writing routine, so carefully preserved at Steventon. Moreover, Jane did not like Bath and may have suffered from depression. Certainly, her failure to find a publisher, despite the efforts of her father and her brother Henry, was discouraging. Her father had submitted *First Impressions* to a London publisher, and it was rejected, obviously unread, by return post. It would be 1811 before her first book was published.

Jane received a proposal of marriage in December 1802 from Harris Bigg-Wither, the brother of friends. He was well off, and the marriage would have been highly convenient for her family. She impulsively accepted the offer but, after a fretful night, announced that she had changed her mind. A loveless marriage did not, in the end, tempt her, and she cherished her personal and artistic freedom, even as she was still financially dependent on her family.

George Austen died in January 1805. The brothers contributed according to their respective means to the maintenance of their mother and two sisters. They were unsettled until 1809, when Jane's wealthy brother, Edward Austen Knight, offered them Chawton Cottage on his estate in Hampshire. The change was definitely a tonic for Jane. She was spared almost all household chores, and she threw herself into revising her earlier books, reading each aloud to her family and gauging their reactions as well as her own.

Sense and Sensibility was published in 1811, sixteen years after the first draft. Henry and Eliza advanced the printing costs, and the book did surprisingly well, making a profit for its anonymous author ("A Lady") of 140 pounds, equivalent to perhaps seventy times that amount today. It was not a huge sum, but it gave Jane some measure of discretion in her spending as well as a welcome confirmation of her talents. *Pride and Prejudice* came out in January 1813 ("By the Author of *Sense and Sensibility*") after a seventeen-year delay. Jane sold the copyright for a mere 110 pounds, which was unfortunate given its popularity. Also unfortunate is that the original manuscripts of those two books were not preserved, so what changes were made for publication is largely guesswork.

Two new books written at Chawton, *Mansfield Park* and *Emma*, were published, also anonymously, in May 1814 and December 1815, respectively. At that point, Jane's authorship was an open secret. Indeed, *Emma* was dedicated, at his request, to the prince regent.

Jane had managed to sell the copyright of *Northanger Abbey* for 10 pounds in 1803. But the publisher took no steps to bring it out. Indeed, ten years later she would write to demand its return so that it could be published elsewhere, only to be told she would have to repay the 10 pounds. That is what she eventually did, but the book was not published until after her death from Addison's disease in July 1817, at the age of forty-one. Through the efforts of Henry and Cassandra, *Northanger Abbey* was published under her name in a four-volume set with *Persuasion*, along with a short biography by her nephew Henry Austen Leigh. A new novel, *Sanditon*, was left unfinished at her death.

Chawton Cottage, where Jane Austen spent the last eight years of her life, saw all six of her novels assume their final form. Established as a museum by the Jane Austen Memorial Trust in 1947, it is a shrine for Janeites everywhere—indeed, for all lovers of English literature.

CATHERINE MORLAND

"No one who had ever seen Catherine Morland in her infancy, would have supposed her born to be an heroine."[11] The opening line of *Northanger Abbey* alerts the reader that its principal character will be altogether different from heroines in the romances and gothic shockers of the day. Such women appear marked from childhood for great adventures by their mysterious parentage, striking beauty, significant artistic talents, and the depth of their feelings. There are no such intimations about Catherine.

Her father is a clergyman, her mother a woman of good sense and mild temper. Her nine siblings are all plain but in good health and high spirits. Catherine herself was unappealing as a young girl, with a thin, awkward figure, sallow skin, lank hair, and strong features. She preferred cricket to dolls and was neither bright nor attentive at her studies. Music and drawing bored her. Her most attractive trait was that she was "noisy and wild, hated confinement and cleanliness, and loved nothing so well in the world as rolling down the green slope at the back of the house."[12]

At fifteen, her features and complexion began to improve, and her figure gained "consequence." Even her parents remarked that, on a good day, she was "almost pretty."[13] She also started reading books, as long as they were "all story and no reflection." Thus began her "training for a heroine."[14] The books, with their sensational plots and implausible characters, filled her head with a succession of silly ideas that bore little relationship to the realities of life in Regency England. She was, in short, wholly unremarkable and yet extremely likeable. "Her heart was affectionate, her disposition cheerful and open, without conceit or affectation of any kind . . . and her mind about as ignorant and uninformed as the female mind at seventeen usually is."[15]

Thus was Catherine Morland on her way to Bath as the invited companion of her equally unremarkable neighbors, Mr. and Mrs. Allen. Yet adventures are to befall her that will require both strength of character and emotional intelligence to master. We are told that "she never could learn or understand anything before she was taught; and sometimes not even then."[16] Yet Catherine Morland will learn to judge and value people based on her own experience rather than to rely wholly on the opinions of others. It is her ability to do so that makes her, in the end, a true (if still formative) Austen heroine.

The plot turns on three brother–sister combinations: Catherine and her brother James, who comes down to Bath from Oxford; Isabella Thorpe, a dowerless beauty who becomes engaged to James, and her brother John, who is James's best college friend; and, finally, Henry Tilney, who is introduced to Catherine by the master of ceremonies at a ball and both dazzles and intimidates her with his wry, mocking humor, and his sister Eleanor, who is modest, shy, and sincere.

In the first half of the book, Catherine must learn to navigate away from the Thorpes and toward the Tilneys, appreciating the virtues of the latter while recognizing the grave flaws of the former. It is a complicated process because women—even heroines—are expected to be passive and powerless in a patriarchal society. In an amusing digression, while they are at a ball, Henry describes the relationship of dancing partners as rather like a marriage, only shorter: "We have entered into a contract of mutual agreeableness for the space of an evening, and all our agreeableness belongs solely to each other for that time."[17] To reinforce the point, he notes that, in both marriage and dancing, "man has the advantage of choice, woman only the power of refusal."[18] It is a clever remark, in keeping with Henry's playful banter. Yet perhaps more clever than sound. Once Henry is introduced to Catherine by the master of ceremonies, after all, he has little choice but to solicit her hand for a dance. Catherine herself, like all Austen heroines, will learn to exercise the advantage of choice even within the social mores of her day.

But first, she must school her judgment. She immediately succumbs to the best-friends-forever blandishments of Isabella. They must be inseparable and share all their most intimate feelings with each other. Catherine, in her naïvete, accepts whatever Isabella tells her, including her pretense that money is wholly unimportant: "My wishes are so moderate, that the smallest income in nature would be enough for me. Where people are really attached, poverty itself is wealth: grandeur I detest."[19] Yet she is clearly disappointed to learn how little James's father is able to do for them—a mere 3,000 pounds. And, in James's absence, she acquiesces in the attentions of Captain Tilney, Henry's older brother and heir to the family's estate.

Perhaps Isabella, who has no fortune, is not wholly blamable in wanting to marry as well as possible. In the absence of an independence— which we will see in *Emma* can have its own drawbacks—a well-chosen marriage was the only way for a woman to make her way in the world. But the casual manner in which Isabella casts off James—"What one means one day, you know, one may not mean the next. Circumstances change, opinions alter"[20]—puts her down as a scheming hypocrite, and not even a good one. Henry sarcastically remarks, "I have too good an opinion of Miss Thorpe's prudence, to suppose that she would part with one gentleman before the other was secured."[21] But she does exactly that. Although the 2007 film version goes beyond any textual warrant in having her sleep with Captain Tilney in her fruitless effort to turn his sexual longing into a positive engagement, she does enough to cause a decisive break with James.

Captain Tilney enjoys his conquest (on whatever level) but has no intention of marrying a pauper. Isabella tries to reverse course and writes to Catherine, "fearful of some misunderstanding," and asks her to reassure James that "he is the only man I ever did or could love."[22] The narrator reassures us that "such a strain of shallow artifice could not impose even upon Catherine."[23] Catherine announces to Henry and Eleanor that "I never was so deceived in anyone's character in my life before."[24] "Among all the great variety that you have known and studied," Henry responds mildly.[25]

Catherine's opinion is more readily formed about John Thorpe. He is boorish and boastful, and she quickly laments "the extreme weariness of his company."[26] Even so, he is her brother's best friend. She doubts her own judgment and continues to engage in outings, riding with him in his carriage (itself a breach of etiquette of which Mrs. Allen fails to warn her) while Isabella rides with James. These outings place her in an awkward position with the Tilneys. Once, when she is scheduled to walk with them, Thorpe convinces her that they have abandoned the project because of ill weather. That is a lie, and as the Tilneys walk to her house, they see her riding away with Thorpe. She later explains to Henry, who pretends not to be offended, that she called out repeatedly to Thorpe to stop, and "if Mr. Thorpe would only have stopped, I would have jumped out and run after you."[27] "Is there a Henry in the world," the narrator notes, "who could be insensible to such a declaration?"[28] On another occasion when Thorpe takes it on himself to cancel her engagement with the Tilneys so that they can go on a different outing, she rushes to their house and straight inside to correct Thorpe's misstatement.

Catherine's forthrightness both delights and bemuses Henry. She is as free of artifice as the girl rolling down the green slope behind her house. She has no idea of, since she has never been taught, the guarded reserve with which a lady should converse with a gentleman. She brings "such fresh feelings of every sort" to society that she breaks through even Henry's ironic detachment, "listening with sparkling eyes to everything he said; and, in finding him irresistible, becoming so herself."[29] When there is still a question of Isabella marrying their brother, Henry offers a mock warning to Eleanor: "Prepare for . . . such a sister-in-law as you must delight in!—Open, candid, artless, guileless, with affections strong but simple, forming no pretensions, and knowing no disguise."[30] "Such a sister-in-law . . . I should delight in," Eleanor responds with a smile, knowing full well that it is Catherine who is in question.

John Thorpe appears to do some serious mischief when he assures General Tilney—the father of Henry, Eleanor, and Captain Tilney—that Catherine stands to inherit great wealth from the childless Allens. This prospect earns her an invitation to visit Northanger Abbey as a presumptively suitable daughter-in-law. Despite General Tilney's constant civilities, she finds him cold and his presence oppressive. So do his children. They are all happier and more open when he is absent. Catherine, of course, views him and the Abbey through the lens of her favorite books, imagining all sorts of dark mysteries. Her foolishness—however necessary for the gothic parody—quickly grows tiresome. But we (and, more important, Henry) still find her appealing. When Catherine is abruptly cast out of the Abbey and left to her own devices to return home, she concludes that, "in suspecting General Tilney of either murdering or shutting up his wife, she had scarcely sinned against his character, or magnified his cruelty."[31]

Well, perhaps a bit. General Tilney, John Thorpe, and Isabella all disappoint. They prove cold and self-centered. Worse, they are insincere. Catherine plaintively remarks to herself regarding General Tilney, "Why he should say one thing so positively, and mean another all the while, was most unaccountable! How were people, at that rate, to be understood?"[32] How indeed. That is a question for all of Jane Austen's heroines to grapple with. How can we come to understand one another despite all the social conventions and restrictions of polite discourse? Catherine is not as fully formed, not as introspective as Austen's other heroines, particularly Anne Elliot and Fanny Price and, in a very different way, Emma, whose imaginative introspection leads her astray as surely as Catherine's infatuation with gothic fiction.

But Catherine does strike a blow against the patriarchy, because there is no question that, in the end, it is she who chooses Henry. The narrator quotes a "celebrated writer," contending that it would be the height of imprudence for a young lady to fall in love "before the gentleman's love is declared."[33] Yet Catherine does precisely that: "Though Henry was now sincerely attached to her, though he felt and delighted in all the excellencies of her character and truly loved her society, I must confess that his affection originated in nothing better than gratitude, or, in other words, that a persuasion of her partiality for him had been the only cause of giving her a serious thought."[34] Like Beatrice and Benedick in *Much Ado About Nothing*, "a persuasion of her partiality" is the spark for their romance. The heroine is not totally passive after all. By choosing Henry, Henry chooses her.

MARIANNE DASHWOOD

Marianne Dashwood is in many ways the opposite of Catherine Morland. She is a born heroine: beautiful, graceful, passionate, and artistic, with a highly developed and much-indulged sensibility, fine-tuned by the nature poetry of William Cowper. There is nothing commonplace about Marianne. Yet she and Catherine share key traits; they are both candid and impetuous. Indeed, Marianne's tumble down the hill behind her family's cottage echoes Catherine's penchant for rolling down the lawn behind her house. It is a reflection of their physical exuberance and willingness to ignore (or, in Catherine's case, ignorance of) social conventions.

Marianne's fall, of course, leads to her rescue by the romantic Willoughby, causing Sir John to jest a bit crudely that "all this tumbling about"—then, as now, a metaphor for sex—is no way to get a husband.[35] Catherine's ingenuousness leads her to a conventional marriage to a somewhat unconventional clergyman. Marianne's refusal to play the passive female nearly leads to disaster and ends in a second-best marriage in which even the woman's "power of refusal" seems denied to her.

Marianne is in some respect punished by her excessive sensibility, just as her sister Elinor suffers the effects of her highly developed sense of what is socially required. "It was impossible for [Marianne] to say what she did not feel, however trivial the occasion; and upon Elinor therefore the whole task of telling lies where politeness required it, always fell."[36] This is Jane Austen at her most caustic. Society demands lies and disguises for the self-interest that renders even our most intimate relationships transactional.

John Dashwood, the half-brother of Elinor and Marianne, promised on the deathbed of his father to support his stepmother and her daughters. It takes only four pages—as brilliant and chilling a four pages as Austen ever wrote—for his wife to whittle away that promise using a series of rationalizations and appeals to interest to justify what is nothing less than an act of theft compounded by the dishonor of repudiating a solemn pledge. Yet the modest sum needed to make the Dashwood women more comfortable would never have been missed from their vast estate.

Reduced to near poverty, Mrs. Dashwood and her daughters move into a cottage provided to them on generous terms by her relative Sir John Middleton. There they live, surrounded by books, music, and drawings—a life of aesthetic and emotional richness that gives them a dignity and interest Fanny Dashwood could never hope to approach. Yet it is a life that Elinor and Marianne both recognize will be incomplete without romantic love and sexual fulfillment. As Marianne insists, with no objection from Elinor, "a compact of convenience . . . a commercial exchange, in which each wished to be benefited at the expense of the other," would be "no marriage at all."[37] They must marry for love rather than money.

The two sisters, however, have starkly different characters. They are both amiable and generous, but Marianne is self-indulgent. She values honesty and deep feeling above all else and will tolerate no moderation of her joys and sorrows. Elinor carefully guards her own feelings. She values discipline, discretion, and propriety. It is not that Elinor has no sensibility or that Marianne no sense, though it sometimes appears that way to the other. But the mixture in each sharply differentiates them.[38] And much of the interest in the novel is in the way they grow more alike over time.

As William Blake writes in his 1794 book, *The Marriage of Heaven and Hell*, "without contraries is no progression."[39] Hegel, too, notes the dialectic between opposing concepts that reveals not only their differences but also their identity at a higher and more complete level of understanding. Neither Marianne nor Elinor is an abstraction. They are vibrant women who are changed by adversity and who reconsider their earliest opinions. But both sense *and* sensibility have their say in this process.

Their chosen suitors are equally antithetical. Edward Ferrars is sweet and thoughtful but unprepossessing and diffident to a fault. Willoughby (Marianne never calls him anything else) is all dash and aggressive self-confidence, with dark good looks and affections seemingly as open and transparent as Marianne's own. Yet both men harbor secrets that will wreak havoc on their relationships with the sisters. And the sisters will react to those secrets each in their own way.

Willoughby has debauched a young girl and then abandoned her. He feels little regret about that, later explaining to Elinor that he "cannot leave you to suppose . . . that because she was injured she was irreproachable, and because I was a libertine, she must be a saint."[40] The more serious consequence is that his aunt cuts him off from his anticipated inheritance, and he immediately drops Marianne to propose to an heiress he does not love. "Her money was necessary to me," he explains, "and in a situation like mine, anything was to be done to prevent a rupture,"[41] including publicly snubbing Marianne at an evening party in London and then sending her a letter—dictated by his fiancée—that disavows any intimacy, past or present, between them.

Marianne, whose "sorrows [and] joys could have no moderation,"[42] is predictably and justly devastated. But she courts her misery: "I must feel—I must be wretched."[43] Enjoined by Elinor to exert herself for the sake of her mother, Marianne replies, "I cannot, I cannot . . . do not torture me so. Oh! How easy for those who have no sorrow of their own to talk of exertion!"[44]

The accusation is unjust to Elinor, who has acute sorrows of her own. Edward, lonely and away from home at school, formed a secret engagement with Lucy Steele, an attachment from which she will not release him despite feeling no particular affection for him. She even uses the engagement as a weapon to wound and ward off Elinor. But Elinor suppresses all outward signs of her affliction: "When she joined [her family] at dinner only two hours after she had first suffered the extinction of all her deepest hopes, no one would have supposed from the appearance of the sisters, that Elinor was mourning in secret over obstacles which must divide her forever from the object of her love."[45] Even when Elinor finally confesses her loss of Edward, it is Marianne who collapses in tears.

"Elinor was to be the comforter of others in her own distresses"[46] and an apologist for Edward as well.

The reader cannot but feel that Elinor is perhaps altogether too measured and rational. And, indeed, the balance does shift over the course of the novel. Marianne's excessive sensibility warrants disapproval at first but wins our increasing sympathy after her humiliation at the hands of Willoughby. We feel admiration for Marianne's forthright avowals. Even her self-indulgence comes to seem a special sort of uncompromising courage.

It is with some sadness, therefore, that we see a subdued and chastened Marianne marry Colonel Brandon, "with no sentiment superior to strong esteem and lively friendship."[47] She is the reward for Brandon's sufferings and constancy and seems herself to have little say in the matter. Even Elinor and Edward owe their ability to marry to the living bestowed by Brandon. "They each felt his sorrows, and their own obligations, and Marianne, by general consent, was to be the reward of all."[48] We are told, as part of the conventional happy ending, that, despite his flannel waistcoat and his rheumatism, "her whole heart became, in time, as much devoted to her husband, as it had once been to Willoughby."[49] But we do not quite believe that. We regret the headstrong, passionate Marianne, whose opinions were all romantic and who never did anything by halves.

Nor does Austen let us forget that the establishments of the two sisters are nothing compared to those of Fanny Dashwood and Lucy Steele. They are cold, grasping, and unscrupulous and meet with every social and financial success. Austen's judgment on Lucy applies to both: "The whole of Lucy's behavior in the affair, and the prosperity which crowned it . . . may be held forth as a most encouraging instance of what an earnest, an unceasing attention to self-interest, however its progress may be apparently obstructed, will do in securing every advantage of fortune, with no other sacrifice than that of time and conscience."[50]

Elizabeth Bennet

Jane Austen famously disparaged *Pride and Prejudice*, her most popular novel: "The work is rather too light, and bright, and sparkling; it wants shade."[51] Heresy to Janeites. Even if the work *lacks* shade, it does not *want* shade. It is too perfect as is for readers to wish any change. To be sure, the villainy of Mr. Wickham, the unembarrassed debauchery of Lydia, the aggressive vulgarity of Mrs. Bennet, the negligent disengagement of Mr. Bennet, the arrogance of Lady Catherine, and even the sad compromise of Charlotte in marrying Mr. Collins are all too insubstantial to cast any real shade over the work. They merely people the stage on which the sun shines with such brilliance on Elizabeth Bennet.

With respect to her heroine, Austen shows no hesitation: "I must confess that I think her as delightful a creature as ever appeared in print, and how I shall be able to tolerate those who do not like *her* at least I do not know."[52] Here, we cannot but agree. Second, perhaps, only to Shakespeare's Rosalind, and like her in wit, spirit, and energy, Elizabeth enchants the novel from beginning to end. This is not to say she is without faults. But, as Mr. Knightley will say of Emma, she is "faultless in spite of all her faults."[53]

Elizabeth is, as Lady Catherine pronounces her, a "headstrong girl."[54] Indeed, she can be quite irritating in her outspoken misjudgments. She takes an instant dislike to Mr. Darcy when he declines to dance with her on their first encounter. "She is tolerable," Elizabeth overhears him saying to Mr. Bingley, "but not handsome enough to tempt *me*; and I am in no humor at present to give consequence to young ladies who are slighted by other men."[55] Elizabeth makes light of this remark among her friends, but it clearly rankles. By contrast, she is immediately attracted to Mr. Wickham, who is handsome, has easy manners, and shows a decided preference for her. These reactions were not wrong. Mr. Darcy was arrogant and insufferable at the ball. At the very least, he was ill at ease and reserved in company (which can seem to amount to pretty much the same thing), whereas Mr. Wickham had an open countenance, a fine figure, and a free (if somewhat breezy) address. These initial impressions incline Elizabeth to credit Mr. Wickham's disparagement of Mr. Darcy. "It was not in her nature to question the veracity of a young man of such amiable appearance as Wickham."[56]

But, of course, her "first impressions"—the initial title of the book—were, if not mistaken, at least only partially correct. They did not touch on the real character of either man, and it takes much of the novel before her judgments find firmer ground.[57] Mr. Darcy's admiration is more readily won by "the beautiful expression of her dark eyes," her "light and pleasing" figure, and her "easy playfulness."[58] As Elizabeth later suggests, her very impertinence attracted him. "The fact is, that you were sick of civility, of deference, of officious attention."[59] This teasing remark is of a piece with that ironic playfulness that Mr. Darcy so soon finds irresistible, even against his will.

Henry Tilney pronounced that "man has the advantage of choice, woman only the power of refusal." Elizabeth exercises that power of refusal on three occasions: first, when she rejects Mr. Collins's proposal; second, when she rejects Mr. Darcy's first proposal; and third, when she rebuffs Lady Catherine's insistence that she renounce any pretensions to marry her nephew. These are three of the turning points in the book, and each demonstrates Elizabeth's spirited independence.

Mr. Collins is a comic character, and his rejection is inevitable. Mrs. Bennet considers it a desirable match (if only to deter Mr. Collins from casting them from their home on the death of Mr. Bennet). But Elizabeth is anything but mercenary, and Mr. Collins manages to be both obsequious and pompous at the same time. He is also oblivious, brushing aside her refusal as "mere[] words" uttered because it is "the established custom of your sex to reject a man on the first application."[60] Since he can offer her what he considers a highly desirable establishment, he cannot believe she would pass up the opportunity, even after she uses harsher words that will echo in her later rejection of Mr. Darcy: "You could not make *me* happy, and I am convinced that I am the last woman in the world who would make *you* so."[61] Even her dual proposals from Mr. Darcy are subtly presaged in her assurance to Mr. Collins "that I am not one of those young ladies (if such young ladies there are) who are so daring as to risk their happiness on the chance of being asked a second time."[62]

Having finally convinced Mr. Collins of her sincerity and her unsuitability for the patronage of Lady Catherine, Elizabeth is shocked when Charlotte announces her own engagement. "Impossible," she exclaims, before checking herself. It is a cruel response and reflects a lack of sympathy for Charlotte's position. She is twenty-seven, not handsome, and without fortune. Her future prospect is as an old maid, a burden on her parents, and an object of ridicule. "I am not romantic," she explains. "I never was. I ask only a comfortable home."[63]

Elizabeth manages to hold her tongue, but she finds Charlotte's sacrifice of "every better feeling to worldly advantage" humiliating.[64] Yet this same Elizabeth is ready to excuse Mr. Wickham when his partiality for her gives way to pragmatism. Deprived of an independence (for which she blames Mr. Darcy), he seeks to acquire one through marriage to a rich young lady. Elizabeth "was ready to allow it a wise and desirable measure for both" Mr. Wickham and herself.[65] She will later make the same allowances for Colonel Fitzwilliam, who all but apologizes, as a younger son, for not being able to pay court to her.

Elizabeth will not marry for money, but she recognizes the folly of marrying without money. It is a fine line indeed, and in policing it she is harsher on her own sex. Clearly, she is troubled by the question of how a woman is to maintain her individual integrity in the marriage marketplace. How can she reserve a power not just of refusal but also of affirmative choice? Or, at least, how can she ensure that acceptance coincides with choice?

Mr. Darcy's first proposal comes at the worst possible time. Elizabeth has been rereading her sister's letters "as if intending to exasperate herself as much as possible against Mr. Darcy."[66] The manner of his address does nothing to soften her mood as he measures the strength of his passion by stressing the inferiority of her connections and the "degradation" that such a marriage would entail. He even admits that he did "everything in my power to separate my friend from your sister. . . . Towards *him* I have been kinder than towards myself."[67] And he offers no defense to her claim that he gravely injured Mr. Wickham's prospects, despite his father's wish to further them.

Elizabeth does not merely exercise the woman's power of refusal; she launches an attack on Mr. Darcy that reduces him to stunned silence. After rehearsing a litany of his flaws and chiding the ungentlemanly manner of his proposal, she ends:

> From the very beginning, from the first moment I may almost say, of my acquaintance with you, your manners impressing me with the fullest belief of your arrogance, your conceit, and your selfish disdain of the feelings of others, were such as to form that ground-work of disapprobation, on which succeeding events have built so immovable a dislike; and I had not known you a month before I felt that you were the last man in the world whom I could ever be prevailed on to marry.[68]

The power and brilliance of this dramatic scene is only heightened by the letter that Mr. Darcy delivers the next morning when Elizabeth is entering the park. The reader is as eager as Elizabeth to know—and as surprised to discover—what defenses Mr. Darcy has to the indictment against him. In these dozen pages, perhaps the finest in any novel, both Mr. Darcy's pride and Elizabeth's prejudice begin to crumble.

By the time they meet again at Pemberley, each has undergone a transformation and is prepared to encounter the other on new terms. "Never . . . had she seen him so desirous to please, so free from self-consequence, or unbending reserve as now."[69] Jane Austen, a great reader of Samuel Johnson, also valued what he called "a disposition to be pleased." Mr. Darcy, having paid as much attention to the substance of her rejection as she has to his letter, is "determined[] to be pleased."[70]

Elizabeth's feelings are more jumbled. She now respects and esteems him. But, above all, she feels "gratitude, not merely for having once loved her, but for loving her still well enough, to forgive all the petulance and acrimony of her manner in rejecting him, and all the unjust accusations accompanying her rejection."[71] When her sister Jane later asks when she first came to love Mr. Darcy, Elizabeth responds, "I believe I must date it from my first seeing his beautiful grounds at Pemberley."[72] She is only partially joking, for her visit to Pemberley completes the process begun with the letter. Seeing not just the tasteful elegance of his house and grounds but also the true character of the man as reflected in the devotion he inspires in his housekeeper, his sister, and his tenants, she realizes that "to be mistress of Pemberley might be something!"[73] What crystalizes these feelings into love is the prospect of losing him as a result of Lydia's thoughtless elopement. Mr. Darcy's apparent coldness on hearing the news does not lead her to condemn him. "It was, on the contrary, exactly calculated to make her understand her own wishes; and never had she so honestly felt that she could have loved him, as now, when all love must be vain."[74]

Her affection is neither blindly sexual (like Lydia's) nor transactional (like Charlotte's) but is founded on a rational appreciation of his character and the ways in which it complements her own. His wealth and consequence are part of that character and certainly no disincentive to affection. But, as Elizabeth comes to know Mr. Darcy better, she learns to know herself better as well and realizes that "he was exactly the man, who, in disposition and talents, would most suit her."[75]

Elizabeth is proud of Mr. Darcy for the part he played in prevailing on "such a man" as Mr. Wickham to marry Lydia, even though she is convinced that the connection must render a second proposal impossible. Yet she will not be bullied by Lady Catherine or social conventions into forswearing the possibility. She remains true to herself and hence to Mr. Darcy. Austen's summation casts a light on marriage that is neither wholly romantic nor wholly pragmatic:

> If gratitude and esteem are good foundations of affection, Elizabeth's change of sentiment will be neither improbable nor faulty. But if otherwise, if the regard springing from such sources is unreasonable or unnatural, in comparison of what is so often described as arising on a first interview with its object, and even before two words have been exchanged, nothing can be said in her defense, except that she had given somewhat of a trial to the latter method, in her partiality for Wickham, and that its ill-success might perhaps authorize her to seek the other less interesting mode of attachment.[76]

FANNY PRICE

There is no want of shade in *Mansfield Park*. Indeed, Fanny Price all but disappears among the shadows where she so often seeks refuge. But there is a certain stolidity in Fanny that verges on the passive aggressive. She declares herself happy "to sit in the shade,"[77] while the other young people are dashing about in the woods of Sotherton like the mismatched lovers in *A Midsummer Night's Dream*. But she resents, even deplores, their activity and, in subtle but unmistakable ways, makes that disapproval known. Fanny is the embodiment of a censorious virtue that continually, but quietly, passes judgment on others. That is why free, indirect speech is so important in the novel; the narrator can give voice to the critical sentiments that Fanny herself will rarely utter aloud.

Fanny's judgments invariably prove sound, but that does not improve the reader's opinion of her. C. S. Lewis calls her "the least attractive of all Jane Austen's heroes."[78] Lionel Trilling goes further: "Nobody, I believe, has ever found it possible to like the heroine of *Mansfield Park*."[79] Kingsley Amis, with typical comic hyperbole, calls her "a monster of complacency and pride" who comes to dominate the novel "under a cloak of cringing self-abasement."[80]

To be sure, unrelenting rectitude is off-putting, boring, and even antisocial. Fanny Price is no Elizabeth Bennet. She is frail, easily fatigued, and excessively timid. A morning picking roses is enough to confine her to the couch with a headache. The prospect of being spoken to in public is a source of genuine terror. Yet there is still something admirable in Fanny's refusal to budge when her inner moral compass bids her to stand firm. Her manner is gentle, but it conceals "the sternness of her purpose,"[81] which is superior to that of every other character in the novel. Both Sir Thomas and Edmund urge her to marry Henry Crawford, even though she is convinced (correctly) that he is not honorable. Henry is still acting.[82] It is his greatest role yet—the faithful suitor and savior—but his lover's vows will not last. Fanny knows that, even though Sir Thomas and Edmund do not.

Schooled by Mrs. Norris to "remember, wherever you are, you must be the lowest and last,"[83] Fanny is convinced that she "can never be important to anyone."[84] Even Sir Thomas laid it down on her first coming to Mansfield Park that, although she can be friends with his daughters, "they cannot be equals."[85] Much of her appeal to Henry is that she is "dependent, helpless, friendless, neglected, forgotten."[86] Fanny does not act; she endures. But Fanny finds consolation in the rare kind word, the occasional smile, and the chance gesture. More important, she has "all the heroism of principle,"[87] which sustains her through neglect, unreasonable demands, and, at the hands of Mrs. Norris, outright cruelty.

But even those to whom she owes the most respect and gratitude cannot take from her a woman's power of refusal. "It ought not to be set down as certain," she explains to Edmund, "that a man must be acceptable to every woman he may happen to like himself."[88] Fanny's own motives are not unmixed. She is in love with Edmund, sufficiently so that she would rather see him suffer the pangs of failed love than wed Mary Crawford, who has all the boldness and vitality of Elizabeth Bennet but lacks the fixed moral purpose that saves Fanny from hypocrisy and selfishness. Mary has many charms and genuinely likes and is kind to Fanny, even protecting her from the malicious assaults of Mrs. Norris. But Mary seeks pleasure, comfort, and consequence. Fanny seeks "a sound intellect and an honest heart."[89] So, too, does Edmund, who ultimately realizes he will find neither in Mary Crawford, who asserts that "a clergyman is nothing";[90] who jokes, half in earnest, that if his brother Tom would only die, Edmund would not need a profession; and who, most gravely, views Maria's adultery as something to be deplored only to the extent that it cannot be covered up.

But why, the reader must ask, would Jane Austen go from the enchanting, if headstrong, Elizabeth Bennett to the drab, if self-consciously virtuous, Fanny Price? Clearly, life is more complicated than *Pride and Prejudice* might indicate. Some notable critics see in *Mansfield Park* a conservative reaction against rapid industrialization and urbanization; an effort by Austen to memorialize and preserve the rural, village world she knew; and a caution that "improvements," whether in estates or society, risk disregarding tradition and ceremony.[91] On this view, *Mansfield Park*, like *Howard's End*, is a book about the true heirs of England. It is a book that celebrates the virtues of quiet, order, and duty, as opposed to the noise, disorder, and impropriety of Plymouth.

There is much truth in that reading, to be sure. But I see something more deliberately playful in the stark contrast between Fanny and Elizabeth and the introduction of a darker version of the latter in Mary Crawford. It is an experiment of sorts and an exploration of the limitations and possibilities of being a woman in the early years of nineteenth-century England. Like Edmund, Austen is trying to determine "whether a very different kind of woman might not do just as well—or a great deal better."[92]

The experiment with Fanny Price is not entirely successful. But the novel is. Kingsley Amis writes that "to invite Mr. and Mrs. Edmund Bertram round for the evening would not be lightly undertaken."[93] *Mansfield Park*, however, would be welcome at any time, which raises the question of whether one must like the heroine to admire the book. Certainly, Jane Austen did not think so. She remarked, only partly in jest, that in her next novel she would "take a heroine that no one but myself will much like."[94]

EMMA WOODHOUSE

There is much to like and even love about "Emma Woodhouse, handsome, clever, and rich, with a comfortable home and happy disposition, [who] seemed to unite some of the best blessings of existence; and had lived nearly twenty-one years in the world with very little to distress or vex her."[95] It just takes time, sympathetic understanding, and a considerable dollop of forbearance to warm to Emma. "The real evils indeed of Emma's situation," the narrator warns us, "were the power of having rather too much her own way, and a disposition to think a little too well of herself."[96] Despite the critical qualifiers—"rather too much" and "a little too well"—she sounds more like Mr. Darcy or, God forbid, Lady Catherine than the bright and brilliant Elizabeth Bennet or the timid yet tenacious Fanny Price.

Fanny always relies on her inner voice to guide her. So, too, does Emma, but her inner voice is often mistaken, if never in doubt. She is wrong in dismissing Robert Martin as a proper suitor for Harriet; she is wrong about the intentions of Mr. Elton; she is wrong about the relationship between Frank Churchill and Jane Fairfax; and, most egregiously, she is wrong about her own feelings for Mr. Knightley and his for her, completely missing or studiously ignoring the romantic tension that underlies their every interaction. Like Elizabeth Bennet, Emma must be schooled out of her misjudgments. She must learn to understand her own heart and the hearts of those around her.

It is tempting to begin every sentence about Emma with the word *yet*. Her every quality has its qualification, her every fault its virtue. She is a Rubik's Cube with no resolution. She is, in short, as thoroughly human and vibrantly alive as any character in fiction. Will the "blessings of existence" or the "real evils" of her situation prevail? Or will they remain in a perplexing equipoise? In this regard, the reader is at one with Mr. Knightley: "There is an anxiety, a curiosity in what one feels for Emma. I wonder what will become of her!"[97]

Certainly, the word *power* is a key to understanding Emma. She reigns over the family estate at Hartfield and is first in consequence among the "large and populous village almost amounting to a town" that is Highbury.[98] She displays her power with an aggressive self-confidence and self-regard that is more frankly masculine than anything found in Austen's other female characters, who, to the extent they wield power, do so in their own, more subtle ways. "I always deserve the best treatment," Emma candidly explains, "because I never put up with any other."[99] Nor should she.

Emma is generous and compassionate with the poor. "She understood their ways, could allow for their ignorance and their temptations, had no romantic expectations of extraordinary virtue from those, for whom education had done so little; entered into their troubles with ready sympathy, and always gave her assistance with as much intelligence as goodwill."[100] There is, to be sure, considerable condescension in her attitude and actions. Indeed, she is more comfortable with—because unquestionably superior to—the poor than with persons closer to her own station, where the lines of demarcation may be less clear. Her charity is another manifestation of her consequence. And yet—there is that word again—she bestows personal attention and genuine kindness as well as material relief.

Most intriguing for a Jane Austen heroine, Emma has no interest in getting married—or at least purports to have none. Her first reason, she explains to Harriet, is that she has never seen anyone superior enough to tempt her and does not in any event think it is in her nature to fall in love. Without that, she would only be changing a good situation for a worse one, as if marriage were purely transactional.

Fortune I do not want; employment I do not want; consequence I do not want: I believe few married women are half as much mistress of their husband's house, as I am of Hartfield; and never, never could I expect to be so truly beloved and important; so always first and always right in any man's eyes as I am in my father's.[101]

But the real reasons for her marital reticence—like everything else about her—are more complicated. She does not want to lose her sense of self-worth and personal integrity. She does not want to follow her sister as "a model of right feminine happiness,"[102] wholly eclipsed by the concerns of her husband and children. But neither does she want to follow the path of Mrs. Elton, who ironically refers to her husband as "my lord and master" while leading him about on a very short leash indeed. Emma must respect her husband. No one but an equal who will treat her as an equal will do, and where is she to find such a man in the small community of Highbury?

An even deeper reason for Emma's hesitancy to commit to any romantic relationship is her fear of her own emotional vulnerability. Having lost her mother as a young child, and with a father who requires, rather than offers, support and protection, Emma's strong façade covers a cauldron of pain and need over which she could easily lose control. She is the one who must hold everything together. But she shows her vulnerability when tears run unchecked down her face after Mr. Knightley chides her rudeness to Miss Bates.

Despite her poverty, Miss Bates is cheerful, fond of everyone, and always ready to count her blessings, however meager. She is also impossibly chatty and banal, which is comical but requires considerable forbearance. Hot, tired, and out of sorts, Emma is clever at Miss Bates's expense on Box Hill. But that moment—which she remedies as best she can by visiting a grateful Miss Bates the next day—does not define her.

Emma needs and seeks approval. She wants to be loved as well as admired, but she wants both on her own terms. She fully understands that "subduing feelings, concealing resentment, and avoiding eclat" are critical elements of the social contract, especially in an "almost . . . town" such as Highbury.[103] Emma is worried about the narrowing of her social circle. Just as "a very narrow income has a tendency to contract the mind, and sour the temper,"[104] so, too, does a very narrow company. Emma must have a positive outlet for her energy and her wit. Otherwise, they will manifest themselves in more hurtful ways.

When Miss Taylor, her longtime friend-cum-governess, becomes Mrs. Weston, Emma and her father dine together with "no prospect of a third to cheer a long evening."[105] Even Emma acknowledges that her father is no companion for her. Virtually a child himself, he is "fond of everybody that he [is] used to," but his crippling anxiety and "habits of gentle selfishness" require everyone else to bend to his special needs.[106] "Gentle selfishness," which is Emma's gloss, is too mild. He is a tyrant of nervous passivity, and the fact that Emma willingly, even happily, bears the consequences is among the strongest marks in her favor and the greatest obstacles to her personal growth. Her father is her excuse for avoiding more dangerous attachments.

So, too, is pretty, empty-headed Harriet. Emma cannot hope to find in her intercourse with Harriet "the equal footing and perfect unreserve" she enjoyed with Miss Taylor.[107] But she can play Pygmalion by forming her opinions and manners and introducing her into society. By planning a match for her protégé, moreover, she can experience the sexual and emotional frisson of romantic attachment without putting her own feelings at risk.[108] Much of the comedy in the novel comes from the repeated overthrowing of Emma's utter confidence in "the skill of such an observer on such a question as herself."[109] She wants to shape her small world, as Jane Austen does, to fit her imagination. "She had taken up the idea . . . [of Mr. Elton loving Harriet] and made everything bend to it."[110] But Emma cannot make her characters bend to her wishes. She must learn to accept them as they are. And that proves a challenge, for Emma is a snob on the order of Lady Catherine. She sets her back against social mobility. She is disdainful of the Coles for trying "to arrange the terms on which the superior families would visit them."[111] She rejects Mr. Knightley's suggestion that Robert Martin is a "respectable, intelligent gentleman-farmer."[112] To her, the Martins are part of the "yeomanry . . . with whom I feel I can have nothing to do."[113] Since Robert Martin does not need her charity, he is "in one sense as much above my notice as in every other he is below it."[114]

Yet even Lady Catherine comes around eventually rather than wall herself off from her nephew. Emma, likewise, chooses not to wall herself off from Highbury. Indeed, she is momentarily panicked at the prospect of not being invited to dinner at the Coles'. And she eventually accepts the fact that Harriet enjoys the greater benefit in her marriage to Robert Martin. Most important, Emma comes to accept the value of community and the need to connect with others. There is a telling passage when Emma is waiting for Harriet to finish some shopping:

> Emma went to the door for amusement.—Much could not be hoped from the traffic of even the busiest part of Highbury;—Mr. Perry walking hastily by, Mr. William Cox letting himself in at the office door, Mr. Cole's carriage horses returning from exercise, or a stray letter-boy on an obstinate mule, were the liveliest objects she could presume to expect; and when her eyes fell only on the butcher with his tray, a tidy old woman traveling homewards from shop with her full basket, two curs quarreling over a dirty bone, and a string of dawdling children round the baker's little bow-window eying the gingerbread, she knew she had no reason to complain, and was amused enough; quite enough still to stand at the door. A mind lively and at ease, can do with seeing nothing, and can see nothing that does not answer.[115]

Emma enjoys a moment of epiphany as she looks out on the almost-town that is her home. So, too, does the reader of Jane Austen. The town may be small, but the complex and sometimes fragile interrelationships are enough to make it a community. We, too, have no reason to complain and are amused enough, quite enough still to stand at the door with Emma.

She soon experiences a second epiphany: "It darted through her, with the speed of an arrow, that Mr. Knightley must marry no one but herself!"[116] Mr. Knightley has been her moral compass. He was right about Robert Martin, right about Mr. Elton, and right about the frivolous insincerity of Frank Churchill and his secret relationship with Jane Fairfax. He has all the insight and delicacy of observation that Emma claims for herself. More important, though, Emma has always been first with him, "first in interest and affection,"[117] which she of course considers only her due until the fear of being supplanted arises in her mind.

Under the guise of a "partial old friend," Mr. Knightley admires her face and figure above all others and confesses frankly to Mrs. Weston, "I love to look at her."[118] But it is not until the ball, after he graciously rescues Harriet from the rudeness of the Eltons, that they exchange a meaningful glance charged with more than friendship. She even asks him to dance with her, explaining that "we are not really so much brother and sister as to make it at all improper." "Brother and sister!" Mr. Knightley responds, "no, indeed."[119]

According to Aristotle, the highest form of friendship is based on shared moral growth. For Jane Austen, it is also the strongest ground for marriage. Mr. Knightley and Emma meet as true equals. Mr. Knightley steadies and affirms Emma; she unsettles and enlivens him.[120] In a stark reversal of established custom, Mr. Knightley even moves to her home so that she need not part from her father. She is worth it. As Mrs. Weston, one among the "small band of true friends who witnessed the ceremony," pronounces, "It was all right, all open, all equal."[121]

ANNE ELLIOT

In Anne Elliot, Austen comes dangerously close to that picture of perfection she claimed to disdain. Anne has "an elegance of mind and sweetness of character, which must have placed her high with any people of real understanding."[122] She has the poetic sensibility of Marianne Dashwood tempered by the prose moralists favored by Elinor. Like Fanny Price, her observations of others are delicate and precise. Like Emma, she harbors deep reserves of passion.

She does not, alas, have the liveliness of Elizabeth Bennet. She made a terrible, life-changing mistake when, at the age of nineteen, she was persuaded by Lady Russell, who had "almost a mother's love, and mother's rights,"[123] to break off her engagement with Captain Wentworth. "Her attachment and regrets had, for a long time, clouded every enjoyment of youth; and an early loss of bloom and spirits had been their lasting effect."[124] She is now twenty-seven, faded, thin, and unmarried. The "nice tone of her mind, the fastidiousness of her taste,"[125] would have precluded a second attachment, even apart from her continuing love of Captain Wentworth: "To retentive feelings eight years may be little more than nothing."[126] Her horizons have narrowed, and her hopes are all but extinguished. Little wonder that she, like Marianne, cherishes the beauty and sadness of autumn.

> Her *pleasure* in the walk must arise from the exercise and the day, from the view of the last smiles of the year upon the tawny leaves and withered hedges, and from repeating to herself some few of the thousand poetical descriptions extant of autumn, that season of peculiar and inexhaustible influence on the mind of taste and tenderness, that season which has drawn from every poet, worthy of being read, some attempt at description, or some lines of feeling.[127]

Anne is more completely isolated than any other Austen heroine. She "was nobody with either father or sister: her word had no weight; her convenience was always to give way;—she was only Anne."[128] She has no close confidant: no Elinor, no Jane, no Miss Taylor, not even an Edmund to whom she can relieve her heart. She also has no Mansfield Park or Hartfield to connect her with a community. Throughout the novel, she is driven by the will of others from Kellynch Hall to Uppercross Cottage to Lyme to Uppercross Great House to Kellynch Lodge and finally to Bath. She is at home nowhere but in her own consciousness, and yet that consciousness pervades the novel. In no other book has the Austenian narrator so thoroughly inhabited the mind of a single character. The reader cannot but share her moral judgments, deplore her lack of consequence, and become invested in the unfolding of her "second spring."[129]

Anne is not bitter. She regrets the advice of Lady Russell but believes she was right to follow it. "She had been forced into prudence in her youth, she learned romance as she grew older—the natural sequel of an unnatural beginning."[130] But Captain Wentworth has not forgiven her. "She had used him ill; deserted and disappointed him; and worse, she had shown a feebleness of character in doing so, which his own decided, confident temper could not endure."[131] It is up to Anne to change his mind and reengage his heart.

Even before Lyme, that process has begun. Her gentleness and unselfish attention to Mary's children gains his notice at Uppercross. Anne is also the quiet repository of everyone's confidences. That is followed at Lyme by her evident kindness to, and ability to draw out, Captain Benwick. But it is her fortitude that strikes Wentworth most. When Louisa has her fall on the Cob, only Anne keeps her composure. Everyone, even Wentworth, looks to her for direction: "no one so proper, so capable as Anne!"[132] The fine wind and the open air, moreover, have restored in her "the bloom and freshness of youth," which strikes, first, William Elliot and then Captain Wentworth, who, with "a glance of brightness," sees the Anne Elliot of eight years earlier.[133]

Anne is not perfect. She even feels a flash of schadenfreude at Louisa's fall. "She thought it could scarcely escape him to feel, that a persuadable temper might sometimes be as much in favor of happiness, as a very resolute character."[134] And when she learns of Louisa's shocking engagement to Benwick and realizes that Captain Wentworth is now free of that entanglement, "she had some feelings which she was ashamed to investigate. They were too much like joy, senseless joy!"[135]

Anne must still engineer the exchange of words that will bring them together again. "Surely," she thinks, "if there be constant attachment on each side, our hearts must understand each other ere long. We are not boy and girl, to be captiously irritable, misled by every moment's inadvertence, and wantonly playing with our own happiness."[136] But, indeed, Captain Wentworth is rendered irritable by wounded pride and is misled by the vexation of William Elliot's attentions and the obvious preference of Anne's family and Lady Russell for a union that will install Anne in her mother's place as the mistress of Kellynch Hall.

It is up to Anne, then, to show firmness of character and the courage to speak, notwithstanding the conventions of female reticence. "If she could only have a few minutes conversation with him again, she fancied she should be satisfied; and as to the power of addressing him she felt all over courage if the opportunity occurred."[137] It does occur, thanks to her efforts and notwithstanding untimely interjections by Mr. Elliot and others.

Anne greets Captain Wentworth at the concert and engages him in conversation despite the hostile looks of her family. She makes clear to him at the White Hart Inn, when responding to questions from Mrs. Musgrove, that she is not at all eager to spend time at an evening party with Mr. Elliot. And when Captain Wentworth suggests that perhaps she has become fond of cards, her response is weighted with enough meaning even for the sometimes slightly obtuse Captain Wentworth: "I am not yet so much changed."[138]

But it is in her dramatic conversation with Captain Harville that Anne swears her faith to Captain Wentworth, overhearing from a nearby table where he is writing a letter. When Harville remarks that his sister would not have forgotten Benwick so easily, Anne responds, "It would not be the nature of any woman who truly loved."[139] And when Harville insists that it is not "more man's nature than woman's to be inconstant and forget those they do love, or have loved," she does not dispute him. "All the privilege I claim for my own sex (it is not a very enviable one, you need not covet it) is that of loving longest, when existence or when hope is gone."[140]

Once they contrive to be alone, "soon words enough had passed between them."[141] The narrator need not provide further details, for enough words have already been spoken by Anne and written by Wentworth to reveal their passion for each other and to settle their future together. They will have neither land nor family nor social position on which to ground and guide their relationship. As Julia Prewitt Brown writes in her wonderful book on the novels, "For the first time in Jane Austen, the future is not linked with the land, and the social order is completely dissociated from the moral order."[142] Anne and Wentworth must forge a new community of the like-minded and openhearted, but also "pay the tax of quick alarm"[143] in a rootless world fraught with contingency.

> They exchanged again those feelings and those promises which had once before seemed to secure everything, but which had been followed by so many, many years of division and estrangement. There they returned again into the past, more exquisitely happy, perhaps, in their

re-union, than when it had been first projected; more tender, more tried, more fixed in a knowledge of each other's character, truth, and attachment; more equal to act, more justified in acting.[144]

6

Stendhal on Love and Death

THE FRENCH NOVELIST AND LITERARY CRITIC ANDRÉ GIDE WAS ASKED to name the best novel ever written. He had no hesitation in choosing the author of that novel—Marie-Henri Beyle, known to us by his pseudonym, Stendhal. Choosing the particular work proved more difficult. But, after repeated readings of each, Gide concluded that *The Charterhouse of Parma* was even greater than *The Red and the Black.* "*The Charterhouse,*" he wrote, "has this one magic quality; every time one goes back to it, it is always a new book one is reading."[1]

One could quibble with the preference for *The Charterhouse,* even after the repeated readings that both novels merit. But the choice is largely a personal one, such as that between *The Iliad* and *The Odyssey* or between *Hamlet* and *The Tempest.* Are we in the mood for a searing tragedy or a lyric romance?[2] Despite its rather grim, truncated ending, *The Charterhouse of Parma,* with its enigmatic "blend of seriousness and farce,"[3] does indeed have the magic quality of seeming ever fresh to us, particularly the scenes at Waterloo and in the prison where Fabrice falls in love with his jailer's daughter. The romance is stripped naked, but its charm never dims.

That does not mean that either book is written in the Romantic style. Stendhal detested the lush, overheated rhetoric of writers such as Chateaubriand and Victor Hugo. He famously bragged that he prepared for writing each day by reading sections of the Napoleonic Code, taking that as his prose model. The result is a dry, even fractured, style that sometimes repels but mostly compels close attention. One passes through the words to get at the reality beneath.

Stendhal's work is a curious mixture of realism and Romanticism, and that mélange is nowhere more evident than in *The Red and the Black*. Its hero, Julien Sorel, is a Romantic determined to be a realist. He is a peasant who resolves to rise, through intelligence and the force of his personal energy, in a society that, in his view, requires all natural feelings to be suppressed in favor of calculated hypocrisy. He "had sworn an oath never to say anything except what seemed false to him."[4] As part of a constant internal dialogue in which he gauges the success of his often-clumsy stratagems, Julien commands himself to display a total lack of human sympathy. Yet somehow his innate innocence and charm, as well as a moral compass he cannot fully suppress, keep him from being odious. We do not love Julien the way we do Fabrice. But he compels our fascination and even the sympathy he would deny to others.

The Red and the Black appears to be a classic bildungsroman, and Julien Sorel is certainly a prototype for Balzac's Eugene de Rastignac and countless other naïfs who arrive from the provinces bursting with talent and seeking fame, fortune, and love, only to lose their illusions in the pitiless grinder of modern life. But, for Julien, there is a critical twist. He is already cynical, hardened, and, in his own view, without illusions. He has steeled himself in advance against any Romantic view of the world. What he finally sheds in the book is that protective armor.

In a critical passage, he exits Mme de Rênal's bedroom after having become her lover:

> Mon Dieu! être heureux, être aimé, n'est-ce que ça? Telle fut la première pensée de Julien, en rentrant dans sa chamber. Il était dans cet état d'étonnement et de trouble inquiet où tombe l'âme qui vient d'obtenir ce qu'elle a longtemps désiré. Elle est habituée à désirer, ne trouve plus quoi désirer, et cependant n'a pas encore de souvenirs.[5]

> (My God! To be happy, to be loved: is that all there is to it? Such was Julien's first thought on returning to his room. He was in that state of astonishment and troubled disquiet into which the soul falls when it

obtains that which it has long desired. Accustomed to desire, it finds nothing more to desire, but does not yet have memories.)[6]

What Julien finds, in the face of death, is a merger of desire and memory in a new form of love. In the process, he finds his own best self. One might call the novel *Les Illusions Retrouvées*.

LIFE

Marie-Henri Beyle was born in Grenoble, France, on January 23, 1783. His father, Chérubin Joseph Beyle, was a highly successful lawyer who also speculated in real estate. His mother, whom he adored, was Henriette-Adelaide-Charlotte Gagnon, daughter of a wealthy local doctor. After giving him two sisters, she died in childbirth in November 1790, when Henri was not yet eight years old. Chérubin, in his grief, sealed her room for a decade and turned for comfort to religion and money. Henri sealed his heart. He hated the cold and emotionally detached father who made no effort to comfort his devastated son. "He was an excessively dislikable man," Henri would later write in one of his many thinly disguised autobiographical writings, "always concerned with the purchase and sale of property, very sharp, accustomed to dealing with peasants."[7]

Chérubin himself was lucky to survive the Reign of Terror that followed the early stages of the French Revolution. He was placed on a local list of suspected counterrevolutionaries, likely by a disgruntled counterparty to one of his real-estate deals. Chérubin was arrested in 1793 and spent at least two brief stints in jail before being finally cleared. The irony, Henri would later note, was that, although the accusation was vilely motivated, it was in fact true. His father favored the *ancien régime* and would have welcomed its return. At home, Henri was forced to disguise his own growing enthusiasm for the revolution and the republic.

The young Henri found little affection after his mother's death. Henriette's younger sister, Seraphie, came to run the household, brusquely asserting her authority while constantly complaining of the burden with which she was saddled. Henri loathed her and was detested in return.

When she died in 1797, at the age of thirty-six, the entire family was relieved, even Chérubin.

Henri had no better luck in his father's choice of the stern and forbidding Abbé Jean-François Raillane as private tutor for his son. "Raillane's tyranny," as Henri called it, lasted two years before Henri was allowed in 1796 to attend L'École Centrale de Grenoble, a school that his maternal grandfather, Dr. Gagnon, helped establish after the Directory succeeded the Terror and liberal principles thrived. The school had an enlightened curriculum that included the sciences, modern languages, and even government legislation. The students could choose their own course of study. Henri's literature teacher taught not only the French classics but also translations of Milton, Dryden, and Shakespeare.

Henri's close relationship with his grandfather was one of the few bright spots in his early years. Dr. Gagnon was beloved by the poor, whom he treated without charge, and respected by the bourgeoisie for his skill. He had a large library, where the lonely boy read constantly and precociously. Henri had to read Rousseau in secret but was otherwise free to choose what books he wished.

Henri was a reserved and prickly young man. He had a few close friends. But he was surly and even fought a duel with one fellow student after an insult led to a shove and then to a slap. It is unclear where these fifteen-year-old boys found the weapons. Both guns failed to fire, but Henri was lionized by his contemporaries for the courage he showed.

Henri graduated in 1799 with the first prize in mathematics. He was offered a scholarship at the prestigious École Polytechnique in Paris. Although he loved the nearby mountains and surrounding countryside, he felt no regrets in leaving Grenoble, which he called "the capital of pettiness." Henri arrived in Paris on November 10, 1799, the day after Napoleon seized power as first consul. The sixteen-year-old boy promptly became a confirmed Bonapartist.

In the midst of such historic turmoil, it is unsurprising that Henri decided not to sit for the entrance exam at the École Polytechnique. He wanted to take Paris by storm as a comic dramatist in the fashion of Molière. That did not happen. His paint-by-the-numbers attempt to model his plays on other successful dramas was a deflating failure. He lacked the experience for original social satire.

Fortunately, a cousin, Pierre Daru, was minister of war under Napoleon and helped find Henri a clerical job at the ministry. Henri showed a talent for administration and rose quickly, traveling through Switzerland to Milan with the minister. Italy was a revelation. He loved the language, the people, the art, and most of all the music, attending the opera at La Scala and in other cities as often as he could. He claims his life was changed when he first heard a performance of Domenico Cimarosa's *Il matrimonio segreto* (*The Secret Marriage*).[8]

Henri served briefly in the French army as a second lieutenant. He even took part in a battle at Castelfranco in early 1801, providing him with material he would need for Fabrice's famous adventures at Waterloo. He soon became *aide-de-camp* of General Michaud, though still only eighteen. On the cessation of hostilities, he was granted a sick leave, returned home to Grenoble, and resigned his commission.

For much of the next decade, Henri tried to make his living as a writer, mostly in Paris but sometimes retreating to Grenoble when his money ran out. He was bitterly annoyed with his father's failure to support the lifestyle to which he aspired. Dr. Gagnon sensibly urged him to once again cultivate and seek employment from his cousin Daru, who Henri affected to despise, and otherwise to make himself more agreeable and search out the best in others.

> Your relationships with several people have inspired you with contempt, an altogether too universal disdain. It is a pleasure to discover honest souls and generous actions; as for you, my dear boy, it seems to me that you delight instead in unveiling perfidy and disgrace.[9]

Though he never conquered his cynical disdain of the majority of humankind, Henri did indeed make himself more agreeable, especially to women. Despite an unprepossessing appearance—he was stout and balding, with a small mouth and a pug nose—Henri began a lifelong series of affairs and friendships with (at least by his account) an astonishing array of women, from actresses to countesses. His brilliant conversation and magnetic presence more than made up for an aggressive awkwardness, and he was welcome even in the best salons, at least until he managed to insult another guest or even the hostess, which happened with some regularity. Henri genuinely loved women and argued for their equality in financial affairs, education, and sexual liaisons.[10]

Daru's intervention was again decisive in obtaining a number of posts for Henri, including a provisional appointment supplying the army. In that position, he spent two years in northern Saxony, where he was exposed to German Romanticism and the cult of sentimental feeling found in the early works of Goethe and the plays of Schiller. He was also with the army when it entered Vienna during the French invasion of Bavaria. There, he reveled in the music and contracted syphilis.

In 1810, Henri was named an auditor of the council of state. He promptly annoyed Daru—now secretary of state and a count—with a lengthy, unauthorized leave of absence to Milan, Rome, and Naples. He also made advances to Daru's wife, who deftly parried them and remained his friend, though never his lover.

Henri participated in Napoleon's disastrous Russian campaign of 1812/1813. Sent to provision the troops, he arrived in Moscow to find the city burning by order of its governor. Henri showed considerable ingenuity, courage, and vigor during the subsequent retreat in which so many French soldiers died. Napoleon was forced to abdicate and was sent to exile on Elba in 1814, when Henri was thirty-one. The allied troops were welcomed in Paris, and Henri was out of a job despite appeals and pledges of loyalty to the restored king, Louis XVIII.

Henri returned to Milan in August 1814 and spent seven reasonably happy and productive years there. He regularly attended the opera, wrote prodigiously, and pursued his many love affairs. Unlike his character Fabrice del Dongo, Henri wisely made no attempt to join in the One Hundred Days that marked the return of Napoleon from Elba until his defeat at Waterloo, a second abdication, a second Restoration, and a harsher banishment to St. Helena. Under the pen name Stendhal, Henri wrote numerous books on art, music, and travel. In his widespread correspondence, he adopted many other pseudonyms. This was part playful, part paranoid, and part a reflection of his dislike for his father. Stendhal, like his hero Julien Sorel, even fantasized about being the natural son of a nobleman. He may also have been a spy or at least an agitator for liberal reforms. Certainly, the Austrian authorities thought so, and he was exiled from his beloved Milan in 1821.

Stendhal spent the next nine years of his life in Paris. He had no job and very little money. His father had died in 1819, but Stendhal's inheritance was much less extensive than he had hoped. Yet another reason to hate his father. He continued writing: a disjointed but psychologically acute "treatise" *On Love* in 1822; a critical comparison of *Racine and Shakespeare* in 1823, in which he annoyed his countrymen by favoring the English poet; an enthusiastic *Life of Rossini*; and his first novel, *Armance*, in 1827, when the author was forty-four. He even wrote opera reviews and several rather bloody short stories set in Italy that were posthumously published as *Italian Chronicles*. His greatest financial success was *Rome, Naples, and Florence*, a mélange of autobiography, travelogue, journalism, and cultural criticism.

There was increasing liberal discontent in Paris with the repressive Bourbon Restoration. Stendhal's circle included the Romantic writer Prosper Mérimée; the painter Eugène Delacroix, whose most famous work would be of Lady Liberty leading the July Revolution of 1830; and Alfred de Musset, poet and lover of the novelist George Sand. Stendhal was sympathetic to their liberal values but also cynical, a mixture he would capture in *The Red and the Black*, published in 1830. The novel manages to be very much about the July Revolution without ever mentioning it.

With the Bourbon dynasty finally at an end, Stendhal was appointed by the new king, Louis-Philippe, as consul to Trieste. After the Austrians refused to grant him an exequatur, he was reappointed to the port city of Civitavecchia. He found the city dreary and boring and spent as much time in Rome as he could while continuing to write book after book. By 1837, he was back in Paris, where he wrote *The Charterhouse of Parma*, in just over seven weeks, from November 4 to December 26, 1939. He made a rough draft section by section and then dictated the final version of each section to a copyist. Honoré de Balzac wrote an extremely favorable review, calling it "a great and beautiful book."[11]

Stendhal died in Paris of a stroke in the early hours of March 23, 1842, at the age of fifty-nine. His chosen epitaph read, "Errico Beyle, Milanese: visse, scrisse, amò" (Henri Beyle, Milanese: he lived, he wrote, he loved).

THE RED AND THE BLACK

Julien Sorel was born too late for the French Revolution and the age of Napoleon. Julien was a child of the Restoration, that fifteen-year hiatus between Napoleon's second abdication in 1815 and the July Revolution of 1830. The promises of the First Republic (liberty, equality, and fraternity) had largely collapsed. The Bourbons were back on the throne. To outward appearances, the *ancien régime* once more held sway. Yet nobles were in a precarious position. Economic conditions and rapid industrialization gave increasing power to the middle class (the so-called bourgeoisie). The social world was open to money as well as rank and title, especially since the latter could be bought. Both middle and upper classes, moreover, had a strong incentive to maintain the status quo and jointly suppress the lowest classes. Aristocrats and plutocrats alike feared a new revolution and a new terror. Political enthusiasm, superior intelligence, and even lively conversation were viewed with suspicion. The parvenu was anathema, unless, of course, success compelled his recognition and incorporation.

That was exactly the task that Julien Sorel, son of a peasant mill owner, set for himself. He was brilliant, ambitious, and desperate to escape his obscure origins. Julien hated his father and his brute brothers, even fantasizing, as Stendhal would do, that his natural father was a nobleman. Interestingly, Fabrice had the inverse and probably correct fantasy—or so the narrator hints—that his true father was not the noble Marquis del Dongo but the lowly Lieutenant Robert during the French occupation of Lombardy that began in 1796.

In the time of Napoleon, Julien would have joined the army and risen by virtue of his natural talent and fierce energy. That route is no longer open to him. He has no money to purchase a commission and no influential friends to secure one for him. Besides, France is at peace, having meekly tolerated occupation by the Allies under the Treaty of Paris of 1815. Julien accordingly will have to rely on his own resources, and that means, first and foremost, disguising his true feelings and thoughts. Julien is disdainful of society post-Napoleon. He believes that it is full of corruption and hypocrisy and resolves to be the consummate hypocrite. Cold calculation will dictate his every stratagem.

For that calculation to work, however, Julien must understand and grapple with the changing social and political conditions of his day. The rules are in flux, and he must reinvent himself in his various roles as tutor, seminarian, and secretary of the Marquis de La Mole, as well as the professed lover of three very different women. Each of the social and political venues in which Julien moves is depicted with great attention to concrete detail, and the characters he encounters are deeply embedded in their historical milieu.[12]

Stendhal has a legitimate claim to be the father of realism in the novel, but that does not make *The Red and the Black* a work of realism. It has the same enigmatic "blend of seriousness and farce" that Irving Howe found in *The Charterhouse*. Much of the comedy of the work lies in Julien's inability to understand the social and political conditions in which he finds himself. Julien is neither pragmatic nor materialistic. He has little interest in bourgeois wealth. He wants recognition and glory. He wants to establish his spiritual and intellectual nobility by forging a new identity. Julien echoes the plaintive cry of Molière's Alceste: "Je veux qu'on me distingue" (I want to be distinguished). Alceste seeks distinction through blunt candor. Julien adopts as his means the religious hypocrisy of a Tartuffe.[13] Yet, somehow, sincerity keeps breaking through. He is spontaneous despite himself. He strives to appear worse than he is and, as a result, is constantly at cross-purposes with himself. He sets out to conquer the world only to discover that it is built on artificial conventions and distinctions of no real worth.

As the good Abbé Pirard tells him, "Il n'y a pas de moyen terme pour vous" (There is no middle ground for you). Julien needs a grand passion for his "ardent . . . spirit."[14] Like his creator, Stendhal, Julien is a Romantic determined to be a realist.

CHEZ RÊNAL

Verrières is a small French town that sits along the Doubs River, close to the mountains of Switzerland. It has grown wealthy from the iconic Mulhouse cotton prints made there. But the idyllic setting is marred by a sawmill on the Doubs and even more by a large nail factory that creates an incessant, deafening racket in the main street, with twenty huge hammers raised by the power of a water wheel and then dropped with a crash to pound slips of iron into nails. The Industrial Revolution has come to the fictional Verrières.

The factory is owned by M. de Rênal, who, since the restoration of the monarchy in 1815 and his election as mayor, "has been ashamed of being in trade."[15] M. de Rênal is a loud, vain, and grasping man who passes for the most aristocratic personage in Verrières. His wife never even admits to herself how boring and vulgar her husband is. She just wants to be left alone in her innocence, to play with her children and wander in the garden.

It is into this far-from Eden that Julien is introduced as the unlikely fruit of M. de Rênal's pride and ambition. Julien, eager to escape his peasant origins and brutal father, has turned himself into something of a prodigy by learning the New Testament in Latin by heart and by studying with equal care a book on the papacy. He "believed as little of one as of the other,"[16] but they are a means of distinguishing himself. His true favorite book is *The Memorial of Saint Helena*, the equivalent of a personal and political testament for the cult of Napoleon. Yet he could not reveal his admiration for Napoleon without being shunned as a Jacobin, so "he never spoke of him without horror."[17]

M. de Rênal decides he must have Julien as a tutor to his sons. Not that he cares particularly about their education: "It's simply one of those expenses that are necessary to keep up a social position."[18] Rênal's archrival, M. Valenod, who is a liberal and director of the poorhouse from which he embezzles large sums, has two fine new horses to show off. Rênal, a conservative, plans to dazzle the town with the sight of his children walking with their tutor. The labels *liberal* and *conservative* have little meaning in a time when political ideas are anathema. They are more like team colors than indications of any genuine political engagement; they mark two opposing forces, each equally bent on the spoils of power.

Julien plays his part to perfection. Dressed in a black suit given to him by M. de Rênal only a few hours earlier, he asks the oldest child, Adolphe, to open the testament at random and read him the first three words. He then recites the rest of the page from memory. That evening, all Verrières comes to witness the marvel, and M. de Rênal's satisfaction is complete.[19]

But it is Mme de Rênal who is Julien's real conquest. She is terrified that the new tutor will beat her children if they do not learn their lessons. When she comes upon him at the time of his arrival, however, he is too timid even to ring the bell. She almost takes him for a girl in disguise, with his slight build, large dark eyes, and lovely features. "Who could have guessed," the Stendhalian narrator interjects, "that that girlish face, so pale and soft, concealed an unshakeable resolution to die a thousand deaths rather than fail to make his fortune!"[20]

Intoxicated by Mme de Rênal's perfume and light summer dress, Julien absurdly decides he must kiss her hand.

> At first he was afraid of his own idea; an instant later he said to himself: It will be cowardice on my part not to carry out a scheme that may be useful to me, and cut down this fine lady's contempt for a laborer just liberated from his sawmill.[21]

Julien totally misreads Mme de Rênal, who is far from feeling any contempt for the young man. She is shocked by his boldness but fails to reproach him. Indeed, she calls him "sir" and does everything to soothe his anxiety and encourage his confidence. His very awkwardness and lack of experience make him endearing in her eyes.

Mme de Rênal is so relieved that Julien is not the severe martinet she imagined that she drops her guard and delights in his company. He chatters incoherently in her presence, but his eyes "were so fine and expressed so ardent a spirit that . . . they gave meaning to words which in themselves had none."[22] She attributes to him virtues simply because he lacks the vices of her husband and M. Valenod. "Gradually, it seemed to her generosity, nobility of spirit, and humanity existed only in the person of this young abbé."[23]

The narrator assures us that if they were in Paris, their situation would soon have been clarified. But things move more slowly in the provinces, particularly among those who read no novels. "Love is the child of novels," after all, which "would have outlined for them the roles to be played" and given them a "model to imitate."[24] Any such knowledge or expectation would have horrified Mme de Rênal. But "thanks to this ignorance, Mme de Rênal, in perfect happiness, occupied herself continually with Julien, and was far from blaming herself in any way."[25]

Julien is no less ignorant but much more calculating. He views all social encounters in terms of military strategy, while ignorant of his own feelings and needs and the feelings and needs of those around him. He thus turns each phase of their growing intimacy into "a heroic duty" and a test of his courage.[26] One evening in the garden, after steeling himself for hours, he takes her hand. She withdraws it, but he seizes it again, and she allows it to rest in his "long enough to count it a definite conquest."[27] Indeed, when she has to rise for a moment, on resettling she returned her hand to his "as if the whole matter were now settled between them."[28] For a moment, Julien forgets to calculate; he fails to gauge his success in military terms.

> For the first time in his life he was carried away by the power of beauty. Lost in a vague delightful dream, wholly foreign to his character, gently pressing that hand which seemed to him perfectly beautiful, he only half heard the rustling of the linden tree in the light night wind and the distant barking of dogs by the mill on the Doubs.[29]

Mme de Rênal, too, is lost in the moment. "With her hand in Julien's, she thought of nothing at all; she allowed herself to live."[30]

It is a seemingly perfect intermezzo. Mme de Rênal, despite being deeply religious, feels no guilt, even after Julien covers her arm with passionate kisses. "No hypocrisy clouded the purity of this innocent spirit, haunted by a passion it had never known before."[31] Until later, that is, when the ugly word *adultery* comes to her mind. Then she is plunged into despair. Julien, too, is recalled to his own situation, for "at the age of twenty, the idea of the world and the effect to be produced there is more important than anything else."[32] He cannot afford to be carried away by love. Mme de Rênal, he reminds himself, is merely a conquest, a step on the ladder (quite literally) measuring his progress in society. Julien decides that he owes it to himself to become her lover and draws up "a highly detailed plan of campaign,"[33] which, of course, completely misfires. When he enters her room at 2:00 a.m., and she angrily reproaches him, he collapses at her feet, grasps her knees, and bursts into tears. He owes to his genuine tears and to the love he had already inspired in her "a victory to which all of his clumsy subtleties would never have conducted him."[34]

It is in the aftermath of this "victory" that Julien asks himself, "Is that all it is?"[35] Yet he comes close to finding it enough. He allows himself to love with the natural ardor of his age, telling Mme de Rênal of his anxieties and even confessing his admiration for Napoleon. She, in turn, reveals to him "an aspect of his own soul of which he had never been aware."[36]

This "vague delightful dream" of Edenic innocence and sensuous delight cannot last, however. It is impossible to keep their intimacy a complete secret. A jealous maid reveals it to M. Valenod, a previously unsuccessful suitor for Mme de Rênal's favors, and he pens anonymous letters to M. de Rênal. Mme de Rênal deftly parries these crude attacks but cannot suppress her own deeply religious and superstitious sense of sin. When her oldest son becomes seriously ill, she blames it on her adultery. These events change the complexion (if not the fervor) of their love. They cannot recover "that delicious serenity, that cloudless felicity, that easy joy of their first falling in love, when Mme de Rênal's only fear was that Julien might not love her enough. Their happiness now wore sometimes the expression of a crime."[37]

The French statesman Talleyrand is said to have reproached Napoleon for the execution of a royalist opponent: "C'est pire qu'un crime, c'est une faute" (It is worse than a crime, it is a mistake). Julien reproaches himself in much the same way. The only thing he sees wrong in his liaison with Mme de Rênal is that it is keeping him from realizing his ambitions. He might have obtained a lasting happiness with Mme de Rênal. But, after he rides a fine horse in the visiting king's honor guard and serves as a deacon at a ceremony conducted by the young bishop celebrating the relics of Saint Clement at the abbey of Bray-le-Haut, Julien cannot suppress his impatience to advance. He will nurture "the sacred fire with which one makes oneself a name."[38] In the process, he must abjure that aspect of his soul cultivated by Mme de Rênal and "create for himself a whole new character."[39]

Julien's first step—since he must leave M. de Rênal's house—is to join a seminary, where he is befriended and protected by the Jansenist Abbé Pirard. Not only is Julien attractive to women, but he also attaches to himself a series of father figures who promote his interests, starting with M. Chelan and ending, disastrously, with M. de La Mole. Julien is completely sincere when he tearfully tells Pirard, "I shall no longer complain of fortune, I have found another father in you."[40] Yet his religious vocation is a sham, as even Pirard understands. Julien believes nothing of what he learns in the seminary, and the irony of a would-be Napoleon joining a religious order does not escape him. But, fired by the example of the young bishop at Bray-le-Haut, he sees the Church as his best means of advance. Under Napoleon, he would be a lieutenant; in the Church, he will be a vicar general and perhaps himself a bishop.

The seminary, however, turns out to be a nest of vipers, and his fellow seminarians just so many enemies. Not that they themselves are sincere in their vocations. Their only interests are warm clothes and regular meals earned "by repeating a few Latin words instead of swinging a pickax."[41] But they despise Julien because he obviously feels—and obviously is—superior to them. "It was useless for Julien to make himself humble and stupid; he could not please, he was too different."[42] If he cannot make his fortune and command their respect, then they will make his life a misery. Again, there is no middle ground. So, when Abbé Pirard is pushed out of his position as director of the seminary, he passes the baton, so to speak, and finds for Julien a position in Paris as secretary to the Marquis de La Mole.

After leaving the seminary, Julien spends two final nights with Mme de Rênal. The ladder to her bedroom is discovered and removed. He makes a narrow escape by jumping from the second-story window and is off to Paris, with barely a look behind him. "At last he was going to make his appearance in the theater of the world."[43]

THE GRAND STAGE

Julien in Paris is high comedy with a serious purpose. His peasant's dream is to conquer the city and win the admiration of beautiful, sophisticated women. He plans to overcome all obstacles through ingenuity and force of will. Who needs noble birth when one has the talent and the energy to succeed?[44] Julien will make his mark or perish in the attempt. Indeed, he will do both.

Julien's awkward manners and extreme sensitivity lead him into a multitude of errors that would have subjected him to ridicule "if he had not been in some sense beneath ridicule."[45] The politeness of Comte Norbert, son of the marquis, is always tinged with irony. Yet Julien manages to disarm criticism by candidly admitting his faults, including his uncertain French spelling—not an encouraging feature in a private secretary—and his lack of experience in social settings. He even treats the dinner table to a self-deprecating account of his fall from a horse when riding with Comte Norbert. On another occasion, he shines when a dinner guest quizzes him on the Roman poets and historians. Even the marquise deigns to notice him.

Julien stumbles into a duel with the Chevalier de Beauvoisis, in which he is wounded but acquits himself well. The chevalier starts a rumor that Julien is the illegitimate son of a rich gentleman in the Franche-Comté who is a friend of the marquis. As the marquis explains, "M. de Beauvoisis didn't want it thought that he had fought with a carpenter's son."[46] This polite fiction allows the chevalier, who has taken a liking to Julien, to exchange visits and introduce him to the opera, always a mark of high favor in Stendhal.

The marquis, who is often confined by gout, also finds qualities in his secretary that intrigue and amuse him. But a Marquis de La Mole does not become intimate with his secretary. So the marquis invents another of those polite fictions so necessary to society during the Restoration. He gives to Julien—always dressed in black as befitting his status as a seminarian—a blue suit and instructs him that when he wears that suit and calls on the marquis, "you will be, in my eyes, the younger brother of the Comte de Retz, that is to say the son of my friend the old duke."[47] So when Julien wears his blue suit, he is treated with exquisite courtesy as an equal; when he returns in his black suit with a portfolio of letters, he is a social inferior and employee. Julien is so baffled by these changes that he fears the marquis is making fun of him. But the marquis is simply embracing the mores of his time. When rank and birth can be readily counterfeited, such marks of distinction are no more significant than Julien's blue suit.[48] Distinction itself becomes just a social convention.

The young Stendhal had hoped but failed to astonish Paris with social comedies in the manner of Molière. Thirty years later, his ear for social satire is now pitch perfect, and France during the Restoration is a target-rich environment. This is nowhere more true than in Julien's affair with Mathilde de La Mole, which is worthy of *Les Précieuses ridicules*.[49] Indeed, the Stendhalian narrator engages in a more direct (though not necessarily more profound) exploration of the ironic gap between inner consciousness and external norms than is possible in a play, even a play by Molière.

Mathilde is first struck by Julien when she overhears him ask Abbé Pirard to get him excused from dining with the family. That was a point of pride (learned from Rousseau) on which he insisted when he was in the house of M. de Rênal. No longer. "For me, sir, it's the most painful part of my job. I was less bored in the seminary."[50] "This fellow wasn't born on his knees," Mathilde thinks.[51]

She also finds in him a welcome respite from the vapidity and interminable platitudes of the mixture of nobles and intriguers who frequent the Hôtel de La Mole. The Parisian salons, which were famous for their prerevolutionary liveliness and wit, are now stultifying and restrained by a fear of controversy. With the Reign of Terror still in memory, everyone goes about on social tiptoes.[52] Even in the circle of Mathilde's admirers, light raillery, reactionary views, and a sneering tone predominate. Any form of enthusiasm would be considered bad form. But Mathilde is an enthusiast, and she recognizes her counterpart, however carefully concealed, in Julien.

Mathilde is beautiful, intelligent, wealthy, and well born. She is also quick with sardonic comments. Men fear her and are fascinated by her. She, in turn, is bored and hence deliberately imprudent. She even writes indiscreet letters to her admirers at a time when (as in Jane Austen) only an engagement would justify direct correspondence between the sexes.

Her ultimate indiscretion, the crowning glory of her imprudence, is her affair with Julien. In that, she intentionally courts disaster. "Exposure to danger," she tells herself, "livens the spirit, and saves one from the bog of boredom in which all my poor admirers seem to be sunk."[53] Julien is not boring. In the library during the day, where Mathilde frequently seeks him out, he will sometimes "forg[e]t to play the depressing part of a resentful plebeian."[54] Julien becomes frank in conversations with her, even opposing and challenging her ideas.

She believes that his innate superiority is apparent even to those who dismiss him as a social inferior. "When these gentlemen," she notes, "make a remark which they consider clever and unexpected, isn't it always Julien at whom they glance?"[55] His smoldering energy strikes terror in others; they view him as a potential Danton, which is precisely his attraction to Mathilde.

Mathilde convinces herself that she is in love with Julien. "The only thing in question, naturally, was a grand passion; frivolous love was unworthy a girl of her age and station."[56] She loves him not despite the fact but because he is poor and without any rank. Otherwise, "it would have none of the qualities of a grand passion: an immense difficulty to be surmounted, and the black uncertainty of the outcome."[57] It is a parody of Romanticism—Marianne Dashwood squared—yet all too real in its consequences.

Mathilde is obsessed with her ancestor, Boniface de La Mole, who had been the lover of Marguerite de Valois during the early years of her marriage to Henry of Navarre. Boniface was beheaded in 1574 when implicated in a plot against the then-reigning king of France, Charles IX. Marguerite, colloquially known as Queen Margot, allegedly kissed his severed head and buried it herself (or preserved it in a jeweled case, depending on the account).

Entering into an affair with a woman for whom the height of romance is to have her lover's head cut off may seem unwise. And so it will prove. But when Mathilde instructs Julien to put a ladder against her window and come to her bedroom at one o'clock in the morning, not even the twinge of guilt he feels at betraying the marquis, or the fear that it might be some sort of complex plot to betray him, allows him to hesitate. He must rise to the challenge. "To tell the truth," the narrator drily remarks, "their transports were a bit *conscious*. Passionate love was still more a model for them to imitate than a reality."[58]

Mathilde suffers extreme remorse. Julien is her first lover, and she is furious with him. "With these bold, proud people, it is always just one step from self-hatred to fury against other people; when this step is taken, transports of rage give them keen pleasure."[59] As soon as she feels secure of his love, Mathilde despises him. The secret, Julien discovers, is to keep her feeling insecure. The battle between these rival egos vacillates between hostility and desire, and they are rarely in sync.

The comic high point of these contretemps is when Julien, having made the fatal mistake of professing his love for Mathilde and being scorned in consequence, follows the advice of his Russian friend, Prince Korasoff, and pays court to another woman. He chooses the beautiful but prudish Mme de Fervaques, daughter of a rich tradesman and widow of a *maréchal*.

Korasoff counsels Julien that he must zealously attend on Mme de Fervaques but without any appearance of passion. "I won't conceal from you, your role is a hard one; you are acting a comedy, and if anyone suspects you of acting, there's no hope for you."[60] The key element in the scheme is to write to her at least once a day, and Korasoff conveniently has six sets of love letters depending on the sort of woman in question. He delivers a numbered set to Julien, carefully designed to wear down the loftiest virtue.

Julien plays his part. He assiduously pays court to Mme de Fervaques, hanging, it would seem, on her every word and talking to her in a serious and somber tone of piety and virtue. Mathilde cannot help herself. She sits close enough to hear the conversation and is amazed by his "perfect insincerity; he never said a single word to the maréchale that was not a lie or at least an abominable distortion of his point of view, which Mathilde knew perfectly well on practically all topics."[61]

The letters, too, have their effect. Julien first made his mark in society by memorizing the Latin New Testament. He will now advance by copying by rote the letters he has been given and playing the part scripted for him. The letters are so boring that he falls asleep while transcribing them. He even forgets once to change references to *London* and *Richmond* in the originals but excuses himself on the grounds that, driven by lofty sentiments, his spirit suffered "a momentary oblivion."[62] She begins to write back; Julien drops the letters unopened in a desk drawer where they are discovered by Mathilde. "Such is the advantage of the emphatic style that Mme de Fervaques was in no way surprised at the lack of connection between letters and answers."[63]

The scheme reignites Mathilde's passion, and when she becomes pregnant, she eventually convinces her furious and deeply wounded father to settle an estate on them both and to secure for Julien a commission as a lieutenant in the cavalry and even a title as the Chevalier de La Vernaye. Yet, on the cusp of success, everything Julien has painstakingly built up unravels with a shocking suddenness that leaves the reader stunned and adrift.

LOVE AND DEATH

Stendhal's initial stimulus for his novel was a newspaper article about one Antoine Berthet, the son of a blacksmith who attended the Grenoble seminary before becoming tutor to the prosperous Michoud family. He was dismissed from that position, apparently after an affair with the wife. He then sent an angry and vaguely threatening letter to Mme Michoud, who responded by getting him fired from a new post, where he had promptly seduced the daughter of the house. Berthet showed up at Mme Michoud's church with a gun, severely wounded her, and then tried but failed to kill himself. The trial received much attention from women attracted by Berthet's youth and delicate good looks. He was sentenced to death and executed in 1828.

One might conclude, then, that the denouement of *The Red and the Black* was preordained, and Stendhal was merely following the script he had set down for himself. But there is nothing tacked on about the ending. It is an integral unveiling and unraveling of the book's three principal characters.

Mme de Rênal is deeply religious and, since Julien's departure, has been under the sway of her stern confessor. When M. de La Mole sends an inquiry to her about Julien, she lets her confessor dictate the response. The marquis cannot bring himself to trust Julien enough to let him marry Mathilde. "Was it authentic, spontaneous love? Or just a vulgar greed to raise himself to a good position?"[64] She answers that question for him in the bluntest terms:

> Born poor and greedy, this man has tried by means of the most consummate hypocrisy, and by the seduction of a weak and wretched woman, to find himself a position and rise in the world. It is part of my painful duty to add that I am forced to believe M. J___ has no religious principles. In all conscience I am obliged to think that his way to rise in a household is to try to seduce the woman who is most influential there. Cloaking himself under the guise of disinterestedness and phrases from novels, he makes it his great and only end to gain control over the master of the house and his fortune. He leaves behind him a trail of misery and eternal regrets.[65]

One has to acknowledge that the religious piety behind this letter is not unmixed with sexual jealousy. Regardless, at the time she sends it, Mme de Rênal is indeed a weak and wretched woman. It is ironic that Julien, the copier of letters, is done in by a letter copied by Mme de Rênal. But the letter is an accurate account of how Julien has wanted to view himself. His self-professed strategy has indeed been one of hypocrisy and seduction: "every man for himself in this desert of selfishness they call life."[66]

Mathilde, too, is fulfilling her character through her dramatic reactions to the letter and its aftermath. She tells Julien that "all is lost," but it is unclear why that should be so. Mathilde is still pregnant, and M. de La Mole still wants to preserve her reputation. All she has to do is tell Julien to let matters die down until the marquis can once again be brought around. She could even elope with Julien, which would force her father's hand. But the situation is tailor-made to Mathilde's tragic sense of self.

Her passion is a role she must play out with one eye on the audience. She is delighted by her pregnancy, not just as a means of getting her way but also as a visible display of her reckless passion. She sees herself as a heroic figure who has shunned the offers of the greatest young nobles in France in preference to a truly superior man without birth or fortune and has thereby demonstrated her own superiority. If Boniface de La Mole seemed to her reborn in Julien, so, too, is Queen Margot reborn in her. Mathilde, Julien recognizes, was "made to live with the heroes of the Middle Ages."[67] Her love "was madness, grandeur of spirit, everything that was most strange."[68] And it unspools in a very public forum, as she visits him in jail, attends his trial and execution, and carries in her lap his severed head, which she will bury with her own hands. Julien's death is her apotheosis as Queen Margot.

It is Julien's character that is the most opaque. His actions seem simultaneously overdetermined and underdetermined. There are a number of ostensible reasons for shooting Mme de Rênal: anger at having his dreams destroyed just as he was about to realize them; dismay in having his character exposed by the very woman he expected to cherish it; and disgust in realizing he has succeeded in becoming what he despises. The letter contains enough truth to enrage Julien and his ego. There is also Julien's Zelig-like nature, which adapts itself to the tragic expectations of Mathilde, just as it once did to the innocent, almost maternal love of Mme de Rênal. He is a man torn between two women and two ways of being in the world. The tension leaves him literally deranged, and he is prepared to destroy the one so as wholly to embrace the other.

The result, however, is just the opposite. Once Julien is in prison, he is exhausted by the constant struggle to be something he is not. He is "tired of heroics" and of Mathilde's "secret need to amaze the public with the splendor of her love and the sublimity of her projects."[69] He is equally tired of trying to repress his own natural affections and present a false front to the world. Julien realizes that his failures as a strategist have been his finest moments as a man. The "novel of my career is over," he tells himself.[70] *Mon roman est fini.*

Julien all but invites the bourgeois jury to condemn him:

Gentlemen, I have not the honor to belong to your social class, you see in me a peasant in open revolt against his humble station. . . . I see before me men who, without ever considering whether my youth merits some pity, are determined to punish in me and discourage forever a certain class of young men—those who, born to a lower social order, and buried by poverty, are lucky enough to get a good education and bold enough to mingle with what the arrogant rich call good society. . . . There is my crime, gentlemen.[71]

This "certain class of young men" will flock to Paris, Milan, and London, determined to make their way by any means necessary. But Julien will no longer be among them. He has realized that the world he hoped to conquer is built on artificial conventions and distinctions of no real worth. "Ambition was dead within his heart."[72] But what will take its place?

The words Julien had memorized and parroted in order to succeed no longer have meaning for him. The Church. Society. The law. All have been perverted to serve private interests. None can offer true guidance. Julien has been liberated from the prison of false ideals, but what is left is "something terrifying," an existence and a consciousness devoid of meaning.[73] "The age was created to bring everything into confusion!" Julien tells himself. "We are on the march toward chaos."[74] Amid the chaos and confusion of the age, there are only two Absolutes (in the Hegelian sense) to fill this void, only two words that gesture toward a reality beyond language: *Love* and *Death*. Julien embraces them both.

He rediscovers his love for Mme de Rênal in prison. "You must know," he tells her, "that I've always loved you, I never loved anyone but you."[75] It is a love beyond language: "Words cannot describe the excess and madness of Julien's devotion."[76] It is a love that displaces religion: "I feel for you," Mme de Rênal explains, "what I should feel only for God: a mixture of respect, love, devotion."[77] Julien, in turn, is undisturbed by the absence of God in his life; "it's the absence of Mme de Rênal that is crushing me."[78] Julien has found his true self in Mme de Rênal: "I am speaking to you as I do to myself."[79] In loving her, Julien has, for the first time in his life, "seen clearly into his own soul."[80]

In the grip of such boundless love, death sinks into insignificance. "Who knows what's to be found in the other world? . . . Perhaps nothing at all." But two months together is something "delectable."[81] Mme de Rênal visits him twice a day while his appeal is pending. During that time, he is "living on love and almost without a thought for the future."[82]

In this state, the transition from life to death, from being to nothingness, is seamless. Of Julien's execution, the narrator says only that "everything proceeded simply, decently, and without the slightest affectation on his part."[83] Although she keeps her promise not to harm herself, Mme de Rênal dies three days later while embracing her children. Their souls are united. Their *liebestod* is complete.

7

Alessandro Manzoni and the Great Italian Novel

ALESSANDRO MANZONI IS NOT WELL KNOWN IN THE UNITED STATES. He is even less read, though that may change with the limpid new translation by Michael Moore of Manzoni's masterpiece *I promessi sposi* (*The Betrothed*). First published in 1827, *The Betrothed* went through nine editions in its first six months. It has been, and is still, read by every schoolchild in Italy. Adults can recite passages they memorized as children, such as the one near the end of chapter 8 when Lucia is driven from her home near the shores of Lake Como:

> Farewell mountains rising from the waters and reaching to the sky; jagged peaks familiar to one who has grown up among you, etched in her mind no less clearly than the faces of those she holds dear. Farewell rivers, whose roaring she knows as well as the voices of home. Farewell small white villages, clinging to the slopes like flocks of grazing sheep. Nothing could be sadder than the footsteps of one who, having grown up among you, must take her leave![1]

Even those of us with limited Italian can appreciate the lyric melody of the lines:

> Addio, monti sorgenti dall-acque, ed elevati al cielo; cime inuguali, note a chi e cresciuto tra voi, e impresse nella sua mente, non meno che lo sia l'aspetto de' suoi piu familiari; torrenti, de' quail distingue lo scroscio,

come il suono delle voci domestiche; ville sparse e bianchedeggianti sul pendio, come branchi di pecore pascenti; addio! Quanto e tristo il passo di chi, cresciuto tra voi, se ne allonttana!

No other Western novel, whether in France or England or the United States, has played such a central role in shaping the culture of a country. Indeed, one might justly say that Manzoni helped to create a united Italy by giving it a national identity and language. At the time he wrote, Italy was barely a concept. The peninsula was broken into ever-shifting spheres of influence from Austria, Spain, and France, along with the Papal States and isolated principalities such as Parma. There were more than twenty dialects, sufficiently different from one another to make communication difficult.

After publication, Manzoni decided that there was too much of the Lombard and Milanese dialects in his work. He wanted it to be a book for all of Italy, so he painstakingly rewrote it in an expanded version of Tuscan, the language of Dante and Machiavelli. The thirteen-year project was Manzoni's own *Risorgimento*. "I have rinsed my rags in the waters of the Arno," he proclaimed, referencing the famous river that bisects Florence.[2] By the time Garibaldi and Mazzini had done their work in creating Italy as a geographic and political unit, the fledgling nation had not only what would remain its greatest novel but also the makings of a common language of uncommon beauty in which to conduct its affairs.

LIFE

Alessandro Manzoni was born in Milan on March 7, 1785. He died in 1873, at the age of eighty-eight, having lived through the French Revolution; the Napoleonic Wars; occupation by Spain, France, and Austria; and the three Italian Wars of Independence that made up the *Risorgimento*, the astonishing unification of the Italian nation, which was largely complete by 1861.

Alessandro's putative father, Count Pietro Manzoni, was a member of the minor nobility. The Manzoni family had long owned a country estate, il Caleotto, some fifty kilometers north of Milan in Lecco on the shores of Lake Como. The lake is shaped like a wishbone, and Lecco is located at the tip of the southeastern branch, where it passes into the Adda River. It is the primary setting of *The Betrothed*.

Alessandro's mother, Giulia, was the daughter of Cesare Beccaria, an important Enlightenment figure in law, philosophy, and economics. She was also the lover of Giovanni Verri, but his family would not let them marry because she had no dowry. Instead, Giovanni's brother arranged for her marriage to the much older Pietro Manzoni in 1782, when she was barely twenty. It was not a happy marriage, and the lively Giulia detested il Caleotto, where she was surrounded by her husband's seven unmarried sisters, who were highly critical of her and suspected her (rightly) of affairs with other men.

It is generally understood that Giovanni Verri was Alessandro's natural father. Giulia paid the boy very little attention. He was sent to be raised by a wet nurse in the countryside. Once he turned six, he was packed off to the first of three religious boarding schools. Homesick and sobbing, he was admonished by the headmaster to stop his sniveling.

Giulia left il Caleotto the following year, 1792, and sought refuge with an uncle before moving to Paris with her new lover, the poet Carlo Imbonati. She received a legal separation from Pietro Manzoni the same year and never returned to il Caleotto until after the death of her former husband in 1807. Giulia did visit Alessandro at his various boarding schools, but only occasionally when she otherwise happened to be back in Italy.

Alessandro's formal education ended in 1801 when he was just sixteen. He alternated his time between il Caleotto and his father's house in Milan, though he was sent briefly to Venice to disrupt a youthful infatuation with the sister of a school friend. The rapidly maturing youth read widely, but his main interest was poetry. He translated Virgil and Horace and wrote poems of his own. He began to make enough of a reputation to draw the interest of his mother and her lover. They invited him to Paris for an extended visit. Imbonati died shortly before Manzoni arrived in 1805, and Manzoni paid tribute to him in the poem "In morte di Carlo Imbonati."

Imbonati left a life interest in his considerable estate to Donna Giulia, as well as complete ownership of a villa in Brusuglio. This bequest left her financially independent, even after she made generous arrangements for Imbonati's sisters and nephews. Mother and son lived together on the Rue Saint-Honoré and found, perhaps to their surprise, that they enjoyed each other's company.

Alessandro spent five years in Paris, mingling freely with his mother's literary and social circles and forging close friendships of his own, most particularly with Claude Fauriel, who would become a distinguished historian. Alessandro loved France the way Stendhal loved Italy and even preferred reading in French to reading in Italian with its many dialects.

In 1807, Don Pietro died, leaving Alessandro as his sole heir. The following year, Alessandro married Henriette (Enrichetta) Blondel, the Calvinist daughter of a wealthy silk merchant. He had written to Fauriel that his recipe for a wife was "a direct, gentle, and sensitive mind . . . a just and cultivated intelligence, simple habits, a calm, even character, no taste for burning pleasures, much taste for country life," and "a good dose of goodness and tolerance."[3] He explained that the tolerance would be needed to "compensate for some of my faults," among which he listed "my fear of embarrassment, my complete isolation from society, my sullen glooms, and my invincible shyness (which sometimes leads me to seem very ridiculous)."[4]

In Henriette, Alessandro seems to have fulfilled his wish. Giulia, too, thoroughly vetted and approved of Henriette, though she later came to resent her daughter-in-law, perhaps in part due to Henriette's conversion to Catholicism in 1810, but mostly, it would seem, out of jealousy as Henriette increasingly absorbed her husband's attention. Alessandro followed Henriette into the church after his extreme anxiety manifested itself as a religious crisis. He and Henriette remarried in a Catholic ceremony by special dispensation in 1810. Alessandro wrote *Inni sacri*, a series of sacred lyrics, admired by both Goethe and Stendhal, as well as a treatise on Catholic morality.

Despite Giulia's increasing hostility, the marriage was a happy one. The couple had nine children, though only two of them survived their long-lived father. They moved to the comfortable and roomy villa at Brusuglio, which they painstakingly restored. It is now known as the Villa Manzoni. There, Manzoni read, wrote, pursued an interest in botany (which he shared with Rousseau and Goethe), and, like Wordsworth, took long walks in the countryside, often covering ten miles or more. He suffered from anxiety and depression, which were only partially relieved by the exercise. "Quant à moi," he wrote to Fauriel: "Je suis entre la famille, les arbres, et les vers" (I live among my family, the trees, and poetry).[5]

Austrian troops had driven out the French and reoccupied northern Italy in 1814. For a time, they were quartered at il Caleotto, Brusuglio, and the house Manzoni had recently acquired in Milan. In 1818, Manzoni was forced to sell il Caleotto, largely due to the failings of the estate manager. He treated the peasants on the estate with great generosity, forgiving their substantial debts and making a gift to them of the coming harvest. But he recognized his own incompetence in matters of business. His mother began to manage the estate at Brusuglio, and her brother handled the rest of his properties. Manzoni's regret at losing il Caleotto is reflected in the beautiful passage, quoted above, when Lucia must leave her native Lecco.

In 1819, Manzoni published his first tragedy, *Il Conte di Carmagnola*, a historical drama about the fifteenth-century *condottiero* Francesco Bussone. The work put him firmly in the Romanticist camp in its deliberate disregard of the classical unities of time, place, and action. Goethe, who had done the same in his 1773 historical drama, *Götz von Berlichingen*, praised the play. Manzoni also wrote a powerful ode, "Il Cinque Maggio" (The Fifth of May), on the death of Napoleon in 1821. The poem had to be smuggled into France, from which it quickly spread throughout western Europe, to the consternation of the Austrian authorities.

Manzoni retreated to Brusuglio. He read the classics, immersed himself in history, and wrote his masterpiece. Influenced by Walter Scott's *Ivanhoe*, Manzoni focused not on major historical figures but on ordinary men and woman who bear the effects of history without changing its course. When he finished the first draft in 1823, he wrote to the ever-faithful Fauriel with a wonderful mixture of pride and modesty:

> All I can tell you of it in conscience is that I have tried to know exactly and to paint sincerely the period and country in which I have placed my

story. The materials are rich; everything that shows up the seamy side of man is there in abundance. Assurance in ignorance, pretension in folly, effrontery in corruption are, alas, among many others of the same kind, the most salient characteristics of that period. Happily there are also men and traits which honor the human race; characters gifted with a strong virtue, remarkable by their attitude to obstacles and difficulties, and by their resistance, and sometimes subservience, to conventional ideas. I've tried to profit by all this; how I've succeeded only God knows. I've stuffed it with peasants, nobles, monks, nuns, priests, magistrates, scholars, war, famine . . . that's to have written a book![6]

The Betrothed was published in three volumes between 1825 and 1827, when Manzoni was forty-two. Not only did it sell out nine editions in six months, but it also spread throughout Europe in translations. Public readings were arranged so that the illiterate could still know the book. It was immediately acknowledged as the greatest Italian novel, a position it would never relinquish, not even to Giuseppe Tomasi di Lampedusa's elegiac *The Leopard*, published in 1958.[7] The composer Giuseppe Verdi called it not only "the greatest book of our period, but one of the greatest books ever to come from a human brain. It is not only a book, it is a consolation for humanity."[8]

No sooner had he finished the novel, however, than Manzoni decided to rewrite it in a more universal Italian language based largely on Tuscan. It took him thirteen years. The revised work was published in ninety-six biweekly installments between 1840 and 1842.

Henriette died on Christmas Day in 1833. She was forty-two and undoubtedly worn out from giving birth nine times. Of their six daughters, one died in infancy and four in their twenties. Manzoni's three sons proved largely feckless and ungrounded. Only one daughter and one son survived him.

Manzoni remarried in 1837 to a thirty-seven-year-old widow, Teresa Borri. It was very much a love match for the fifty-one-year-old Manzoni, who was smitten by the attractive and literary Teresa. He also grew close to her son Stefano, a painter and musician. The couple had stillborn twins in 1845. Teresa died in 1861.

Manzoni remained at Brusuglio for the rest of his life. He rose between 5:00 and 6:00 a.m., made himself a hot chocolate, attended an early mass, and then wrote and read before his long afternoon walk. In the evening, he received intimate friends. Manzoni did not participate in the liberation movement that led to the unification of Italy, but he was a passionate (if passive) observer.

On May 7, 1873, the eighty-eight-year-old Manzoni attended an early mass and fell on the steps of the church. He died of complications from the fall on May 22, 1873. A national day of mourning was declared. The highest government officials marched in the funeral procession. Verdi wrote his great *Requiem Mass* in honor of Manzoni. It was performed at the Church of San Marco in Milan on the first anniversary of his death.

A SEVENTEENTH-CENTURY PORTRAIT GALLERY

The Betrothed is set in Lombardy between 1628 and 1631. It is presented as the work of an anonymous chronicler. The ostensible narrator simply undertakes the heroic effort of transcribing the "faded chicken scratch" of that ancient manuscript.[9]

This metafictional conceit is at least as old as *Don Quixote*, which was claimed to be translated from an Arabic text by the Moorish historian Cide Hamete Benengeli. It allows the transcriber cum translator to address the reader directly and to interject comments and reactions of his own to the supposedly historical account, ironically underscoring the fiction within the fiction.

But Manzoni's narrator adds an additional twist. The manuscript he purports to transcribe is written in the language of the seventeenth century, which is full of "bombastic declamations, composed of pedestrian solecisms, and everywhere the ambitious awkwardness so characteristic of the writing of that century."[10] He gives a vivid illustration of that language in the first couple of pages, which open as follows:

> History can veritably be defined as an illustrious war against Time, for by emancipating the years it has imprisoned, and indeed reduced to corpses, it restores them to life, musters them for review and sends them forth into battle anew.[11]

The Wisdom of the Romantics

The chronicler complains, however, that historians focus only on the great and the powerful: "The illustrious Champions of History . . . plunder only the most glittering and opulent spoils, embalming with ink the Exploits of Princes and Potentates as well as other Eminences, embroidering gold and silk threads with the finest needle of their genius to form a perpetual tapestry of glorious Deeds."[12] Unworthy of recording such glorious deeds, he will take a different approach, for "having chanced upon news of memorable events that befell, admittedly, humble laborers of low birth, I gird myself to bequeath such memory to Posterity by relating the Tale, or rather the Report, in its unadorned Truth."[13]

After giving this sample of the anonymous chronicler's extravagant and labored diction, the transcriber realizes that modern readers will find it unpalatable. Rather than abandon such a beautiful story, however, he resolves to translate it into the current language of everyday life. This is a gentle dig at Sir Walter Scott, whom Manzoni in fact greatly admired, but whose characters speak in an archaic language that sometimes borders on the risible. It also makes an important point. Our transcriber has become an author. He will not merely copy the work of another but will "take the series of events from the manuscript and rewrite them."[14] As an author, he takes on the burden of verisimilitude in the use of history. Accordingly, he tells us that he "pored through the records of the time, to see if that really was the way of the world in those days."[15]

This introduction serves as a manifesto of sorts for historical fiction. It should accurately portray the period in question, in minute details as well as broader events. It should be written in contemporary language for contemporary readers. It should contain a metanarrative that allows for commentary on the events and people portrayed. And, most important of all, it should tell a compelling story stuffed with vivid characters, both invented and historical, from every walk of life: peasants and nobles, bravos and monks, heroes and villains, scholars and magistrates, rich and poor, oppressors and oppressed, all of them deeply embedded in their historical period. That's to have written a book. And that is precisely the book Manzoni wrote.

Lorenzo Tramaglino, known to all as Renzo, and Lucia Mondella are the central characters of this book. Renzo was orphaned when still

ALESSANDRO MANZONI AND THE GREAT ITALIAN NOVEL

an adolescent but followed his father's trade as a silk worker. He is in demand despite an economic recession, and he supplements his stores with a bit of farmland that he owns next to his house in the village of Lecco. Renzo reads only with difficulty, but he is a hard worker and very much in love with Lucia, who lives with her mother in the same village. Lucia is devout and modest but as firmly committed to Renzo as he is to her.

Renzo and Lucia are ordinary peasants until circumstances show them not to be ordinary at all, but rather heroic in their perseverance and fidelity to each other. As the book opens, they are prepared to marry. It is a simple thing. Couples do it every day, building a life and raising children together. But chance, malevolence, and weakness open a crack in their plans, which grows into a fissure and becomes a massive chasm through which history passes, separating the two lovers.

It starts when Don Rodrigo, a local nobleman, and his cousin happen upon Lucia one day as she is returning home from her job in a silk-spinning mill. He makes crude remarks to her, and as Lucia hurries away, she hears Don Rodrigo's cousin laugh, and Don Rodrigo respond, "How much do you want to bet?"[16] Just that casually and callously, Lucia and Renzo's plans begin to unravel.

Don Rodrigo sends two of his bravos—hired thugs in the entourage of any nobleman of note—to warn the local priest, Don Abbondio, not to marry the pair. Don Abbondio, of course, has a solemn duty to perform the sacraments for the members of his congregation, and marriage is among the most sacred. But Don Abbondio did not become a priest in order to stand up to the wicked and powerful. The duties of his profession were the furthest thing from his mind. He sought only a life of ease and the protection of a revered profession. He made it past sixty in a violent and lawless society by avoiding conflict whenever possible and, when forced to choose, always favoring the stronger party, while pretending not to notice its abuses and reproaching the weaker side for stirring up trouble. His favorite saying is "No harm comes to an honest man who minds his own business and knows his place."[17]

Don Abbondio accordingly resents Renzo and Lucia for putting him in such a position. And when Renzo arrives on the day appointed for

THE WISDOM OF THE ROMANTICS

their marriage to set the time for going to church, Don Abbondio puts him off with an array of feeble excuses about his health and the formalities that must still be observed. He even resorts to Latin phrases in an effort to overawe the young peasant. But Renzo is not to be deterred. He gets most of the story out of Perpetua, Don Abbondio's voluble housekeeper, and the rest when he corners and confronts the terrified Don Abbondio. Religion has failed to defend the rights of the young couple. Yet Don Abbondio is certainly correct that it won't help him either. He can write a letter seeking the protection of the archbishop, but the archbishop won't be there to interpose between Don Abbondio and a bullet. At the end of the day, Don Abbondio is left with only one option: he bars the door and takes to his bed.

That is no option for Renzo, however. After first considering the impractical and likely fatal option of muscling through a score of bravos to confront Don Rodrigo directly and grab him by the throat, Lucia's mother, Agnese, convinces him to seek redress from the law. So, with four chickens in hand, Renzo goes to see Professor Argle-Bargle—as he is nicknamed—one of many minor characters in the novel, like Agnese and Perpetua, who are, as in Shakespeare, vividly and memorably portrayed with a comic exaggeration we would now consider Dickensian, but without ever losing their authenticity.

When asked whether it is a crime to threaten a priest into refusing to perform a marriage, Professor Argle-Bargle calls it "a clear-cut case, provided for in a hundred decrees,"[18] which he proceeds to show and read to Renzo. And, indeed, the decrees do seem to cover the case exactly, providing for serious penalties ranging from banishment to the galleys and even death for "forc[ing] a priest not to perform his duties."[19] Best of all, the decrees apply without regard to position or influence. "Listen, listen," says Professor Argle-Bargle. "All these and other such criminal acts, whether committed by feudal lords, noblemen, burghers, farmers, or commoners—No one's left out: It's like the Last Judgment!"[20]

Despite the clarity of the decrees, the lawyer promises Renzo—who he assumes did the threatening—that he can get him off: "If you know how to manipulate the decrees, no one's guilty and no one's innocent."[21] With skilled obfuscation, a well-placed gratuity, and a threat or two directed at the victim, the matter can be resolved in the defendant's favor "so long as you didn't attack a person of standing."[22] Of course, as soon as Renzo corrects the misunderstanding and explains that it was Don Rodrigo who caused the threats to be made, the lawyer drives the young man from his office: "Don't go trying to ambush an honest man with such surprises."[23] He even takes the extraordinary step of returning the chickens given to the housekeeper.

So much for the resort to justice. All the decrees in the world won't help when those charged with enforcing them have "sold their inaction or even their collusion to the powerful . . . and reserved the exercise of their detested authority and the powers they enjoyed for occasions when there was no danger; namely, the oppression and harassment of the law-abiding and defenseless."[24] It is the universal lament through the centuries of those too poor, too weak, and too obscure to command equal protection of the laws.

Yet Lucia is undaunted. "The Good Lord also looks out for the poor," she insists.[25] If human justice eludes them, they will seek help from God's chosen representatives on earth. She is not forgetting that the Church, in the character of Don Abbondio, has already failed them. But she places her hopes in a very different sort of man, Padre Cristoforo, whose faith invests him with courage, compassion, and a firm belief in divine providence, notwithstanding his clear-eyed recognition of the miseries, both man-made and natural, that devastate so many lives.

Padre Cristoforo gets his own backstory in chapter 4. He is a forerunner of Father Zosima from Dostoevsky's *The Brothers Karamazov*.[26] Both were young men of fortune, but not noble birth, who were hot-tempered and jealous of their prerogatives, and both ended up in duels that led them to enter monasteries where they became renowned for their holiness.

Padre Cristoforo, whose Christian name was Lodovico, is quite literally cold-shouldered as a mere tradesman's son. One day, a trivial dispute over who takes precedence as they walk toward one another leads to a brawl between Lodovico, an arrogant aristocrat, and their respective retainers. The situation is deliberately reminiscent of the swordfight that leads to the death of Mercutio and Tybalt in *Romeo and Juliet*.

THE WISDOM OF THE ROMANTICS

Outnumbered by the aristocrat's bravos, Lodovico is twice wounded, and the aristocrat moves in for a killing sword thrust. But a longtime family steward, Cristoforo, interposes himself between them and is stabbed in his stead. Enraged, Lodovico drives his own sword though the stomach of his attacker. With two men dead, the bravos scatter, and the wounded Lodovico is carried to a nearby Capuchin monastery where he can seek sanctuary from both the law and the dead nobleman's relatives.

Lodovico is transformed. Horrified that his temper has led to two deaths, one by his own hand and the other in his place, he resolves to become a monk. He gives his entire fortune to Cristoforo's widow and children and then takes on the dead steward's name as a constant reminder of his sin. Even as a monk, though, Padre Cristoforo still feels an "instinctive, sincere horror at injustice and bullying."[27] In addition to preaching and ministering to the sick and dying, therefore, Padre Cristoforo takes on two further obligations: "to settle disputes and to protect the oppressed." In doing so, "vestiges of his warrior spirit" are still to be found.[28]

Too many vestiges, perhaps. When Padre Cristoforo confronts Don Rodrigo, his resolve to remain calm and patient quickly dissipates after Don Rodrigo sarcastically offers to take Lucia under his protection. In a fury, and in front of his guests, Padre Cristoforo calls Don Rodrigo a man forsaken by God, with a curse hanging over his house and divine justice ready to descend on him. Despite the feeling of dread aroused by this prophecy, Don Rodrigo furiously orders the padre out of his house, doubles down on his bet, and resolves to abduct Lucia.

At the same time, Agnese and Renzo settle on a scheme to effect the marriage even without any active participation by Don Abbondio. Under settled custom, in the presence of the parish priest and two witnesses, if the man says, "This is my wife," and the woman says, "This is my husband," they will be married in the eyes of God and the Church without the priest so much as lifting two fingers to give them a blessing.

The abduction plot and the marriage plot comically intersect, however. While Agnese distracts Perpetua with some local gossip, the two witnesses gain access to the priest under the pretense of paying a long-overdue debt. Renzo and Lucia, after sneaking into the room behind the pair, pop out, and Renzo says, "Father, this is my wife." But the priest is too quick and too wily for them. Before the timid Lucia can get beyond "And this . . . ," Don Abbondio knocks over the lamp, throws a table covering over her head, and clamps a hand on her mouth. In the ensuing darkness and confusion, Don Abbondio feels his way into another room, locks the door behind him, and begins shouting for help from the window. His shouts raise the town, the sexton begins ringing the church bell by way of alarm, and the villagers, thinking that thieves have invaded, hastily arm themselves with whatever weapons they can find. Meanwhile, the bravos lying in wait for Lucia believe that their own plot has been discovered and flee back to the palace of Don Rodrigo.

Agnese, Lucia, and Renzo make their way to the monastery, where Padre Cristoforo, who had learned of the plot to kidnap Lucia and sent a boy to warn them, has already made plans for their escape. He has arranged for a boatman to take them across the Adda, where a cart will be waiting. He gives Agnese and Lucia a letter to the father guardian at a monastery near Monza, where they can obtain refuge. He gives Renzo a letter to another monastery in Milan, where they will help him find work.

Lucia and Renzo must part from their village and from each other. The famous passage of farewell quoted at the start of this chapter is mostly focused on geography and a sense of place. But Lucia is also invested with a much more personal sense of loss and longing:

> Farewell childhood home, where lost in private thoughts, she had learned to hear the difference between normal footsteps and the footsteps of the youth she awaited with a mysterious fear. Farewell home she might never know, at which she had stolen many a blushing glance; the home where she had envisioned a married life, serene and lifelong. Farewell church, where peace of mind had so often returned while singing the Lord's praises. Where her marriage banns had been posted and the Mass prepared. Where the secret yearning of her heart was supposed to be solemnly blessed and love ordained and made holy. Farewell![29]

Padre Cristoforo expresses his faith that their parting "is what God has ordained."[30] They should trust in divine providence, and the day will

The Wisdom of the Romantics

come when they find peace. "My heart tells me we shall soon meet again" are his final words.[31] The irony is palpable, particularly since the private troubles of the two young lovers are about to be submerged in a series of historic catastrophes that appear to display God's utter indifference to human suffering.

The Maelstrom of History

The Italian writer, critic, and journalist Italo Calvino perceived a geometric structure in *The Betrothed*. In the first part of the book (until they depart Lecco), Renzo and Lucia are caught in an equilateral triangle formed by Don Rodrigo, Don Abbondio, and Padre Cristoforo. Don Rodrigo represents human malevolence; Don Abbondio represents indifference to or active collusion in that malevolence; and Padre Cristoforo is the representative of the good church that strives for social justice and ministers to the afflicted. These are what Calvino calls the "ratios of power," in the face of which Renzo and Lucia are largely defenseless.[32]

The ratios of power seem largely fixed in Part I: Padre Cristoforo cannot compel Don Rodrigo to abandon his designs on Lucia or convince Don Abbondio to do his duty as a priest. Without such an improbable change of heart, all he can do is put Lucia and Renzo out of reach. But, in doing so, he launches them from the timeless village of Lecco into the maelstrom of history, where the star-crossed lovers must face war, famine, political upheaval, and pestilence, as well as the petty violence and tyranny of a lawless era. In response, Renzo and Lucia are forced to play more active roles in their own destinies, and the line between divine providence and human striving grows ever fainter.

The ratios of power are repeated and intensified in the second part of the book, by the larger triangle of L'Innominato (the Nameless One), Cardinal Borromeo, and the Nun of Monza. Unlike the fictional trio in Part I, however, these three are actual historical figures to whom the story line is adapted as they interact with the fictional characters. The interweaving of history and fiction helps to universalize the first trio and the predicament of Renzo and Lucia. In the process, however, the ratios of power—reflecting individual concerns—are overwhelmed by history. "The real forces at work in the novel," Calvino notes, "stand revealed as natural and historical disasters of slow incubation and sudden conflagration, upsetting the little game of the ratios of power."[33]

Each member of the second triangle also has his or her own backstory. L'Innominato is allegedly based on Francesco Bernardino Visconti, a wealthy nobleman cum warlord ensconced in an impregnable mountain fortress guarded by dozens of well-armed bravos. Don Rodrigo is a petty thug in comparison to the power and the history of violence displayed by L'Innominato.

> To do whatever the law prohibited or any power opposed; to declare oneself the arbiter, the master, of other people's affairs, for no good reason other than the thrill of command; to be feared by all, and deferred to by those more accustomed to receiving deference: These had always been his main passions.[34]

Cardinal Federico Borromeo was beloved for his saintly demeanor and good works. He was archbishop of Milan during the famine of 1627/1628 as well as the plague of 1630. He could readily have fled the city for the relative safety of a country estate, as many nobles did. But he stayed in Milan even as his household was decimated by the plague and eight out of every nine priests died. He sought to feed the hungry and minister to the sick and dying, even visiting the lazarettos, where those infected by the plague were confined.

The infamous Nun of Monza was a lively, willful, and anything-but-pious girl forced into a convent by her father, who wanted to avoid paying any dowry for her to marry. Her tortured history is introduced to the reader in a thirty-plus-page short story that, in its psychological acumen and range of emotions, excels even the best of Boccaccio's *Decameron*.

> There were moments when a careful observer might deduce that those eyes were pleading for affection, for sympathy, for pity. There were others when he might think he had caught a sudden glimpse of a deep and long-repressed hatred, something vaguely menacing and cruel.[35]

After becoming a nun, she entered into an affair with Egidio, a compatriot of L'Innominato who had taken sanctuary in a house adjacent to the convent that overlooked a courtyard where she liked to walk. As the narrator demurely explains, "He dared to call out to her. And she gave her fateful reply."[36] This is the woman to whose protection Padre Cristoforo has unwittingly consigned Lucia. This is the new triangle, with its increasingly unstable ratios of power, within which Lucia is precariously confined.

Meanwhile, Renzo has arrived in Milan, where the city is in an uproar. It is the second year of a bad harvest. The weather has been poor. The ravages and waste of war have left many fields abandoned. And even after the meager harvest was stored, "the provisioning of the army, and the waste that always accompanies it, left such a hole that shortages were immediately felt, and with the shortages came a rise in prices: painful, corrective, and inevitable."[37]

Note the word *corrective* here. Painful and inevitable as they are, high prices are self-correcting because they invite imports from other cities and states with a more plentiful harvest. They also encourage more farmland to be put into production. But the people will tolerate only so much of a rise in prices before they become convinced that the problem is not a shortage, but rather grain hoarders deliberately driving up the cost of bread and making windfall profits. To appease the people, decrees are passed setting maximum prices, penalizing hoarders, and so forth. "Yet no measure in the world, no matter how vigorous," the narrator explains, "has the power to lower the need for food, nor to obtain crops out of season. And they certainly had no power to extract it from non-existent surpluses."[38] The acting Spanish governor stepped in and set by fiat a maximum price for bread that might have been fair if grain cost 33 lire a bushel, when in reality it sold for 80. "He acted like an aging woman who thinks she can be young again by simply altering her birth certificate."[39]

Bread was suddenly cheap but only because the bakers were required to produce it and sell it at a price well below their costs. The situation was both unfair and unsustainable. Eventually, a government-appointed commission reluctantly decided to raise the price of bread. This change leads to the bread riots in Milan on November 11 and 12, 1628. Delivery

ALESSANDRO MANZONI AND THE GREAT ITALIAN NOVEL

boys and bakeries are attacked. Looting is commonplace and violence is threatened. Fires are deliberately set, as if burning bakeries could create more bread. Renzo enters the city and is immediately swept up in the riot and confusion. As a peasant suspicious of those in power, he naturally takes the side of the people crying out for bread. He does his best to tamp down the violence and supports efforts to control the crowd. But stirred by the wrongdoing that drove him and Lucia from Lecco, he addresses a large group:

> Bakeries aren't the only places cheating us. If there's one thing we've learned today, it's that when we raise our voices, we get justice. We have to keep going until every wrong has been made right, and the world is a little more humane.[40]

Because of his activity, Renzo is noticed by a government informer who follows him to his inn, where he encourages the excited Renzo to drink and run off at the mouth about the rights of the people to revolt against tyranny. The informer, to puff up his own importance, describes Renzo in an arrest warrant as an outside agitator who came to Milan specifically to incite the riot. He is arrested the next morning and led toward the nearest police station. Renzo escapes only by appealing to the still volatile crowd: "Boys, they're dragging me off to prison for shouting 'bread and justice' yesterday. I didn't do anything. I'm an honest man. Help me! Don't abandon me, boys!"[41]

Luigi Einaudi, an economist who later became president of the fledgling Italian republic, called the portion of *The Betrothed* dealing with the bread riots "one of the best treatises on political economy ever written."[42] It is certainly worthy of Adam Smith in its attack on price controls as counterproductive. Rising prices attract more output, which in turn leads to lower prices rather than artificial scarcity. But at what human cost in the meantime?

In any event, *The Betrothed* is a novel, not an economic treatise or even a history of the two-day bread riots that actually occurred in Milan. It is an artistic rendering of a mob divided against itself: "primed for cruelty or mercy, to detest or adore, if and when the occasion arises to fully feel

213

one way or the other."[43] Such a mob can readily be moved toward or away from violence, depending on which of the competing forces can harness its energy.

> They set their sights on whoever is best at spreading the rumors most apt to excite passions, to steer movements toward one purpose or the other; whoever is best at finding the piece of information that will arouse indignation or dampen it, that will rekindle hopes or fears; whoever can find the slogans that, when repeated by the many and the strong, simultaneously express, attest to, and create the vote of the majority, for one side or the other.[44]

The true brilliance of the treatment of the bread riots in *The Betrothed* is to be found in neither economic acumen nor historical accuracy—though both are undoubtedly present—but in the portrayal of the ever-shifting moods of the crowd itself and Renzo's stumbling efforts to be guided by his own moral compass.

Renzo is freed by the crowd, which angrily drives off the informer and the two policemen he has summoned. Renzo makes his way out of Milan, eventually crossing the Adda and fleeing to Bergamo, in the Venetian Republic, where he need not fear a Milanese arrest warrant and is able to find work with an old friend.

There we shall leave him, returning to the far greater perils of Lucia, who is at the mercy of the Nun of Monza. Lucia's mother has returned home thinking Lucia is in safe hands. Padre Cristoforo, through the machinations of a powerful uncle of Don Rodrigo, has been transferred to far-off Rimini. But Don Rodrigo still can't get at Lucia while she remains in the convent. He seeks an audience with L'Innominato, who promises to arrange the abduction and turn the helpless girl over to Don Rodrigo. L'Innominato in turn directs Egidio to coerce the Nun of Monza, on threat of disclosing their affair, to send Lucia on an errand along a largely deserted road to a nearby monastery. On the way, the terrified Lucia is bundled into a waiting coach and taken to the castle of L'Innominato.

Alessandro Manzoni and the Great Italian Novel

But L'Innominato himself is suffering a midlife crisis, a credible (if convenient) plot device that is nonetheless based on the historical character.

> For some time now, he had been feeling, if not remorse, then a certain disquiet over his evil ways. A lifetime of crime had amassed in his memory, if not in his conscience, which was reawakened with each new act, pressing down on him in all its ugliness and multitude, an already uncomfortable burden growing heavier and heavier.[45]

He cannot help but rehearse in his mind the litany of his crimes. He has lived "as if there were no God,"[46] but the prospect of being judged before God now terrifies him. He is deeply and inexplicably moved by Lucia's desperate pleas. "God will forgive many things for an act of mercy!" she tells him repeatedly.[47] She promises always to pray to God to deliver him. "I can see that you have a good heart, that you feel pity for me, this poor creature."[48]

To his own amazement, he does pity her despite having turned a deaf ear to a lifetime of such pleas. After a sleepless night, he hears distant bells ringing in celebration. He learns that they honor Cardinal Borromeo and resolves to go see him, where he is welcomed with open arms and a full heart.

The conversion of L'Innominato by Cardinal Borromeo is a historical fact, given fictional form here. That has not kept it from being criticized by some critics as an implausibly sudden and overly contrived event in the fictional history of Lucia and Renzo. Conversions, however, are by definition sudden, as were the two most famous and significant conversions in Catholic history: those of Saint Paul and Saint Augustine. Martin Luther, too, resolved to become a monk when he was exposed on horseback in the midst of a violent thunderstorm. Manzoni's own conversion was equally sudden. And the psychological groundwork for L'Innominato's conversion is carefully laid, as it is in Saint Augustine's *Confessions*. Manzoni is fully justified as a matter of history, psychology, and aesthetics in portraying and employing such an event—as he does with the bread riots, the war, and the plague—though, as discussed below,

THE WISDOM OF THE ROMANTICS

he comes to have second thoughts about the inherent tension between historical accuracy and the aesthetic demands of art.

From Lucia's perspective, of course, L'Innominato's conversion is nothing less than a miracle by the divine intercession of the Virgin Mary, to whom she prayed so fervently throughout the night. Lucia even resolved, if rescued, to sacrifice to the Virgin Mary what is for her the most important thing in her life: "I vow to you to remain a virgin for the rest of my life, and to renounce my poor love forever, and belong to no one but you."[49] After her unexpected salvation, she must now live, or at least try to live, with the consequences of her vow. "It's as if God Himself wanted to keep us apart," she laments.[50]

Whether interposed by God or man or happenstance, the obstacles to their reunion remain great. Lucia is offered shelter from the continuing threat posed by Don Rodrigo by a noble couple—pious but overly officious—with a vacation home near Lecco. Renzo still has an arrest warrant outstanding if he returns to the duchy of Milan. He is living in Bergamo under an assumed name and cannot be located even by the good auspices of Cardinal Borromeo.

One of their biggest obstacles, however, is illiteracy. Renzo can read printed pages with difficulty but handwriting not at all. His own penmanship is limited to painstakingly writing his name. So when he wants to send a letter to Lucia to let her know where he is, Renzo must find a scribe he can trust and a method of delivery that is uncertain at best, which means he must obscure sensitive information in case the letter falls into other hands. His first attempt, placed inside an envelope addressed to Padre Cristoforo, yields no response. But a second letter sent to a relative close to Lecco eventually reaches Agnese, who goes through the whole process in reverse. She obliquely describes the dangers Lucia faced, coming to the vow only at the end of the letter, which advises Renzo to "set his heart at peace and think no more about it."[51] Renzo—in his rage and confusion—responds, "I have no intention of setting my heart at peace, and I never will."[52] He will not rest until Lucia is his bride.

Their communication is halting, uncertain, and indirect. But it is enough to reestablish their fragile connection, a connection all the more important as they are "swept up by new, more widespread, powerful, and extreme circumstances."[53]

The famine that led to the bread riots has not abated. To the contrary, barren fields still abound, devastated by the War of the Mantuan Succession (1628–1631), which was itself just a sidebar of the Thirty Years' War that raged throughout Europe from 1618 to 1648. The dislocation of citizens is exacerbated by the heavy taxation levied to fund the war and by the looting of the troops. Migrants, driven from their homes in search of food, work, and some semblance of safety, numbly pass one another on the roads, each blindly hoping that where they are going will be better than where they have left. In fact, what lies ahead for most of them is the plague, brought into Lombardy by German troops on their way to and from the duchy of Mantua. The plague hit Milan in 1629, killing almost half the population of the city over the next two years and 30–35 percent of those in northern Italy, generally.

Manzoni had not himself experienced a plague, but he studied historical documents and likely read a French translation of Defoe's *Journal of the Plague Year*, which offers a quasi-fictional, quasi-historical description of the Great Plague of London in 1665. He was also familiar with Thucydides's famous account in his *History of the Peloponnesian War* of the plague that hit Athens in 430 BCE. Manzoni's retelling is the most vivid of the three.

The city authorities had directed all vagrants, whether healthy or sick, to the lazaretto of Milan, a large square enclosure surrounded by a ditch and further separated from the city walls by a moat. Some came willingly in hopes of charity; others who fell sick in the city were simply deposited there. In these increasingly crowded conditions, the plague spread rapidly among already malnourished and weakened inhabitants. Despite strict orders from the Tribunal of Health that those from plague-infested areas should be forbidden to enter Milan, the Spanish governor decreed a two-day festival to celebrate the birth of the first son of King Philip IV. The death rate soared. Yet the population disregarded the pleas of these precursors to Dr. Anthony Fauci to isolate cases, avoid public events, and destroy contaminated clothing. "In the public squares, in the workplace, or at home, anyone who dared to hint at the danger, and who attributed

The Wisdom of the Romantics

the deaths to the plague, was treated to angry contempt and jeers of disbelief."[54] Even many doctors derided the warnings of the few: "They trotted out the names of common illnesses to explain away every case of plague they were called upon to treat, regardless of the signs or symptoms."[55] Still, the plague spread, and so, too, eventually, did panic. The populace swung from denial to false accusations, attributing cases to dark arts, satanic rituals, and deliberate efforts to infect others. Foreigners were readily singled out and accused of being "anointers" who smeared infected unguents on doors and public places. No one could enter the city without an official health certification.

The magistrates finally awoke to the danger, ordering possessions burned, houses sequestered, and families sent to the lazaretto. In some cases, they went so far as to nail shut the doors of houses with whole families, sick and well alike, still inside. Two new professions sprang up. The *monatti* were charged with transporting the dead on carts to be dumped in common graves without funeral rights, mourners, or even clothes, which had to be burned to avoid infection. The sick were taken to the lazaretto. Most of the *monatti* had already survived the plague and hence were protected against further contagion. The *apparatori* walked ahead of these carts piled with naked bodies while ringing a bell to warn others to keep away.

Looting and other crimes increased. Yet so did instances of conspicuous virtue, especially among health care workers who performed their duties despite the risks. The Capuchin monks were asked and agreed to take over management of the lazaretto. Most of them died in that service.

> There was beauty in their very acceptance of this assignment, for no other reason than that no one else would, and for no other purpose than to serve, with no other hope in this world than to die a death more enviable than envied.[56]

Renzo, still in Bergamo, contracts the plague and recovers. He then resolves to find Lucia, if still alive, and hear from her directly about her vow. He ignores the warrant for his arrest on the correct assumption that the authorities have far more important concerns. On the road, he encounters a postapocalyptic scene of devastation—houses looted by marauding troops and now inhabited only by rats, fields overgrown with brambles, and, in his depopulated village, a broken Don Abbondio, who tells him that Lucia went to Milan with the couple who had offered her refuge.

Renzo manages to slip into Milan even without the requisite health card. He finds a world from which human compassion and decency have largely fled. Bodies are scattered randomly: people who had died in the streets or whose lifeless forms had been tossed from the windows of locked houses or had fallen off the carts of the *monatti*. The normal sounds of life in a city—carriages rattling, vendors crying, neighbors chatting—are gone. "Only rarely was the deathly silence broken by any sounds other than those of funeral processions, the moaning of the poor, the anguish of the sick, the howls of the dying, and the shouts of the monatti."[57] Three times a day, the church bells ring and people come to their windows to recite their prayers in unison, as Italians stepped out on their balconies during the COVID-19 lockdown to applaud the selfless work of those caring for the sick and dying and to feel some connection with their neighbors through song or prayer or simply by tapping "crude rhythms" on "a cracked kettle."[58]

In his search for Lucia, Renzo comes across a rare scene of activity, where four carts are gathered at an intersection, and the *monatti* are entering houses and exiting with their grim burdens. Bent as he is on his own concerns, Renzo cannot but stop to watch as a lovely young, but obviously ill, mother comes out carrying her lifeless daughter, carefully groomed and dressed in white. Even the hardened *monatti* clear a space on the cart for the girl and let her mother arrange her on it, kissing her forehead and covering her with a white sheet. She bids the *monatti* to return that night for herself and her youngest child.

When Renzo finally locates the house where Lucia was living and where he will learn whether she is alive or dead, he is so paralyzed with fear that "he would rather have remained completely in the dark and gone back to the beginning of the journey that was finally about to end."[59] But he steels himself and knocks on the door regardless, only to learn that Lucia herself had fallen ill and was taken to the lazaretto. As

THE WISDOM OF THE ROMANTICS

he lingers there at the door, a passerby screams that he is an anointer. A hostile crowd quickly forms, and he escapes only by jumping onto one of the carts of the *monatti* and riding in safety to the lazaretto. The very disease that so terrifies them becomes his protective armor.

Primo Levi, who survived a different sort of plague in the death camp at Auschwitz, writes:

> I have just finished rereading the famous scene in Manzoni's novel *The Betrothed* where Renzo, having recovered from the plague, returns to Milan to search for Lucia. These are splendid pages, sure, rich with a strong and sad human wisdom, which enriches you and which you feel is valid for all times: not only for those in which the story unfolds but for Manzoni's times and for ours.[60]

For Levi, understandably, the death camp that is the lazaretto is not a redemptive experience. He sees in it neither "Catholic realism" nor "Socialist realism" rendering literary craftsmanship "subservient to the aims of propaganda."[61] Manzoni does not shrink from describing the full scope of human misery or attributing it to the joint forces of malign government and natural catastrophe. Sixteen thousand people are jammed into this limited space, the dead and the living jumbled together on pallets or heaps of straw.

Yet the novel seems to suggest, however inexplicably, that even in the lazaretto, divine providence—or at least human mercy—is at work. The Capuchin friars and lay volunteers together, though they cannot stop the dying, do their best to ease the suffering. There is even a section for babies who are suckled by goats in lieu of their mothers' milk. Occasionally, a procession of those who have recovered departs the lazaretto to finish their quarantine elsewhere, though their places are quickly taken by even more new arrivals herded by the *monatti*.

The lazaretto—though a potent symbol for how degraded human life can become—is also a place of reunion and even salvation for the novel's main characters. Renzo, in his frantic search for Lucia, finds Padre Cristoforo, his body broken and ravaged by illness but held together by fierce willpower as he cares for the children of the sick and dying. "Only his eyes were the same as before, if not even brighter and livelier. It was as if charity, sublimated by this extreme sacrifice, and rejoicing to feel so close to its maker, had given him a purer and more ardent flame than the one that his illness was slowly extinguishing."[62]

Together, Padre Cristoforo and Renzo pray over the nearly lifeless, lesion-covered body of Don Rodrigo, abandoned by all his retainers when he fell ill and reduced to the commonest level in the lazaretto. Padre Cristoforo directs Renzo to the women's area, telling him to "go prepared to receive grace or to make a sacrifice" and "to praise God whatever the outcome of your search may be."[63] Renzo is not put to that impossible test, for he finds Lucia alive and recovered from the contagion. The scene of their reunion contains some of the most moving pages in all of literature, rendered more so by its simplicity: "You're asking why I came? Do I have to tell you? Am I not Renzo? Are you not Lucia?"[64]

Padre Cristoforo's heartfelt conviction that they would all meet again has been validated. He proceeds to release Lucia from her vow, noting that "if ever two people were united by God, it seemed to me that it was you."[65] Even the once-reluctant Don Abbondio is persuaded to perform the ceremony, though only after Don Rodrigo's death is confirmed.

THE HISTORICAL NOVEL

The Betrothed ends on a note of optimism, not just for Renzo and Lucia but for all Italy. The plague is washed away in a torrent of cleansing rain. Greenery flourishes. Houses and businesses reopen. Couples line up to marry. Life seems to begin anew, and the series of catastrophes that mark the book—both natural and man-made—recede in time and memory. On Renzo's return to his village, "everything he saw—the mountains, the nearby Resegone, and the Lecco territory—had become something that belonged to him."[66] Just as *Howards End* is a book about who will inherit England, *The Betrothed* anticipates a united Italy free of foreign misgovernment and foreign wars.

The Betrothed shows the commitment of two young people to each other when an entire world seems intent on keeping them apart. It also reflects the commitment of the Italian people to a single nation when the entire world seems intent on tearing it apart. And just as Renzo and

Lucia, when separated by circumstances, could not directly communicate with each other without writing, the Italians of various regions could not bridge their many dialects. Renzo will insist that their children learn to read and write so that they need not be at the mercy of scribes. Manzoni likewise insisted that the Italian people needed a living, universal language, fed both by natural speech and by literary tradition. He set out to provide such a language with the dedication of Samuel Johnson preparing his dictionary. Building on the Tuscan dialect of Dante, Boccaccio, and Machiavelli—which Manzoni considered the "richest speech capable of expressing the highest thoughts most adequately"—he turned his home into a "linguistic laboratory," with collaborators sifting through examples of common usage. He sought "a living language, which is by its nature a mixture of the actual and the potential" and "is, in consequence, the sum, never however determinable, of what is universally accepted and what can be most easily accepted."[67] The result of his efforts was a language of consummate beauty that was gradually and increasingly used in daily conversation and governmental affairs throughout Italy, as well as in the grander efforts of history, philosophy, literature, and, of course, the great Italian genre, opera.[68]

Manzoni is by no means naïve; he is not expecting any sort of utopia, either for Renzo and Lucia or for the nation as a whole. But his narrator believes in the possibility of kindness, humanity, and love, even while recognizing that they will not immunize us from violence and oppression. In a typical romantic comedy, the young couple must overcome numerous obstacles in order to find happiness in marriage. Here, as in Shakespeare's problem plays, the obstacles are harrowing and the darkness never fully lifts. But as Prospero cautions in *The Tempest*, after the political and romantic resolutions are reached, "Let us not burthen our remembrance with / A heaviness that's gone."[69] "Quiet days, fair issue and long life"[70] will bring us as close to paradise as one might hope in an imperfect world. Having reached this state of fulfillment, Renzo and Lucia fade back into the historical background.[71]

Goethe, who otherwise heaped generous praise on *The Betrothed*, thought the historical events—the bread riots, the war, and the plague—were treated in too much detail, sacrificing the aesthetic to the factual. To

Alessandro Manzoni and the Great Italian Novel

that one can only say, even Goethe nods. The historical canvas is not just a backdrop for the concerns of the fictional characters; history itself is both protagonist and antagonist in this modern epic. As Calvino wryly puts it, "the part of Providence is played by the plague."[72] The classical unities are no longer needed when poetry is embedded in history. *The Betrothed* is a masterful synthesis of historic reality and aesthetic invention.

Manzoni never attempted a second novel. In his final years, following the death of his second wife and all but two of his children, he devoted himself to history, religious philosophy, and linguistics. He also wrote a curious book, *On the Historical Novel* (1859), that seemed to discount even the possibility of his great achievement. In that work, Manzoni notes "two diametrically opposite criticisms" of the historical novel based on what he calls "the inherent contradiction of its premises and . . . its resulting inability to take on a convincing and stable form."[73] First, because in "certain historical novels . . . fact is not clearly distinguished from invention," the reader is left wondering which of the events described are historical and which are invented.[74] Second, when the historical novel does "plainly distinguish factual truth from invention," it "destroys the unity that is the vital condition of this or any other work of art."[75] In short, you can have history or poetry, truth or beauty, but not both.

Manzoni's prediction of the demise of historical fiction was reasonably accurate, though Victor Hugo's *Les Misérables* and Tolstoy's *War and Peace* were still to come. The historical novel formed a critical bridge between the eighteenth-century social novel and the realism of the latter half of the nineteenth century. Starting at least with the French Revolution and accelerating through the Industrial Revolution, history became a more visible force in daily life. Whether directly or by osmosis, the writers of historical fiction began to see human life in Hegelian terms as conditioned by and embedded in history. For Georg Lukács, the Marxist literary critic, "what is important is that Scott and Manzoni, Pushkin and Tolstoy, were able to grasp and portray popular life in a more profound, authentic, human and concretely historical fashion."[76]

Scott and Manzoni, Pushkin and Tolstoy, did not want to write pure history. They wanted, and strove for, that very synthesis of history and poetry, fact and invention, of which Manzoni in his old age despaired.

That synthesis speaks to us today, as individuals continue to seek quiet days, fair issue, and long life amid war, famine, civil unrest, environmental degradation, inflation, desperate migration, pandemic, oppression, and injustice.

"What, in the end, does history give us?" Manzoni had earlier asked.

> Events that are known only, so to speak, from the outside, what men have done. But what they have thought, the feelings that have accompanied their decisions and their plans, their successes and misfortunes, the words by which they have asserted—or tried to assert—their passions and wills on those of others, by which they have expressed their anger, poured out their sadness, by which, in a word, they have revealed their individuality: all that, more or less, is passed over in silence by history: and all that is the domain of poetry.[77]

Manzoni, who knew Homer only in poor translations, was a passionate admirer of Virgil's *Aeneid*. He recognized that the genre of epic poetry was long past, but, as its highest exemplar, the *Aeneid* will always survive the genre that gave it birth. Manzoni considered the historical novel a successor of epic poetry, combining fact and invention in the service of a new foundational myth. While remaining faithful to the story of Renzo and Lucia, Manzoni presents us with both the tragedy and the hopes of the Italian people,[78] just as Virgil did for the Romans and as Tolstoy would do for the Russian people.

The historical novel is not as outmoded as epic poetry. One can point to modern examples such as Patrick O'Brian's *Aubrey/Maturin* series and Larry McMurtry's *Lonesome Dove*, our modern *Aeneid*. Indeed, one could argue that every realistic novel is told against a backdrop that seeks to be faithful to the time in question, and even if that time is the present, it will quickly become the past. Only if the work effects a synthesis of poetry and reality will it survive. *The Betrothed*, as one of the greatest exemplars of the historical novel, will always survive the genre that gave it birth. In it, as in Keats's poetry, beauty and truth have become one.

8

John Keats and the Great Odes

JOHN KEATS DIED OF TUBERCULOSIS IN 1821, AT THE AGE OF twenty-five. He had, at most, three years as a fully mature poet. One year in particular—September 1818 to September 1819—produced almost all the poems that guaranteed his place in the pantheon of English poets with Shakespeare (who lived to fifty-two), Milton (sixty-five), and Wordsworth (eighty). What he might have written if he had their longevity is a question to tease us out of thought.

Keats himself feared that the beauties and possibilities of English poetry had already been exhausted. There was nothing left to say, nor any way to say it, that was not simply a rehash. His *Letters* provide a remarkable account of his struggle to overcome what W. Jackson Bate would call "the burden of the past" and Harold Bloom "the anxiety of influence." Yet somehow, in that "living year," Keats found a way to combine the seriousness of Shakespeare, the condensation of Milton, and the emotional intimacy of Wordsworth into a poetry peculiarly his own.

"If Poetry comes not as naturally as the Leaves to a tree," Keats wrote, "it had better not come at all."[1] In this sense, he echoes Shakespeare, who wrote, "Poesy is as a gum which oozes / From whence 'tis nourished."[2] Neither meant that the poet should sit around and wait for inspiration to present him with fully polished verses. Keats studied his predecessors with the greatest care and set himself to write as many as forty verses a day, even while recognizing that his judgment was as yet unprepared: "I leaped headlong into the Sea, and thereby have become better acquainted with the Soundings, the quicksands, & the rocks, than

THE WISDOM OF THE ROMANTICS

if I had stayed upon the green shore, and piped a silly pipe, and took tea & comfortable advice."[3]

As Shakespeare also wrote, in Keats's favorite play, "ripeness is all."[4] That Keats, at such a young age, reached his own season of mellow fruitfulness, in which the verses fell so naturally from his pen, is a source of both wonder and joy.

EARLY LIFE

John Keats was born on October 31, 1795. He was the oldest of five children, born at two-year intervals to Thomas and Frances Keats. The others were George (1797); Tom (1799); Edward (1801), who died in infancy; and Fanny (1803), their only daughter.

Frances, by all accounts, was both beautiful and rebellious. Her parents, John and Alice Jennings, ran a successful livery stable on the outskirts of London, known as the Swan and Hoop. Thomas worked there as the chief stable hand. The couple eloped when Frances was only nineteen. Thomas was a good, steady employee and took over the family business when Frances's parents retired to the country in 1802. Thomas and Frances then moved with their growing family into an apartment above the livery.

There is very little information about Keats's early years. Apparently, he delighted in word games and would often respond with a rhyme on the last word spoken to him. He and his brother George were sent in 1803 to board at John Clarke's Academy, around ten miles from London in the town of Enfield. The boys were still quite young (eight and six, respectively), but their Jennings grandparents lived nearby and could keep an eye on them. They were taught math, science, Latin, and French. Their father visited the boys regularly. Younger brother Tom later joined them there. All three boys were popular with their fellow students. John was short, just over five feet, but stocky and very handy with his fists when needed.

The Keats children seemed destined to enjoy a solid middle-class existence, perhaps even with a chance for the boys to attend university when the time came. But their lives took a sudden turn for the worse in 1804 when their father fell from his horse while returning to London from Enfield. The cause of the accident, which occurred close to home, was unclear. Thomas was an expert horseman. His horse might have slipped on the cobblestones. He might have been drinking. He could even have been attacked. But that is all speculation. What is clear is that Thomas Keats fractured his skull in the fall and died shortly thereafter. The family's prospects fell with him.

Frances was unstable, wayward, and a heavy drinker. This behavior seemed to predate her husband's death. According to one anecdote, the five-year-old Keats once stood in the doorway with a sword to try to keep her from going out of the house. She abandoned her children to deal with the death of their father as best they might, leaving John and George at Enfield and depositing the two youngest, Tom and Fanny, with her parents. Two months after her husband's death, she married the much younger William Rawlings, a banker's clerk with his eyes clearly on her inheritance as well as her person.

John and Alice Jennings unsurprisingly disapproved of the match and changed their wills accordingly. John and George remained at school; Tom and Fanny moved in with their maternal grandparents. Meanwhile, Rawlings, who had neither experience nor ability with horses, mismanaged the stables.

John Jennings unfortunately died in March 1805. He was quite well off, but his will was badly drafted and Frances and her new husband sued the estate, claiming that her inheritance was inadequate. The suit was not decided for two decades, by which time most of the principals were dead, thus depriving John and his siblings of money they would have found extremely useful. Charles Dickens allegedly used the suit as his inspiration for the endless chancery litigation in *Bleak House*.

Frances's new marriage predictably fell apart. She left her husband in 1806, thereby abandoning her marital property to Rawlings and further impoverishing her children. She had had no contact whatsoever with them for three years.

She began an affair with another man, but she drank too much and had no money. She was also showing symptoms of the tuberculosis that would kill all three of her sons. Frances eventually moved in with her widowed mother in 1809, when John was fourteen. He would sit by her

The Wisdom of the Romantics

on visits from Enfield, giving her medicine, cooking her food, and reading to her. She died in March 1810, at the age of thirty-five, while the boys were at school. The heartbroken Keats crawled under the headmaster's desk at Enfield and refused to come out.

Yet another disaster, though less immediately apparent, came in 1810, when the children's grandmother, Alice Jennings, chose two legal guardians for the children, one of whom, John Rowland Sandell, largely neglected his duties, and the other, Richard Abbey, was cold, censorious, and at best insufficiently active on their behalf; at worst, he speculated with and never repaid money from the estate.

Alice Jennings died in 1814. John Keats was only nineteen. He had lost a little brother, his father and mother, two maternal uncles, and both his maternal grandparents. He would later write, "I must think that difficulties nerve the Spirit of a Man—they make our Prime Objects a Refuge as well as a Passion."[5] Poetry, his prime object, would become both his refuge and his passion.

Without sufficient funds, however, there was no possibility of a university education such as Wordsworth, Coleridge, Byron, and Shelley all enjoyed, at least until Shelley was expelled from University College, Oxford, for writing a pamphlet titled *The Necessity of Atheism*. Ironically, once he became famous—and dead—his college reclaimed him with a mawkish statue of the drowned Shelley.

Keats read voraciously in his last two years of school, as if to make up for the brevity of his education. At age sixteen (in 1811), he left school and was apprenticed by Abbey as an apothecary to Thomas Hammond, the family doctor. It was tedious, menial work, mostly grinding pills, but he also learned how to dress wounds and otherwise assist the surgeons at Guy's Hospital in London. He often visited Clarke's Academy, where his good friend Charles Cowden Clarke, son of the headmaster, taught.

George, though only fourteen, was also pulled from Enfield in 1811 and sent to work in Abbey's counting house. Tom joined him there when he turned sixteen. The three boys were close and tried to live with one another as much as possible. They also sought to remain close to their sister, Fanny, but Abbey either considered the boys a bad influence or did not want them inquiring into his handling of her finances. Regardless, he did his best to keep them apart, even forbidding Fanny to visit Tom when he was near death. Fanny was removed from school, over Keats's objections, when she was fifteen and required to live with the Abbeys. She was a virtual prisoner in that house until a young Spanish admirer of her brother, John, who had met him in Rome shortly before his death, arrived in 1821 with a letter of introduction from Joseph Severn, Keats's companion on the final, fatal journey to Rome. Fanny, eager to escape Abbey's house, married Valentin Llanos y Gutiérrez in 1826 and moved with him to Madrid. She died in 1889, at the age of eighty-six.

THE PRENTICE POET

Keats passed his medical exam in the summer of 1816, which allowed him to work as a surgeon and apothecary. But by then he was already deep into poetry. His first published work, in 1816, was the sonnet that begins "O Solitude! if I must with thee dwell, / Let it not be among the jumbled heap / Of murky buildings."[6] It was standard Romantic fare, obviously influenced by Wordsworth and the Lake Poets. But it caught the eye of Leigh Hunt, a poet, essayist, and, most important, editor of the radical journal *Examiner*. The circle that formed around Hunt included the painter Robert Haydon and such literary figures as William Hazlitt, Charles Lamb, John Reynolds, and Percy Bysshe Shelley, who was only three years older than Keats. They all became more or less close friends with Keats, whom Reynolds called "the sincerest Friend,—the most lovable associate,—the deepest Listener to the griefs & disappointments of all around him."[7]

Hunt was caught up in the conservative reaction to the French Revolution and the Napoleonic Wars that were its aftermath. He unwisely called the prince regent a "libertine" and suggested that he had lived "half a century without one claim on the gratitude of his country, or the respect of posterity."[8] Hunt was prosecuted for libel in 1816 and sentenced to two years in prison. As a "gentleman," he was allowed to furnish his cell with comfortable furniture, books, busts of famous poets, and even a piano. He received visitors and continued to edit the *Examiner*. Keats endeared himself to Hunt by writing a not particularly impressive sonnet, "Written on the Day That Mr. Leigh Hunt Left Prison."

The Wisdom of the Romantics

Late in 1816, Keats wrote his first truly memorable poem, "On First Looking into Chapman's Homer." In it, Keats notes that, despite studying many poets, he knew of Homer only by reputation until he encountered George Chapman's verse translation of both the *Iliad* and the *Odyssey*:

> Then felt I like some watcher of the skies
> When a new planet swims into his ken;
> Or like stout Cortez when with eagle eyes
> He star'd at the Pacific—and all his men
> Look'd at each other with a wild surmise—
> Silent, upon a peak in Darien.[9]

The poem beautifully captures Keats's awestruck encounter with the greatness and power of the poetic tradition. Keats himself is stout Cortés gazing with wild surmise on this vast realm that he is eager to explore and determined to conquer.

Overeager, perhaps. Keats prematurely put together a book of thirty poems and sonnets, including "Chapman's Homer," which was published under the title *Poems* in 1817. It contained a hastily written dedicatory sonnet to Hunt, which showed loyalty (if not marketing savvy). The book, of course, was praised by Hunt and his coterie but savaged by the conservative critical establishment. Keats himself thought little of the book over time. But the last poem, the 404-line "Sleep and Poetry," hints at his future development. He will not imitate other poets, but rather will immerse himself in the original sources of poetry and recapture their spirit.[10] He is confident that he can stand apart, yet equally on high.

> Is there so small a range
> In the present strength of manhood, that the high
> Imagination cannot freely fly
> As she was wont of old?[11]

Keats asks only for the time and the freedom he needs.

O for ten years, that I may overwhelm
Myself in poesy; so I may do the deed
That my own soul has to itself decreed.[12]

He would not get ten years. Nor anything close to that. But his high imagination and the strength of his understanding would allow him to probe the depths of the human heart and accomplish much that his soul had to itself decreed.

In the spring of 1817, at the age of twenty-one, Keats left medicine to write poetry full time. Despite the bad reviews of his book, and with little to warrant the boast even a year later, he confidently predicted to his brother George that he would be "among the English Poets" after his death.[13]

Abbey did not share that confidence, telling Keats that "your Book is hard to understand & good for nothing when it is understood."[14] In the time-honored tradition of philistines, Abbey advised Keats to get a real job, if not as a surgeon, then—he actually suggested this!—as a hatter, perhaps one of the maddest bits of advice in literary history. Worse, Abbey failed to alert Keats to the existence of funds from his grandmother's estate that should have been available to him when he turned twenty-one and that would have allowed him to live more comfortably, despite his generous habit of lending what little money he had to others.

Keats, in a friendly competition with Shelley, decided to undertake an immense project in April—an epic romance of four thousand lines—to build up his poetic muscles and endurance. He duly finished *Endymion*—with fifty lines to spare—on November 28, 1817. Shelley's poem, the 4,818-line *Revolt of Islam*, was published in December.

Endymion recounts the love of a shepherd prince and the Moon Goddess. It is largely unreadable straight through, but portions are exquisite, including its famous opening lines:

A thing of beauty is a joy for ever:
Its loveliness increases; it will never
Pass into nothingness; but still will keep

> A bower quiet for us, and a sleep
> Full of sweet dreams, and health, and quiet breathing.[15]

The poem combines classical elements—a pastoral setting, the hymn to Pan, a visit to the underworld, the love of mortal and immortal—with Romantic themes of dream-like joy, passion, and loss.

Endymion was harshly received by critics but not unjustly, as Keats himself would come to acknowledge. He did not regret writing the poem because of what he learned in the process, but he did regret publishing it. When he met William Wordsworth at Hunt's house, Keats was implored by the assembled company to read aloud the "Hymn to Pan" in book 1. He did so, and the group looked expectantly at Wordsworth, who only remarked, "A very pretty piece of Paganism."[16] The cold response was undoubtedly deflating for the young poet but in keeping with two other encounters with Wordsworth. Told that Sir Walter Scott was going to write a novel on Rob Roy, Wordsworth read aloud his own ballad, "Rob Roy's Grave," and added, "I do not know what more Mr. Scott can have to say upon the subject."[17] On the other occasion, Keats offered a word of reinforcement to something Wordsworth was saying, and Wordsworth's wife put her hand on Keats's arm, cautioning him, "Mr. Wordsworth is never interrupted."[18]

Keats greatly admired Wordsworth for "think[ing] into the human heart"[19] but shunned what he called "the wordsworthian or egotistical sublime."[20] For Wordsworth, the cult of poetry too readily became the cult of personality. In several of his most brilliant letters, Keats argues that "the poetical Character itself"[21] should disappear into the poem.

> At once it struck me, what quality went to form a Man of Achievement especially in Literature & which Shakespeare possessed so enormously—I mean *Negative Capability*, that is when man is capable of being in uncertainties, Mysteries, doubts, without any irritable reaching after fact & reason.[22]

Keats disparages neither fact nor reason. But he has "never yet been able to perceive how anything can be known for truth by consecutive reasoning."[23] Truth manifests itself in lived experience. He wants to combine ideas rather than parse them. The "chameleon poet" should be open to all that exists. Imagination should rule over ratiocination, for "what the imagination seizes as Beauty must be truth."[24] "O for a Life of Sensations rather than of Thoughts!" he concludes.[25]

In search of such sensations, Keats took an extended walking tour of England and Scotland with his friend Charles Brown in the summer of 1818. They covered 640 miles over rugged country, averaging twelve miles a day, despite a persistent sore throat that ultimately forced Keats to curtail the hike in August.

Keats came home to find his brother Tom in an advanced stage of consumption, despite his having reassured the absent Keats that he was much improved. Tom suffered a massive hemorrhage shortly after Keats's return. Keats cared for Tom, as he had for their mother, until his death on December 1, 1818.

Keats's other brother, George, was also absent. He had married Georgiana Augusta Wylie in May 1818, and they decided to move to the United States the following month to pursue whatever opportunities presented themselves. George promptly lost most of his money in a fraudulent business scheme proposed by the naturalist John James Audubon. He returned to London briefly in 1820 to try to collect from Abbey his share of Tom's estate. He left with money that was likely owed to John. George ultimately prospered in Louisville, Kentucky, with a lumber mill and a flour mill. He had seven children before dying of tuberculosis in 1841, when he was forty-four. After the brief visit in 1820, however, Keats never saw him again.

With Tom dead, George overseas, and Fanny secluded in Abbey's house, Keats had no family left on which to lean. This might explain, in part, the intensity of his attachment to the eighteen-year-old Fanny Brawne, which began in September 1818. The Brawnes—a widowed mother and her three children—had rented half of Charles Brown's house in Hampstead, where the three Keats brothers had often stayed. Keats seemed indifferent to Fanny at first, but, as early as December, he described her in a letter to George as "beautiful and elegant, graceful, silly, fashionable and strange."[26] She soon became his muse, the point where poetry and reality, beauty and truth, would meet in his imagination.

"THE EVE OF ST. AGNES"

Eager to capitalize on the popular and monetary success of verse romances by Scott and Byron, Keats worked on a number of longer projects in 1818. These included a rather gruesome story, inspired by Boccaccio, called *Isabella; Or, The Pot of Basil*, and an epic poem, *Hyperion*, in the spirit of Milton, on the overthrow of Saturn and the Titans by Jove and his new Olympian gods. Despite many brilliant touches, neither poem was transformative; indeed, *Hyperion* stalled after two books, and Keats ultimately abandoned it.

Then, in early 1819, something remarkable happened, corresponding in time with his increasing attachment to Fanny Brawne. Keats wrote a pitch-perfect blend of romantic passion and erotic fantasy, "The Eve of St. Agnes." The mood of the narrative is beautifully set in its opening lines:

> St. Agnes' Eve—Ah, bitter chill it was!
> The owl, for all his feathers, was a-cold;
> The hare limp'd trembling through the frozen grass,
> And silent was the flock in woolly fold:
> Numb were the Beadsman's fingers, while he told
> His rosary, and while his frosted breath,
> Like pious incense from a censer old,
> Seem'd taking flight for heaven, without a death,
> Past the sweet Virgin's picture, while his prayer he saith.[27]

According to legend, if a young virgin goes to bed on St. Agnes's Eve without supper and follows various prescribed rituals, she might have a dream vision of her future lover. Madeline slips away from the party her parents are hosting in their castle. She disdains the living men eager to court her in favor of the vision promised by St. Agnes. Enter young Porphyro, from a rival family, who is in love with Madeline. If he is seen by the assembled company, "a hundred swords / Will storm his heart."[28] But an ancient servant, who has long known him, is persuaded after many promises and pleas "to lead him, in close secrecy, / Even to Madeline's chamber, and there hide / Him in a closet, of such privacy / That he might see her beauty unespied, / And win perhaps that night a peerless bride."[29] The real Porphyro seeks to take the place of the promised vision.

Madeline enters her chamber, and, after kneeling and saying her prayers, she readies herself for bed.

> Of all its wreathed pearls her hair she frees;
> Unclasps her warmed jewels one by one;
> Loosens her fragrant bodice; by degrees
> Her rich attire creeps rustling to her knees:
> Half-hidden, like a mermaid in sea-weed,
> Pensive awhile she dreams awake, and sees,
> In fancy, fair St. Agnes in her bed,
> But dares not look behind, or all the charm is fled.[30]

Once Madeline is fully asleep, Porphyro slips from his hiding place, heaps an array of exotic delicacies on a table beside her bed, and, sinking his arm into her pillow, whispers:

> "And now, my love, my seraph fair, awake!
> Thou art my heaven, and I thine eremite."[31]

But Madeline is so deeply asleep "it seem'd he never, never could redeem / From such a steadfast spell his lady's eyes."[32] He picks up her lute and plays close to her ear an ancient tune:

> Wherewith disturb'd, she utter'd a soft moan:
> He ceased—she panted quick—and suddenly
> Her blue affrayed eyes wide open shone:
> Upon his knees he sank, pale as smooth-sculptured stone.[33]

Though her eyes are open, Madeline still beholds the image of her sleep and finds the reality before her a "painful change."[34] The "looks immortal" in her dream are here "pallid, chill, and drear."[35] Yet she confirms that Porphyro is the one of whom she dreamed and pleads with him never to leave her:

> Beyond a mortal man impassion'd far
> At these voluptuous accents, he arose,
> Ethereal, flush'd, and like a throbbing star
> Seen mid the sapphire heaven's deep repose;
> Into her dream he melted, as the rose
> Blendeth its odour with the violet,—
> Solution sweet: meantime the frost-wind blows
> Like Love's alarum pattering the sharp sleet
> Against the window-panes; St. Agnes' moon hath set.[36]

Wide awake now, Madeline feels betrayed and deceived and fears he will forsake her. But Porphyro calls her his bride and pledges himself as her vassal: "Awake! arise! my love, and fearless be, / For o'er the southern moors I have a home for thee."[37] They both choose a real love, however imperfect, over an empty dream.

The two lovers quickly dress and "glide, like phantoms,"[38] through the hall, past the unconscious revelers, and out the massive door.

> And they are gone: ay, ages long ago
> These lovers fled away into the storm.[39]

Porphyro and Madeline have passed from dream to reality and into legend.

The poem was controversial when Keats wrote it and is still controversial today. Even some of his friends and admirers thought the consummation of their love in stanza 36 was too openly erotic. Academics today are inclined to chastise Porphyro as a voyeur and rapist insofar as Madeline was still in a dreamlike state and therefore an unwilling (or at least unwitting) participant in their lovemaking—all of which seems rather beside the point. Madeline's innocence is violated in the way that all dreams are violated in contact with reality. But we cannot live in dreams. We must find our happiness in reality, and the two lovers seize theirs both physically and emotionally. They make love only after she calls him "my Porphyro" and "my Love."[40]

The *Romeo and Juliet* setting of the young lovers, their warring families, and the impossibility of ever meeting openly, blending with the legend of St. Agnes's Eve and their successful, eager elopement, surely licenses all what went before. Obviously, they had met previously—fleetingly, perhaps, but enough to spark their respective passions. It is clear, moreover, that Porphyro was the St. Agnes vision for which Madeline longed. Her disappointment on awakening is a function of the way we idealize those we love, especially if separated from them. Yet Madeline quickly recognizes that the reality of Porphyro more than compensates for the loss of her dream. She is betrayed (by her nurse) and deceived (by Porpyhro), but she can also now translate her dream into a reality, however imperfect, that they will share together. There is a perfect symmetry in the ending of the poem, as the two lovers leave behind them the "nightmar'd" baron and his guests, the old servant who has "died palsy-twitch'd," and the beadsman, who "aye unsought for slept among his ashes cold."[41]

Harold Bloom, who reads the poem as a prototype of a Wallace Stevens antireligious allegory, notes that "warmth and sexual passion glow more brightly against the Beadsman's death-in-life."[42] A fair observation. But "The Eve of St. Agnes" is not antireligious so much as it is pro–young love. It is a poem of wish fulfillment, written just after Keats and Fanny Brawne became engaged. Given the many obstacles to their union—her mother's opposition, his lack of money, and, most of all, his uncertain health—Keats longs, like Porphyro, to glide past all such obstacles so that the two lovers can consummate their passion and escape together from the forces arrayed against them. The poem urges Fanny, like Madeline, to transmute that dream into reality. Alas, that will never happen.

"The Eve of St. Agnes" is a poem for lovers to read aloud together, as my wife and I first did more than forty years ago. We can be sure that Keats read it aloud to Fanny Brawne. There is no more romantic poem— or, given its poignant context, no sadder poem—in the English language.

"La Belle Dame sans Merci"

When Porphyro takes up Madeline's lute to awaken her, he plays a fifteenth-century French ballad known as "La Belle Dame sans Merci." Keats borrowed that title for his next major poem. Yet the new poem could not be more different from "The Eve of St. Agnes." The setting of "St. Agnes" is richly described and fully envisioned, right down to the litany of candied fruits spread before the sleeping Madeline. The landscape of "La Belle Dame" is as sparse and stripped of color as Ingmar Bergman's *Seventh Seal*. In "St. Agnes," the lovers are triumphant in their flight. In "La Belle Dame," the solitary knight is left despairingly rooted in place and time. All he needs is a chessboard for his duel with death.

This is a hauntingly beautiful poem of obsession and loss, perfectly captured in the ballad format of twelve quatrains, each of which begins with three lilting lines of iambic tetrameter followed by a shortened, deliberately abrupt line of stressed syllables ("and no birds sing"; "on the cold hill's side") that carries the rhyme. The sonnets aside, it is the most readily memorized and melodic of Keats's poems.

As late as March 19, 1819, Keats wrote to George and Georgiana, "I am . . . straining at particles of light in the midst of a great darkness."[43] It is an apt description of the mood of "La Belle Dame sans Merci," which Keats wrote in a single afternoon and evening in late April.

The poem opens on a desolate landscape at the onset of winter:

> O what can ail thee, knight-at-arms,
> Alone and palely loitering?
> The sedge has withered from the lake,
> And no birds sing.
>
> O what can ail thee, knight-at-arms,
> So haggard and so woe-begone?
> The squirrel's granary is full,
> And the harvest's done.
>
> I see a lily on thy brow
> With anguish moist and fever dew,

And on thy cheeks a fading rose
Fast withereth too.[44]

The fall harvest is over, the sedge—a grass-like plant—has died, and the birds have fled. Yet the knight-at-arms remains. Note the phrase *palely loitering*. It is a form of literary synesthesia—applying words appropriate to one sense to another context—of which Keats was particularly fond. Loitering does not have a color, and yet the phrase perfectly captures the listlessness and depression of the knight-at-arms. Note, too, how well the third stanza in particular describes the later stages of consumption—the pale skin, the wasting away, the night sweats, and the red cheeks with their feverish but fading glow.

This is not a poem about the cause and course of Keats's tuberculosis or that of his recently deceased brother, Tom. But it is a poem that confronts the relentless decay of human life. There is a void at the center of the knight's existence that he cannot fill.

The question raised by the first three stanzas is: Why is the knight-at-arms so woebegone? The answer is both straightforward and an unsolvable mystery. "I met a lady in the meads," he explains, "full beautiful, a fairy's child, / Her hair was long, her foot was light, / And her eyes were wild."[45] The knight-at-arms becomes infatuated with this unearthly love. "I set her on my pacing steed, / And nothing else saw all day long, / For sidelong would she bend, and sing / A fairy's song."[46]

The contrast with "St. Agnes" continues: Whereas Porphyro piled up exotic delicacies for Madeline, the belle dame gives to the knight something less than human food: "roots of relish sweet, / And honey wild, and manna dew."[47] The sexual dynamic has also changed. Whereas Porphyro had to secrete himself in Madeline's bed chamber, the belle dame leads the knight directly to her elfin grot. And while Madeline was still half-asleep and dreaming, the belle dame "look'd at me as she did love, / And made sweet moan."[48] Most important, it is the knight-at-arms who has the dream vision:

I saw pale kings, and princes too,
Pale warriors, death pale were they all;

THE WISDOM OF THE ROMANTICS

They cried—"La Bell Dame sans Merci
Hath thee in thrall!"

I saw their starved lips in the gloam
With horrid warning gaped wide,
And I awoke and found me here
On the cold hill's side.[49]

The knight awakens, not in the elfin grot where he was lulled to sleep but alone "on the cold hill's side." Which, then, was the dream and which the reality? Was it the fairy's child, who is a product of fantasy, or the warning of the pale warriors? Surely both and neither. Madeline had to give up her dream to embrace Porphyro as her reality. The fairy's child has become the reality of the knight-at-arms, the only reality he can accept, but not one he can retain or command. She is all things beautiful—passion, nature, love, and, most of all, poetry—things that could, but never will completely, fill the void of existence. She is also terrifying. The knight-at-arms has joined the company of the pale warriors in thrall to beauty, which is without mercy. He claims the fairy's child loves him—"sure in language strange she said— / I love thee true"[50]—but he cannot even understand her words, much less the destructive power of her love. The poet has seen some "particles of light in the midst of a great darkness." But he has not learned to combine them into a living reality. The fairy's child is immortal; the knight-at-arms cannot cheat death.

And this is why I sojourn here,
Alone and palely loitering,
Though the sedge is wither'd from the lake,
And no birds sing.[51]

The last stanza is structured as an answer to the first stanza ("this is why"). But there is no closure. Nothing is explained. We remain haunted by the knight's sense of failure and loss. Keats himself is palely loitering, hoping to cheat death long enough to fill the emptiness with beauty and truth, with poetry and love. That is exactly what he sets out to do in the great odes.

THE GREAT ODES[52]

In the spring of 1819, Keats wrote the series of odes on which his dizzyingly high reputation largely rests. Though only one or two of these poems can be dated exactly, the overall order of composition appears to be "Ode on Indolence," "Ode to Psyche," "Ode to a Nightingale," "Ode on a Grecian Urn," and "Ode on Melancholy." The first odes were written in a roughly four-week period in April and May. A final ode, "To Autumn," followed in September of that same year.

After "La Belle Dame," Keats was looking for a new way of grappling with the aesthetic, personal, and intellectual concerns that obsessed him. A single sonnet was too confining. But he found himself unable to complete an epic. Besides, he was ready for something more personal, even confessional. He settled on the ode, an ancient hymn of praise to a god or Olympic victor, or even just a wealthy patron. The form dated back to Pindar and Horace but had been revived by the older Romantics—Coleridge ("Dejection: An Ode," 1802) and Wordsworth ("Ode: Intimations of Immortality," 1804). It was also seized on by Shelley in one of his most memorable poems ("Ode to the West Wind," 1819). As their titles indicate, the odes of the Romantics were intimate revelations of daily life, more in keeping with the Horatian odes than the Pindaric celebrations of victory or status.

The ode was a spacious but still disciplined form that allowed for both external description and inward contemplation. In Keats's hands, each stanza was generally a ten-line sonnet, starting with a Shakespearean quatrain (rhyme scheme *abab*), followed by a Petrarchan sextet (*cdecde*). In "To Autumn," the sextet becomes a sestet (*cdecdde*).

The number of stanzas vary from ode to ode; there are eight in "Ode to a Nightingale," five in "Ode on a Grecian Urn," and only three in "To Autumn." Since these three odes are rightly and almost universally considered Keats's greatest, we will focus on them.

The Wisdom of the Romantics

"Ode to a Nightingale"

The first thing to note about this ode is its first word, *my*, which is repeated at the beginning of the second line for emphasis. This poem is going to report on Keats's (qua narrator) personal experience and the changes to his sensibility as he listens to the song of a nightingale:

> My heart aches, and a drowsy numbness pains
> My sense, as though of hemlock I had drunk,
> Or emptied some dull opiate to the drains
> One minute past, and Lethe-wards had sunk.[53]

The second thing to note is that Keats's senses are dulled rather than heightened by the nightingale's song. Keats, as listener, is benumbed, as if drugged by hemlock or some other opiate. Socrates was ordered to drink hemlock, thus extinguishing the most inquisitive mind in classical philosophy. Socrates was the opposite of *negative capability*. He refused to rest "in uncertainties, Mysteries, doubts"; his entire life was an "irritable reaching after fact & reason"—so irritable, to his interlocutors at least, that he was condemned to die.

The song of the nightingale moves in the opposite direction from Socrates. It is nonrepresentational and nonconceptual. There are no lyrics to decipher. No mysteries to decode. No doubts to resolve. Music is the purest form of art, unmixed with fact or reason. The song comes to the nightingale, as Keats thought poetry should, "as naturally as the Leaves to a tree." There is not even any history to relive. In Dante's Christianized mythology, the River Lethe flows through the earthly paradise at the top of the mountain of purgatory. One drink from the river will eliminate all memory of past sins and prepare one for the celestial paradise. The nightingale and its song live in the present; neither past nor future weighs on them.

In absorbing the nightingale's "draught of vintage," Keats hopes to "leave the world unseen, / And with thee fade away into the forest dim."[54] The words "leave the world unseen" have the double meaning that Keats would no longer see, or be seen by, the world. Keats, like the

242

nightingale, would, in an ultimate gesture of negative capability, altogether disappear into the song.

> Fade far away, dissolve, and quite forget
> What thou among the leaves hast never known,
> The weariness, the fever, and the fret
> Here, where men sit and hear each other groan;
> Where palsy shakes a few, sad, last gray hairs,
> Where youth grows pale, and spectre-thin, and dies;
> Where but to think is to be full of sorrow
> And leaden-eyed despairs.[55]

These powerful images echo those in Shakespeare's Sonnet 73. But they have a special meaning for Keats, who nursed his brother Tom through the last stages of consumption and, by this time, expected to follow him to the grave. As he explained in his first letter to Fanny Brawne, "I have never known any unalloy'd Happiness for many days together: the death or sickness of some one has always spoilt my hours."[56]

In Shakespeare, the "bare ruin'd choirs" that signify the coming of death are redeemed by love: "This thou perceiv'st, which makes thy love more strong, / To love that well which thou must leave ere long."[57] But even love disappoints in "Ode to a Nightingale," "where Beauty cannot keep her lustrous eyes, / Or new Love pine at them beyond to-morrow."[58] The passage of time erases all.

Yet Keats hopes to transcend sorrow, "not charioted by Bacchus . . . , / But on the viewless wings of Poesy,"[59] which he now explicitly equates with the song of the nightingale. Poetry does not decay with time. It stands apart in a state not unlike death. The nightingale lives deep in the forest, among "shadows numberless," where "there is no light, / Save what from heaven is with the breezes blown / Through verdurous glooms and winding mossy ways."[60] Keats is no longer "straining at particles of light in the midst of a great darkness." He is content to savor the soft sounds and rich smells in the "embalmed darkness" of the bower where he rests, "half in love with easeful Death."[61]

The Wisdom of the Romantics

Now more than ever seems it rich to die,
To cease upon the midnight with no pain,
While thou art pouring forth thy soul abroad
In such an ecstasy![62]

The nod toward death is qualified: "half in love"; "seems it rich." Keats recognizes that, in death, he will no longer hear the nightingale. In death, all is silence.

Still wouldst thou sing, and I have ears in vain—
To thy high requiem become a sod.[63]

Again, the echo of Shakespeare, this time from Claudio in *Measure for Measure*:

Ay, but to die, and go we know not where,
To lie in cold obstruction and to rot,
This sensible warm motion to become
A kneaded clod.[64]

There is no celestial paradise on the other side of the Lethe. In death, we become merely another kneaded clod. Only art escapes mortality. The song of the nightingale is immune from the passage of time.

Thou wast not born for death, immortal Bird!
No hungry generations tread thee down;
The voice I hear this passing night was heard
In ancient days by emperor and clown:
Perhaps the self-same song that found a path
Through the sad heart of Ruth, when, sick for home,
She stood in tears amid the alien corn;
The same that oft-times hath
Charm'd magic casements, opening on the foam
Of perilous seas, in faery lands forlorn.[65]

Art is universal; it can charm both "emperor and clown." It can soothe sad hearts. And it can work its magic even in lands forlorn when no human creature is left to hear. But, in the end, "the fancy cannot cheat so well / As she is fam'd to do."[66] Even if we avert our eyes from it, human suffering remains. Death is death, not a transition to another state.

The Keatsian narrator all but disappears into the beauty of the song and then reasserts itself: "Forlorn! the very word is like a bell / To toll me back from thee to my sole self!"[67] We can attempt to shun fact, reason, and memory. But the appreciation of beauty, whether in art of nature, requires consciousness, and with consciousness comes suffering. Art may be eternal, but the enjoyment of art is fleeting. Keats as narrator asks himself the same question posed by Madeline and the knight-at-arms: "Was it a vision, or a waking dream? / Fled is that music:—Do I wake or sleep?"[68]

The answer to that question doesn't actually matter, for the one thing we know is that, however much art seems to lift us out of our bodily form, it cannot halt time. Time can include interludes of "dance, and Provençal song, and sunburnt mirth!"[69] But it leads inexorably to decay and death. Art doesn't change the often-harsh reality of our condition. It is a consolation but not a cure for what ails us. Keats will nonetheless choose even an unhappy consciousness, provided it knows passion and love, over the erasure of consciousness, which is death.

"Ode on a Grecian Urn"

> Thou still unravish'd bride of quietness,
> Thou foster-child of silence and slow time,
> Sylvan historian, who canst thus express
> A flowery tale more sweetly than our rhyme.[70]

"Ode to a Nightingale" opens with a repetition of the word *my*; "Ode on a Grecian Urn" repeats the word *thou*. The poet in "Nightingale" attempts to explain the aesthetic effect on him of the immortal bird's song. The poet in "Grecian Urn" attempts to understand and explain what the urn itself has to say to us. It is not an ode "to" a Grecian urn, but rather an ode "on" a Grecian urn. Indeed, the figurative ode is quite literally baked onto the surface of the urn and tells its pastoral tale even more sweetly than the poet can do in his rhyme.

Other contrasts between the two poems are equally striking. Both focus on a single sense; in one it is hearing, in the other it is sight. The nightingale's song is accordingly progressive. It unfolds in time. The urn is static. The scenes it portrays are unaffected by time. Most significantly, the song of the nightingale is a purely natural phenomenon. It blossoms forth from the bird like "the Leaves to a tree." It can be experienced and appreciated, but not deciphered. The urn, by contrast, is a conscious product of human craftsmanship. It is an intentional artifact, and understanding its intentionality is critical to the aesthetic experience.

The imaginary urn of the ode—presumably an idealized composite of other urns viewed by Keats and the Elgin Marbles, newly arrived in Britain—depicts a series of three scenes that are directly before the spectator. The scenes are representational, which immediately raises the question of what is being depicted, and how well. Whereas "Nightingale" focuses purely on sensation (beauty), "Grecian Urn" adds the dimension of representation (truth). The two values must coalesce for the ode to succeed. It is a very different and far more complex aesthetic experience than listening to the song of a nightingale.

The urn itself is the "still unravish'd bride of quietness," in both senses of the word *still*: she is unmoving, and she has not yet been ravished. She has not yet yielded her most precious secrets. The urn functions, albeit silently, as a "Sylvan historian" of the three pastoral settings it depicts.

Because the urn is circular, there is no necessary starting point. Each scene leads into another, and the sequence can be endlessly repeated. Thus, each scene must be "read" and understood not only on its own terms but also in conjunction with the other two. We follow the poem's narrator through this process, enriching our understanding of the whole, just as we do when we read each of Keats's odes, not in isolation but in light of the others. In essence, Keats is telling us how to understand a work of art that aspires to truth as well as beauty.

The narrator begins by asking the urn questions about one of the scenes it depicts:

What leaf-fring'd legend haunts about thy shape
Of deities or mortals, or of both,
In Tempe or the dales of Arcady?
What men or gods are these? What maidens loth?
What mad pursuit? What struggle to escape?
What pipes and timbrels? What wild ecstasy?[71]

The first thing the viewer needs to know is what he is looking at. What is being depicted? Is this a historical scene or something out of Greek mythology? The poem speaks of "men or gods," "mad pursuit," "maidens loth," "pipes and timbrels," and "wild ecstasy." These terms suggest satyrs and nymphs and Dionysian excess. Understanding that setting is an important first step in understanding and judging the work of art. It is the same for the poem, which in most editions has footnotes explaining terms such as *Sylvan*, *Tempe*, *Arcady*, and *timbrels*. Understanding the words used in it is a necessary first step in understanding any poem.

But it is only a step. The second stanza begins by establishing the claims for art that can be only seen (or read) rather than heard:

Heard melodies are sweet, but those unheard
Are sweeter; therefore, ye soft pipes, play on;
Not to the sensual ear, but, more endear'd,
Pipe to the spirit ditties of no tone.[72]

The urn portrays the playing of music, but the urn itself is silent and, therefore, we must, and are free to, imagine the beauties of the music. This is the second time the ode has used the term *sweeter* or *more sweetly*. The silent urn tells us a tale and plays us a melody that is sweeter than any actual rhyme or audible music. Yet the idealized urn is itself a product of the poet's imagination. The artist/poet accordingly must draw us into that imaginary world and give us, through empathy, a reason to embrace it. That happens when we contemplate a second scene, in which a young man courts a maiden to the accompaniment of a piper:

The Wisdom of the Romantics

Fair youth, beneath the trees, thou canst not leave
Thy song, nor ever can those trees be bare;
Bold Lover, never, never canst thou kiss,
Though winning near the goal—yet, do not grieve;
She cannot fade, though thou hast not thy bliss,
For ever wilt thou love, and she be fair![73]

It is a beautiful but disturbing image. Keats as narrator is both the bold lover and the melodist who can never leave his song. But life as depicted on the urn is frozen in time. Love and passion will not fade, but neither can they be realized. The third stanza calls this state "happy," because the love depicted is

For ever warm and still to be enjoy'd,
For ever panting, and for ever young;
All breathing human passion far above,
That leaves a heart high-sorrowful and cloy'd,
A burning forehead, and a parching tongue.[74]

But in what sense is unfulfilled passion happy? Is anticipation better than fulfillment? Would we really prefer to paralyze our "breathing human passion" before it leads to a sorrowful heart, a burning forehead, and a parching tongue? Or is Keats merely saying that representational art is uniquely positioned to capture that "for ever panting" state? Such art is beautiful. But is identification with the two unfulfilled lovers a sufficient form of aesthetic appreciation?

We have viewed a scene of bacchanalian excess and a scene of tender young love and the imaginary music appropriate to each. We responded to the first by seeking to establish the factual or mythological history of the story being told. We gathered facts and attached labels; where necessary, we drew analogies. We responded to the second with empathy; we identified so strongly with the young lovers that we became caught in their stasis of longing. We literally held our breathing human passion. Helen Vendler calls both of those responses to the work of art "naive" and "incompatible" with each other,[75] which seems unduly dismissive

248

and ultimately incorrect. They are important steps in a unified process of interpretation that only become clear in the third scene.

> Who are these coming to the sacrifice?
> To what green altar, O mysterious priest,
> Lead'st thou that heifer lowing at the skies,
> And all her silken flanks with garlands drest?[76]

The third scene is a sacrificial procession. It is in movement from town to a green altar somewhere in the fields or woods. The only music imagined now is the heifer lowing at the skies—a haunting image. We know nothing of the mysterious priest or the green altar or the little town where there is "not a soul to tell." And yet there is a spiritual solemnity to the procession that must be recognized—a "greeting of the spirit," as Keats likes to say—that draws us in. We do not rest frozen with the procession on the frieze. Our thoughts extend back to its origins and forward to its future.

> What little town by river or sea shore,
> Or mountain-built with peaceful citadel,
> Is emptied of this folk, this pious morn?
> And, little town, thy streets for evermore
> Will silent be; and not a soul to tell
> Why thou art desolate, can e'er return.[77]

This pagan procession is itself an ode, with its own music, its own motion, and its own obscure meaning. We must accept that "uncertainties, Mysteries, doubts" are a critical part of what it conveys, a critical part of what any work of art conveys. We are all, as Vendler rightly points out, "members of a linked cultural procession of pious folk."[78]

Keats's apostrophe on the urn and what it teaches us about art and love and life are among his most famous lines:

> O Attic shape! Fair attitude! with brede
> Of marble men and maidens overwrought,

With forest branches and the trodden weed;
Thou, silent form, dost tease us out of thought
As doth eternity: Cold Pastoral!
When old age shall this generation waste,
Thou shalt remain, in midst of other woe
Than ours, a friend to man, to whom thou say'st,
"Beauty is truth, truth beauty,"—that is all
Ye know on earth, and all ye need to know.[79]

Keats begins by shifting to an objective perspective on the urn, its Attic shape, its fair attitude—yes, the urn, like any work of art, can have an attitude. Keats is not focused now on its individual scenes. He is not concerned with the story it tells or the self-identification it provokes. He views it as a spectator conscious of being a spectator. It is a work of art, complete in and of itself. As such, it teases out of thought the same way that eternity does. It is a cold pastoral because we can never fully penetrate its mysteries. The bride is still unravished.

But that does not mean that the urn has nothing to teach us, even if what it says is neither what we expected nor all we hoped. The words Keats finally coaxes from the silent urn are as obscure as a Delphic oracle: "Beauty is truth, truth beauty."

Beauty and truth, as used here, are not Platonic abstractions that meet in the unchanging, transcendent realm of the forms. That would be too much of "the wordsworthian sublime," which is not Keats's register. He remains thoroughly grounded and attentive to human concerns. He is also fully aware of our limitations and imperfections. But a work of art must aspire to the union of beauty and truth. Beauty (Romanticism) and truth (realism) can coalesce, in life as well as art. Each is necessary. This is all we can know and all we need to know. We don't require a more developed philosophy or religion. And we won't find it in any event. Consecutive reasoning will not lead us to any greater understanding.

Harold Bloom protests that the truth of art "is not a saving truth. If this is all we need to know, it may be that no knowledge can help us."[80] But that is surely a false dichotomy. Art cannot save us in a religious sense. It won't grant us eternal life. But there is no question in Keats's mind that art is our shared cultural vessel, our pagan procession, and our highest form of worship. Keats is content, as Helen Vendler puts it, that "a beautiful train of anonymous figures led by a mysterious priest from obscure origins to an ultimate sacrificial rite in an unknown place is all we know of beauty and truth on earth."[81] Who are we to gainsay him? What do we have to replace that knowledge? The urn speaks to each new generation, as Keats's poems do. It is a greeting of the spirit, and what it tells us is of vital importance, if we but listen.

"To Autumn"

Keats wrote his last great lyric poem in September 1819. Harold Bloom calls "To Autumn" "as close to perfection as any shorter poem in the English language."[82] Jackson Bate is only slightly more measured, claiming that "each generation has found it one of the most nearly perfect poems in English."[83] Both men, however, are careful in their choice of praise. They do not contend that "To Autumn" is one of the best poems in the English language. They don't even claim that it is Keats's best poem. "Ode on a Grecian Urn" is a stronger candidate in both categories. But "To Autumn" may be Keats's most beloved poem, and it is certainly his most integrated. It is also thoroughly English in its setting and diction. There is no chasing after classical allusions, which frankly can become tedious in some of Keats's lesser works. And the poem is solidly grounded in the English countryside, a field outside Winchester, where Keats had recently been walking.

There are three stanzas, each displaying a different scene. The three scenes together constitute a procession of the seasons that constantly loops back on itself and hence need never end. It is a poem that celebrates nature as an eternal recurrence.

The first stanza speaks of ripeness and plenitude. The season, matured by the still warm sun, loads the vines with fruit, weights the trees with apples, swells the gourds, plumps the hazel shells, and provides late flowers for the bees, whose hives overflow with honey. The period of growth, begun in spring, is reaching its climax. Nature is fully laden.

Season of mists and mellow fruitfulness,
Close bosom-friend of the maturing sun;
Conspiring with him how to load and bless
With fruit the vines that round the thatch-eves run;
To bend with apples the moss'd cottage-trees,
And fill all fruit with ripeness to the core;
To swell the gourd, and plump the hazel shells
With a sweet kernel; to set budding more,
And still more, later flowers for the bees,
Until they think warm days will never cease,
For Summer has o'er-brimm'd their clammy cells.[84]

The second stanza presents a personification of autumn, sitting careless on the granary floor, or drowsy in a half-reaped furrow, or gleaning the remains left by the harvesters, or watching over the cider press.

Who hath not seen thee oft amid thy store?
Sometimes whoever seeks abroad may find
Thee sitting careless on a granary floor,
Thy hair soft-lifted by the winnowing wind;
Or on a half-reap'd furrow sound asleep,
Drows'd with the fume of poppies, while thy hook
Spares the next swath and all its twined flowers:
And sometimes like a gleaner thou dost keep
Steady thy laden head across a brook;
Or by a cyder-press, with patient look,
Thou watchest the last oozings hours by hours.[85]

These brief glimpses of autumn participating in the harvest humanize nature without mythologizing it. Autumn, careless and fecund, does not resent the harvesters but generously shares her bounty, her hair "soft-lifted by the winnowing wind." The harvest is as natural as the ripening.

In the third stanza, the harvest is complete, and late autumn will soon turn to winter. "Where are the songs of Spring?" we ask, already turning our minds ahead as if autumn has no more to offer us. But that is not the case. Indeed, the beauties of autumn, both visible and aural, are more exquisite than ever.

> Where are the songs of Spring? Ay, where are they?
> Think not of them, thou hast thy music too,—
> While barred clouds bloom the soft-dying day,
> And touch the stubble-plains with rosy hue;
> Then in a wailful choir the small gnats mourn
> Among the river sallows, borne aloft
> Or sinking as the light wind lives or dies;
> And full-grown lambs loud bleat from hilly bourn;
> Hedge-crickets sing; and now with treble soft
> The red-breast whistles from a garden-croft;
> And gathering swallows twitter in the skies.[86]

Unlike the song of the nightingale, which leaves the world unseen, the music of late autumn connects us to the earth. The wailful choir of the gnats, the loud bleat of the lambs, the song of the hedge crickets, the whistles of the robins, and the twitter of the swallows are all living sounds of nature. Despite the postharvest approach of winter, there is no thought of death—only of a cycle of life that will restore and replenish itself. Keats here reaches his apotheosis of negative capability. There is no sign of the poet; there is only the poem and the natural world it portrays and on which it bestows its grace.

By the time he wrote "On Autumn," Keats had no money and no prospects. He seriously considered abandoning poetry before concluding that he was fit for nothing else. But he would write no more great poems, at least none that could stand comparison to the odes. He put together a volume in 1820 that included the odes titled *Lamia, Isabella, The Eve of St. Agnes and Other Poems*. Shockingly, the odes didn't even get top billing. Keats did not seem to recognize the summit of his achievement.

His attention was now on Fanny Brawne and his failing health. The two became engaged in the summer of 1819, which freed him to write to her directly. The series of love letters he wrote beginning July 1, 1819,

The Wisdom of the Romantics

bears comparison, for both their passion and their frankness, with those of Heloise to Abelard.[87]

> You fear sometimes, I do not love you so much as you wish? My dear Girl I love you ever and ever and without reserve. The more I have known you the more have I lov'd. In every way—even my jealousies have been agonies of Love, in the hottest fit I ever had I would have died for you. I have vex'd you too much. But for Love! Can I help it? You are always new. The last of your kisses was ever the sweetest; the last smile the brightest; the last movement the gracefullest.[88]

That letter was written shortly after Keats had a severe hemorrhage in the lungs. His doctors advised him to write no more poetry (because of the strain on his nerves), to subsist on a near-starvation diet (lest he "feed" the consumption), and to undergo regular bleeding (to rid the body of impurities). Perhaps the only sound advice they gave him was to spend the following winter in Italy, with its more temperate climate. But even that suggestion proved a mistake given his greatly weakened condition and the arduous travel.

Keats had no money to travel to Rome. He sold all his copyrights but still had to borrow from friends, one of whom, the painter Joseph Severn, agreed at the last moment to accompany him when it was clear that Keats was in no condition to travel alone. They left in mid-September but did not arrive in Rome until November 15 after a miserable voyage and a ten-day quarantine in Naples.

They moved into the famous house, now a museum, at 26 Piazza di Spagna, toward the bottom of the Spanish Steps. The best Keats could manage were occasional walks, but soon he was too weak even to leave the house. "How long," he plaintively asked the doctor who was treating him; "How long is this posthumous life of mine to last?"[89] Not long, as it turned out. After a series of increasingly severe hemorrhages, Keats died on February 23, 1821.

> He remained quiet to the end, which made the death-summons more terrible. . . . He died with the most perfect ease. He seemed to go to sleep. On the 23rd, Friday, at half-past four, the approach of death came

on. "Severn—I—lift me up, for I am dying. I shall die easy. Don't be frightened! Thank God it has come." . . . He gradually sank into death, so quiet, that I still thought he slept.[90]

Severn made a deathbed charcoal sketch of the poet. It is haunting and unbearably sad. John Keats was twenty-five years old. At that age, Shakespeare was still writing his apprentice trilogy on Henry VI. All of his greatest work lay ahead.

9

Alexander Pushkin and the Descent into Prose

ALEXANDER PUSHKIN, LIKE ALESSANDRO MANZONI, WAS CONFRONTED with an underdeveloped national language and an uncertain literary tradition. Educated Russians spoke French in society and at court. They preferred to read and write in French as well. Many native Russians, like Tatiana in *Eugene Onegin*, were not even comfortable with the Russian language.

Pushkin set out to change that. He was remarkably studious, building, during his all-too-short life, a library of four thousand volumes in fourteen different languages.[1] He put that knowledge to work, combining disparate linguistic elements in a new Russian language capable of great expressive and poetic power. And he put that language to work in an astonishing variety of genres and styles. As the novelist Ivan Turgenev explains, "There is no doubt that he created our poetic, our literary language and that we and our descendants can only follow the path laid down by his genius."[2]

It is commonly said that Pushkin was to Russia what Shakespeare was to England and Goethe to Germany. He was Russia's national poet. But his prose may have been even more influential than his poetry. With his compelling blend of Romanticism shading into realism, Pushkin's true heirs were the great prose writers of nineteenth-century Russia: Mikhail Lermontov, *A Hero of Our Time* (1840); Nikolai Gogol, *Dead Souls* (1842), along with his array of absurdist short stories; and Turgenev,

Fathers and Sons (1862). Most important, Pushkin carved a path for the novels of Leo Tolstoy and Fyodor Dostoevsky, as well as the plays of Anton Chekhov. He helped fashion a national literature that was the envy of the world.

Pushkin was equally influential in the development of Russian opera. More than twenty operas were based on his works, starting with Mikhail Glinka's *Ruslan and Lyudmila* (1842), a landmark in Russian music. Other notable examples include *Boris Godunov* (1874), by Modest Mussorgsky; *Eugene Onegin* (1879) and *The Queen of Spades* (1890), both composed by Pyotr Ilyich Tchaikovsky; and *Mozart and Salieri* (1897), by Nikolai Rimsky-Korsakov. Several of these operas were, and still are, better known outside Russia than the Pushkin works on which they were based.

As a lyric poet, narrative poet, playwright, historian, teller of folk tales, and master of short stories and novels alike, Pushkin demonstrates what Dostoevsky calls "the universality and panhumanity of his genius."[3] The Russian poet, critic, and translator Apollon Grigorev sums it up nicely: "Pushkin is our all."[4]

EARLY LIFE

Alexander Pushkin was born in Moscow on June 6, 1799.[5] He had an older sister, Olga, and a younger brother, Lev. Five other children died in infancy.[6]

Pushkin's father, Sergei, was from a noble but now impoverished line of boyars with a six-hundred-year lineage of which Pushkin was inordinately proud. The boyars, many of them wealthy landowners, were at the highest rank of the military feudal aristocracy before Peter the Great's economic reforms ushered in a new, more commercial elite.

Pushkin's mother, Nadezhda Ossipovna Gannibal, had a more exotic background. Her grandfather, Ibrahim Gannibal, was of African origin. Enslaved by, and then purchased from, a sea captain, Ibrahim was brought to Moscow at the age of five by the Russian ambassador to the Ottoman Empire as a gift to Peter the Great, who stood as godfather to the boy and saw to his education. Ibrahim had a long and distinguished career in the Russian military, rising to the rank of general. He adopted the name Gannibal, after the Carthaginian general Hannibal, who drove his elephants over the Alps and stymied the Roman legions in battle after battle. Pushkin wrote about his ancestor in an unfinished historical novel titled *The Moor of Peter the Great*. Ibrahim spent his final twenty years on a country estate in Mikhailovskoye surrounded by books. Pushkin, who would later be confined to the same estate, noted that his great-grandfather, "the black African who had become a Russian noble, lived out his life like a French philosophe."[7]

Ibrahim's third son, Osip, married Marya Pushkina in the year 1773. Nadezhda was their only child. Osip later fled the family and made a bigamous marriage in Pskov with a young widow. The abandoned Marya filed a complaint against Osip, which was ultimately granted. His second marriage was annulled, and the two estates he had since inherited from his father (at Kobrino and Mikhailovskoye) were transferred in trust to Nadezhda. Meanwhile, Marya moved to St. Petersburg, where Nadezhda learned excellent French, read widely, and was introduced into society through her mother's relatives. She was known as "the beautiful Creole," and she married Sergei Pushkin, a distant cousin on her mother's side, at the Kobrino estate in 1796.

Alexander was largely neglected by his parents. Indeed, his mother seems to have been actively hostile toward him. She also bullied his father, so perhaps her ill temper was indifferent as to its target, but it certainly complicated Pushkin's relationship with women. He would have an equally long and complicated relationship with authority. When still a baby in the keeping of his nurse, the emperor Paul happened upon them in a St. Petersburg park. He reproached the nurse for not removing Pushkin's cap in the presence of royalty and gruffly removed it himself.

Pushkin's first language was French, the main language in society during the time of Catherine the Great, who reigned from 1762 to 1796. Pushkin learned Russian from the serfs on his father's estate and, in particular, from his nanny, a freed serf named Arina Rodionovna, who instilled in him a love of Russian folk tales of which she seemed to have an endless supply. The boy also took refuge in his father's library, which was extensive. He read Homer in a French translation and worked his way through volumes of eighteenth-century French literature. He also wrote poems. His uncle Vasily (on his father's side) was a poet himself and recognized and encouraged his brilliance. Pushkin's maternal grandmother, Marya, lived with the family and ran the household. She arranged a succession of French tutors but herself spoke Russian with the boy.

In 1811, at the age of twelve, Pushkin attended a new lycée established by Tsar Alexander I to educate the sons of the aristocracy and prepare them for service in the various state ministries. There were thirty boys in the first class. The school was in Tsarskoe Selo, home of the famous Catherine Palace, a mere sixteen miles from St. Petersburg but several days' journey from Pushkin's home in Moscow. Over their six-year course of study, the boys were never allowed to leave the school, even during the holidays. Not even the 1812 French invasion of Russia and the burning of Moscow interrupted their studies.

Pushkin excelled in Russian and French literature and fencing but was otherwise an indifferent student. He was abysmal at mathematics, but his poems dazzled his teachers and found their anonymous way into several publications. During the examinations at the end of the junior course, Pushkin recited his "Recollections in Tsarskoe Selo" to a distinguished audience that included Vasily Zhukovsky, a leading figure in Russian literature. Zhukovsky was effusive in his praise, calling Pushkin a "future giant" and "the hope of our literature."[8] Pushkin was also befriended there by the fifty-year-old Nikolay Karamzin, whose twelve-volume *History of the Russian State* would be a watershed in Russian letters. In a post-Waterloo world, Russia was now a pan-European power and would soon become one in literature as well, thanks in large part to Pushkin.

When he graduated in 1817, Pushkin was given a minor post in St. Petersburg at the ministry of foreign affairs. The actual work was negligible, or at least Pushkin treated it as such. He spent the next three years writing poetry, drinking, gambling, and womanizing. He had intermittent bouts of venereal disease and fought several duels, fortunately without injury. Pushkin could fall in love at the turn of a head, and he boasted of many conquests, though the true number is uncertain. Pushkin was short, swarthy, and generally considered unattractive, if not positively ugly, with bushy, black, mutton chop sideburns. But he had a magnetic personality and was an incisive and entertaining conversationalist, welcomed everywhere, despite a tendency toward crudeness.

Pushkin joined two literary societies in St. Petersburg in which the members discussed the latest poems, read reviews, and talked radical politics. Liberal sentiments—promoting free speech and open elections, while decrying serfdom and autocracy—were particularly common among officers returned from the occupation of France. Pushkin shared such views and was remarkably indiscreet in voicing them. He wrote reams of lyric poems, almost like a diary of the various periods of his life. One was an ode, "Liberty," which opens:

> Away now, limp Cytherean muse,
> I order you to flee!
> Come to me, you who menace tsars,
> Proud bard of Liberty!
> Come, tear the garland from my head
> And drown my minstrelsy . . .
> I wish to scourge the vice on thrones
> And sing of Liberty.[9]

Politics aside, "Liberty" is interesting because it shuns the ancient mythology so beloved of Romantic poets, such as Keats, in favor of a more direct confrontation with the world. But poems have consequences, particularly in an autocratic state. Pushkin was not reckless enough actually to publish this poem (no one would have published it in any event), but it, along with other similar poems, circulated widely in manuscript form and their authorship was no secret to the Russian authorities. One that particularly offended the tsar was an exquisite patriotic paean to a free Russia that most young military officers and technocrats learned by heart.

> While we yet with freedom burn,
> While our hearts yet live for honor,
> My friend, let us devote to our country

The sublime impulses of our soul!
Comrade, believe: it will arise,
The star of captivating joy,
Russia will start from her sleep,
And on the ruins of autocracy
Our names will be inscribed![10]

The tsar was appalled that the school he founded to bolster and modernize the Russian state was apparently rife with such sentiments. Pushkin, he concluded, had "flooded Russia with seditious verses"[11] and must be exiled to Siberia. Only the intervention of Karamzin and other influential friends—aided by Pushkin's growing fame as Russia's premier poet—convinced the tsar simply to "transfer" Pushkin in 1820 to a post in the south of Russia near the Black Sea, where the great Roman poet Ovid was banished for similar indiscretions by the emperor Augustus in 8 CE.

EXILE

Having grown tired of St. Petersburg and his mounting debts there, Pushkin rather enjoyed his exile at first. He was befriended by General Nikolay Raevsky, a hero of the Napoleonic Wars, and spent three months traveling with Raevsky's family in the Caucasus and Crimea. In the midst of this second family, he felt a warmth and support he had never known before.

> Judge whether I was happy: a free and untroubled life in the circle of a kind family—the kind of life I love so much and that has never before been mine to enjoy; a happy, southern sky; charming surroundings; scenery which gratifies the imagination: mountains, orchards, the sea.[12]

The exile also proved a boon for his poetry. He held another nominal post and continued his somewhat dissolute life, but he wrote more regularly, and his fame increased. Before his banishment, he had already completed *Ruslan and Lyudmila*, an epic Russian fairy tale in verse inspired by the stories his nanny had told him. Published in 1820, it was extremely popular. Two decades later, it was turned into an opera by Mikhail Glinka.

General Raevsky's oldest son exposed Pushkin to Byron, whose Romanticism provided a powerful (if ambivalent) influence. Indeed, Pushkin was inclined to romanticize his exile as that of a heroic, Byronic outcast. Pushkin wrote two mostly praised narrative poems: *The Captive of the Caucasus* and *The Fountain at Bakhchisaray*. His foray into narrative poetry had more commercial and critical success than Keats, even if it fell short of Scott and Byron. He also began work on his masterpiece, *Eugene Onegin*, which is not a narrative poem, Pushkin insisted, but a novel in verse—"a devilish difference," he explained in writing to a friend.

Pushkin spent four years in southern Russia, first in Ekaterinoslav, in what is now Ukraine; then Kishinev, in Moldova; and finally Odessa, where he passed a year and fell in love, twice. Unfortunately, one of those affairs was with the wife of Count Mikhail Vorontsov, governor general of South Russia, of whom Pushkin also wrote a mocking epigram that was widely circulated. Karamzin wrote of Pushkin, "He really has a splendid talent: what a pity that there is no order and peace in his soul and not the slightest sense in his head."[13] The modern reader cannot but agree, especially in light of Pushkin's future follies.

Vorontsov complained to Tsar Alexander and asked that Pushkin be moved elsewhere. The tsar seemed unmoved by Vorontsov's humiliation but was himself enraged by an intercepted letter in which Pushkin announced he was "taking lessons in pure atheism"[14] from an English philosopher. Any undermining of the state religion, the tsar believed, would undermine his own authority.

Pushkin was accordingly dismissed from the foreign ministry in 1824. Exiled from his exile, he was sent to live on his mother's estate at Mikhailovskoye in northwestern Russia, near the border of what is now Estonia. Pushkin spent considerable time with his former nanny, who fed him more tales of ancient Russia. There, he again proved remarkably productive, writing two new narrative poems, *The Gypsies* and *Count Nulin*, which marked a significant move away from Romanticism, as well as his first and most important play, *Boris Godunov*, in 1825. He also had an affair with and impregnated his bailiff's nineteen-year-old daughter. Pushkin tried to make arrangements for the support of the child, but the infant, a boy, died within three months of his birth.

263

This final exile likely saved Pushkin's life. On the death of Alexander I on December 1, 1825, the line of succession was unclear, and a group of Russian officers, accompanied by three thousand troops, gathered in Senate Square in St. Petersburg to declare the end of autocracy. This ill-planned "Decembrist Revolt," as it was called, was quickly quashed by the new emperor, Nicholas I. Five of the conspirators were hanged; another 125 were sentenced to hard labor in Siberia.

Most of the Decembrists knew Pushkin's ode "Liberty" and other lyric poems by heart. They were inspired by his writings, and he was in turn inspired by their activism. Asked by Nicholas what he would have done had he been in St. Petersburg, Pushkin boldly insisted that he would have stood with the Decembrists in Senate Square. The tsar seemed to appreciate Pushkin's honesty or, perhaps, having already made an example of others, thought it best to treat Russia's best-known poet with leniency. Nicholas pardoned "my Pushkin" and allowed him to leave the family estate at Mikhailovskoye in September 1826. He also relieved Pushkin from having to submit his works to the official censors before publication. The tsar volunteered that he himself would serve as Pushkin's "personal censor." In fact, this apparent courtesy became a source of endless frustration for Pushkin, because the tsar largely delegated the job to the decidedly unliterary chief of his secret police, Count Benckendorff, whose first act was to preclude publication of *Boris Godunov*.

Godunov had become tsar in 1598 after serving as regent for the impaired Feodor I and having, by most accounts, already murdered Feodor's younger brother, Dmitry, in 1591. A monk posing as Dmitry led a popular uprising against Godunov in 1605. The uprising succeeded due only to the untimely death of Godunov. The "false Dmitry" then murdered Godunov's wife and son and seized the throne, only to be murdered in his turn by a group of boyars. Two other "false Dmitries" unsuccessfully sought the throne during this Time of Troubles. Perhaps it was no wonder that Count Benckendorff precluded publication of the play. Pushkin even received a reprimand for reading the unpublished play to small groups of friends. Modest Mussorgsky turned it into an opera that premiered in 1874.

MARRIAGE

Pushkin was released from his six-year exile in September 1826. He was only twenty-seven and seemed determined to make up for lost time. He lived alternately in Moscow and St. Petersburg, where he frequented the theater, opera, and ballet, and was lionized in society, both for his poetry and for his exile. He also resumed his ways—if he ever abandoned them—as a compulsive gambler and serial womanizer.

The four years between his release and his marriage were not especially productive by Pushkin's standards. He continued writing reams of lyric poetry, of course, publishing a first collection in 1826. He would sometimes walk the sixteen miles to Tsarskoye Selo and back while composing verses in his head. In 1829, he wrote an exquisite poem (untitled) for Anna Olenina, to whom he had proposed marriage, only to be brusquely rejected by her parents.

> I loved you: in my heart, perhaps,
> Love may not be extinguished yet;
> But I will weary you no more,
> Nor cause you sadness or regret.
> I loved you not in words, or hope,
> But shyly, and in jealous torture;
> My love was tender, it was true,
> As may God grant you from another.[15]

In 1827, Pushkin published *Poltava*, a long narrative poem on the eponymous 1709 battle between Sweden and Russia. A second collection of his lyric poems followed in 1829. But tastes were changing away from lyric poetry and verse tales toward prose.[16] "The age impels toward stern prose," Pushkin wrote in *Eugene Onegin*. "The age chases away that imp, rhyme."[17] Historical novels in both French and English were proving to be a more compelling way to explore the human condition, as would Gogol's short stories, which Pushkin himself promoted. Accordingly, deep in debt and unable to publish *Boris Godunov*, Pushkin began his self-described "descen[t] into prose" in 1830.[18]

He made what was supposed to be a short visit to his small estate in Boldino in the fall of 1830 but was confined there for three months due to a cholera epidemic. During this "Boldino Autumn," he finished *Eugene Onegin* and wrote, among other works, a series of fascinating short plays known as *The Little Tragedies*, including *Mozart and Salieri*, which portrays Mozart's rival composer, Antonio Salieri, as considering Mozart unworthy of his effortless talent.

> O heaven! Where is justice,
> When a sacred gift, when immortal genius
> Is not sent as a reward of ardent love,
> Of self-denial, labor, zeal, and prayer,
> But shines upon the head of a madcap,
> An idle reveler? . . . Oh, Mozart, Mozart![19]

At the end of the play, consumed by envy, Salieri poisons Mozart. Baseless rumors to that effect had circulated in the decades following Mozart's early death. Peter Shaffer followed Pushkin in dramatizing those rumors in his 1979 play *Amadeus*. Inevitably, Pushkin's play had long since been turned into an opera by Nikolai Rimsky-Korsakov.

Pushkin also tried his hand at short stories in *The Tales of Belkin*—of particular note were "The Station Master" and "The Blizzard," which anticipate Guy de Maupassant with their ironic reversals. Tolstoy, too, claimed to be heavily influenced by their dark ironies and unadorned prose. Pushkin was finally allowed to publish a heavily bowdlerized version of *Boris Godunov* in 1831 but to only modest success.

The most momentous change in Pushkin's life began in 1829, when he met the sixteen-year-old Natalya Goncharova. He proposed marriage on very little acquaintance. She and her family turned him down but relented the following year. The main reason for their change of heart appears to have been their deteriorating financial condition. Natalya was by all accounts a great beauty, but she was also a frivolous social butterfly who wasted Pushkin's substance (both monetary and literary) and whose extended flirtation with a French officer ultimately got him killed.

They married in 1831 and had four children: Maria (born in May 1832), Alexander (1833), Grigory (1835), and Natalya (1836). Signs were not good from the outset. Property promised to the couple by Natalya's grandfather was so severely encumbered as to make it worthless. Her family had to borrow the agreed-on dowry from Pushkin, which was never repaid. His mother-in-law constantly nagged and disparaged him, and the rest of her extended family repeatedly sought loans from the already deeply indebted Pushkin.

Pushkin had expected his household expenses to treble after marriage; instead, they increased ten-fold, largely because Natalya insisted on cutting a figure in society, especially at the court balls attended by Nicholas, with whom some assumed she was having an affair. Pushkin wanted to retrench by moving to Boldino for several years where he could work unimpeded, minimize expenses, and recoup his many debts. But Natalya would not hear of it.

It was an unhappy period in Pushkin's life, as reflected in an untitled poem from 1834:

It's time, my love, it's time! The heart seeks peace—
Day chases day, the hours and minutes seize
Fragments of our existence; you and I
Make plans for life—and suddenly, we die.
There is no happiness on earth; but freedom
And peace there are. Long have I dreamt of Eden—
A weary slave, long meditated flight
To some far realm of work and pure delight.[20]

Pushkin revived both as a poet and as a man when he slipped away to Boldino by himself for four weeks in the fall of 1833. There, he was once again remarkably productive. He wrote *The Bronze Horsemen*—a study in how individual lives and loves can so readily be crushed by state power and the indifferent and inexorable footfalls of history. Many consider it Pushkin's most perfect narrative poem. He also wrote a series of folk tales in verse and finished the *History of the Pugachev Rebellion*, about the Cossack Yemelyan Pugachev's unsuccessful popular uprising against

Catherine the Great in 1773/1774. The first complete edition of *Eugene Onegin*, which had appeared only in serial form between 1825 and 1832, was published in 1833. It was the novel-in-verse where Romanticism went to die.

EUGENE ONEGIN

There are four principal characters in *Eugene Onegin*. Each is introduced with care, laying the foundation for the interactions that follow.

The entire first chapter—consisting of fifty-five ten-line stanzas[21]—is devoted to delineating the daily life and character of the eponymous "hero"—though that term will prove bitterly ironic. The chapter is written in the voice of one "Pushkin," who introduces himself as a "friend" of Onegin while at the same time exposing his faults with shocking clarity. After chapter 1, "Pushkin" the friend will depart, to be replaced by a more standard, omniscient narrator, but one who still purports to show a partisan preference for Onegin while instilling the opposite in the reader. This unreliable narrator adds a very modern layer of complexity and moral ambiguity to the story.

Eugene Onegin has many gifts, starting with a large inheritance from his ailing uncle to whom, in his private thoughts, he shows little devotion:

> But, oh my God, what desolation
> To tend a sick man day and night
> And not to venture from his sight!
> What shameful cunning to be cheerful
> With someone who is halfway dead,
> To prop up pillows by his head,
> To bring him medicine, looking tearful,
> To sigh—while inwardly you think:
> When will the devil let him sink?[22]

"Pushkin" acknowledges that Onegin is "a youthful scapegrace,"[23] with no proper moral training, but succumbs to his charm, nonetheless. Indeed, Onegin manages to dazzle society generally despite a questionable background. He has money, after all, along with good looks, good clothes, and sufficient wit to mimic the qualities valued in the *beau monde*:

> With hair trimmed to the latest fashion,
> Dressed like a London *dandy*, he
> At last saw high society.
> In French, which he'd by now perfected,
> He could express himself and write,
> Dance the mazurka, treading light
> And bow in manner unaffected.
> What more? Society opined:
> Here was a youth with charm and mind.[24]

What more, indeed! He is a good listener, with a light touch in polite conversation, who can be counted on to delight the ladies with a sudden epigram. While no scholar, Onegin commands a smattering of Latin sufficient for an occasional, mangled quotation. He also knows enough about economics to pass as a devotee of Adam Smith. Where he truly excels, however, is in "the art of tender passion."[25]

> How soon he learned the skill of feigning,
> Of seeming jealous, hiding hope,
>> Inspiring faith and undermining,
>> Appearing somber and to mope,
> Now acting proud and now submissive,
> By turns attentive and dismissive!
> . . .
> How self-forgetting he could be!
> How rapid was his look and bashful,
> Tender and bold, while off and on
> With an obedient tear it shone.[26]

Onegin seduces their wives and yet remains friends with the cuckolded husbands.

In short, "Pushkin" paints his "friend" and "hero" as a consummate but effective rake—that is, as someone rather like Pushkin himself. "Madame Bovary, c'est moi," Flaubert will say of his deeply flawed but still fascinating character. "Eugene Onegin, c'est moi," Pushkin might equally say, at least of the social Onegin.

But "Pushkin" was a poet—a devotee of the "lofty passion . . . / That sacrifices life to rhyme."[27] He was also an acute observer of contemporary mores, surpassed in that respect, among his contemporaries, only by Balzac. By contrast, Onegin goes through life without noticing or, worse, valuing anything but his own convenience. As a consequence, he is bored, and boredom makes him nasty. He will readily annihilate a rival with a "train of malice, spite and slander!"[28]

A typical day underscores the hollowness of Onegin's pursuits. He gets up late and peruses his various invitations for the evening. Then, dressed with care and sporting a broad-brimmed Bolivar hat, he drives out and strolls until dinner at a fashionable restaurant where he is sure to encounter acquaintances and where the wine and champagne flow freely to accompany an array of French dishes. Hearing someone praise a new ballet, Onegin rushes to the theater. Pushkin describes the entire scene beautifully:

> The house is full; the boxes brilliant;
> Parterre and stalls—all seethe and roar;
> Up in the gods they clap, ebullient,
> And, with a swish, the curtains soar.
> Semi-ethereal and radiant,
> To the enchanting bow obedient,
> Ringed round by nymphs, Istomina
> Stands still; one foot supporting her,
> She circles slowly with the other,
> And lo! a leap, and lo! she flies,
> Flies off like fluff across the skies,
> By Aeolus wafted hither thither;
> Her waist she twists, untwists; her feet
> Against each other swiftly beat.[29]

It would be impossible to find a more exquisite account of the full theater, the eager patrons, and the godlike dancer defying gravity with consummate grace.

But where is Onegin? Late, of course. He arrives after Istomina has danced to great applause. "Treading on toes at every stall,"[30] he reaches his place only to pull out his eyeglass and survey the various boxes. With barely a glance at the stage, he once again declares himself bored. An utter lack of enthusiasm seems to be a social necessity.

As the ballet progresses, the narrator offers a description of the coachmen outside the theater, weary and cold, awaiting the departure of their masters. But Onegin—indifferent to that scene as well—has already gone home to undress and dress again, a three-hour process described with defensive good humor by "Pushkin."

This same "Pushkin" then spends seven stanzas describing not the ball that Onegin attended, which was already in full swing, but rather "Pushkin's" own love of balls: the *billet-doux* and assignations, "the youthfulness and madness, / The crush, the glitter and the gladness."[31] Of Onegin's own feelings, however, we learn nothing. He only reappears driving sleepily through the city streets on his way home. It is as if the entire experience is lost on him. And so, too, is the gradually awakening city, which "Pushkin" describes with loving attention: the busy merchants, the hawkers calling, the young girl carrying a jug of milk though the snow, the German baker unlocking his shutters, the smoke rising from chimneys. For "Pushkin," this "early-morning noise is cheering."[32]

Yet Onegin once again ignores the scene playing out before him, as if he has no connection with ordinary life. On the morrow he will do it all again. He will do it, but not because the freedom, the conquests, the feasting, and the pageantry make him happy. To the contrary, his feelings are numbed by boredom and overpowered by ever-increasing spleen. Onegin tries to write but has nothing to say, or at least he finds the persistent effort too painful. He amasses a library and reads to "mak[e] other minds his own,"[33] but even that grows wearisome.

It is when Onegin is "emptied / Of all attachment to this life"[34] that he and "Pushkin" become companions. They share an indifference to public opinion and the same low assessment of humanity. Onegin's "humor halfway mixed with bile"[35] finds a ready counterpart:

> We both had known the play of passions,
> By life we both had been oppressed;
> In each the heart had lost its zest;
> Each waited for the machinations
> Of men, and blind Fortuna's gaze,
> Blighting the morning of our days.[36]

Having surfeited on the blandishments of St. Petersburg, the two resolve to travel abroad in search of new adventures, like a pair of Byronic heroes. But "there are no more enchantments."[37] Onegin's father dies, and he is besieged by creditors of the heavily indebted estate. Rather than preserve his family legacy, Onegin abandons it to the creditors, counting on his uncle to die in short order. Indeed, he is soon summoned urgently by his uncle's steward and jumps into a carriage, in which he prepares "for sighs and boredom and deception / For money's sake."[38] But Onegin is spared the odious task of nursing his uncle that he had imagined, for by the time he arrives, the uncle is already laid out on a table, ready for burial. Onegin is rich, settled in the country, and "Pushkin" disappears from the novel, but not before he bids farewell to Romanticism, his former muse. "Dead ashes cannot be replenished," he sadly but soberly notes.[39]

"For two whole days," Onegin is enchanted with the woods, the meadows, and the burbling brooks surrounding his new estate.[40] But boredom once again sets in. He dabbles in estate management and, much to the annoyance of his neighbors, institutes a quick rent system that frees the serfs from their traditional services. He quickly loses interest in improvements, however, as well as in his neighbors, whom he deliberately evades and ignores. Until, that is, a new landowner, Vladimir Lensky, arrives, fresh from the University of Göttingen, a hotbed of German Romanticism. He is a parody of the Romantic figure with his fervent, yearning spirit, his exalted feelings, and his "curling, shoulder-length black hair."[41] Inevitably, Lensky writes poetry. He sings of love, maidens' thoughts, the moon, and the dim beyond. He even sings "of life's decaying scene, / While he was not yet quite eighteen."[42] In a passage worthy of Jane Austen, the narrator explains that, as a young, wealthy, handsome, and, above all, single youth, Lensky was deemed the property of all those neighbors with eligible daughters. "Such in the country was the custom."[43]

Lensky and Onegin become friends, despite being as different from each other as "ice and flame," "stone and water," "verse and prose."[44] The stark differences in their personalities, like those of Darcy and Bingley, are no obstacle to their growing friendship. They ride out together every day and become inseparable, even though Onegin, like Darcy, is condescending to his friend. Onegin tolerates Lensky's passionate effusions and even confesses some of his own regrets at the waning of his Romantic attachments.

But it is Lensky who "la[ys] his trusting conscience bare"[45] by disclosing his love for his childhood sweetheart, Olga Larina, and the promises they have made to each other. Olga is blonde, with blue eyes and a slender waist. But the narrator cannot be bothered to offer anything more than a generic description. "Just glance / At any novel at your leisure," he explains. "You'll find her portrait there."[46]

The narrator dismisses Olga as boring and turns to her older sister, Tatiana, "a wayward, silent, sad young maiden"[47] who lacks Olga's fresh beauty and has a dark, contemplative nature. Tatiana, who rises before dawn to watch from her balcony as the night fades and the morning arrives, would contentedly "at a window silently / Sit on her own throughout the day."[48] She is a reader and favors the Romantic works of Rousseau, Goethe, and others. She sees the world in their terms.

Lensky makes the fatal mistake of introducing Onegin to the Larin family. After the visit, during which he was transparently bored, Onegin speaks slightingly of Olga:

In Olga's looks there's no more life
Than Van Dyck has in his madonnas:
Her countenance is round and fair
Just like the daft moon shining there
Above the daft horizon on us.[49]

The Wisdom of the Romantics

Although the otherwise marvelous translator, Stanley Mitchell, has to strain for the rhyme (madonnas / on us), the remark is aimed to wound, and does wound, Lensky. Onegin's spleen is returning, perhaps out of jealousy that Lensky is capable of love, however foolish. Onegin expresses his own preference, not the least bit convincing, for the pensive Tatiana.

Tatiana herself falls in love with the worldly and sophisticated Onegin. She was ready for it. Her heart, full of longing and fueled by many novels, has finally found its object. She sees in him "the characters that she most prizes,"[50] including Saint-Preux from Rousseau's *La Nouvelle Héloïse* and Werther from Goethe's eponymous novel. She is now the heroine of her self-composed novel. Heroines write letters candidly revealing the depth and strength of their love, and she resolves to do the same.

Before we turn to Tatiana's famous letter, however, the narrator-poet treats us to a lecture on the harmful absurdity of "woebegone romanticism."[51] He resolves, going forward, to write a novel of a very different kind. Perhaps, he notes, "I shall no longer be a poet."[52] By that he means both that people will no longer consider him a poet when he eschews the "hopeless egotism" of a Byron and that he will "settle to prosaic labors," quite literally writing in prose or at least in a poetry that depicts in plain terms and "grim relief" a Russian family and its "rural ways."[53] In short, he promises us a new sort of realism, which will break forth in works like *The Captain's Daughter*, *The Tales of Belkin*, and, of course, *Eugene Onegin* itself.

But "Tatiana, dear Tatiana,"[54] is still at this point a strikingly Romantic figure.

> The moon was radiating
> A languid light, illuminating
> Tatiana's graces, pale with care,
> Her loosened and unruly hair.[55]

She wanders endlessly through the gardens, filled alternately with dazzling hope and dark despair; each robs her of sleep and composure.

ALEXANDER PUSHKIN AND THE DESCENT INTO PROSE

Tatiana writes to Eugene a letter such as Julie wrote to Saint-Preux once she finally abandoned her false reserve.[56] It is a letter such as Heloise wrote to her Abelard, refusing to accept his contention that their passionate affair had been a mistake.[57] With neither inhibition nor guile, Tatiana artlessly confesses her love for Onegin and consigns her honor to his protection. She "gives up herself without conditions / Like a small child, defenselessly."[58] In the process, she demonstrates the superiority of her soul to all the society women adopting the tropes of Romanticism. Tatiana has transcended the genre.

Alas, Onegin is no more worthy of Tatiana than Abelard is of Heloise. He is silent for two days, leaving her in anguished uncertainty before he finally confronts her in the garden. Tatiana's letter—"a trusting soul's confession"[59]—moved him, and he endeavors to let her down easily. His rhetoric is even a bit exalted in praise of her, but his message is thoroughly pedestrian and egoistic: It's not you, it's me. I am not capable of happiness. I cannot sustain love, and your tears "would fail to touch my heart and would / Only infuriate my mood."[60] He ends by warning her to be more discreet—"naiveté risks a dangerous end"—and blandly assuring her with misplaced confidence, "You'll fall in love again, I know."[61]

Onegin knows nothing of Tatiana. He cannot sound the depths of her soul because his own is so empty. The world-weary Onegin retreats further into himself, while Lensky is occupied day and night with Olga. Onegin is genuinely delighted when Lensky finally visits him. He commands a fine meal and the best champagne, and the two friends talk late into the night. Onegin even asks after "the Larin girls." Lensky, of course, effuses over Olga but eventually notes that Tatiana's name day is soon and that Onegin is invited. Onegin demurs, claiming he is unfit for crowds, but Lensky assures him that it's just a family affair and urges Onegin to come as a favor to Lensky.

The name-day celebration proves to be a large social affair, and Tatiana all but faints when Onegin is seated across from her and gives her a tender look. Her discomposure is remarked by the other guests, and Onegin is enraged with Lensky. He takes his revenge by flirting openly with Olga and engaging her for dance after dance. Lensky can barely credit what he sees. They are due to be married in a fortnight, and yet

Olga seems content to play the coquette with the man he thought was his friend. Lensky storms out, and Onegin is left to be bored by the now mortified Olga.

A duel follows. It is not inevitable. Onegin feels some remorse for his behavior and might have apologized to Lensky, but by that point Lensky has engaged a second, and Onegin—who pretends to hold public opinion in contempt—cannot bear to be the subject of gossip and ridicule. So he immediately agrees to a duel. Lensky prepares for the duel by writing a very bad poem, a parody of Romanticism, that ends:

> When daybreak comes with rays ascending
> And sparkling day dispels the gloom,
> Then I, perhaps—I'll be descending
> Into the mystery of the tomb
> Slow Lethe will engulf forever
> My young poetical endeavor;
> I'll be forgot, but you'll return
> To weep on my untimely urn,
> And, maid of beauty, in your sorrow,
> You will reflect: he loved me, sworn
> To me alone in his sad dawn,
> Bereft now of its stormy morrow! . . .
> Come, heartfelt friend, come, longed-for friend,
> I'll be your husband to the end.[62]

The verse is risible and yet unbearably touching. It stands in deliberate and painful contrast to the detailed, realistic description of the loading of the guns and the measuring of the field.

The whole scene develops in the most matter-of-fact terms, and all the more powerfully for that. Onegin is an hour late for the duel. Lensky, who is only eighteen, is left to shiver in the winter morning, nursing his nerves. As they advance toward each other, Onegin raises his gun first, pointing it at Lensky's breast, and continues to advance, further discomforting the inexperienced youth, who now understands that this is not to be a duel in which the antagonists aim at the legs and honor is to be satisfied by a wound. Onegin fires before Lensky can even finish raising his gun. "Well then, he's dead," Lensky's second indifferently remarks.[63] Onegin has murdered his young friend. There is really no other way to express it. Symbolically, he is Pushkin killing Romanticism. But no symbolism can atone for such a deed.

The narrator speculates on what Lensky might have become, with his high aspirations and ardent desires. Perhaps he would have been a famous poet beloved and honored by his countrymen. "Then again," the narrator suggests, he might have become a commonplace squire, fat and happy despite wearing a cuckold's crown.[64] We can never know. All that remains of Lensky is a simple monument placed by a brook in the deepest shade, where a visitor might pause on a morning ride, read the inscription, and shed a brief tear.[65] That visitor would not be Olga, who all too soon, "forsaking / A grief that went not very deep," married a young lancer and moved away.[66]

Onegin, too, has moved away, ostensibly crushed by his own guilt. Only Tatiana remains, season after season, taking her long walks without purpose or comfort and repulsing the various suitors who long to court her. She even takes to visiting Onegin's house and, sitting in his study, with its portrait of Lord Byron, examining the well-thumbed volumes of Byron and other poets whom Onegin once valued. She reads his soul in their markings and begins to wonder whether his Byronic manner is simply an affectation, "a parody, when said and done."[67]

Eventually, Tatiana is persuaded by her mother—eager to find Tatiana a husband—to spend a season in Moscow with relatives. She bids farewell to the familiar fields and woods with all the tender regret that Lucia expressed on leaving her native village of Lecco. Yet, in Moscow, she attracts not only the confidences of women but also the admiration of many men, including "a certain general of substance,"[68] a hero in the Napoleonic Wars who is also a prince and cannot take his eyes off her. When her attention is directed to him by her aunts, she responds, "Who? That fat general, you mean?"[69] Yes, indeed, and it is with this "weighty general"[70] in tow that, two years later, Tatiana reencounters Onegin at a ball.

Unable to bear the constant reminders of Lensky's death, Onegin left his country estate and traveled aimlessly. But travel only increased his dejection, and he finally returns after several years abroad to find that Tatiana, in her quiet, graceful way, has captured Moscow society and married a prince.[71]

Pushkin famously remarked, "My Tatiana has gone and got married! I should never have thought it of her."[72] The quote is meant to emphasize that characters in a novel take on a life of their own and cannot always be made to bow to the author's whim—not if realism is to be preserved. But why does Tatiana marry? Has she despaired of Onegin or found his Byronic posturing unworthy of her love? Perhaps it is some combination of the two, or perhaps she wanted the security and position of an advantageous marriage? Surely, too, we feel she must genuinely admire the weighty general, for Tatiana would never marry where she does not feel both respect and affection.

Onegin is reintroduced to Tatiana by the prince himself:

> The Princess looks
> At him . . . and whatsoever shakes
> Her soul, whatever her impression
> Of him or the astonishment
> She feels or the bewilderment,
> Nothing betrays her self-possession.[73]

It is now Onegin's turn to lose his famous self-possession. He is frozen in place, while Tatiana is a model of composure, chatting briefly with Onegin as with a distant acquaintance before taking her husband's arm and retiring.

Onegin becomes as obsessed with Tatiana as she once was with him. But the reader is understandably uneasy about Onegin's sudden transformation.

> What, deep down in him,
> Has stirred his sluggish soul to fever?

Pique? Vanity? Or, once again,
Could it be love, that youthful pain?[74]

Onegin spurned Tatiana when she was a shy and simple country girl. Is it only because others now admire her that he has changed his mind? Or perhaps her unattainability is what attracts him. His emotions are as difficult to pinpoint as her own. She, who loved him to distraction, now treats his attentions with barely polite indifference. These are not just "lovers who are out of phase with one another," as Harold Bloom suggests.[75] These are two people who, at the deepest level, are fundamentally incompatible with each other. Tatiana has outgrown her youthful infatuation with Romantic novels; Onegin merely switches from one genre (the weary Byronic hero) to another (the impassioned Werther). Tatiana sees the world and Onegin with clearer eyes.

Onegin inevitably writes to Tatiana, but he still doesn't understand or fully appreciate her. His letter is as far from hers in frank and generous passion as Abelard's to Heloise. He predicts that she will greet his confession with "bitter scorn" and perhaps "wicked merriment."[76] He also continues to paint himself in the terms of a Romantic hero, as an "alien soul,"[77] who was unwilling to forfeit his prized freedom and then was condemned by the death of Lensky (as if Onegin himself were not responsible for it) to be a stranger to all tender feelings. Most egregiously, he implies that Tatiana hasn't experienced the love he feels: "If you but knew the frightful torment / To languish after your beloved."[78] Tatiana must have read those words with appalled astonishment and an acute sense of irony. Unsurprisingly, she offers no response. A second and third letter fare no better.

Onegin once again confronts her alone, this time in an empty reception room. She is in tears, holding a letter, presumably one of the ones he sent to her. He kneels at her feet and repeatedly kisses her hand. But she orders him to get up and recalls to him the avenue in the garden where he lectured and rejected her. "Today it is my turn to speak," she says,[79] and the power of those seven words fixes Onegin in place.

Tatiana questions the motive behind this change of heart, now that she is wealthy and renowned, and suggests that he is seeking the "seductive notoriety"[80] of conquest. Worse, she at least felt respected by his "cold, unsparing homily."[81] "But now, I see / You at my feet in coward fashion? / How with the heart and mind you have / Can you be paltry feeling's slave?"[82] In other words, she liked him better in his youthful Byronic arrogance. "That time," she claims, "was so auspicious / And happiness so near."[83] But we don't really believe in that happiness. In any event, it didn't come then and cannot come now. She is married. Indifferent to her fate, she gave in to the tears and entreaties of her mother to marry the prince.

> I love you (why should I disguise it?),
> But I am someone else's wife,
> To him I shall be true for life.[84]

The very strength of Tatiana's moral character—a character insufficiently valued by the younger Onegin—precludes an illicit attachment. Not for her the romantic fantasies of a Madame Bovary or the grand adulterous passion of an Anna Karenina.[85] Those women belong to later novels and a grittier time. But even the earlier, seemingly innocent passion of a Mme de Rênal is not available to Tatiana. All three of those affairs end disastrously. Tatiana, like Pushkin, is torn between the illusions of Romanticism and the disappointments of realism. She is too thoroughly grounded to embrace either extreme.

DEATH IMITATING ART

In 1833, the year *Eugene Onegin* was finally published, Pushkin was appointed by Tsar Nicholas as a *kammerjunker*, a junior gentleman of the chamber usually awarded to young aristocrats in their twenties. Pushkin was insulted by the appointment but could hardly turn it down. It seems to have been designed to keep his beautiful wife in society. But court life was expensive and time consuming. Pushkin impulsively sought to withdraw in 1834 so that he could move more or less full time to Boldino. The tsar considered the request an insult, and Pushkin was told he would lose all marks of imperial favor, including use of the archives in researching a proposed history of Peter the Great. Pushkin quickly and apologetically reversed course.

He was still producing works of genius, including "The Queen of Spades," his haunting tale of gambling and obsession, and his historical novel, *The Captain's Daughter*, in 1836, in which the Cossack Pugachev plays a major and largely sympathetic role. *The Captain's Daughter* exercised a powerful influence on *War and Peace*. *The Queen of Spades* and *Eugene Onegin* became Tchaikovsky's greatest operas.

But Pushkin felt keenly his humiliation at court, as well as his wife's constant flirtation with other men. Pushkin rebuked her in no uncertain terms: "You are glad that dogs run after you, as after a bitch, raising their tails like a poker and sniffing your arse; that is really something to be glad about!"[86] Pushkin smoothed over this breach with a milder reproach and a pleading appeal to their dependence on each other, as well as a concession that "you can . . . sparkle to your heart's content, as is fitting at your age and with your beauty."[87]

The situation would grow dramatically worse. In February 1836, Baron Georges d'Anthes was introduced into Russian society by the Dutch ambassador, with whom the much younger d'Anthes was apparently sexually intimate. Although French by birth and upbringing, d'Anthes obtained a commission in the Russian Chevalier Guards. He quickly singled out Natalya as the object of his attentions. She appeared to welcome them, but only up to a point. D'Anthes twice tried to seduce Natalya and was twice rebuffed. He enlisted the Dutch ambassador to plead his case. He sent a letter begging her to run away with him. Most egregiously, he contrived through a woman friend to trick Natalya into entering a drawing room where d'Anthes alone was present. He pulled out a pistol and threatened to shoot himself if she did not give herself to him; she escaped only on the chance entry of the woman's four-year-old daughter.

D'Anthes boasted that Natalya was in love with him even if she would not violate her duties to Pushkin. The relationship, of course, invited open gossip. An anonymous letter was sent to Pushkin and many of his acquaintances, nominating him as "Grand Master of the Order of Cuckolds and historiographer of the Order."[88] Pushkin was convinced that d'Anthes was the author—which appears unlikely. Regardless, after Natalya confessed to the various ways that d'Anthes had been harassing her, Pushkin challenged him to a duel. At the urging of the Dutch ambassador, and to avoid a growing scandal, d'Anthes proposed marriage to Natalya's sister, Yekaterina. Pushkin withdrew his challenge, albeit reluctantly. When rumors spread that d'Anthes proposed to Yekaterina only to escape the duel, d'Anthes himself sent a challenge to Pushkin. Friends convinced both parties to stand down. The tsar himself apparently intervened and forbade Pushkin to fight in any duels.

But, after marrying Yekaterina and steering clear of Natalya for a period of time, d'Anthes again paid conspicuous attention to Natalya at a ball attended by the tsar. He not only danced and flirted with her—attentions that, astonishingly, she did not rebuff—but also made a joke about his "lawful wife," implying that Natalya was his unlawful one. The next day, Pushkin sent a highly insulting letter. D'Anthes renewed his challenge, and they met with their seconds on February 8, 1837. The barriers were unusually close, a mere ten paces apart instead of the standard minimum of fifteen. The short distance all but guaranteed a fatality.

D'Anthes took the first shot as the two men advanced on the barriers. The ball struck Pushkin in the stomach, and he fell, dropping his weapon. Propping himself up on one elbow, Pushkin called for his second pistol. He aimed carefully and hit d'Anthes in the chest, but the bullet deflected off a button on d'Anthes's military tunic, and he was largely unharmed.

Pushkin was taken to his apartment by coach and physicians were summoned, but there was nothing they could do. He lingered for two days. "Don't worry, it isn't your fault," he told Natalya over and over.[89] He wrote a note seeking forgiveness from the tsar and begging protection for his wife and children.

Alexander Pushkin died on February 10, 1837. He was thirty-seven. More than ten thousand people went to the apartment to pay their respects. The funeral was massive, even though students were forbidden to attend lest there be a public disturbance.

The tsar provided generously for Pushkin's family and arranged for the publication of his complete works. Natalya remarried in 1844 and lived until 1863, age fifty-one. D'Anthes was condemned for his role in the duel, but his sentence was commuted to court martial and banishment. He lived to be eighty-three.

Following Horace, Pushkin effectively wrote his own epitaph in the 1836 poem "*Exegi monumentum*" (I have built my own monument).

Not all of me shall die—for in my cherished lyre
My soul shall outlive my dust, it shall escape decay—
In the sublunary world my fame shall be unending
    As long as a single poet holds sway.[90]

10

Balzac and the *Comédie Humaine*

The nineteenth century, as we know it, is largely an invention of Balzac.[1]

Oscar Wilde's famous *bon mot* is only partly facetious. Indeed, Wilde is often at his most serious when seemingly at his most facetious, as in his related saying: "Life imitates art far more than art imitates life."

It is the opposite view, of course, that prevails in most literary criticism. Erich Auerbach titled his magisterial study *Mimesis: The Representation of Reality in Western Literature*. He maintains that Balzac, together with Stendhal, "can be regarded as the creator of modern realism."[2] Although Balzac was still of the Romantic generation, Auerbach notes that he "seized upon the representation of contemporary life as his own particular task."[3] Balzac himself says as much of *Père Goriot*: "This drama is not fictional, it's not a novel. All is true—so true you'll be able to recognize everything that goes into it in your own life, perhaps even in your own heart."[4]

Yet Balzac, too, is being deliberately paradoxical. Of course, *Père Goriot* is fictional. Of course, it is a novel. But it is also a depiction of a particular time in the life of France, and for Balzac this social history is as important as the lives of the principal characters, rooted as they are in the material, cultural, and economic conditions of France. The novel is set in 1819, during the Bourbon Restoration, but it was written in 1835, after the July Revolution of 1830, which, as in *The Red and the Black*, looms large over its characters even though it is never directly mentioned. The goal of the narrator is to convince the reader of the emotional, moral, and economic truth of what is presented. The plot is Romantic, but the setting is realistic.

In the great procession of novelists from Richardson, Fielding, and Jane Austen through Dickens, Flaubert, and George Eliot, Balzac is a crucial hinge connecting the Romantics and the realists. His *Comédie Humaine*—a collection of more than ninety intersecting novels and stories—explores the full range of the human condition as well as the human heart. The trilogy of *Père Goriot*, *Lost Illusions*, and *The Splendors and Miseries of Courtesans*, in particular, is one of the great milestones in the history of the novel. It changed our view of what we can expect from a work of fiction. Small wonder that both Henry James and Émile Zola resort to comparisons with Shakespeare to describe Balzac's ability to take in so much of human life.[5] Speaking for his fellow writers, Henry James frankly acknowledges Balzac as "the master of us all."[6]

LIFE[7]

Honoré de Balzac was born on May 20, 1799, in the French city of Tours. His father, Bernard-François Balssa, was from a peasant family in southern France. But Bernard-François was too ambitious to work in the fields as did his father and a solid line of ancestors before him. He learned to read and found work as a clerk in a law office. He also altered his last name to Balzac, after an ancient noble family. The aristocratic *de* was yet a later, equally unjustified, addition at a time when such social sobriquets were in flux.

Anticipating a number of his son's fictional characters, Bernard-François left the provinces to seek his fortune in Paris. He was remarkably successful, serving in a series of distinguished positions. Even more remarkably, he navigated the French Revolution, the ensuing Reign of Terror, the Napoleonic era, and even the Bourbon Restoration with chameleonic ease. He became a quartermaster for the French army and was eventually transferred to Tours, where he managed the hospital.

In 1797, at the age of fifty, Bernard-François married Anne-Charlotte-Laure Sallambier, an eighteen-year-old Parisian from a family of haberdashers. A first child died shortly after birth. Honoré was born in 1799. His beloved sister Laure was born a year later, and another sister, Laurence, arrived two years after that. Balzac was sent out to nurse and was largely neglected by his highly social mother. He judged her harshly, and she in turn rarely missed an opportunity to belittle him. Like Pushkin (who was born the same year), Balzac claimed, with some justification, that his mother hated him. He got on somewhat better with his mother's mother, who came to live with the family after the death of her husband.

Balzac began attending a nearby day school before he turned five. Three years later, he was sent away to the highly regarded Collège de Vendôme, about thirty-five miles from Tours. He spent six years there and saw his mother only twice in that entire time. Balzac received a secular, post-Revolutionary education. But he was rebellious, resistant to assigned work, and frequently punished. Though withdrawn at first, he gradually made friends. He also won a prize for Latin prose and received extra tutoring in mathematics. He was inspired by two of his teachers but was largely an autodidact. His intense, eclectic reading already reflected the encyclopedic range of interests revealed in his novels. Balzac made Vautrin, his most famous Byronic villain/hero, into a graduate of Vendôme.

Mme Balzac had a number of affairs, which were tolerated by her much older husband. She gave birth to an illegitimate son, Henry, when Balzac was eight, shortly after he left for school. Henry's father, a local landowner, would leave 200,000 francs to his natural son. Balzac's mother doted on Henry, which increased Balzac's bitterness and sense of rejection.

Balzac returned home at the age of fourteen. His father was transferred to Paris, where Balzac briefly attended the Lycée Charlemagne and even saw Napoleon during a parade in the Tuileries. His mother returned with her children to Tours in the spring of 1814 when the Napoleonic Empire was teetering on the edge of military disaster. Shortly thereafter, Napoleon was forced to abdicate, and the Balzacs returned to Paris after the restoration of Louis XVIII.

Balzac was enrolled in the Lepitre boarding school in January 1815, but his further education was quickly interrupted by the return of Napoleon during the famous Hundred Days. Balzac joined other students in hailing Napoleon's escape from Elba and triumphant return to Paris in March 1815. But this brief interlude before Waterloo and the Second Restoration had little effect other than to feed continued feelings of insecurity among the nobility, who were eager to ally themselves with successful bourgeoisie against a dangerous working class. A new aristocracy was arising based on money. Social mobility was increasingly tied to economic success, and titles became another form of currency. Marriage was more a marketplace than ever. Buy the right clothes. Adopt the proper manners. Solicit the best connections. Add a *de* to your name and marry (or at least have an affair with) a wealthy, preferably aristocratic woman. In today's parlance, "fake it until you make it"—exactly the path that would be taken by the ultimate *parvenu/arriviste*, Balzac's Eugène de Rastignac.

Balzac finished his formal education in September 1816 at the Collège Charlemagne. He was apprenticed as a clerk in the law offices of Victor Passez, a friend of his father, and began to study law at the École de Droit. He managed to obtain a bachelor of law degree in 1819, and Passez generously offered him the chance to take over his practice. But Balzac had no intention of working as a lawyer. His surprisingly indulgent parents allowed him to remain in Paris and pursue his fortune as a man of letters. He was granted two years to prove himself as a writer. In the event, it was a much longer process.

In the tradition of literary aspirants such as Samuel Johnson and Voltaire, in 1819 Balzac wrote a tragedy, *Cromwell*, hoping to introduce himself to the larger world as a blazing new talent. Cromwell was a convenient stand-in at a time when writing directly about Napoleon or the monarchy was hazardous. His own character, Lucien de Rubempré, will do the same in Part II of *Lost Illusions*, Balzac's devastating critique of the soul-destroying commercialization of literature. Neither Balzac nor Lucien finds success in the classical format. Victor Hugo will write his own highly acclaimed play by the same name, which he prefaced with a paean to Romanticism. Hugo's 1830 play, *Hernani*, caused a riot at the

Comédie-Française by deliberately rejecting all the classical unities of time, place, and action.

Balzac's failure as a tragedian found consolation in an affair with Laure de Berny, which began in 1821. At forty-four, she was twice his age and a friend and adviser as well as a lover. She was married but, like Balzac's mother, in an open marriage with a much older man. Balzac clearly considered her a substitute mother figure. Unsurprisingly, Balzac's real mother strongly disapproved of the relationship and tried, without success, to separate the two lovers. Laure would remain a loyal friend throughout Balzac's life, despite his array of other lovers.

At the time, novels were widely disparaged as written for, and often by, women. They were not considered serious literature. But they paid, as Sir Walter Scott demonstrated. Hoping to capitalize on that commercial success, between 1822 and 1826 Balzac wrote a series of pseudonymous gothic novels. He called it "dirtying paper,"[8] but he wrote at a rate of twenty pages per day. "It is absolute pigswill," he confessed; "I now know its true worth, though pride still whispers to me that it's as good as all the other stuff that's published."[9] It was a useful apprenticeship, recalling Jane Austen's early fascination with gothic novels, though her *Northanger Abbey* was anything but pigswill and showed a promise that would be hard to discern in Balzac's potboilers. He managed to make some money, though not as much as he spent on clothes and furnishings. Balzac's extravagance and obsession for collecting was already evident. Mme de Berny helped to support him, but he was in need of a more lucrative enterprise and more aristocratic connections.

In 1826, Balzac met and laid siege to the Duchess d'Abrantès. Her introductions allowed Balzac access to some of the most selective salons in Paris, a fact that turned his head as surely as Rastignac's introduction into society by his cousin Mme de Beauséant. Balzac ultimately convinced the duchess to become his lover. Mme de Berny had full knowledge of the affair and often discussed it with Balzac, but she never deviated from her attachment to him.

In 1827, Balzac abandoned novel writing and decided to make his fortune as a publisher. He sought, among other projects, to publish complete, pocket-sized editions of French classical authors, an idea that would, a century later, lead to the great *Pléiade* series. In the process, he acquired a detailed understanding of the printers' trade that would inform the last part of *Lost Illusions*. He also met many important literary figures, including Victor Hugo. But Balzac's publishing house failed under a mountain of debt after two years, for which we can only be grateful because it sent him back to novel writing. Throughout his life, Balzac's attempts to stay one step ahead of his creditors provided the spur for further works. His publishing debts included 50,000 francs to his mother and another 50,000 to Mme de Berny, who proved to be more astute at business than Balzac. She took over the bankrupt business, enlisted her son to run it, and it became one of the largest and most successful publishers in Paris. As would be the case for other quixotic ventures, Balzac's scheme was sound, but his timing and execution were not.

Balzac returned to writing with a prolonged intensity rarely matched in the history of great literature. Between 1829 and his death in 1850, he wrote more than ninety novels and novellas as part of his projected *Comédie Humaine*, a comprehensive account of French life in the second quarter of the nineteenth century. Balzac did not want to write historical novels in the manner of Sir Walter Scott; he wanted to explore—with the precision of a sociologist and the imagination of a supreme artist—the rapidly shifting moral, social, and economic landscape of contemporary France.

Balzac ensured the unity of his vision by employing overlapping characters in his many novels. Once his overall plan had matured, he even revised earlier novels to introduce characters from later novels. In the real world, we come across individuals at different times and in different circumstances to form a fuller, more realized understanding of their natures. Balzac decided to do the same in his novels as a means of imposing order on his two-thousand-plus characters. The cross references solidify their existence. For example, forty-eight characters in *Père Goriot* appear in other novels, including two of his most celebrated: Eugène de Rastignac and the arch-criminal Jacques Collin, colloquially known as Vautrin. Even more marginal characters, such as the physician Horace Bianchon, the moneylender Gobseck, and the lawyer Derville, are met with in book after book as their characters gradually unfold. Balzac made a full genealogy to keep track of them all and constantly revised his works to replace historical characters with fictional ones who were even more real to him and to us, his readers, because they are so deeply embedded in their social context.

Balzac augmented the concrete reality of his characters by exhaustive descriptions of their clothes (and the various gradations of dress that signify status), their furnishings (such as the oft-cited description of Mme Vauquer's shabby-genteel boarding house), their mode of transportation (there are few things more socially demoralizing than arriving at an elegant house on foot, spattered with muddy water and horse manure), their subjects of conversation, the food and drink they consume, and the theaters they frequent. With revenues and expenses calculated to the last franc, Balzac's detailed exploration of the economic conditions that determine one's place in society was hailed by Karl Marx and Friedrich Engels as a powerful, if unintended, critique of capitalism. Most important, all the characters share in the intensity of their creator. As the poet Charles Baudelaire explains in a passage that shows why Balzac is still counted among the Romantics despite his gift for realistic description:

> All his characters are gifted with that ardor of life that animated himself. All his fictions are as deeply colored as dreams. From the highest peaks of the aristocracy to the lowest depths of the people, all the actors of his *Comedy* are more greedy for life, more active and cunning in the struggle, more patient in misfortune, more gluttonous in the gratification of desire, more angelic in devotion than they appear in the comedy of the real world. In Balzac, even the door-keepers have genius. All his minds are weapons loaded to the muzzle with will. Just like Balzac himself.[10]

Balzac's standard practice, fueled by endless cups of coffee, was to rise at one in the morning and work until eight. After a short nap and some refreshment, he started in again until four in the afternoon, when he would have dinner and receive visitors. After dinner, he went straight to bed. As he aged, he felt an increased sense of urgency and began to work up to eighteen hours a day on his grand project.

But Balzac did not give up all society in preference to work. He was a noted conversationalist, not as a competitive sport, but rather in an out-pouring of intellect and good cheer. As one contemporary noted, "he was so trusting, so kind, so naive and so candid that it was impossible not to love him. And the most extraordinary thing about him was his perpetual good humor."[11] All these traits would be reaffirmed in the diary of his longtime love and eventual wife, Countess Eveline Hanska.

In February 1832, Balzac received an anonymous letter from Odessa both lauding his work and urging him to moderate his treatment of women. He responded by placing an ad in the *Gazette de France*, regret-ting his inability to reply. Thus began a lengthy correspondence with Countess Hanska. She came from a prominent Polish family but, for financial reasons, was pressed by her family to marry a count twenty years her senior. At first, she wished to remain anonymous—she signed herself "L'Étrangère"—but soon revealed her identity and invited Balzac to meet her in Neuchâtel the following year. Other rendezvous followed in Geneva and Vienna. Her husband was present for most of these encounters and himself greatly enjoyed Balzac's company. After 1836, Balzac and Eveline did not see each other for seven years but maintained a voluminous and intimate correspondence. Marrying Eveline became his great object.

That is not to say that Balzac was monogamous. He began an affair with Countess Frances-Sarah Guidoboni-Visconti in 1834. She gave birth to a son, Lionel-Richard Guidoboni-Visconti in 1836, who was widely regarded as Balzac's natural son.

As if he were not busy enough, Balzac purchased a controlling interest in a weekly magazine, the *Chronique de Paris*, in 1835. Displaced by the advent of daily newspapers, the magazine lasted less than a year and added significantly to his debts. A later *Revue Parisienne* managed only three issues. Two more get-rich schemes had thus failed, but they gave Balzac an intimate (if jaded) knowledge of journalism, which he promptly put to good use in *Lost Illusions*. Other, equally futile schemes for enrichment would involve dairy, manure, and wine. Balzac was con-stantly prey to what Samuel Johnson, speaking of second marriages, called the triumph of hope over experience. He was also a compulsive collector of paintings, furniture, vases, and other bric-a-brac. An inventory of his tangible personal property prepared by Balzac ran forty-seven pages.[12]

In January 1842, Balzac received a letter from Eveline announcing the death of her husband. His hopes that they would quickly marry were disappointed, however, by complications with her husband's estate, legal resistance from a cousin who considered Balzac a gold digger, and Eveline's own understandable reluctance to trade the life she had forged for herself in Russia for an uncertain future in Paris with Balzac. They saw each other on a number of occasions, usually in Paris or St. Petersburg. Eveline paid his debts and for their trips together. More important, she became his business manager and imposed some form of financial discipline on the free-spending Balzac. She delivered a stillborn child in 1846. But the proposed marriage was repeatedly delayed. It was unclear whether she would be able to keep her estate if she married a foreigner. She also wanted to ensure that her daughter, Anna, was properly married before any potential scandal arose from her marriage to Balzac.

Balzac was popular in Russia, earning praise from both Pushkin and Dostoevsky. At one point, he spent eighteen months in Russia with Eveline. They were extremely happy together and would frequently talk through the night after he finished his writing. Although his productivity suffered, he produced *La Cousine Bette* and *Le Cousin Pons*, his last great works, published in 1846 and 1847, respectively.

Balzac returned to Paris just in time to be a spectator at the Revolution of 1848. Industrialization, though still in its early phases, had already caused a large shift from rural to urban areas, resulting in unemployment, overcrowding, and hunger. On February 22, a demonstration against the government spread rapidly. The national guard not only failed to suppress the marchers but even took their side and neutralized the army. Two days later, Louis-Philippe abdicated and fled to England. The Second Republic was declared. It lasted through the remainder of Balzac's life but ultimately led, in 1852, to the autocratic Second Empire. Louis Napoleon, nephew of Bonaparte, was elected president and became Emperor Napoleon III.

In 1849, Balzac applied to fill an empty seat in the Académie Française but received only four votes, though one was from his greatest contemporary, Victor Hugo. Balzac shared the honor of rejection with Descartes, Rousseau, Diderot, and Molière, among others. Flaubert and Marcel Proust would also be rejected.

Eveline finally agreed to marry Balzac in March 1850. She abandoned her Ukrainian estate to Anna and her husband and moved to Paris to take care of Balzac. Balzac himself called it "a heroic resolution."[13] He was already suffering from numerous gastrointestinal and cardiac problems that were undoubtedly exacerbated by his constant consumption of strong coffee.

Balzac survived the marriage for only five months. He died on August 18, 1850. He was fifty-one years old. Famously, though perhaps apocryphally, on his deathbed, the delirious Balzac asked that the great but fictional doctor, Horace Bianchon, who appears in more than thirty books, be summoned to attend him.[14]

Balzac was buried in Père Lachaise Cemetery, where Rastignac vowed to conquer Paris and where Balzac's other fictional characters Père Goriot and Lucien de Rubempré, among others, were buried. Eveline lived for another thirty-two years before she was laid to rest in the same grave with Balzac.

Père Goriot

Père Goriot, like King Lear, is in many respects the tragic hero of the work that bears his name. But Lear is a king. Goriot is a maker of vermicelli. Aristotle insisted that a proper tragic hero must be of noble birth and character. Yet, despite their vastly different statures, Lear and Goriot share the same tragic flaw (*hamartia*) that leads to their downfall. They give everything to their daughters, reversing the natural order of things, and become the supplicants of their own children, whose affections they have gravely misjudged.

Goriot seized the pasta business where he worked when its owner was executed during the Revolution. Food shortages and rapidly rising prices post-Revolution allowed him to make a fortune. But, on the death of his beloved wife, Goriot transferred his affections to his daughters. He gave each a dowry of 500,000 to 600,000 francs so they could make distinguished marriages. The older, Anastasie, chose the aristocratic Comte de Restaud. The younger, Delphine, chose the wealthy banker Baron de Nucingen. Such marriages were purely transactional. Money and title changed hands; love was nowhere to be found.

But Goriot, like Lear, counted on his generosity to guarantee his daughters' continued affection, "thinking they'd always be his daughters, and that he'd have manufactured two new homes for himself, two homes where he'd always be adored, and fussed over."[15] And, indeed, his sons-in-law and their wives were happy enough to welcome and embrace the wealthy merchant post-Revolution and even during the Napoleonic Empire. But, once the Bourbons were restored to power in 1814, having a relative in trade became a social embarrassment. The daughters and their husbands pressed him to give up his vermicelli business. Worse, they "not only . . . refuse[d] to take him into their own houses, but even to openly receive him there."[16]

The daughters continue to meet with Goriot secretly but only to plead for more money—Anastasie to pay the gambling debts of her lover and Delphine to satisfy her aspiration to be accepted in aristocratic society. They demand more and more from him, and he is powerless to say no. "To give always is what makes one a father," he believes.[17] That is how he taught his own daughters to regard him. The extent of his love was measured by the money he dispensed. Small wonder that, "once the lemon was well squeezed, his daughters tossed the peel into the gutter."[18]

The unceasing and ever-increasing demands made on him force Goriot to drastically lower his own standard of living. Anastasie moves freely among the aristocracy thanks to her titled husband. Delphine is part of the wealthy Parisian bourgeoisie, bolstered by her banker husband. But their father occupies a single room in a shabby boarding house run by Mme Vauquer in a neighborhood where "poverty rules, and there's no poetry to alleviate it."[19] The boarding house is to Goriot what the heath is to Lear: the realm of an outcast.

Of the three levels in the social hierarchy, however, the boarding house is by far the most interesting because of the variety of its occupants, most of whom are vainly scheming to move up in society through chance or circumstance, including the landlady herself, who insists on inserting a *de* in her name and lays claim to a distinguished (if vague) past. Balzac's gifts for description are nowhere shown to greater effect than in his detailed depictions of Mme Vauquer, her boarding house (with its faded and eclectic furnishings), and her clients.

Among the boarders is Eugène de Rastignac. The noble Rastignac family had their fortune invested in the Indian Trading Company, which was nationalized by the Revolution. They were lucky to come through it with their lives and a very modest estate. Eugène goes to Paris to reestablish the family fortune, carrying in his pocket a letter of introduction to his cousin, the Vicomtesse de Beauséant, one of the most celebrated and sought-after hostesses in Paris. The hopes of his mother and sisters rest on his shoulders. His initial plan is to study law and become a magistrate, but he finds the pursuit tedious and slow. Eugène longs instead to shine in society and make a spectacular marriage. His looks, his bearing, and his manners all indicate noble origins and a good education. But he quickly realizes that his clothes bespeak poverty, which will bar him from fashionable society. A good tailor is the critical but expensive means of passage, so he implores his mother and his two sisters to send him money, claiming that despair would drive him to suicide if the necessary funds are not forthcoming. "Our entire future depends on this money," he tells them, "which I need so I can start my campaign: life here in Paris is indeed perpetual warfare."[20]

Eugène has two completely different mentors in this "campaign." Yet their message is essentially the same. First, he visits his cousin, the vicomtesse, who takes a liking to the handsome, ambitious young man and tells him that, if he is to succeed, he must harbor no illusions:

> The more coldly you calculate, the farther you'll go. Strike without pity, and you'll be feared. Think of men and women simply as post-horses to be discarded in a ditch, each time you change to a fresh team, and you'll get exactly what you long for. Understand you'll never be anything, here in Paris, without a woman's backing. You need someone who's young, rich, and elegant. But also remember: if you have any genuine feelings, hide them like treasure; never let anyone so much as suspect them, or you're lost. Instead of being the executioner, you'll be the victim. And if you ever fall in love, keep that absolutely secret![21]

Vautrin, an arch-criminal and fellow boarder at the maison Vauquer, is also attracted to the fresh-faced Rastignac. In the garden of the boarding house, as night falls, Vautrin delivers an equally harsh lesson in the realities of Parisian life, but one with surprising affinities to the elegant vicomtesse. "It's a strange mud pit," replies Vautrin.

> If you get that dirt on you while you're driving around in a carriage, you're a very respectable fellow, but if it splatters all over you while you slog along on foot, then you're a good-for-nothing rogue. Make the mistake of grabbing anything out of the mud, no matter how insignificant, and they'll pillory you in the courts of law. But steal millions, and they'll point you out as a hero, in the very best houses. That's an ethical system you pay the cops and the judges thirty million a year to keep in good working order.[22]

Behind every great fortune, Vautrin concludes, is a great crime, and he promptly proposes one to Rastignac. "I'll make you an offer you can't refuse," Vautrin tells him.[23] He rightly sees that Eugène is too impatient to follow the slow path to success paved by deep learning and hard work, as his friend, the medical student Horace Bianchon, will do.

Vautrin's plan revolves around a young, innocent girl, Victorine Taillefer, who also lives at the maison Vauquer. Victorine's mother has died, and her wealthy father, suspecting that she is illegitimate, neglects her and plans to leave his entire estate to her brother. The father will not even see her. In a complete reversal of Goriot's story, Victorine is indifferent to her father's fortune but wants only to show her love and obedience. Victorine is the good-child equivalent to *King Lear*'s Cordelia.

In *King Lear*, the plot is doubled. Lear is rejected by his daughters Goneril and Regan, and he has in his turn misguidedly banished his only faithful daughter, Cordelia. So, too, the Earl of Gloucester is the victim of his evil son, Edmund, and has mistakenly shunned his faithful son, Edgar.

The same double structure is present in *Père Goriot*, with one twist. M. Taillefer has rejected his faithful daughter in favor of his grasping son. Goriot is abused by his two daughters. But one space is empty. Goriot has no faithful child to fill the role of Cordelia or Edgar. That is where

Eugène de Rastignac comes in. He views himself as a defender of Goriot, just as he views himself as the protector of the women in his family. Goriot even calls Eugène "my son."[24]

Yet Rastignac is a deeply ambiguous figure, neither as good as Cordelia and Edgar nor as evil as Goneril, Regan, and Edmund. He is not, in any event, as calculating as Vautrin wants him to be. Eugène proves quite prepared to sacrifice his conscience to his ambitions. But even so, there are limits.

Vautrin proposes to enlist a criminal acquaintance—a master swordsman and expert shot—to provoke Victorine's brother into a duel in which he will be killed. The father will then shift his affection to his only remaining child, who is clearly in love with Rastignac. They will marry. Rastignac will become a millionaire and, by prior agreement, pay 20 percent of that amount to Vautrin. Vautrin guarantees Rastignac that he will be completely insulated from the murder itself.

Rastignac chooses to treat this proposal as a joke, and he responds rather piously. "I want a fortune I've earned," he claims. "Maybe it will be the slowest of fortunes, but every night I'll lay my head on my pillow, knowing my conscience is clear."[25] Vautrin openly mocks him as "the kind of idiot who believes in absolutes. But there are no principles, just things that happen; there are no laws, either, just circumstances, and the superior man espouses both events and circumstances, so he can guide them."[26]

Indeed, Rastignac's good intentions are short-lived. Once he has donned the elegant clothes paid for by his family, "finding himself the object of an attention virtually admiring, he stopped thinking about his sisters or the aunt he'd despoiled, or about his virtuous horror."[27] He realizes that to be both a doctor of laws and a fashionable young man is simply not possible. Too impatient to rise slowly within the law, Rastignac decides, in keeping with Vicomtesse de Beauséant's advice, that marriage—or at least an affair with a distinguished woman—is the best path to success. Meanwhile, he continues to flirt with Mlle Taillefer and doesn't positively reject Vautrin's plan. Laughing it off is not the same as a categorical rejection; it is a way (at least subconsciously) of hedging his bets and preserving plausible deniability.

Through his cousin, the vicomtesse, Rastignac meets Anastasie de Restaud. He is subsequently introduced by others to Delphine de Nucingen. Fascinated by their unlikely connection with Goriot, he courts all three and finds that the surest way into Goriot's confidence is to talk to him about his daughters. The converse is not true, and Rastignac grows very cautious about making unwelcome references to their father. But he has a different form of leverage, at least with Delphine, who wants desperately to be introduced into aristocratic society, a privilege deliberately blocked by Anastasie. Eugène obtains for Delphine an invitation to the final and most magnificent ball of the season, to be hosted by the vicomtesse. Delphine's affections are thus secured, at least for the time being.

But, as the ball approaches, it becomes a further occasion for the two daughters to hector their father for more money, each vying for the finest diamonds to wear. Goriot is mortally ill, but he wants to hide that fact from his daughters, concerned they would give up the ball to stay with him. Rastignac sees more clearly, "underneath both sisters' diamonds, . . . the straw pallet on which their father was lying."[28] Yet Eugène sacrifices his own conscience to his would-be mistress. "He had the sense that, in order to get to this ball, [Delphine] was capable of walking right over her father's body, and he lacked the strength to try to be her guide, just as he lacked the courage to displease her, and the valor to simply leave her."[29] It is a damning description of Rastignac's character, fully borne out in the remainder of his career.

When Lear eventually recognizes that Goneril and Regan not only do not love him but actively despise him, he rages against a universe that creates such ungrateful children:

> You see me here, you gods, a poor old man
> As full of grief as age, wretched in both.
> If it be you that stirs these daughters' hearts
> Against their father, fool me not so much
> To bear it tamely. Touch me with noble anger,
> And let not women's weapons, water drops,
> Stain my man's cheeks.—No, you unnatural hags,
> I will have such revenges on you both

THE WISDOM OF THE ROMANTICS

That all the world shall—I will do such things—
What they are yet I know not, but they shall be
The terrors of the Earth! You think I'll weep.
No, I'll not weep.
I have full cause of weeping, but this heart
Shall break into a hundred thousand flaws
Or ere I'll weep.—O Fool, I shall go mad![30]

Eventually, Goriot, too, reaches his Lear-like revelation: He has been a fool; his daughters have never loved him and will not come to his deathbed. But Goriot speaks more in sadness than in anger:

You have to die to understand what children are! Ah! my friend, don't get married, don't have children! You give them life, and they give you death. You bring them into the world, they chase you out of it. No, they're not coming! I've known that for ten years. I told myself as much, sometimes, but I didn't dare believe it.[31]

Goriot rightly is the focus of the drama that unfolds in the book. But *his* end is not *the* end. Balzac presents us with an open-ended universe in which one closure marks another beginning. The comedy of human wants, needs, and desires in the first half of the nineteenth century will continue with an ever-shifting cast. There is no closure of the sort found in Julien's death in *The Red and the Black* or in any of Jane Austen's novels, where marriage takes the place of death as the proper end of the novel.

The finest elegy spoken over Père Goriot is delivered by the surgeon attending him with Bianchon. "We still have to change his bed linen," he explains. "There may be no hope, but we must respect him as a human being."[32] That respect is something his daughters and his sons-in-law fail to afford him. Indeed, they do not even attend the funeral, sending empty carriages in their stead. Nor do they contribute a single sou to the pauper's funeral, which is all the impoverished students, Rastignac and Bianchon, can afford to give Goriot.

But the end of Goriot's story launches Rastignac's campaign of social conquest. He keeps his eyes on the main chance. Rastignac tells himself that Delphine's husband, the wealthy financier Baron de Nucingen, is "fairly rolling in golden opportunities, so he could help me rake in a fast fortune."[33] That is precisely how events will unfold in the *Comédie Humaine*. Eugène will become extremely rich and even a minister of state thanks to participating in Nucingen's shady dealings. Eventually, he will marry Delphine's daughter, Augusta, who, in light of Eugène's lengthy affair with Delphine, is likely his own daughter as well. So much for the "simple, sustained, uncomplicated happiness" his family had once enjoyed, despite their poverty.[34] Success is all that will matter to him going forward.

> Left alone, Rastignac walked to the highest part of the cemetery and looked down at the heart of Paris, winding tortuously along both banks of the Seine, where night lights were beginning to gleam. . . . He looked at that swarming beehive, his very glance seeming to suck out its honey, and then declared, grandly, "Now it's just the two of us!—I'm ready!"[35]

And then, for the first challenge he hurls at society, Rastignac goes to dinner with Mme de Nucingen.

LOST ILLUSIONS

Balzac can be considered, with Pushkin, the last of the Romantics or, with Stendhal, the first of the realists. Both strands are evident in his three-part novel, completed in 1843, which follows Lucien de Rubempré's journey from the provinces to Paris, from poetry to journalism, from innocence to corruption, from exaltation to despair.

The reader is not inclined to like Lucien. He is selfish and vain. He expects others to bow before his genius and tend to his needs. Worse, he has a unique ability to destroy the lives of those who love him. Yet Lucien's soul quivers in response to tones unheard by most. He worships love, beauty, and art. He tries to cling to these ideals when confronted by a culture in which money and position are the measures of all value and where even literature is treated as just another commodity. Lucien's fall from grace is shockingly steep and rapid. He deserves no less, but we nonetheless mourn the loss.

Lucien's mother is a midwife in the small town of Angoulême, in southwestern France. She is the last of an impoverished aristocratic line, the de Rubempré family, who avoided the guillotine only through the efforts of Major Chardon, a former surgeon in the republican army struck by her beauty. After he was wounded and discharged, Major Chardon started a pharmacy but died before he could build any sort of estate. His wife and two children, Lucien and a daughter, Ève, can barely subsist on the proceeds from the sale of the pharmacy combined with the mother's modest income and Ève's work as a laundress. But what little they have is devoted to Lucien. Mme Chardon and her daughter "believed in Lucien the way Mohammed's wife believed in her husband; their devotion to him and his future was absolute."[36]

With his feminine features and slender build, Lucien might have been mistaken for a girl in disguise, like Julien Sorel, whose first appearance proved so striking to Mme de Rênal. "His face had the lines of ancient, classical beauty: a Greek forehead and nose, the velvety white skin of a woman, eyes so black they were blue, eyes rich with love, their whites as clear and pure as a child's."[37] Women and even some men fall instantly in love with him. Lucien is the epitome of the Byronic Romantic hero except that there is nothing heroic about him. He has, as his loyal friend and brother-in-law, David Séchard, reluctantly recognizes, a "deadly instability of character."[38]

Lucien has written a historical novel, *The Archer of Charles IX*, and a book of poems, *Marguerites*, with which he plans to take the literary world by storm. They are Romantic set pieces, designed by Balzac to recall Wordsworth's golden daffodils and Scott's historical novels. They mark Lucien as an imitative rather than original writer. His concern is for instant literary success rather than the sustained hard work and accompanying hardship necessary for literary greatness. "He's the type," David perceptively observes, "who wants the fruits of the harvest without having to do any of the harvesting work."[39]

Lucien's immediate goal is to mingle with and be considered equal or even superior to the provincial aristocracy of Angoulême. He is patronized by Louise de Bargeton, the most important (if sometimes ridiculed) figure in what passes for Angoulême society. Like Proust's

Mme Verdurin, who will plainly be drawn after her, Mme de Bargeton has a passion or at least affects a passion for music and literature. She wants to be the center of a salon and "exhaust[s] herself with constant enthusiasms."[40] Lucien is her prime catch, and she aspires to play the role of his muse, like Dante's Beatrice or Petrarch's Laura. She praises him as a genius, above the trivial laws of society, whose only duty is to follow that genius. Like Rastignac, but more naïvely and less effectively, Lucien will learn to regard men and women as post-horses in his ride to glory.

The book takes place during the Bourbon Restoration, when aristocrats clung all the more jealously to their tenuous prerogatives. By force of her own status, Mme de Bargeton can give an *entree* to Lucien. She even urges him to use his mother's aristocratic last name, de Rubempré. But others resent the upstart, especially the bourgeoisie who are vainly hoping for a similar ascent.

The story unfolds in a series of vivid vignettes, beautifully strung together, albeit with great liberties, in the 2021 movie version of the novel directed by Xavier Giannoli. Mme de Bargeton's poetry soiree, designed to introduce Lucien to Angoulême society, falls flat from the studied indifference of the audience and is capped by a devastating, if carefully prepared, witticism from the bishop. After Lucien modestly explains the long gestation period necessary to writing poetry, another guest chimes in, "Your labor is going to be a tough one."[41] The bishop then adds, "And your excellent mother will be able to help."[42] Angoulême society makes no effort to hide its satisfaction with the put-down.

A second *mise-en-scène* is created by the Baron du Châtelet, a rival for Louise's affections, who manages to introduce a talkative busybody, Stanislas de Chandour, into her boudoir when she is alone with Lucien. De Chandour finds them in a compromising position, with Lucien on his knees, in tears, and his head in her lap. De Chandour tells the story, with numerous embellishments, to anyone who will listen. Louise's obedient husband challenges de Chandour to a duel and shoots him through the neck. Louise, finding her position untenable, leaves for Paris with Lucien in tow.

Lucien expects Paris to welcome him like a beautifully dressed woman with arms open wide. In his imagination, "illustrious men would step forward with gestures of fraternal welcome. There everything smiled upon genius. There he would find no petty aristocrats tossing off insults to humiliate the writer, nor any imbecilic indifference to poetry."[43] He even believes that the publishing houses, after reading just a few pages of his novel, will open their cash drawers to him.

Needless to say, he is sorely disappointed. Dozens of clever young men from the provinces arrive in Paris every day with a book of poems or a novel in their hands and dreams of literary glory in their hearts. But they quickly learn that Paris is indifferent to their self-proclaimed genius and that, without aristocratic patronage or (like Lord Byron) inherited wealth, they cannot live on literature. Even if they could find a publisher, which only established writers can do, and even if their work were to strike a chord with an easily distracted public, copyright law is murky and difficult to enforce. Literature, Lucien finds, has become a "brutal and purely material" commodity to be bought and sold like so many bonnets.[44]

Lucien and Mme de Bargeton, too, quickly grow disenchanted with each other. In the bright glare of Paris, Louise appears dowdy, and Lucien looks like an awkward shopkeeper in his Sunday best.[45] Louise puts herself under the guidance of her cousin, the Marquise d'Espard, and soon becomes the model of a refined and elegant Parisian aristocrat. But Lucien's untutored attempt to be fashionable—using money that his mother and sister can ill afford—meets with astonished ridicule when he joins Louise and Mme d'Espard at the opera. Eugène de Rastignac, who appears in this novel as well, is from the same town as Lucien. But Rastignac has already navigated the shoals of Parisian social life and is part of the smart set. He is more than happy to shut every door in the face of his provincial compatriot by informing others that the preposterous young man is the son of a pharmacist and a midwife, who has no right to use the de Rubempré name. Mme d'Espard flees her own box in horror, with Louise meekly following, leaving Lucien in shocked dismay. The following day, the two women snub Lucien as he walks on the Champs-Élysées, and Lucien discovers that they are never to be "at home" when he calls.

Abandoned by his supposed patroness, Lucien must navigate Paris on his own. He explores two pathways and, of course, chooses badly. Or does he? That ambiguity is part of what makes the novel so compelling.

The first option is to follow the higher calling of literature and philosophy. Lucien—dining at Flicoteaux, where the food is cheap and the bread plentiful—makes the acquaintance of a group of young intellectuals known as "Le Cénacle," a term that generally refers to a reclusive religious house gathered around a single dominant figure. In the novel, that figure is the philosopher-poet Daniel d'Arthez. In real life, Victor Hugo was the focal point of the most famous Cénacle.

The members of Balzac's Cénacle will include some of the most illustrious figures in French literature and science—or at least Balzac will portray them as such, as they weave in and out of his fictional universe. They are a serious, dedicated bunch that never flinches at poverty. "There's no bargain price for achieving greatness," as Daniel explains.[46] Literature is, for them, a sacred calling.

> And so it was that in that frigid attic room, all the finest dreams of friendship were realized. There these brothers, equally strong in their different branches of knowledge, expressed themselves to each other with good faith, holding nothing back, even their worst thoughts, all of them men of immense learning, all of them tried in the crucible of poverty.[47]

But Lucien was not made for hardship. Even a month of privation exhausts his patience. Through Étienne Lousteau, another frequenter of Flicoteaux, Lucien is seduced by the easy world of journalism, that most extreme example of the commercialization and prostitution of the written word.

In the dawning days of the daily newspaper, Balzac was already fully attuned to its dangers as a partisan tool of misinformation and attack. His condemnation of that era's version of social media could easily be echoed today.

THE WISDOM OF THE ROMANTICS

A paper no longer exists in order to enlighten the reader, only to flatter his opinions. Soon enough, all the papers will be amoral, hypocritical, brazen, dishonest, and murderous: they will be the murderers of ideas, of philosophical systems, or men, and they will flourish for doing so.[48]

Lucien succumbs to the allure of journalism in a scene that paints it in its worst but most seductive light. He listens to the veteran newsman speak candidly about their calling, revealing their cynicism, their irreverence, and their manipulation of public opinion, as they sell their well-worn pens to the highest bidder. They make or break books, plays, and actors with no attempt—or perhaps even ability—to appreciate genuine merit. Money, sex, and power are their only gods; if ever there were a profane calling, it is journalism.

"But instead of being seized with horror . . . [Lucien] was intoxicated by and delighted with the witty company among which he found himself. . . . They all seemed superior to the grave, sober men of the Cénacle."[49] And who can blame him? The newspaper is a place of instant payment, false fellowship, and facile good cheer. "The Cénacle, that heavenly constellation of noble intellect, could not hope to compete with so thoroughgoing a temptation."[50] Oscar Wilde will mimic Lucien when he proclaims in *Lady Windermere's Fan*, "I can resist everything except temptation."[51]

Much of the brilliance of *Lost Illusions*, as Wilde recognized, is that the reader's sympathies involuntarily go with Lucien despite his myriad flaws. The journalists are having much more fun than the grimly determined Cénacle, and Lucien proves a master of the game. He throws in his lot with the liberal press and freely does their bidding. Despite initial scruples, he agrees to trash books he admires and praise those he despises. He even does both for the same book in successive unsigned reviews. Lucien makes a specialty of ridiculing aristocrats, particularly the powerful Marquise d'Espard, Mme de Bargeton, and Baron du Châtelet. His malicious wit is both admired and feared, and his articles are a delicious form of revenge. He also takes a mistress, the beautiful actress Coralie, whose career he promotes and into whose luxurious apartment he moves. Together they run up huge debts, and Lucien begins to gamble. But one of the sweetest moments of Lucien's life is when he and Coralie encounter the astonished d'Espard and de Bargeton while riding in an elegant carriage to the admiration of all Paris.

With his vanity and simplicity, however, Lucien is easily lured into a fatal trap. He is courted and invited to the soirees of the nobility, who assure him that if he would only switch sides and write for the royal press, the king would certify his use of the name *de Rubempré* with a patent of nobility. A royal pension and a lucrative marriage would surely follow. "Child that he was, he actually believed he was a deep and cunning politician for concealing his plan so well, and he was counting heavily on governmental largesse to deal with his debts."[52] He falls for every contrived compliment. But his own fall is soon in coming.

Once he makes his move to the royalist press, Lucien is ferociously attacked, along with Coralie, by his onetime liberal friends, who have long harbored jealousy and resentment of his success. They further betray him by publishing, under his name, an antiroyalist article that he had been compelled to write on promise of anonymity. The royalists (who never had any intention of granting him a patent of nobility) now shun him as well. The creditors close in, and everything in their apartment is repossessed as Coralie sinks under the consumption that will soon kill her. Like a stunned child who still expects everyone to love and pet him, Lucien descends into a lethargic but insightful despair.

> He saw that he was the puppet of envious people, grasping and duplicitous people. But who was he in that world that seethed with ambition? A child, running after the pleasures and thrills of vanity, sacrificing everything for them; a poet with no capacity for serious reflection, flitting from one pretty flower to another like a butterfly, with no fixed destination, the slave of circumstances, acting foolishly even when his reasoning was good.[53]

In desperation, Lucien forges his brother-in-law's name to three bills for 1,000 francs each. But the theft can only defer the inevitable. As with Père Goriot, there is barely enough money left to pay for a pauper's funeral for Coralie. Indeed, the poorly attended burial scene at Père Lachaise will parallel that of the old man, but with Lucien rather than Rastignac left alone to contemplate Paris: "Lucien stayed on alone until the sun began to set, up on that height from which he could see Paris spread out below him."[54] Rastignac, from that same vantage, had vowed to conquer Paris; Lucien acknowledges defeat and will slink back to Angoulême just in time to ruin the prospects of brother-in-law David, who has invented a cheaper process for making paper. The debts incurred by Lucien push David into bankruptcy and allow rival printers, the Cointet brothers, to steal his valuable invention by having David arrested for debt.

In a frank letter to Ève, written at her request, Daniel d'Arthez offers a devastating but accurate portrait of his onetime friend.[55] He is "addicted to being admired" and has no willpower "that would allow him to withstand the temptations of sensuality or of his most trivial desires."[56] "He would," Daniel concludes, "sell his soul to the devil tomorrow, if the pact promised him a few years of fame and luxury."[57] In fact, even after all that has happened, Lucien will do exactly that.

Vautrin

Any Romantic work benefits from a good villain, at least since Shakespeare's Lady Macbeth, Milton's Satan, and Byron's famous array of antiheroes. Balzac provides us with one of the best in all of literature. He introduces him as "Jacques Collin, who is, so to speak, the vertebral column whose evil influence stitches together *Père Goriot* with *Lost Illusions*, and *Lost Illusions* with the present work."[58] Jacques Collin also goes by the name of Vautrin, as we knew him in *Père Goriot*, in which Eugène de Rastignac barely escaped his control. Vautrin is also known among his fellow convicts as *trompe-la-mort*, or "death cheater." But when we meet him again at the end of *Lost Illusions*, he is disguised as the Spanish priest and diplomat Father Carlos Herrera.

Vautrin is "heavy and short, with large hands, a thick chest, Herculean strength, and a terrifying expression."[59] But it is the power of his will and his native cunning and audacity that most strike us. He had just recently escaped from the penal colony where he was sent at the end of *Père Goriot*.

Vautrin enters Lucien's life just as Lucien has resolved to end it. Having lost Coralie, met with disgrace in Paris, and destroyed the hopes of his family, Lucien sets off from Angoulême to commit suicide. As a poet, he wishes to end his life poetically.[60] He therefore heads to a charming and picturesque pond nearby, where he will fill his pockets with rocks and drown himself. His resolve is absolute, but then again, this is Lucien, and he is no match for Vautrin, whom he meets along the road, disguised as the Spanish priest. Vautrin is in the area to look up Rastignac, whose family estate is nearby. But when Lucien suddenly appears on the road, Vautrin is immediately struck by his melancholy beauty and descends on him like a hunter on his prey. Rastignac is soon forgotten.

Vautrin has little difficulty in convincing Lucien to defer his project—"I really do have plenty of time to kill myself," Lucien admits[61]—and he divulges his entire life story under the gentle, sympathetic questioning of Father Herrera. Vautrin proffers the same sort of advice that he and the Vicomtesse de Beauséant gave to Rastignac with such good effect. Success is the only criterion for judging an action. Always "project a brilliant exterior,"[62] and never let society peer beneath the surface. Had Lucien kept his relationship with Coralie discreet and stayed focused on the main chance, Vautrin explains, he could easily have married Mme de Bargeton and received the king's ordinance making him Lucien de Rubempré.

"Ensnared by the charm of this cynical discourse, Lucien began to cling more vigorously to life, feeling that a powerful arm had reached out and snatched him from the water's edge."[63] Vautrin's attraction to Lucien, as it was to Rastignac, has a strong erotic component. But it is still remarkably disinterested. Vautrin wants to live through and in Lucien. Echoing Dr. Frankenstein, Vautrin vows, "I want to love my creation, to fashion it, to sculpt it to my own uses—to love the way a father loves his child."[64] Lucien's success will be his success.

In *Lost Illusions*, Lucien is vain, weak, and selfish. But he is not a bad person; indeed, he remains as charmingly innocent as a child even in the face of social iniquity. He admires the writers of the Cénacle, though he cannot match their dedication. He glories in the lively baubles of journalism and the theater. He delights in the game of dress-up that garners him such admiring looks. Most important, he loves Coralie and stands by her even when it is contrary to his own interests.

But Vautrin will allow no such sentimentality to interfere with his grand plans for Lucien's future, which unfold in the third volume of this saga, *Splendeurs et misères des courtisanes*. The otherwise excellent translation I use in text bizarrely gives the title as *Lost Souls*, on the excuse that the French title "loses its subtleties and its tonalities when carried directly into English."[65] Quite the contrary, *The Splendors and Miseries of Courtesans* carries over a critical point in the use of the plural: both Esther and Lucien are courtesans in this book, loved for their beauty but given no independent scope for their wills, except in death.[66] Lucien's cherished ordinance granting him the noble title "Lucien de Rubempré" and Esther's police certificate striking her from the rolls of prostitutes are both empty formalities and yet crucial metaphors.

Prostitution is, for Balzac, a symbol that everything in the modern world has been made into a commodity. But Esther finds purity in her love for Lucien, just as Lucien finds nobility in his own end. Though long lost, both regain their souls by virtue of a shared vision. Lucien's "poetic nature, extreme in all things by its nature, had divined the angel in the prostitute, only brushed by corruption, not actually corrupted: he saw her always white and winged, pure and mysterious—just as she had fashioned herself for him, knowing this is what he wanted."[67]

It is this inner purity that frustrates Vautrin's plans for Lucien to make a grand marriage and rise to an exalted position. Lucien and Esther can be true to each other only by being false to Vautrin. That is what makes this magnificent three-novel series such a pillar of Romanticism, like the love-death in Wagner's *Tristan and Isolde*. The collapse of Romantic ideals is itself the greatest Romantic theme, from Goethe and Rousseau through Stendhal and Pushkin. It reaches its apotheosis in Balzac, highlighted against his realistic descriptions of the social, political, and economic milieu that indifferently crushes Lucien and Esther.

When Vautrin learns of Lucien's death, he utters a terrifying cry and falls on the body, "embracing it with such desperation that the three onlookers trembled at the force and passionate intensity of the embrace."[68] Once again, Wilde captures the essence of the moment:

BALZAC AND THE *COMÉDIE HUMAINE*

One of the greatest tragedies of my life is the death of Lucien de Rubempré. It is a grief from which I have never been able completely to rid myself. It haunts me in my moments of pleasure. I remember it when I laugh.[69]

Acknowledgments

I have not tried to document every source for the ideas in this book. Regardless, my extensive debt to generations of Romantic scholars and translators will be obvious to those in the field. I have tried to list the books and articles on which I most relied, as well as those from which general readers would most benefit, in the section "Suggestions for Further Reading." I also cite there, and in the notes, the many excellent translations from which the quotations in the text are derived.

Darrin Leverette once again worked through the entire manuscript, checking the citations, the facts, and the prose, and saved me from numerous errors. His intelligence, attention to detail, ability to track down obscure sources, and sensitivity to the nuances of language have been indispensable. So, too, was the work of Susan Cohen, who carefully and thoughtfully read each chapter. My longtime assistant, Marilyn Williams, kept me and the entire project on schedule and put the manuscript in its final form. I would also like to thank my copyeditor, Jacqueline Plante Wilson, for her close reading and thoughtful suggestions.

I have dedicated this book to my three children—Baird, Cole, and Camille—who have sustained, encouraged, and inspired me throughout the writing of the books in this series and bring me joy on a daily basis.

Notes

Introduction

1. Michael K. Kellogg, *The Wisdom of the Enlightenment* (Lanham, MD: Prometheus Books, 2022), vii.

2. Isaiah Berlin, *The Roots of Romanticism*, ed. Henry Hardy (Princeton, NJ: Princeton University Press, 1999), 21–22.

3. Quoted in Tim Blanning, *The Romantic Revolution: A History* (New York: Modern Library, 2012), 15.

4. Berlin, *Roots of Romanticism*, 16–18.

5. Ibid., 18.

6. See Michael K. Kellogg, *Three Questions We Never Stop Asking* (Amherst, NY: Prometheus Books, 2010), 72–77.

7. Ludwig Wittgenstein, *Philosophical Investigations*, trans. G. E. M. Anscombe, third edition (New York: Macmillan, 1973), sec. 65.

8. Ibid., sec. 66.

9. Ibid., sec. 67.

10. Michael Ferber, *Romanticism: A Very Short Introduction* (Oxford: Oxford University Press, 2010), 9; see also Berlin, *Roots of Romanticism*, 19.

11. Andrea Wulf, *Magnificent Rebels: The First Romantics and the Invention of the Self* (London: John Murray, 2022), 18.

12. See, for example, Ferber, *Romanticism*, 12; Eric Hobsbawm, *The Age of Revolution, 1789–1848* (New York: Vintage Books, 1996), chap. 14; Berlin, *Roots of Romanticism*, 6, 8.

13. Berlin, *Roots of Romanticism*, 1.

14. Hobsbawm, *Age of Revolution*, 1.

15. Ibid., 53.

16. Quoted in Charles Breunig, *The Age of Revolution and Reaction, 1789–1850* (New York: W. W. Norton, 1970), 255.

17. William Vaughan, *Romanticism and Art* (1978; repr., London: Thames and Hudson, 1994), 13.

18. See Richard Holmes, *The Age of Wonder: How the Romantic Generation Discovered the Beauty and Terror of Science* (New York: Vintage Books, 2010), xvi–xix.

CHAPTER 1

1. Jean-Jacques Rousseau, *The Confessions*, trans. J. M. Cohen (London: Penguin Books, 1953), 65.

2. Jean-Jacques Rousseau, "Discourse on Inequality," in *The Essential Rousseau*, trans. Lowell Bair (1974; repr., New York: New American Library, 1983), 195.

3. Ibid., 150.

4. Rousseau, *Confessions*, 19.

5. Ibid., 20.

6. Ibid., 25–26.

7. Ibid., 52.

8. Ibid., 58.

9. Jean-Jacques Rousseau, *The Reveries of the Solitary Walker*, trans. Charles E. Butterworth (1979; repr., Indianapolis, IN: Hackett, 1992), 29.

10. Rousseau, *Confessions*, 189.

11. Ibid., 215.

12. Ibid.

13. See Michael K. Kellogg, *The Wisdom of the Enlightenment* (Lanham, MD: Prometheus Books, 2022), chap. 7.

14. Rousseau, *Confessions*, 385–86.

15. Quoted in Leo Damrosch, *Jean-Jacques Rousseau: Restless Genius* (Boston: Houghton Mifflin, 2007), 332.

16. Rousseau, *Confessions*, 327.

17. The opera is still available on CD or on Spotify, and the libretto can be found, in French, on Kindle.

18. Rousseau, *Confessions*, 25.

19. Jean-Jacques Rousseau, *The Social Contract*, in *Essential Rousseau*, 8.

20. Rousseau, *Discourse on Inequality*, in *Essential Rousseau*, 180.

21. Ibid., 182.

22. Ibid., 196.

23. Ibid., 144.

24. Ibid., 173.

25. Ibid., 165.

26. Ibid., 164.

27. Jean-Jacques Rousseau, *Emile: or On Education*, trans. Allan Bloom (New York: Basic Books, 1979), 84.

28. Rousseau, *Discourse on Inequality*, in *Essential Rousseau*, 141.

29. Ibid., 173.

30. Ibid., 150.

31. Ibid., 141.

32. Rousseau, *Social Contract*, in *Essential Rousseau*, 9.

33. Ibid.

34. Ibid., 13.

35. Ibid., 36.

36. Ibid., 37.

NOTES

37. Quoted in Damrosch, *Restless Genius*, 347.

38. Rousseau, *Social Contract*, in *Essential Rousseau*, 17.

39. Ibid., 20.

40. Ibid., 17.

41. Ibid., 22.

42. Ibid., 31.

43. Ibid., 28.

44. Ibid., 19.

45. Ibid., 27.

46. Ibid., 35.

47. Ibid.

48. Ibid., 58.

49. Ibid., 35.

50. Ibid., 36.

51. Ibid., 38.

52. Rousseau, *Emile*, 120.

53. Rousseau, *Social Contract*, in *Essential Rousseau*, 30.

54. Jean Starobinski, *Jean-Jacques Rousseau: Transparency and Obstruction*, trans. Arthur Goldhammer (Chicago: University of Chicago Press, 1988), 121.

55. See Michael K. Kellogg, *The Wisdom of the Middle Ages* (Amherst, NY: Prometheus Books, 2016), chap. 5.

56. Jean-Jacques Rousseau, *La Nouvelle Héloïse: Julie, or the New Eloise*, trans. Judith H. McDowell (University Park: Pennsylvania State University Press, 1987), Pt. I, letter 11, 47.

57. Ibid., Pt. I, letter 2, 29.

58. Ibid., Pt. I, letter 26, 75.

59. Ibid., Pt. I, letter 23, 65.

60. Starobinski, *Transparency and Obstruction*, 83.

61. Rousseau, *La Nouvelle Héloïse*, Pt. II, letter 2, 163.

62. Ibid., Pt. I, letter 26, 72.

63. Ibid., Pt. II, letter 7, 180.

64. Jean-Jacques Rousseau, *Julie, or the New Heloise*, trans. Philip Stewart and Jean Vaché (Lebanon, NH: Dartmouth College Press, 1997), Pt. III, letter 18, 282-83.

65. Rousseau, *La Nouvelle Héloïse*, Pt. I, letter 3, 31.

66. Ibid., Pt. I, letter 21, 61.

67. Ibid., Pt. II, letter 7, 181.

68. Ibid., Pt. II, letter 16, 201.

69. Ibid., Pt. V, letter 11, 369-70.

70. Ibid., Pt. VI, letter 3, 391.

71. Starobinski, *Transparency and Obstruction*, 93.

72. See Judith N. Shklar, "Rousseau's Images of Authority," in *The Cambridge Companion to Rousseau*, ed. Patrick Riley (Cambridge: Cambridge University Press, 2001), 156-57.

73. Rousseau, *La Nouvelle Héloïse*, Pt. III, letter 20, 260.

The Wisdom of the Romantics

74. Ibid., Pt. VI, letter 12, 405.

75. Ibid.

76. Donald M. Frame, trans., *The Complete Essays of Montaigne* (Stanford, CA: Stanford University Press, 1965), 3.2, 611.

77. Rousseau, *Confessions*, 17.

78. Giovanni Pico della Mirandola, *On the Dignity of Man*, trans. Charles Glenn Wallis (1965; repr., Indianapolis, IN: Hackett, 1998), 5.

79. Rousseau, *Confessions*, 262.

80. Quoted in Damrosch, *Restless Genius*, 438.

81. Rousseau, *Confessions*, 262.

82. Ibid., 17, 65.

83. Ibid., 17.

84. Ibid., 597–98.

85. James Boswell, *The Life of Samuel Johnson* (New York: Heritage, 1963), 1:355.

86. Rousseau, *Confessions*, 17.

87. Ibid.

88. Ibid., 23.

89. Damrosch, *Restless Genius*, 58.

90. Rousseau, *Confessions*, 19.

91. Ibid., 30.

92. Ibid.

93. Ibid., 31.

94. Ibid., 136.

95. See Jean Starobinski, "Windows: From Rousseau to Baudelaire," *Hudson Review* 40, no. 4 (Winter 1988): 551–60.

96. Rousseau, *Confessions*, 145.

97. Ibid.

98. Ibid., 149.

99. Ibid., 232.

100. Ibid., 247.

101. Ibid., 87.

102. Ibid., 88.

103. Ibid., 128.

104. Ibid., 130.

105. Ibid.

106. Ibid., 89.

107. Rousseau, *Reveries of the Solitary Walker*, 123; see also Rousseau, *Confessions*, 332–35.

108. Rousseau, *Confessions*, 248.

109. Ibid., 249.

110. Ibid., 250.

111. Ibid., 257.

112. Ibid., 50.

113. Ibid., 600.

Notes

114. Ibid., 263.
115. Ibid.
116. Ibid.
117. Ibid., 262.
118. See Starobinski, *Transparency and Obstruction*, 77–79.
119. Rousseau, *Reveries of the Solitary Walker*, 6–7.
120. Ibid., 5.
121. Ibid.
122. See Michael K. Kellogg, *The Roman Search for Wisdom* (Amherst, NY: Prometheus Books, 2014), 75, 104–5.
123. Rousseau, *Reveries of the Solitary Walker*, 68.
124. Ibid.
125. Ibid., 68–69.
126. Ibid., 69.
127. Ibid., 98, 103.
128. Ibid., 103.
129. Ibid., 69.

Chapter 2

1. Quoted in Jeremy Adler, *Johann Wolfgang von Goethe* (London: Reaktion Books, 2020), 7.
2. Quoted in Ritchie Robertson, *Goethe: A Very Short Introduction* (Oxford: Oxford University Press, 2016), xiii.
3. John Milton, *Paradise Lost*, ed. Gordon Teskey (New York: W. W. Norton, 2005), 11. 349–50.
4. Johann Wolfgang von Goethe, *Faust: A Tragedy*, ed. Cyrus Hamlin, trans. Walter Arndt, second edition (New York: W. W. Norton, 2001), l. 6272.
5. *Pascal's "Pensées,"* trans. W. F. Trotter (New York: E. P. Dutton, 1958), no. 139, 39.
6. *Sturm und Drang* was the name of a 1777 play by Friedrich Maximilian Klinger.
7. Adler, *Goethe*, 134.
8. See Michael K. Kellogg, *The Roman Search for Wisdom* (Amherst, NY: Prometheus Books, 2014), 167–73.
9. Johann Peter Eckermann, *Conversations with Goethe*, trans. Gisela C. O'Brien (New York: Frederick Ungar, 1964), 154.
10. Quoted in Robertson, *Short Introduction*, 70.
11. Johann Peter Eckermann, *Conversations with Goethe*, ed. J. K. Moorhead, trans. John Oxenford (1930; repr., London: Dent, 1971), 157.
12. Peter Boerner, *Goethe*, trans. Nancy Boerner (London: Haus, 2013), 91.
13. Eckermann, *Conversations with Goethe*, 245–46 (Oxenford translation).
14. Quoted in Robertson, *Short Introduction*, 82.
15. Eckermann, *Conversations with Goethe*, 94 (O'Brien translation).
16. Johann Wolfgang von Goethe, *The Sufferings of Young Werther*, ed. and trans. Stanley Corngold (New York: W. W. Norton, 2013), 104–5.

17. See, for example, Malcolm Gladwell, "Something Borrowed," *New Yorker*, November 14, 2004; Robert Kolker, "Who Is the Bad Art Friend?" *New York Times Magazine*, October 5, 2021.

18. Quoted in Johann Wolfgang von Goethe, *The Sorrows of Young Werther*, trans. Victor Lange (New York: Holt, Rinehart, 1971), ix.

19. Goethe, *Sufferings of Young Werther*, 116.

20. Ibid., 3.

21. Oscar Wilde, *The Importance of Being Earnest*, ed. Russell Jackson (1980; repr., London: A & C Black, 2004), 1.3-6.

22. Goethe, *Sufferings of Young Werther*, 3.

23. Ibid., 13.

24. Ibid., 66.

25. Ibid., 36.

26. Ibid., 9.

27. Ibid., 58.

28. Ibid., 3.

29. Ibid.

30. David E. Wellbery, "Afterword to *The Sorrows of Young Werther*," in *Sufferings of Young Werther*, 185.

31. Goethe, *Sorrows of Young Werther*, 49.

32. Ibid.

33. Excerpt from *A Lover's Discourse*, by Roland Barthes, in *Sufferings of Young Werther*, 148.

34. Goethe, *Sorrows of Young Werther*, 12.

35. Ibid., 14.

36. Ibid., 19.

37. Excerpt from "*Werther*, Goethe, and the Formation of Modern Subjectivity," by Dirk von Petersdorff, in *Sufferings of Young Werther*, 202.

38. Goethe, *Sorrows of Young Werther*, 102.

39. Ibid., 76.

40. Ibid., 118.

41. Ibid., 120.

42. Ibid., 124.

43. Hans Rudolf Vaget, "Werther, the Undead," in *Sufferings of Young Werther*, 188-89.

44. Goethe, *Sorrows of Young Werther*, 128.

45. Wellbery, "Afterword," in *Sufferings of Young Werther*, 185; von Petersdorff, "*Werther*, Goethe," in *Sufferings of Young Werther*, 204.

46. Goethe, *Sorrows of Young Werther*, 86.

47. Excerpt from *My Life: Poetry and Truth*, by Johann Wolfgang von Goethe, in *Sufferings of Young Werther*, 118.

48. Ibid.

49. Goethe, *Sorrows of Young Werther*, 95.

50. Ian Watt, *Myths of Modern Individualism: Faust, Don Quixote, Don Juan, Robinson Crusoe* (Cambridge: Cambridge University Press, 1997).

Notes

51. Harold Bloom, *The Western Canon: The Books and School of the Ages* (New York: Riverhead Books, 1995), 194.

52. Excerpt from *The Philosophy of Art*, by Friedrich Schelling, in *Faust*, 556.

53. Excerpt from *The Romantic School*, by Heinrich Heine, in *Faust*, 563.

54. Christopher Marlowe, prologue to *Doctor Faustus*, in *The Complete Plays of Christopher Marlowe*, ed. Irving Ribner (New York: Odyssey, 1963).

55. Ibid., 1.3.90–95.

56. Ibid., 2.1.32.

57. Ibid., 5.1.99–100.

58. Ibid., 5.2.133–87.

59. Johann Wolfgang von Goethe, *Faust, Part I*, trans. David Luke (Oxford: Oxford University Press, 2008), 5.1066–67.

60. Ibid., 4.382–84.

61. Ibid., 4.501–9.

62. Ibid., 4.652–55.

63. Ibid., 5.1116–17.

64. Ibid., 4.769–70.

65. Ibid., 4.772–74.

66. Ibid., 7.1604–6.

67. Ibid., 6.1338.

68. Ibid., 7.1765–75.

69. Ibid., 7.1780–84.

70. Ibid., 7.1785.

71. See Michael K. Kellogg, *The Wisdom of the Enlightenment* (Lanham, MD: Prometheus Books, 2022), chap. 4.

72. Goethe, *Faust, Part I*, 8.2160–67.

73. Ibid., 9.2354–55.

74. Ibid., 9.2603–4.

75. Ibid., 14.3054.

76. Ibid., 14.3055.

77. Ibid., 15.3188–94.

78. Ibid., 26.10.

79. Ibid., 26.45.

80. Ibid., 28.4607–9.

81. Ibid., 28.4612.

82. Johann Wolfgang von Goethe, *Faust, Part II*, trans. David Luke (Oxford: Oxford University Press, 2008), 1.1.4622–25.

83. Ibid., 1.1.4679–85.

84. Ibid., 1.1.4725–27.

85. Goethe, *Faust, Part I*, 6.1379–80.

86. Goethe, *Faust, Part II*, 1.2.4893–94.

87. Ibid., 1.4.6084.

88. Ibid., 1.4.6125.

89. Ibid., 1.5.6197–98.

The Wisdom of the Romantics

90. Ibid., 1.5.6201.

91. Ibid., 1.5.6211–14.

92. Ibid., 1.7.6431–32.

93. Ibid., 1.7.6553.

94. Eckermann, *Conversations with Goethe*, 384–85 (Oxenford translation).

95. Goethe, *Faust, Part II*, 2.10.7433.

96. Ibid., 2.9.6925–26.

97. Ibid., 2.10.7071–77.

98. Ibid., 2.10.7444–45.

99. Ibid., 3.13.9625–26. Goethe equated Euphorion with the English poet George Gordon (Lord Byron), who died in Greece at the age of thirty-six during the fight for Greek independence from the Ottoman Empire. Goethe, *Faust*, 531.

100. Goethe, *Faust, Part II*, 3.13.9940.

101. Ibid., 3.13.9941–44.

102. Ibid., 4.14.10201.

103. Ibid., 4.14.10228–31.

104. Ibid., 5.17.11116.

105. Ibid., 5.17.11092–97.

106. See Kellogg, *Roman Search for Wisdom*, 190.

107. Ovid, *Metamorphoses*, trans. Charles Martin (New York: W. W. Norton, 2005), 8.997–99.

108. Goethe, *Faust, Part II*, 5.18.11239–42.

109. Ibid., 5.19.11382.

110. Ibid., 5.19.11371–72.

111. Ibid., 5.17.11137.

112. Ibid., 1.5.6272–74.

113. Ibid., 5.21.11578–82.

114. Ibid., 5.21.11583.

115. Ibid., 5.20.11433–52.

116. Ibid., 5.23.11938–39.

117. Ibid., 5.21.11597–603.

118. William Shakespeare, *Macbeth*, 5.5.29–31, https://shakespeare.folger.edu/shakespeares-works/macbeth/entire-play/.

119. Bloom, *Western Canon*, 206.

120. Eckermann, *Conversations with Goethe*, 414 (Oxenford translation).

121. Quoted in Bloom, *Western Canon*, 194.

Chapter 3

1. Mark Twain, *A Connecticut Yankee in King Arthur's Court* (San Francisco, CA: Chandler, 1963), 280.

2. Frederick Beiser, *Hegel* (New York: Routledge, 2005), 1.

3. William Wallace, trans., *The Logic of Hegel: Translated from the Encyclopaedia of the Philosophical Sciences*, second edition (Oxford: Clarendon, 1892), sec. 13.

Notes

4. See Michael K. Kellogg, *The Wisdom of the Enlightenment* (Lanham, MD: Prometheus Books, 2022), chap. 10.

5. See Terry Pinkard, *Hegel: A Biography* (Cambridge: Cambridge University Press, 2000), 101.

6. Quoted in Peter Singer, *Hegel: A Very Short Introduction* (Oxford: Oxford University Press, 2001), 2.

7. Quoted in Norman Davies, *Europe: A History* (Oxford: Oxford University Press, 1996), 687.

8. G. W. F. Hegel, *Phenomenology of Spirit*, trans. A. V. Miller (Oxford: Oxford University Press, 1977), sec. 2.

9. Ibid., sec. 4.

10. Ibid., sec. 2.

11. Kellogg, *Wisdom of the Enlightenment*, chap. 10.

12. Immanuel Kant, *Critique of Pure Reason*, trans. Norman Kemp Smith, unabridged edition (New York: St. Martin's, 1965), A51, B75.

13. Ibid., Bxviii.

14. See P. F. Strawson, *The Bounds of Sense: An Essay on Kant's "Critique of Pure Reason"* (London: Routledge, 1975). The title is a quadruple pun, since "sense" covers both experience and meaning, and "bounds" covers both the limits and the leaps of speculative thought.

15. Quoted in Ivan Soll, *An Introduction to Hegel's Metaphysics* (Chicago: University of Chicago Press, 1969), 66.

16. G. W. F. Hegel, *Encyclopedia of the Philosophical Sciences in Basic Outline, Part I: Science of Logic*, ed. and trans. Klaus Brinkmann and Daniel O. Dahlstrom (Cambridge: Cambridge University Press, 2015), sec. 10.

17. Ibid.

18. Ibid.

19. Ibid., sec. 22.

20. Plato, *Republic*, 511b, trans. G. M. A. Grube, rev. C. D. C. Reeve, in *Complete Works*, edition John M. Cooper, 4 vols. (Norwalk, CT: Easton, 2001), 3:971. For a fuller explanation of Plato's thinking, see Michael K. Kellogg, *Three Questions We Never Stop Asking* (Amherst, NY: Prometheus Books, 2010), chap. 1.

21. Aristotle, *Physics*, 2.3, trans. R. P. Hardie and R. K. Gaye, in *The Complete Works of Aristotle: The Revised Oxford Translation*, ed. Jonathan Barnes (Princeton, NJ: Princeton University Press, 1984), 1:332–34; Aristotle, *Metaphysics*, 5.2, trans. W. D. Ross, in Barnes, *Complete Works*, 2:1600-601.

22. Aristotle, *Physics*, 2.3, in Barnes, *Complete Works*, 1:332-34; Aristotle, *Metaphysics*, 5.2, in Barnes, *Complete Works*, 2:1600-601.

23. Hegel, *Science of Logic*, sec. 12.

24. Ibid., sec. 87.

25. Ibid., sec. 88.

26. Ibid.

27. Ibid., sec. 82.

28. Hegel, *Phenomenology*, sec. 177.

The Wisdom of the Romantics

29. Hegel, *Science of Logic*, sec. 81.

30. Ibid., sec. 82.

31. Quoted in Michael Forster, "Hegel's Dialectical Method," in *The Cambridge Companion to Hegel*, ed. Frederick C. Beiser (Cambridge: Cambridge University Press, 1993), 133.

32. Hegel, *Science of Logic*, sec. 6.

33. Thomas E. Wartenberg, "Hegel's Idealism: The Logic of Conceptuality," in Beiser, *Cambridge Companion to Hegel*, 106.

34. Ludwig Wittgenstein, *Philosophical Investigations*, trans. G. E. M. Anscombe, third edition (New York: Macmillan, 1973), sec. 309.

35. Ibid., sec. 89.

36. Hegel, *Science of Logic*, sec. 24.

37. See Robert Stern, *The Routledge Guidebook to Hegel's "Phenomenology of Spirit"* (New York: Routledge, 2013), 14.

38. Hegel, *Science of Logic*, sec. 32.

39. Ibid.

40. Marcus Aurelius, *Meditations*, trans. Maxwell Staniforth (1964; repr., London: Folio Society, 2002), 6.10.

41. Quoted in Walter Kaufmann, *Hegel: Reinterpretation, Texts, and Commentary* (Garden City, NY: Doubleday, 1965), 365.

42. Hegel, *Phenomenology*, sec. 91.

43. Ibid., sec. 91.

44. Ibid., sec. 92.

45. Ibid., sec. 98.

46. Ibid.

47. Ibid., sec. 110.

48. Ibid., sec. 102.

49. Ibid.

50. See Kellogg, *Three Questions*, 77–85.

51. Hegel, *Phenomenology*, sec. 109.

52. Ibid., sec. 96.

53. Ibid., sec. 110.

54. Ibid.

55. Ibid., sec. 111.

56. Ibid.

57. Ibid., sec. 112.

58. Ibid., sec. 113.

59. Ibid., sec. 122.

60. Ibid., sec. 127.

61. Ibid., sec. 129.

62. Ibid., sec. 173.

63. Ibid., sec. 186.

64. Ibid., sec. 178.

65. Ibid., sec. 179.

Notes

66. Ibid., sec. 191.
67. Ibid., secs. 193, 195.
68. Ibid., secs. 178–96.
69. Ibid., sec. 177.
70. Ibid., sec. 199.
71. Ibid.
72. Quoted in Singer, *Hegel*, 104.
73. Hegel, *Science of Logic*, sec. 216.
74. Hegel, *Phenomenology*, sec. 438.
75. Ibid., sec. 110.
76. Hegel, *Science of Logic*, sec. 214.
77. Hegel, *Phenomenology*, sec. 654.
78. Ibid., sec. 759.
79. Hegel, *Science of Logic*, sec. 214.
80. Quoted in Soll, *Hegel's Metaphysics*, 72.
81. Hegel, *Science of Logic*, sec. 213.
82. Ibid.
83. Wallace, *Logic of Hegel*, sec. 13.
84. J. N. Findlay, foreword to *Phenomenology*, xviii.
85. T. S. Eliot, "Little Gidding," www.columbia.edu/itc/history/winter/w3206/edit/tseliotlittlegidding.html.

Chapter 4

1. William Wordsworth, preface to *Lyrical Ballads, with Other Poems*, in *Wordsworth's Poetry and Prose*, ed. Nicholas Halmi (New York: W. W. Norton, 2013), 85.
2. William Wordsworth, advertisement to *Lyrical Ballads, with a Few Other Poems*, in *Poetry and Prose*, 8.
3. William Wordsworth, *The Prelude*, 10.692–93, in *Poetry and Prose*, 337.
4. William Wordsworth, "It is a beauteous Evening, calm and free," in *Poetry and Prose*, 404.
5. Samuel Taylor Coleridge, "Frost at Midnight," ll. 44–49, in *The Norton Anthology of Poetry*, ed. Alexander W. Allison et al., third edition (New York: W. W. Norton, 1983), 566–67.
6. Samuel Taylor Coleridge, "Dejection: An Ode," ll. 21–24, in *Norton Anthology*, 582.
7. The poem is available in its original form in the *Norton Anthology of Poetry*.
8. Wordsworth, preface to *Lyrical Ballads*, in *Poetry and Prose*, 92.
9. John Milton, *Paradise Lost*, ed. Gordon Teskey (New York: W. W. Norton, 2005), 12.645–49.
10. Wordsworth, *Prelude*, 1.15, in *Poetry and Prose*, 168.
11. William Wordsworth, "My heart leaps up," ll. 7–9, in *Poetry and Prose*, 418.
12. William Wordsworth, "Surprised by joy," in *Poetry and Prose*, 528.
13. See Arthur Miller, *Death of a Salesman* (Oxford: Heinemann, 1994), 38–39 (Linda Loman: "I don't say he's a great man. Willy Loman never made a lot of money. His name was never in the paper. He's not the finest character that ever lived. But he's a human

being, and a terrible thing is happening to him. So attention must be paid. He's not to be allowed to fall into his grave like an old dog. Attention, attention must be finally paid to such a person").

14. Wordsworth, preface to *Lyrical Ballads*, in *Poetry and Prose*, 92.

15. Ibid.

16. Ibid., 78.

17. Ibid., 78–79.

18. Ibid., 78.

19. Ibid., 77.

20. Ibid., 79.

21. Ibid., 80.

22. Ibid., 82.

23. Ibid., 87.

24. Ibid., 86–87.

25. William Wordsworth, "The Ruined Cottage," ll. 68–79, in *Norton Anthology*, 527.

26. Ibid., ll. 211–12, in *Norton Anthology*, 530.

27. Ibid., ll. 130–32, in *Norton Anthology*, 528.

28. Ibid., ll. 95–96, in *Norton Anthology*, 528.

29. Ibid., ll. 134–37, in *Norton Anthology*, 528–29.

30. Ibid., ll. 151–53, in *Norton Anthology*, 529.

31. Ibid., ll. 264–73, in *Norton Anthology*, 531.

32. Harold Bloom, *The Western Canon: The Books and School of the Ages* (New York: Harcourt Brace, 1993), 247.

33. Wordsworth, "Ruined Cottage," l. 410, in *Norton Anthology*, 534.

34. Ibid., l. 447, in *Norton Anthology*, 534.

35. Ibid., ll. 491–92, in *Norton Anthology*, 535.

36. Ibid., ll. 221–26, in *Norton Anthology*, 530.

37. Ibid., ll. 227–31, in *Norton Anthology*, 530.

38. William Wordsworth, "The Old Cumberland Beggar," ll. 12–21, in *Selected Poems*, ed. John O. Hayden (London: Penguin Books, 1994), 72.

39. Ibid., ll. 67–73, in *Selected Poems*, 73–74.

40. Ibid., ll. 73–79, in *Selected Poems*, 74.

41. Ibid., l. 83, in *Selected Poems*, 74.

42. Ibid., ll. 114–16, in *Selected Poems*, 75.

43. Ibid., ll. 148–54, in *Selected Poems*, 76.

44. Harold Bloom, ed., *William Wordsworth* (New York: Chelsea House, 1985), 4.

45. William Wordsworth, "Resolution and Independence," ll. 108–12, in *Poetry and Prose*, 400.

46. William Wordsworth, "Michael, a Pastoral Poem," ll. 61–79, in *Poetry and Prose*, 147.

47. Ibid., ll. 154–57, in *Poetry and Prose*, 149.

48. Ibid., ll. 167–68, in *Poetry and Prose*, 149.

49. Ibid., l. 213, in *Poetry and Prose*, 150.

50. Ibid., ll. 223–24, in *Poetry and Prose*, 150.

51. Ibid., l. 412, in *Poetry and Prose*, 155.

NOTES

52. Ibid., ll. 417–27, in *Poetry and Prose*, 155.

53. Excerpt from *Romanticism and the Forms of Ruin: Wordsworth, Coleridge, the Modalities of Fragmentation*, by Thomas McFarland, in Bloom, *Wordsworth*, 159.

54. Wordsworth, "Michael," l. 431, in *Poetry and Prose*, 155.

55. Ibid., ll. 451–56, in *Poetry and Prose*, 156.

56. Ibid., ll. 457–75, in *Poetry and Prose*, 156.

57. William Wordsworth, "Ode: Intimations of Immortality," l. 205, in *Norton Anthology*, 555.

58. Quoted in Susan J. Wolfson, "Poem upon the Wye," in *The Oxford Handbook of William Wordsworth*, ed. Richard Gravil and Daniel Robinson (Oxford: Oxford University Press, 2018), 193.

59. William Wordsworth, "Lines Written a Few Miles above Tintern Abbey, on Revisiting the Banks of the Wye during a Tour," ll. 24–50, in *Poetry and Prose*, 66–67.

60. Ibid., ll. 134–35, in *Poetry and Prose*, 69.

61. Ibid., ll. 75, 82–83, in *Poetry and Prose*, 68.

62. Ibid., ll. 85–86, in *Poetry and Prose*, 68.

63. Ibid., ll. 89–94, in *Poetry and Prose*, 68.

64. Ibid., l. 92, in *Poetry and Prose*, 68.

65. Ibid., ll. 110–12, in *Poetry and Prose*, 68–69.

66. Ibid., ll. 96–97, in *Poetry and Prose*, 68.

67. Ibid., ll. 94–100, in *Poetry and Prose*, 68.

68. Ibid., ll. 101–3, in *Poetry and Prose*, 68.

69. "Tintern Abbey" was too early to have been influenced directly by Hegel, whose *Phenomenology* was not published until 1807. But Wordsworth, through Coleridge, was fully aware of the stirrings of the post-Kantian German idealism discussed in the previous chapter.

70. Wordsworth, "Tintern Abbey," ll. 64–64, in *Poetry and Prose*, 67.

71. Ibid., l. 64, in *Poetry and Prose*, 67.

72. Ibid., ll. 117–20, in *Poetry and Prose*, 69.

73. Coleridge's last stanza, directed at his sleeping baby, reads:

> Therefore all seasons shall be sweet to thee,
> Whether the summer clothe the general earth
> With greenness, or the redbreast sit and sing
> Betwixt the tufts of snow on the bare branch
> Of mossy apple tree, while the night thatch
> Smokes in the sun-thaw; whether the eave-drops fall
> Heard only in the trances of the blast,
> Or if the secret ministry of frost
> Shall hang them up in silent icicles,
> Quietly shining to the quiet Moon.

Coleridge, "Frost at Midnight," ll. 65–74, in *Norton Anthology*, 567.

74. Wordsworth, "Tintern Abbey," ll. 135–43, in *Poetry and Prose*, 69.

75. Ibid., l. 146, in *Poetry and Prose*, 69.

76. Ibid., ll. 155–56, in *Poetry and Prose*, 70.

77. Ibid., ll. 156–60, in *Poetry and Prose*, 70.

78. Wordsworth, "Ode," ll. 1–9, in *Norton Anthology*, 551–52.

79. Ibid., ll. 17–18, in *Norton Anthology*, 552.

80. Ibid., l. 23, in *Norton Anthology*, 552.

81. See, for example, Lionel Trilling, *The Liberal Imagination* (New York: Harcourt Brace, 1979), 132.

82. Wordsworth, "Resolution and Independence," ll. 77, 142–47, in *Poetry and Prose*, 399, 401.

83. Wordsworth, "Ode," l. 26, in *Norton Anthology*, 552.

84. Ibid., ll. 32–33, in *Norton Anthology*, 552.

85. Ibid., ll. 37–38, in *Norton Anthology*, 552.

86. T. S. Eliot, "The Love Song of J. Alfred Prufrock," ll. 124–25, https://www.bartleby.com/198/1.html.

87. Wordsworth, "Ode," ll. 57–58, in *Norton Anthology*, 552.

88. Ibid., ll. 60–67, in *Norton Anthology*, 552–53.

89. Ibid., ll. 68–78, in *Norton Anthology*, 553.

90. Ibid., l. 100, in *Norton Anthology*, 553.

91. Ibid., ll. 128–30, in *Norton Anthology*, 554.

92. William Shakespeare, *The Merchant of Venice*, 5.1.62–73, https://shakespeare.folger.edu/shakespeares-works/the-merchant-of-venice/entire-play/.

93. Wordsworth, "Ode," l. 183, in *Norton Anthology*, 555.

94. Ibid., l. 136, in *Norton Anthology*, 554.

95. Ibid., ll. 156–58, in *Norton Anthology*, 554.

96. Ibid., ll. 179–88, in *Norton Anthology*, 555.

97. Quoted in Halmi, *Poetry and Prose*, 433.

98. Wordsworth, "Ode," l. 200, in *Norton Anthology*, 555.

99. Ibid., ll. 202–5, in *Norton Anthology*, 555.

100. Wordsworth, *Prelude*, 1.61–63, in *Poetry and Prose*, 169.

101. Ibid., 1.85–86, in *Poetry and Prose*, 169.

102. Ibid., 1.266–74, in *Poetry and Prose*, 174.

103. Ibid., 1.274–88, 1.308–9, in *Poetry and Prose*, 174–75.

104. Ibid., 2.263–64, in *Poetry and Prose*, 189–90.

105. Ibid., 2.232, in *Poetry and Prose*, 189.

106. Ibid., 1.357–60, in *Poetry and Prose*, 176.

107. Ibid., 1.354–58, in *Poetry and Prose*, 176.

108. Ibid., 2.208–209, 2.211–12, in *Poetry and Prose*, 188.

109. Ibid., 11.258–65, in *Poetry and Prose*, 353.

110. Martin Heidegger, *Being and Time*, trans. John Macquarrie and Edward Robinson (San Francisco, CA: HarperSanFrancisco, 1962), 26.

111. Wordsworth, *Prelude*, 1.616, in *Poetry and Prose*, 182.

112. Ibid., 5.619–29, in *Poetry and Prose*, 238.

Notes

113. Quoted in Leo Damrosch, *Jean-Jacques Rousseau: Restless Genius* (Boston: Houghton Mifflin, 2007), 438.

114. Wordsworth, *Prelude*, 11.274–79, in *Poetry and Prose*, 353.

115. Ibid., 1.391–92, in *Poetry and Prose*, 176.

116. Ibid., 1.413–15, in *Poetry and Prose*, 177.

117. Ibid., 1.422–23, in *Poetry and Prose*, 177.

118. Ibid., 1.463–67, in *Poetry and Prose*, 178.

119. Ibid., 1.477–92, in *Poetry and Prose*, 178–79.

120. Ibid., 11.348–50, in *Poetry and Prose*, 355.

121. Ibid., 11.367–68, in *Poetry and Prose*, 356.

122. Ibid., 11.372, in *Poetry and Prose*, 356.

123. Ibid., 6.541, in *Poetry and Prose*, 253.

124. Ibid., 2.419–24, in *Poetry and Prose*, 193.

125. Ibid., 2.376–77, in *Poetry and Prose*, 192.

126. Ibid., 13.71–73, in *Poetry and Prose*, 367.

127. Jonathan Roberts, "Wordsworth on Religious Experience," in Gravil and Robinson, *Oxford Handbook*, 703.

128. Wordsworth, *Prelude*, 1.431–34, in *Poetry and Prose*, 177–78.

129. Ibid., 8.757–59, in *Poetry and Prose*, 295.

130. Ibid., 13.152, in *Poetry and Prose*, 370.

131. Ibid., 1.440–44, in *Poetry and Prose*, 178.

CHAPTER 5

1. Austen to Fanny Knight, March 23, 1817, in Sarah Chauncey Woolsey, *Letters of Jane Austen* (Boston: Little, Brown, 1908), 209.

2. Quoted in Jane Austen, *Pride and Prejudice*, ed. Donald Gray and Mary A. Favret, fourth edition (New York: W. W. Norton, 2016), 401.

3. Ibid., 243.

4. David Nokes, *Jane Austen: A Life* (New York: Farrar, Straus and Giroux, 1997), 43.

5. Jane Austen, *Emma*, ed. George Justice, fourth edition (New York: W. W. Norton, 2012), 70.

6. Nokes, *Jane Austen*, 86.

7. Jane Austen, *Northanger Abbey*, ed. Susan Fraiman (New York: W. W. Norton, 2004), 22.

8. Ibid., 22–23.

9. Quoted in Claire Tomalin, *Jane Austen: A Life* (New York: Vintage Books, 1999), 120.

10. Quoted in Jan Fergus, *Jane Austen: A Literary Life* (New York: St. Martin's, 1991), 77.

11. Austen, *Northanger Abbey*, 5.

12. Ibid., 6.

13. Ibid.

14. Ibid., 7.

15. Ibid., 9.

16. Ibid., 6.

17. Ibid., 51.
18. Ibid.
19. Ibid., 83.
20. Ibid., 99.
21. Ibid., 141.
22. Ibid., 149.
23. Ibid., 150.
24. Ibid., 142.
25. Ibid.
26. Ibid., 44.
27. Ibid., 63.
28. Ibid.
29. Ibid., 53, 90.
30. Ibid., 141–42.
31. Ibid., 170.
32. Ibid., 145.
33. Ibid., 17.
34. Ibid., 168.

35. Jane Austen, *Sense and Sensibility*, ed. Claudia L. Johnson (New York: W. W. Norton, 2002), 35; see Alice Chandler, "'A Pair of Fine Eyes': Jane Austen's Treatment of Sex," in *Jane Austen*, ed. Harold Bloom (New York: Chelsea House, 1986), 36.

36. Austen, *Sense and Sensibility*, 89.

37. Ibid., 30.

38. Tony Tanner, *Jane Austen* (Cambridge, MA: Harvard University Press, 1986), 77.

39. Ruth Roberts, "*Sense and Sensibility*, or Growing up Dichotomous," in Bloom, *Jane Austen*, 47.

40. Austen, *Sense and Sensibility*, 228.

41. Ibid., 233.
42. Ibid., 8.
43. Ibid., 134.
44. Ibid., 131.
45. Ibid., 100.
46. Ibid., 184.
47. Ibid., 268.
48. Ibid., 267.
49. Ibid., 268.
50. Ibid., 266.
51. Quoted in Tanner, *Jane Austen*, 137.
52. Ibid., 105.
53. Austen, *Emma*, 298.
54. Austen, *Pride and Prejudice*, 243.
55. Ibid., 9.
56. Ibid., 61.
57. See Tanner, *Jane Austen*, 114.

Notes

58. Austen, *Pride and Prejudice*, 17.
59. Ibid., 260.
60. Ibid., 78.
61. Ibid., 77.
62. Ibid.
63. Ibid., 89–90.
64. Ibid., 90.
65. Ibid., 105.
66. Ibid., 130.
67. Ibid., 131, 133.
68. Ibid., 134.
69. Ibid., 179.
70. Ibid., 178.
71. Ibid., 180.
72. Ibid., 255.
73. Ibid., 166.
74. Ibid., 189.
75. Ibid., 212.
76. Ibid., 189–90.
77. Jane Austen, *Mansfield Park*, ed. Claudia L. Johnson (New York: W. W. Norton, 1998), 68.
78. C. S. Lewis, "A Note on Jane Austen," in *Selected Literary Essays*, ed. Walter Hooper (New York: Cambridge University Press, 2013), 182.
79. Excerpt from *The Opposing Self: Nine Essays in Criticism*, by Lionel Trilling, in Austen, *Mansfield* Park, 425.
80. Kingsley Amis, "What Became of Jane Austen?" in *Jane Austen: A Collection of Critical Essays*, ed. Ian Watt (Englewood Cliffs, NJ: Prentice-Hall, 1963), 144.
81. Austen, *Mansfield Park*, 222.
82. Tanner, *Jane Austen*, 155.
83. Austen, *Mansfield Park*, 151–52.
84. Ibid., 21.
85. Ibid., 10.
86. Ibid., 203.
87. Ibid., 181.
88. Ibid., 239.
89. Ibid., 181.
90. Ibid., 66.
91. Trilling, *Opposing Self*, in Austen, *Mansfield Park*, 424–25; Tanner, *Jane Austen*, 146–47.
92. Austen, *Mansfield Park*, 319.
93. Amis, "What Became of Jane Austen?" in Watt, *Critical Essays*, 142.
94. Quoted in Richard Jenkyns, *A Fine Brush on Ivory: An Appreciation of Jane Austen* (Oxford: Oxford University Press, 2004), 109.
95. Austen, *Emma*, 5.

96. Ibid.
97. Ibid., 30.
98. Ibid., 6.
99. Ibid., 326.
100. Ibid., 63.
101. Ibid., 62.
102. Ibid., 99.
103. Ibid., 98.
104. Ibid., 62.
105. Ibid., 5.
106. Ibid., 7.
107. Ibid., 6.
108. Tanner, *Jane Austen*, 182.
109. Austen, *Emma*, 49.
110. Ibid., 95.
111. Ibid., 144.
112. Ibid., 45.
113. Ibid., 22.
114. Ibid.
115. Ibid., 161.
116. Ibid., 281.
117. Ibid., 286.
118. Ibid., 29.
119. Ibid., 228.
120. Julia Prewitt Brown, "Civilization and the Contentment of *Emma*," in Bloom, *Jane Austen*, 94.
121. Austen, *Emma*, 322, 333.
122. Jane Austen, *Persuasion*, ed. Patricia Meyer Spacks, second edition (New York: W. W. Norton, 2013), 5.
123. Ibid., 20.
124. Ibid., 21.
125. Ibid.
126. Ibid., 44.
127. Ibid., 60.
128. Ibid., 5.
129. Ibid., 87.
130. Ibid., 22–23.
131. Ibid., 44.
132. Ibid., 82.
133. Ibid., 75.
134. Ibid., 84.
135. Ibid., 118.
136. Ibid., 157.
137. Ibid., 127.

Notes

138. Ibid., 159.

139. Ibid., 164.

140. Ibid., 165, 166.

141. Ibid., 170.

142. Julia Prewitt Brown, *Jane Austen's Novels: Social Change and Literary Form* (Cambridge, MA: Harvard University Press, 1979), 146.

143. Austen, *Persuasion*, 178.

144. Ibid., 170.

Chapter 6

1. André Gide, "The Ten French Novels Which I . . . ," *Virginia Quarterly Review* 5, no. 4 (Autumn 1929). Gide was asked to name the ten best French novels, but he decided to answer "without bothering about their origin."

2. Of course, no one would seriously suggest that *The Tempest* is a greater play than *Hamlet*. But, after repeated encounters with the dismal prince, even the most ardent admirer of Shakespeare's tragedies might prefer the autumnal glories of *The Tempest*, which, in both its romantic fantasy and its political alienation, bears a striking relationship to *The Charterhouse*.

3. Irving Howe, "Stendhal: The Politics of Survival," in *Stendhal: A Collection of Critical Essays*, ed. Victor Brombert (Englewood Cliffs, NJ: Prentice-Hall, 1962), 93.

4. Stendhal, *The Red and the Black*, ed. Susanna Lee, trans. Robert M. Adams, second edition (New York: W. W. Norton, 2008), 120.

5. Stendhal, *Le Rouge et le Noir* (Paris: Garnier-Flammarion, 1964), 111.

6. My translation.

7. Jonathan Keates, *Stendhal* (New York: Carroll & Graf, 1997), 7 (quoting Stendhal, *Vie de Henri Brulard*).

8. Though overshadowed by Mozart and Rossini, on each of whom he had a profound influence, several of Cimarosa's operas are still performed today, including *Il matrimonio segreto*, and are available on Spotify. So, too, is the aria "Quelle pupille tenere" from *Gli Orazi e i Curiazi* that Henri treated as a talisman of transcendence in several of his works, including *The Charterhouse*.

9. Quoted in Keates, *Stendhal*, 94.

10. See Simone de Beauvoir, "Stendhal or the Romantic of Reality," in Brombert, *Stendhal*, 147–56.

11. Quoted in Keates, *Stendhal*, 404.

12. Erich Auerbach, *Mimesis: The Representation of Reality in Western Literature*, trans. Willard R. Trask (Princeton, NJ: Princeton University Press, 1968), 463.

13. See Michael K. Kellogg, *The Wisdom of the Enlightenment* (Lanham, MD: Prometheus Books, 2022), chap. 3.

14. Stendhal, *Red and the Black*, 41.

15. Ibid., 9.

16. Ibid., 22.

17. Ibid., 33.

18. Ibid., 16.

19. Ibid., 33.
20. Ibid., 25.
21. Ibid., 30.
22. Ibid., 41.
23. Ibid., 36.
24. Ibid., 36–37.
25. Ibid., 42.
26. Ibid., 51.
27. Ibid., 50.
28. Ibid.
29. Ibid., 59.
30. Ibid., 50.
31. Ibid., 58.
32. Ibid., 59.
33. Ibid., 70.
34. Ibid., 74.
35. Ibid., 75.
36. Ibid., 61.
37. Ibid., 98.
38. Ibid., 65.
39. Ibid., 150.
40. Ibid., 197.
41. Ibid., 147.
42. Ibid., 157.
43. Ibid., 177.
44. See Howe, "Politics of Survival," in Brombert, *Stendhal*, 77.
45. Stendhal, *Red and the Black*, 219.
46. Ibid., 225.
47. Ibid., 225–26.
48. Excerpt from *Realism and Revolution: Balzac, Stendhal, Zola and the Performances of History*, by Sandy Petrey, in *Red and the Black*, 564.
49. See Kellogg, *Wisdom of the Enlightenment*, chap. 3.
50. Stendhal, *Red and the Black*, 210.
51. Ibid.
52. Auerbach, *Mimesis*, 456.
53. Stendhal, *Red and the Black*, 256–57.
54. Ibid., 252.
55. Ibid., 260.
56. Ibid., 257.
57. Ibid., 259.
58. Ibid., 285.
59. Ibid., 304.
60. Ibid., 326.
61. Ibid., 342.

Notes

62. Ibid., 341.
63. Ibid., 345.
64. Ibid., 366.
65. Ibid., 371.
66. Ibid., 268.
67. Ibid., 374.
68. Ibid., 383.
69. Ibid., 387.
70. Ibid., 368.
71. Ibid., 397.
72. Ibid., 388.
73. Ibid., 365.
74. Ibid., 362.
75. Ibid., 404.
76. Ibid., 413.
77. Ibid., 404.
78. Ibid., 412.
79. Ibid., 405.
80. Ibid., 413.
81. Ibid., 405.
82. Ibid., 415.
83. Ibid., 417.

CHAPTER 7

1. Alessandro Manzoni, *The Betrothed*, trans. Michael F. Moore (New York: Modern Library, 2022), 140.
2. Ibid., xxvi.
3. Quoted in Archibald Colquhoun, *Manzoni and His Times* (New York: E. P. Dutton, 1954), 76.
4. Ibid., 77.
5. Ibid., 107.
6. Quoted in Colquhoun, *Manzoni*, 169–70.
7. Arguably, the third greatest "Italian" novel was *The Charterhouse of Parma*, written in French by a Frenchman in 1839.
8. Quoted in Colquhoun, *Manzoni*, 256.
9. Manzoni, *Betrothed*, 4.
10. Ibid., 4–5.
11. Ibid., 3.
12. Ibid.
13. Ibid.
14. Ibid., 5.
15. Ibid.
16. Ibid., 39.
17. Ibid., 20.

18. Ibid., 44.
19. Ibid., 45.
20. Ibid.
21. Ibid., 47.
22. Ibid.
23. Ibid., 48.
24. Ibid., 18.
25. Ibid., 41.
26. Unsurprisingly, Pope Francis has said that his two favorite novels are *The Brothers Karamazov* and *The Betrothed*.
27. Manzoni, *Betrothed*, 58.
28. Ibid., 68–69.
29. Ibid., 141.
30. Ibid., 138.
31. Ibid., 139.
32. Italo Calvino, "Manzoni's *The Betrothed*: The Novel of Ratios of Power," in *The Uses of Literature*, trans. Patrick Creagh (San Diego: Harcourt Brace Jovanovich, 1986), 202.
33. Ibid., 208.
34. Manzoni, *Betrothed*, 321.
35. Ibid., 147.
36. Ibid., 181.
37. Ibid., 203.
38. Ibid., 204.
39. Ibid., 205.
40. Ibid., 233.
41. Ibid., 263.
42. Quoted in Alberto Mingardi, "Living Language," *City Journal*, February 3, 2023, https://www.city-journal.org/article/living-language.
43. Manzoni, *Betrothed*, 222.
44. Ibid.
45. Ibid., 329.
46. Ibid., 330.
47. Ibid., 344.
48. Ibid., 345.
49. Ibid., 349.
50. Ibid., 435.
51. Ibid., 447.
52. Ibid.
53. Ibid., 455.
54. Ibid., 512.
55. Ibid., 514.
56. Ibid., 518.
57. Ibid., 572.

NOTES

58. See Gustave Flaubert, *Madame Bovary*, trans. Francis Steegmuller (New York: Vintage Books, 1992), 224 ("Human speech is like a cracked kettle on which we tap crude rhythms for bears to dance to, while we long to make music that will melt the stars").

59. Manzoni, *Betrothed*, 571.

60. Primo Levi, *Other People's Trades*, trans. Raymond Rosenthal (New York: Summit Books, 1989), 147–48.

61. Ibid., 151.

62. Manzoni, *Betrothed*, 589.

63. Ibid., 597.

64. Ibid., 604.

65. Ibid., 613.

66. Ibid., 620.

67. Quoted in Colquhoun, *Manzoni*, 216, 218.

68. The role of opera in Italian culture in many ways substituted for the tradition of the novel in countries like England, France, and Russia; hence, Manzoni's outsized cultural influence in filling this vacuum. Italy's other great novelist, Giuseppe Tomasi di Lampedusa, is said to have lamented that, in Italy, everything was "opera, opera, opera." I owe this anecdote to the poet Dana Gioia. There was, inevitably, an opera of *I promessi sposi*, composed by Amilcare Ponchielli in 1856. There is also now an opera of Lampedusa's *The Leopard*, by the American composer Michael Dellaira, which premiered in March 2022 during the COVID-19 pandemic.

69. William Shakespeare, *The Tempest*, ed. Frank Kermode (1954; repr., London: Routledge, 1988), 5.1.198–99.

70. Ibid., 4.1.24.

71. See Bernard Wall, *Alessandro Manzoni* (New Haven, CT: Yale University Press, 1954), 49.

72. Calvino, "Manzoni's *Betrothed*," in *Uses of Literature*, 208.

73. Alessandro Manzoni, *On the Historical Novel*, trans. Sandra Bermann (Lincoln: University of Nebraska Press, 1984), 63, 81.

74. Ibid., 63.

75. Ibid., 65.

76. Georg Lukács, *The Historical Novel*, trans. Hannah Mitchell and Stanley Mitchell (1963; repr., Lincoln: University of Nebraska Press, 1983), 333.

77. Quoted in introduction to Manzoni, *Historical Novel*, 23.

78. Lukács, *Historical Novel*, 70.

CHAPTER 8

1. Keats to John Taylor, February 27, 1818, in *Keats's Poetry and Prose*, ed. Jeffrey N. Cox (New York: W. W. Norton, 2009), 128.

2. William Shakespeare, *Timon of Athens*, 1.1.27–28.

3. Keats to J. A. Hessey, October 8, 1818, in *Poetry and Prose*, 287.

4. William Shakespeare, *King Lear*, 5.2.12.

5. Keats to B. R. Haydon, May 1817, in *Poetry and Prose*, 84.

6. John Keats, "To Solitude," ll. 1–3, in *Poetry and Prose*, 52.

THE WISDOM OF THE ROMANTICS

7. Quoted in W. Jackson Bate, *John Keats* (Cambridge, MA: Harvard University Press, 1963), 105.

8. Ibid., 41.

9. John Keats, "On First Looking into Chapman's Homer," ll. 9–14, in *Poetry and Prose*, 55.

10. Bate, *John Keats*, 124.

11. John Keats, "Sleep and Poetry," ll. 162–65, in *Poetry and Prose*, 62.

12. Ibid., ll. 96–98, in *Poetry and Prose*, 61.

13. Keats to George and Georgiana Keats, October 25, 1818, in *Poetry and Prose*, 289.

14. Quoted in Bate, *John Keats*, 118.

15. John Keats, *Endymion*, ll. 1–5, in *Poetry and Prose*, 148–49.

16. Quoted in Bate, *John Keats*, 265.

17. Ibid., 266.

18. Ibid.

19. Keats to J. H. Reynolds, May 3, 1818, in *Poetry and Prose*, 245.

20. Keats to Richard Woodhouse, October 27, 1818, in *Poetry and Prose*, 295.

21. Ibid., 294–95.

22. Keats to George and Tom Keats, December 1817, in *Poetry and Prose*, 109.

23. Keats to Benjamin Bailey, November 22, 1817, in *Poetry and Prose*, 102.

24. Ibid.

25. Ibid.

26. Keats to George and Georgiana Keats, December 1818, in *Poetry and Prose*, 299.

27. John Keats, "The Eve of St. Agnes," ll. 1–9, in *Poetry and Prose*, 445–46.

28. Ibid., ll. 83–84, in *Poetry and Prose*, 448.

29. Ibid., ll. 163–67, in *Poetry and Prose*, 450.

30. Ibid., ll. 227–34, in *Poetry and Prose*, 452.

31. Ibid., ll. 276–77, in *Poetry and Prose*, 453.

32. Ibid., ll. 286–87, in *Poetry and Prose*, 454.

33. Ibid., ll. 294–97, in *Poetry and Prose*, 454.

34. Ibid., l. 300, in *Poetry and Prose*, 454.

35. Ibid., ll. 311, 313 in *Poetry and Prose*, 454.

36. Ibid., ll. 316–24, in *Poetry and Prose*, 455.

37. Ibid., ll. 350–51, in *Poetry and Prose*, 455.

38. Ibid., l. 361, in *Poetry and Prose*, 456.

39. Ibid., ll. 370–71, in *Poetry and Prose*, 456.

40. Ibid., ll. 312, 315, in *Poetry and Prose*, 454.

41. Ibid., ll. 372–78, in *Poetry and Prose*, 456.

42. Harold Bloom, *The Visionary Company: A Reading of English Romantic Poetry*, rev. ed. (Ithaca, NY: Cornell University Press, 1971), 380.

43. Keats to George and Georgiana Keats, March 19, 1819, in *Poetry and Prose*, 322.

44. John Keats, "La Belle Dame sans Merci," ll. 1–12, in *Poetry and Prose*, 341–42.

45. Ibid., ll. 13–16, in *Poetry and Prose*, 342.

46. Ibid., ll. 21–24, in *Poetry and Prose*, 342.

47. Ibid., ll. 25–26, in *Poetry and Prose*, 342.

NOTES

48. Ibid., ll. 19–20, in *Poetry and Prose*, 342.

49. Ibid., ll. 37–44, in *Poetry and Prose*, 343.

50. Ibid., ll. 27–28, in *Poetry and Prose*, 342.

51. Ibid., ll. 45–48, in *Poetry and Prose*, 343.

52. My discussion of the odes has greatly benefited from the work of Helen Vendler, W. Jackson Bate, and Harold Bloom, among others.

53. John Keats, "Ode to a Nightingale," ll. 1–4, in *Poetry and Prose*, 457.

54. Ibid., ll. 11–20, in *Poetry and Prose*, 458.

55. Ibid., ll. 21–28, in *Poetry and Prose*, 458.

56. Keats to Fanny Brawne, July 1, 1819, in *Poetry and Prose*, 349.

57. William Shakespeare, "Sonnet 73," https://www.poetryfoundation.org/poems /45099/sonnet-73-that-time-of-year-thou-mayst-in-me-behold.

58. Keats, "Ode to a Nightingale," ll. 29–30, in *Poetry and Prose*, 458.

59. Ibid., ll. 32–33, in *Poetry and Prose*, 458.

60. Ibid., ll. 9, 38–40, in *Poetry and Prose*, 458–59.

61. Ibid., ll. 43, 52, in *Poetry and Prose*, 459.

62. Ibid., ll. 55–58, in *Poetry and Prose*, 459.

63. Ibid., ll. 59–60, in *Poetry and Prose*, 459.

64. William Shakespeare, *Measure for Measure*, 3.1.133–36.

65. Keats, "Ode to a Nightingale," ll. 61–70, in *Poetry and Prose*, 459.

66. Ibid., ll. 73–74, in *Poetry and Prose*, 460.

67. Ibid., ll. 71–72, in *Poetry and Prose*, 460.

68. Ibid., ll. 79–80, in *Poetry and Prose*, 460.

69. Ibid., l. 14, in *Poetry and Prose*, 458.

70. John Keats, "Ode on a Grecian Urn," ll. 1–4, in *Poetry and Prose*, 461.

71. Ibid., ll. 5–10, in *Poetry and Prose*, 461.

72. Ibid., ll. 11–14, in *Poetry and Prose*, 461.

73. Ibid., ll. 15–20, in *Poetry and Prose*, 461–62.

74. Ibid., ll. 26–30, in *Poetry and Prose*, 462.

75. Helen Vendler, *The Odes of John Keats* (Cambridge, MA: Harvard University Press, 1983), 120.

76. Keats, "Ode on a Grecian Urn," ll. 31–34, in *Poetry and Prose*, 462.

77. Ibid., ll. 35–40, in *Poetry and Prose*, 462.

78. Vendler, *Odes of John Keats*, 142–43.

79. Keats, "Ode on a Grecian Urn," ll. 41–50, in *Poetry and Prose*, 462.

80. Harold Bloom, ed., *John Keats* (New York: Chelsea House, 2007), 7.

81. Vendler, *Odes of John Keats*, 135.

82. Bloom, *Visionary Company*, 432.

83. Bate, *John Keats*, 581.

84. John Keats, "To Autumn," ll. 1–11, in *Poetry and Prose*, 472.

85. Ibid., ll. 12–22, in *Poetry and Prose*, 472–73.

86. Ibid., ll. 23–33, in *Poetry and Prose*, 473.

87. See Michael K. Kellogg, *The Wisdom of the Middle Ages* (Amherst, NY: Prometheus Books, 2016), 149–54, 161–63.

THE WISDOM OF THE ROMANTICS

88. Keats to Fanny Brawne, March 1820, in *Poetry and Prose*, 405.

89. Bate, *John Keats*, 687.

90. Quoted in Stanley Plumly, *Posthumous Keats* (New York: W. W. Norton, 2008), 33.

CHAPTER 9

1. Robert Chandler, *A Short Life of Pushkin* (London: Pushkin, 2017), 39.

2. Quoted in T. J. Binyon, prologue to *Pushkin: A Biography* (New York: Vintage Books, 2003), xxvi.

3. Ibid., xxvii.

4. Ibid., xxv.

5. Russia used the Julian calendar rather than the Gregorian ("New Style") until 1917. To avoid the complication of providing all dates according to both calendars, the Gregorian calendar has been used throughout this chapter.

6. Biographical details are drawn largely from Binyon and Chandler.

7. Quoted in Chandler, *Short Life of Pushkin*, 10.

8. Quoted in Binyon, *Pushkin*, 35.

9. Alexander Pushkin, "Liberty: An Ode," ll. 1–8, in *Selected Poetry*, trans. Antony Wood (London: Penguin Books, 2020), 7.

10. Quoted in Binyon, *Pushkin*, 61.

11. Ibid., 100.

12. Quoted in Chandler, *Short Life of Pushkin*, 26.

13. Quoted in Binyon, *Pushkin*, 149.

14. Quoted in Chandler, *Short Life of Pushkin*, 31.

15. Alexander Pushkin, [no title], in *Selected Poetry*, 47–48.

16. Excerpt from *Pushkin: A Comparative Commentary*, by John Bayley, in *Alexander Pushkin*, ed. Harold Bloom (New York: Chelsea House, 1987), 63.

17. Quoted in Boris Eikhenbaum, "Pushkin's Path to Prose," in Bloom, *Pushkin*, 120.

18. Richard Pevear and Larissa Volokhonsky, trans., *Novels, Tales, Journeys: The Complete Prose of Alexander Pushkin* (New York: Vintage Books, 2017), xv.

19. Alexander Pushkin, *Mozart and Salieri*, in *"Boris Godunov," "Little Tragedies" and Others: The Complete Plays*, trans. Richard Pevear and Larissa Volokhonsky (New York: Vintage Books, 2023), 153.

20. Alexander Pushkin, [no title], in *Selected Poetry*, 67.

21. The numbering reaches sixty, but five of the stanzas were dropped by Pushkin.

22. Alexander Pushkin, *Eugene Onegin*, trans. Stanley Mitchell (London: Penguin Books, 2008), 1.1. References are to chapter and stanza.

23. Ibid., 1.2.

24. Ibid., 1.4.

25. Ibid., 1.8.

26. Ibid., 1.10.

27. Ibid., 1.7.

28. Ibid., 1.12.

29. Ibid., 1.20.

30. Ibid., 1.21.

Notes

31. Ibid., 1.30.
32. Ibid., 1.35.
33. Ibid., 1.44.
34. Ibid., 1.38.
35. Ibid., 1.46.
36. Ibid., 1.45.
37. Ibid., 1.46.
38. Ibid., 1.52.
39. Ibid., 1.59.
40. Ibid., 1.54.
41. Ibid., 2.6.
42. Ibid., 2.10.
43. Ibid., 2.12.
44. Ibid., 2.13.
45. Ibid., 2.19.
46. Ibid., 2.23.
47. Ibid., 2.25.
48. Ibid.
49. Ibid., 3.5.
50. Ibid., 3.9.
51. Ibid., 3.12.
52. Ibid., 3.13.
53. Ibid., 3.12, 3.13.
54. Ibid., 3.15.
55. Ibid., 3.20.
56. See Jean-Jacques Rousseau, *La Nouvelle Héloïse: Julie, or the New Eloise*, trans. Judith H. McDowell (University Park: Pennsylvania State University Press, 1987), Pt. I, letter 4.
57. See Betty Radice, trans., *The Letters of Abelard and Heloise*, rev. M. T. Clanchy (London: Penguin Books, 2003), letter 2.
58. Pushkin, *Eugene Onegin*, 3.25.
59. Ibid., 4.12.
60. Ibid., 4.14.
61. Ibid., 4.16.
62. Ibid., 6.22.
63. Ibid., 6.35.
64. Ibid., 6.39.
65. Ibid., 6.40.
66. Ibid., 7.10.
67. Ibid., 7.24.
68. Ibid., 7.54.
69. Ibid.
70. Ibid., 8.14.
71. Ibid.

THE WISDOM OF THE ROMANTICS

72. Quoted in Chandler, *Short Life of Pushkin*, 82. Bloom attributes to Pushkin a somewhat different remark: "Do you know my Tatyana has rejected Onegin. I never expected it of her." Quoted in Bloom, *Pushkin*, 1. Since neither Bloom nor Chandler footnotes the quotes, it is hard to choose between them. But, knowing Pushkin, perhaps he said both things at one time or another.

73. Pushkin, *Eugene Onegin*, 8.18.

74. Ibid., 8.21.

75. Bloom, *Pushkin*, 5.

76. Pushkin, *Eugene Onegin*, 8.32.

77. Ibid.

78. Ibid.

79. Ibid., 8.42.

80. Ibid., 8.44.

81. Ibid., 8.45.

82. Ibid.

83. Ibid., 8.47.

84. Ibid.

85. Excerpt from *The Poets of Russia, 1890–1930*, by Renato Poggioli, in Bloom, *Pushkin*, 15.

86. Quoted in Binyon, *Pushkin*, 407.

87. Ibid., 408.

88. Ibid., 539.

89. Ibid., 600.

90. Alexander Pushkin, *"Exegi monumentum,"* ll. 5–8, in *Selected Poetry*, 75.

Chapter 10

1. Quoted in Richard Ellmann, *Oscar Wilde* (New York: Vintage Books, 1988), 303.

2. Erich Auerbach, *Mimesis: The Representation of Reality in Western Literature*, trans. Willard R. Trask (Princeton, NJ: Princeton University Press, 1968), 468.

3. Ibid.

4. Honoré de Balzac, *Père Goriot*, ed. Peter Brooks, trans. Burton Raffel (New York: W. W. Norton, 1997), 6.

5. Excerpt from *Les Romanciers Naturalistes*, by Émile Zola, in *Père Goriot*, 237 ("Shakespeare alone was able to create as large and lively a humanity as Balzac"); Graham Robb, *Balzac: A Biography* (New York: W. W. Norton, 1995), 3 (Balzac "took in more of human life than anyone since Shakespeare") (quoting Henry James).

6. Excerpt from *Literary Criticism: French Writers, Other European Writers; Prefaces to the New York Edition*, by Henry James, in *Père Goriot*, 258.

7. Biographical details are taken largely from Graham Robb's *Balzac: A Biography*. Stefan Zweig's *Balzac* (unfortunately out of print) beautifully captures Balzac's boundless energy and the breadth of his enthusiasms.

8. Robb, *Balzac*, 78.

9. Ibid., 91.

10. Quoted in Robb, *Balzac*, 415.

342

Notes

11. Ibid., 148–49.

12. Ibid., 373.

13. Quoted in Robb, *Balzac*, 403.

14. Ibid., 255.

15. Balzac, *Père Goriot*, 60.

16. Ibid., 71.

17. Quoted in David Bellos, *Balzac: "Old Goriot"* (Cambridge: Cambridge University Press, 1987), 82.

18. Balzac, *Père Goriot*, 61.

19. Ibid., 9.

20. Ibid., 66.

21. Ibid., 62.

22. Ibid., 39.

23. Ibid., 86.

24. Ibid., 183.

25. Ibid., 91.

26. Ibid., 89.

27. Ibid., 93.

28. Ibid., 196–97.

29. Ibid., 192.

30. William Shakespeare, *King Lear*, 2.4.313–27.

31. Balzac, *Père Goriot*, 202.

32. Ibid., 210.

33. Ibid., 101.

34. Ibid., 192.

35. Ibid., 217.

36. Honoré de Balzac, *Lost Illusions*, trans. Raymond N. MacKenzie (Minneapolis: University of Minnesota Press, 2020), 18.

37. Ibid., 22.

38. Ibid., 120.

39. Ibid., 83.

40. Ibid., 33.

41. Ibid., 78.

42. Ibid.

43. Ibid., 116.

44. Ibid., 163.

45. Ibid., 145.

46. Ibid., 170.

47. Ibid., 179.

48. Ibid., 254.

49. Ibid., 257.

50. Ibid.

51. Oscar Wilde, *Lady Windermere's Fan*, ed. Susan L. Rattiner (Mineola, NY: Dover, 1998), 5.

The Wisdom of the Romantics

52. Balzac, *Lost Illusions*, 334.

53. Ibid., 374.

54. Ibid., 384.

55. Ibid., 412–13.

56. Ibid.

57. Ibid., 412.

58. Honoré de Balzac, *Lost Souls*, trans. Raymond N. MacKenzie (Minneapolis: University of Minnesota Press, 2020), 382.

59. Balzac, *Lost Illusions*, 529.

60. Ibid., 514.

61. Ibid., 518.

62. Ibid., 525.

63. Ibid., 524.

64. Ibid., 532.

65. Balzac, *Lost Souls*, vii.

66. Other popular translations give the title as *A Harlot High and Low* and *A Harlot's Progress*. Both, again, ignore the importance of the plural. It would be better to stick with the original French, which is transparent, whether one knows the language or not.

67. Balzac, *Lost Souls*, 44.

68. Ibid., 353.

69. Oscar Wilde, *The Decay of Lying* (quoted in Robb, *Balzac*, xvi).

Suggestions for Further Reading

Introduction

Berlin, Isaiah. *The Roots of Romanticism*. Edited by Henry Hardy. Princeton, NJ: Princeton University Press, 1999.

Blanning, Tim. *The Romantic Revolution: A History*. New York: Modern Library, 2012.

Cranston, Maurice. *The Romantic Movement*. Oxford: Blackwell, 1994.

Ferber, Michael. *Romanticism: A Very Short Introduction*. Oxford: Oxford University Press, 2010.

Hobsbawm, Eric. *The Age of Revolution, 1789–1848*. New York: Vintage Books, 1996.

Holmes, Richard. *The Age of Wonder: How the Romantic Generation Discovered the Beauty and Terror of Science*. New York: Vintage Books, 2010.

Vaughan, William. *Romanticism and Art*. 1978. Reprint, London: Thames and Hudson, 1994.

Wulf, Andrea. *Magnificent Rebels: The First Romantics and the Invention of the Self*. London: John Murray, 2022.

Rousseau

Primary Sources

The Essential Rousseau. Translated by Lowell Bair, with an introduction by Matthew Josephson. 1974. Reprint, New York: New American Library, 1983.

Rousseau, Jean-Jacques. *The Confessions*. Translated with an introduction by J. M. Cohen. London: Penguin Books, 1953.

Rousseau, Jean-Jacques. *Emile: or On Education*. Translated with an introduction and notes by Allan Bloom. New York: Basic Books, 1979.

Rousseau, Jean-Jacques. *La Nouvelle Héloïse: Julie, or the New Eloise*. Translated and abridged by Judith H. McDowell. University Park: Pennsylvania State University Press, 1987.

Rousseau, Jean-Jacques. *The Reveries of the Solitary Walker*. Translated with a preface and notes by Charles E. Butterworth. 1979. Reprint, Indianapolis, IN: Hackett, 1992.

Secondary Sources

Damrosch, Leo. *Jean-Jacques Rousseau: Restless Genius.* Boston: Houghton Mifflin, 2007.

Melzer, Arthur M. *The Natural Goodness of Man: On the System of Rousseau's Thought.* Chicago: University of Chicago Press, 1990.

Riley, Patrick, ed. *The Cambridge Companion to Rousseau.* Cambridge: Cambridge University Press, 2001.

Starobinski, Jean. *Jean-Jacques Rousseau: Transparency and Obstruction.* Translated by Arthur Goldhammer, with an introduction by Robert J. Morrissey. Chicago: University of Chicago Press, 1988.

Wokler, Robert. *Rousseau: A Very Short Introduction.* Oxford: Oxford University Press, 2001.

GOETHE

Primary Sources

The Autobiography of Johann Wolfgang von Goethe. Translated by John Oxenford, with an introduction by Karl J. Weintraub. 2 vols. Chicago: Chicago University Press, 1974.

Eckermann, Johann Peter. *Conversations with Goethe.* Translated by Gisela C. O'Brien, with an introduction by Hans Kohn. New York: Frederick Ungar, 1964.

Eckermann, Johann Peter. *Conversations with Goethe.* Edited by J. K. Moorhead, translated by John Oxenford. 1930. Reprint, London: Dent, 1971.

Goethe, Johann Wolfgang von. *Faust: A Tragedy.* Edited by Cyrus Hamlin, translated by Walter Arndt. Second Norton Critical Edition. New York: W. W. Norton, 2001.

Goethe, Johann Wolfgang von. *Faust, Part I.* Translated with an introduction and notes by David Luke. Oxford: Oxford University Press, 2008.

Goethe, Johann Wolfgang von. *Faust, Part II.* Translated with an introduction and notes by David Luke. Oxford: Oxford University Press, 2008.

Goethe, Johann Wolfgang von. *Italian Journey.* Translated with an introduction by W. H. Auden and Elizabeth Mayer. London: Penguin Books, 1970.

Goethe, Johann Wolfgang von. *Maxims and Reflections.* Edited with an introduction and notes by Peter Hutchinson, translated by Elisabeth Stopp. London: Penguin Books, 1998.

Goethe, Johann Wolfgang von. *The Sorrows of Young Werther.* Translated with an introduction by Victor Lange. New York: Holt, Rinehart, 1971.

Goethe, Johann Wolfgang von. *The Sufferings of Young Werther.* Edited and translated by Stanley Corngold. Norton Critical Edition. New York: W. W. Norton, 2013.

Secondary Sources

Adler, Jeremy. *Johann Wolfgang von Goethe.* London: Reaktion Books, 2020.

Armstrong, John. *Love, Life, Goethe: Lessons of the Imagination from the Great German Poet.* New York: Farrar, Straus and Giroux, 2007.

Bloom, Harold, ed. *Johann Wolfgang von Goethe.* Broomall, PA: Chelsea House, 2003.

Bloom, Harold. *The Western Canon: The Books and School of the Ages.* New York: Riverhead Books, 1995.

Boerner, Peter. *Goethe.* Translated by Nancy Boerner. London: Haus, 2013.

SUGGESTIONS FOR FURTHER READING

Robertson, Ritchie. *Goethe: A Very Short Introduction*. Oxford: Oxford University Press, 2016.
Sharpe, Lesley, ed. *The Cambridge Companion to Goethe*. Cambridge: Cambridge University Press, 2002.

HEGEL
Primary Sources
Hegel, G. W. F. *Encyclopedia of the Philosophical Sciences in Basic Outline, Part I: Science of Logic*. Edited and translated by Klaus Brinkmann and Daniel O. Dahlstrom. Cambridge: Cambridge University Press, 2015.
Hegel, G. W. F. *Introductory Lectures on Aesthetics*. Edited with an introduction and commentary by Michael Inwood, translated by Bernard Bosanquet. 2004. Reprint, London: Penguin Books, 2004.
Hegel, G. W. F. *Phenomenology of Spirit*. Translated by A. V. Miller, with a foreword by J. N. Findlay. Oxford: Oxford University Press, 1977.
Hegel, G. W. F. *The Philosophy of Right*. Translated by Alan White. Newburyport, MA: Focus, 2002.
Hegel: Texts and Commentary. Edited and translated by Walter Kaufmann. Garden City, NY: Anchor Books, 1966.
Hegel's "Lectures on the History of Philosophy." Translated by E. S. Haldane and Frances H. Simson, with an introduction by Tom Rockmore. Atlantic Highlands, NJ: Humanities Press, 1996.

Secondary Sources
Beiser, Frederick. *Hegel*. New York: Routledge, 2005.
Beiser, Frederick C., ed. *The Cambridge Companion to Hegel*. Cambridge: Cambridge University Press, 1993.
Bungay, Stephen. *Beauty and Truth: A Study of Hegel's "Aesthetics."* Oxford: Oxford University Press, 1987.
Fox, Michael Allen. *The Accessible Hegel*. Amherst, NY: Humanity Books, 2005.
Houlgate, Stephen. *Hegel's "Phenomenology of Spirit": A Reader's Guide*. London: Bloomsbury, 2013.
Kojève, Alexandre. *Introduction to the Reading of Hegel*. Ithaca, NY: Cornell University Press, 1980.
Norman, Richard J. *Hegel's "Phenomenology": A Philosophical Introduction*. 1976. Reprint, Hampshire, UK: Gregg Revivals, 1991.
Pinkard, Terry. *Hegel: A Biography*. Cambridge: Cambridge University Press, 2000.
Singer, Peter. *Hegel: A Very Short Introduction*. Oxford: Oxford University Press, 2001.
Soll, Ivan. *An Introduction to Hegel's Metaphysics*. Foreword by Walter Kaufmann. Chicago: University of Chicago Press, 1969.
Stern, Robert. *The Routledge Guidebook to Hegel's "Phenomenology of Spirit."* New York: Routledge, 2013.

WORDSWORTH
Primary Sources
The Norton Anthology of Poetry. Edited by Alexander W. Allison, Herbert Barrows, Caesar R. Blake, Arthur J. Carr, Arthur M. Eastman, and Hubert M. English Jr. Third edition. New York: W. W. Norton, 1983.

William Wordsworth: Selected Poems. Edited by John O. Hayden. London: Penguin Books, 1994.

Wordsworth, William, and Samuel Taylor Coleridge, *Lyrical Ballads, 1798 and 1802.* Edited with an introduction and notes by Fiona Stafford. Oxford: Oxford University Press, 2013.

Wordsworth's Poetry and Prose. Edited by Nicholas Halmi. Norton Critical Edition. New York: W. W. Norton, 2013.

Secondary Sources
Bate, Jonathan. *Radical Wordsworth.* London: William Collins, 2021.

Bloom, Harold. *The Western Canon: The Books and School of the Ages.* New York: Harcourt Brace, 1993.

Gravil, Richard, and Daniel Robinson, eds. *The Oxford Handbook of William Wordsworth.* Oxford: Oxford University Press, 2018.

Modern Critical Views: William Wordsworth. Edited with an introduction by Harold Bloom. New York: Chelsea House, 1985.

Trilling, Lionel. *The Liberal Imagination.* New York: Harcourt Brace, 1979.

AUSTEN
Primary Sources
Austen, Jane. *Emma.* Edited by George Justice. Fourth Norton Critical Edition. New York: W. W. Norton, 2012.

Austen, Jane. *Mansfield Park.* Edited by Claudia L. Johnson. Norton Critical Edition. New York: W. W. Norton, 1998.

Austen, Jane. *Northanger Abbey.* Edited by Susan Fraiman. Norton Critical Edition. New York: W. W. Norton, 2004.

Austen, Jane. *Persuasion.* Edited by Patricia Meyer Spacks. Second Norton Critical Edition. New York: W. W. Norton, 2013.

Austen, Jane. *Pride and Prejudice.* Edited by Donald Gray and Mary A. Favret. Fourth Norton Critical Edition. New York: W. W. Norton, 2016.

Austen, Jane. *Sense and Sensibility.* Edited by Claudia L. Johnson. Norton Critical Edition. New York: W. W. Norton, 2002.

Secondary Sources
Brown, Julia Prewitt. *Jane Austen's Novels: Social Change and Literary Form.* Cambridge, MA: Harvard University Press, 1979.

SUGGESTIONS FOR FURTHER READING

Copeland, Edward, and Juliet McMaster, eds. *The Cambridge Companion to Jane Austen.* Second edition. Cambridge: Cambridge University Press, 2011.

Gard, Roger. *Jane Austen's Novels: The Art of Clarity.* New Haven, CT: Yale University Press, 1992.

Modern Critical Views: Jane Austen. Edited with an introduction by Harold Bloom. New York: Chelsea House, 1986.

Nokes, David. *Jane Austen: A Life.* New York: Farrar, Straus and Giroux, 1997.

Tanner, Tony. *Jane Austen.* Cambridge, MA: Harvard University Press, 1986.

Tomalin, Claire. *Jane Austen: A Life.* New York: Vintage Books, 1999.

Watt, Ian, ed. *Jane Austen: A Collection of Critical Essays.* Englewood Cliffs, NJ: Prentice-Hall, 1963.

STENDHAL
Primary Sources
Stendhal. *The Charterhouse of Parma.* Translated by Richard Howard. New York: Modern Library, 1999.

Stendhal. *On Love.* Translated by Vyvyan Beresford Holland. Garden City, NY: Doubleday Anchor Books, 1957.

Stendhal. *The Red and the Black.* Edited by Susanna Lee, translated by Robert M. Adams. Second Norton Critical Edition. New York: W. W. Norton, 2008.

Stendhal. *Le Rouge et le Noir.* Paris: Garnier-Flammarion, 1964.

Secondary Sources
Brombert, Victor, ed. *Stendhal: A Collection of Critical Essays.* Englewood Cliffs, NJ: Prentice-Hall, 1962.

Keates, Jonathan. *Stendhal.* New York: Carroll & Graf, 1997.

Modern Critical Interpretations: Stendhal's "The Red and the Black." Edited with an introduction by Harold Bloom. New York: Chelsea House, 1988.

MANZONI
Primary Sources
Manzoni, Alessandro. *The Betrothed.* Translated with an introduction by Michael F. Moore. New York: Modern Library, 2022.

Manzoni, Alessandro. *On the Historical Novel.* Translated with an introduction by Sandra Bermann. Lincoln: University of Nebraska Press, 1984.

Secondary Sources
Calvino, Italo. *The Uses of Literature.* Translated by Patrick Creagh. San Diego: Harcourt Brace Jovanovich, 1986.

Colquhoun, Archibald. *Manzoni and His Times.* New York: E. P. Dutton, 1954.

Levi, Primo. *Other People's Trades.* Translated by Raymond Rosenthal. New York: Summit Books, 1989.

Lukács, Georg. *The Historical Novel*. Translated by Hannah Mitchell and Stanley Mitchell, with an introduction by Frederic Jameson. 1963. Reprint, Lincoln: University of Nebraska Press, 1983.

Wall, Bernard. *Alessandro Manzoni*. New Haven, CT: Yale University Press, 1954.

KEATS

Primary Sources

Keats's Poetry and Prose. Edited by Jeffrey N. Cox. Norton Critical Edition. New York: W. W. Norton, 2009.

Letters of John Keats. Edited by Robert Gittings. 1970. Reprint, Oxford: Oxford University Press, 1987.

The Poems of John Keats. Edited by John Strachan. Routledge Literary Sourcebook. London: Routledge, 2003.

Secondary Sources

Bate, W. Jackson. *John Keats*. Cambridge, MA: Harvard University Press, 1963.

Bloom, Harold. *The Visionary Company: A Reading of English Romantic Poetry*. Revised edition. Ithaca, NY: Cornell University Press, 1971.

Miller, Lucasta. *Keats: A Brief Life in Nine Poems and One Epitaph*. New York: Alfred A. Knopf, 2022.

Modern Critical Views: John Keats. Edited with an introduction by Harold Bloom. Updated edition. New York: Chelsea House, 2007.

Plumly, Stanley. *Posthumous Keats*. New York: W. W. Norton, 2008.

Roe, Nicholas. *John Keats: A New Life*. New Haven, CT: Yale University Press, 2013.

Vendler, Helen. *The Odes of John Keats*. Cambridge, MA: Harvard University Press, 1983.

PUSHKIN

Primary Sources

Alexander Pushkin: Selected Poetry. Translated with an introduction and notes by Antony Wood. London: Penguin Books, 2020.

"Boris Godunov," "Little Tragedies" and Others: The Complete Plays of Alexander Pushkin. Translated by Richard Pevear and Larissa Volokhonsky. New York: Vintage Books, 2023.

Novels, Tales, Journeys: The Complete Prose of Alexander Pushkin. Translated by Richard Pevear and Larissa Volokhonsky. New York: Vintage Books, 2017.

Pushkin, Aleksandr. *Eugene Onegin: A Novel in Verse*. Translated with an introduction by Vladimir Nabokov, with a foreword by Brian Boyd. Princeton, NJ: Princeton University Press, 2018.

Pushkin, Alexander. *Eugene Onegin*. Translated with an introduction and notes by Stanley Mitchell. London: Penguin Books, 2008.

Suggestions for Further Reading

Secondary Sources
Binyon, T. J. *Pushkin: A Biography*. New York: Vintage Books, 2003.
Briggs, A. D. P. *Pushkin: "Eugene Onegin."* Cambridge: Cambridge University Press, 1992.
Chandler, Robert. *A Short Life of Pushkin*. London: Pushkin, 2017.
Modern Critical Views: Alexander Pushkin. Edited with an introduction by Harold Bloom. New York: Chelsea House, 1987.

BALZAC
Primary Sources
Balzac, Honoré de. *A Harlot High and Low*. Translated with an introduction by Rayner Heppenstall. Harmondsworth, UK: Penguin Books, 1970.
Balzac, Honoré de. *Lost Illusions*. Translated with an introduction by Raymond N. MacKenzie. Minneapolis: University of Minnesota Press, 2020.
Balzac, Honoré de. *Lost Souls*. Translated with an introduction by Raymond N. MacKenzie. Minneapolis: University of Minnesota Press, 2020.
Balzac, Honoré de. *Père Goriot*. Edited by Peter Brooks, translated by Burton Raffel. Norton Critical Edition. New York: W. W. Norton, 1997.

Secondary Sources
Bellos, David. *Balzac: "Old Goriot."* Cambridge: Cambridge University Press, 1987.
Brooks, Peter. *Balzac's Lives*. New York: New York Review Books, 2020.
Modern Critical Views: Honoré de Balzac. Edited with an introduction by Harold Bloom. Broomall, PA: Chelsea House, 2003.
Robb, Graham. *Balzac: A Biography*. New York: W. W. Norton, 1995.

Index

abandonment, Rousseau and, 13–14, 17–18, 35–36
Abbey, Richard, 228, 231
Abelard, Peter, 27–29, 275, 279
absolutes: Balzac and, 298; Goethe and, 52, 54, 61; Hegel and, 76, 80, 82, 89, 91–93, 100–102; Stendhal and, 194
aesthetics, Keats and, 245–51
affairs: Balzac and, 289, 292–93, 303–4, 306; Goethe and, 43–46; Pushkin and, 263, 269, 279–80; Rousseau and, 14–15, 17–18, 34, 36; Stendhal and, 174–75, 177–78, 185, 188, 190, 192, 198; Wordsworth and, 108
Alexander I, tsar of Russia, 261–62, 263–64
ambition, Stendhal and, 186, 194
ambivalence, Romanticism and, 7
Amis, Kingsley, 160, 162
amour propre, Rousseau and, 23
anamnesis, 131
Aristotle, 24, 81, 86–88, 167, 294
Arnold, Matthew, 41
art: Goethe and, 44, 50, 66–67; Hegel and, 102; Keats and, 244–51; in Romantic era, 6–7; Schelling and, 78
artisans, Rousseau and, 13, 19
atheism: Pushkin and, 263; Shelley and, 228
attention: Miller and, 326n13; Wordsworth and, 114–24
Audubon, John James, 233
Auerbach, Erich, 285

Augustine, saint, 9, 49, 215
Augustus, emperor of Rome, 262
Austen, Jane, 139–71; life of, 140–46
authenticity: Austen and, 149–50, 156; Rousseau and, 10, 30; Stendhal and, 181, 188; Wordsworth and, 114–15
authority: Balzac and, 287; Pushkin and, 259; Rousseau and, 13, 33
autobiography: Goethe and, 41, 48–50; Rousseau and, 12, 30–8; Wordsworth and, 112, 132–37
autumn: Austen and, 168; Keats and, 251–53

ballet, Pushkin and, 270–71
Balzac, Honoré de, 270, 285–311; life of, 286–94; Stendhal and, 174, 179
Barthes, Roland, 52
Bastille, storming of, 3, 4, 77, 107
Bate, W. Jackson, 225, 251
Baucis and Philemon, 69–70, 71
Baudelaire, Charles, 291
beauty, 7; Austen and, 168; Goethe and, 68–69; Keats and, 231, 233, 243, 246, 250, 253; Stendhal and, 184; Wordsworth and, 125–26, 130–31
Beccaria, Cesare, 199
becoming, Hegel and, 88, 101
Beethoven, Ludwig van, 6, 76
Begriff, term, 88. *See also* concepts
being: Hegel and, 88, 90; Rousseau and, 39; Wordsworth and, 136

353

belief: Goethe and, 58–59; Romanticism and, 84. *See also* faith

"La Belle Dame sans Merci" (Keats), 238–41

Bellini, Vincenzo, 6

Bennet, Elizabeth (character), 154–59

Berlin, Isaiah, 2, 3

Berthet, Antoine, 191

The Betrothed (Manzoni), 197–224

Beyle, Marie-Henri. *See* Stendhal

Blake, William, 6, 152

Bloom, Harold: on Goethe, 56, 73; on Keats, 225, 237, 250–51; on Pushkin, 279; on Wordsworth, 120

Boris Godunov (Pushkin), 263–66

Borromeo, Federico, 210–11, 215, 216

botany, 7; Manzoni and, 200–201; Rousseau and, 20, 39

Bourbon Restoration, 5; Balzac and, 285, 295, 303; Stendhal and, 179, 181, 182, 188

Brawne, Fanny, 233–34, 237, 253–54

bread riots, Milan, 212–14

Brown, Charles, 233

Brown, Julia Prewitt, 170

Buff, Charlotte, 43–44, 49

Burke, Edmund, 107–8

Bussone, Francesco, 201

Byron, George Gordon, lord, 74, 105, 263, 277, 322n99

Calvino, Italo, 210–11, 223

The Captain's Daughter (Pushkin), 281

Catherine the Great, empress of Russia, 259, 268

Catholic Church, Rousseau and, 15, 19

causes, Hegel and, 87–88, 93

censorship: Pushkin and, 264, 266; Rousseau and, 20

chapbooks, 55

Chapman, George, 230

Charles X, king of France, 6

The Charterhouse of Parma (Stendhal), 173, 179

children: Balzac and, 299–300; Coleridge and, 109; Goethe and, 46; Hegel and, 79–80; Pushkin and, 267; Rousseau and, 17–18, 33, 36; Wordsworth and, 108–9, 111, 113

choice, Austen and, 148, 150–51, 156–57, 161–64, 169–70

Cimarosa, Domenico, 177, 333n8

civil society, Rousseau and, 23

Clarissa (Richardson), 49

Clarke, Charles Cowden, 228

classical antiquity, 7; Goethe and, 46, 66–69; Keats and, 231–32, 245–51; Pushkin and, 261

class issues: Balzac and, 286, 288, 295–96, 303, 306–7; Manzoni and, 207; Rousseau and, 12–13; Stendhal and, 182, 187–88, 193–94, 198

clergy: French Revolution and, 4; Manzoni and, 205–6, 207–9; Rousseau and, 11, 15

Coleridge, Samuel Taylor, 105, 109–10, 112, 113, 127, 132, 327n73

color, Goethe and, 65

Comédie Humaine (Balzac), 285–311

commercialization of literature, Balzac and, 289, 301–8

commitment, Manzoni and, 221–22

communication, Manzoni and, 216–17, 222

communion of souls: Austen and, 169; Rousseau and, 28, 34; Stendhal and, 195

communitarianism, Rousseau and, 26–27

community: Austen and, 165–66, 170; Rousseau and, 24, 29

concepts: Hegel and, 75, 88, 90–91, 94, 96, 102–3; Plato and, 86–87

Confessions (Rousseau), 12, 17, 21, 27, 30–38

conscience, Hegel and, 102

consciousness: Austen and, 168; Hegel and, 93–99, 101–3; Keats and, 245

354

INDEX

contentment: Goethe and, 53–54;
Rousseau and, 38–39
contradiction(s): Austen and, 152; Goethe
and, 52, 73; Hegel and, 87–92, 100;
Kant and, 90; Romanticism and, 2
conversation: Austen and, 169–70; Balzac
and, 292; Rousseau and, 38; Stendhal
and, 198
conversion, Manzoni and, 215–16
Cook, James, 7
correspondence. *See* letters
corruption: Balzac and, 310; Rousseau
and, 10–11, 18, 21–22
COVID-19, 219
Cowper, William, 142, 151
Cromwell (Balzac), 288
cynicism: Balzac and, 296, 298, 306, 309;
Pushkin and, 272

D'Alembert, Jean le Rond, 17
Damrosch, Leo, 32
d'Anthes, Georges, 281–83
Daru, Pierre, 177, 178
Darwin, Charles, 7
Dashwood, Elinor and Marianne (characters), 151–54
death: Balzac and, 294, 307–8, 309,
310–11; Goethe and, 54, 64; Keats
and, 242–45, 254–55; Manzoni and,
218–20; Pushkin and, 276–77, 280–83;
Stendhal and, 191–95; Wordsworth
and, 112–13, 135
Decembrist Revolution, 264
deception: Balzac and, 309; Rousseau and,
23, 35. *See also* hypocrisy
Declaration of the Rights of Man, 4–5
Defoe, Daniel, 217
"Dejection: An Ode" (Coleridge),
110, 241
Delacrois, Eugène, 7, 179
de La Mole, Boniface, 189, 193
Dellaira, Michael, 337n68
democracy, Rousseau and, 24–26

depression: Austen and, 145; Coleridge
and, 110; Keats and, 239; Manzoni
and, 201
Le Devin du village (Rousseau), 18–19
dialectic: Hegel and, 75–76, 81, 86, 90, 92,
152; Plato and, 86
Dickens, Charles, 4, 227
Diderot, Denis, 17, 18
Donizetti, Gaetano, 6
Dostoevsky, Fyodor, 207, 258, 293
dreams, Keats and, 236–37, 239–40, 245

Eckermann, Johann, 41, 47, 48, 74
economic issues: Austen and, 148–49,
152, 153, 157, 163, 170; Balzac and,
288–93, 299, 307; Goethe and, 66;
Manzoni and, 201, 212–14, 217;
Romanticism and, 4–6; Rousseau
and, 21, 23; Stendhal and, 182;
Wordsworth and, 122
education: Austen and, 141–42; Balzac
and, 287–88; Goethe and, 43;
Hegel and, 77; Keats and, 226, 228;
Marlowe and, 57; Pushkin and, 257,
259–60, 269; Rousseau and, 12, 16, 18;
Stendhal and, 176, 182, 187
ego: Austen and, 155, 158; Goethe and,
53–54; Keats and, 232; Pushkin and,
274, 280; Stendhal and, 190, 193;
Wordsworth and, 112, 124, 232
Einaudi, Luigi, 213
Einstein, Albert, 91
Eliot, T. S., 129
Elliot, Anne (character), 167–71
Emile (Rousseau), 12, 18, 20, 27
Emma (Austen), 146, 162–67
emotions, 7; Austen and, 139–40, 146–54,
164–65; Rousseau and, 15, 27–31;
Stendhal and, 178, 185; Wordsworth
and, 106, 114, 116–17, 120–24. *See also*
sensibility
Encyclopedia, Rousseau and, 19
Endymion (Keats), 231–32

355

THE WISDOM OF THE ROMANTICS

energy: Austen and, 155; Goethe and, 74; Stendhal and, 187

Engels, Friedrich, 291

England: and French Revolution, 107–8; and Industrial Revolution, 4; Keats and, 251; Rousseau and, 20; Wordsworth and, 106–7

Enlightenment: Hegel and, 100–101; versus Romanticism, 1; Rousseau and, 9–10, 18

ennui, Pushkin and, 270–71, 273

epic poetry, Manzoni and, 224

epistemology, Kant and, 83

equality, 5; Austen and, 164, 167, 171; Hegel and, 77; Rousseau and, 10, 21–27, 29; Wordsworth and, 115

"Die Erlkönig" (Goethe), 48

Eugene Onegin (Pushkin), 263, 265–66, 268–80, 281

"The Eve of St. Agnes" (Keats), 234–37

exile/flight: Pushkin and, 262–64; Rousseau and, 14, 20; Stendhal and, 179

experience: Goethe and, 59–62; Hegel and, 95–96; Kant and, 78, 83

exploration, in Romantic era, 7

faith: Manzoni and, 215; Wordsworth and, 126, 131. *See also* belief

family: Austen and, 140–41, 143–44; Balzac and, 286–87; Goethe and, 42–43; Hegel and, 76–77; Keats and, 226–29; Manzoni and, 198–200; Pushkin and, 258; Rousseau and, 12–14; Stendhal and, 175–76, 179; Wordsworth and, 107, 111–13, 122. *See also* children

family resemblances, and Romanticism, 2–3, 7

fashion, Balzac and, 296

Fauriel, Claude, 200, 201

Faust (Goethe), 48, 55–74

Fichte, Johann, 65, 78, 79, 84

Findlay, J. N., 103

Fischer-Dieskau, Dietrich, 48

Flaubert, Gustave, 270, 337n58

folk tales, Pushkin and, 259, 262, 263

force, Hegel and, 97

forms, Plato and, 86, 88

France: Balzac and, 285, 290; Manzoni and, 200; Romantic era in, 4–6; Stendhal and, 179; Wordsworth and, 113

Francis, pope, 336n26

fraternity, 5, 10, 77

freedom: Austen and, 145–46, 148, 150–51, 155–56; Goethe and, 44; Hegel and, 99; Rousseau and, 10, 33. *See also* liberty

French Revolution, 4–5, 26–27; Goethe and, 46–47; Hegel and, 77; Wordsworth and, 107–8

Friedrich, Caspar David, 6–7

friendship: Aristotle and, 167; Austen and, 148, 154

"Frost at Midnight" (Coleridge), 109, 127, 327n73

Gannibal, Ibrahim, 258–59

gender issues. *See* women

general will, Rousseau and, 10, 24–25

genius: Balzac and, 303; Goethe and, 60; Hegel and, 102; Romanticism and, 48–49

George IV, king of Great Britain, 146, 229

German idealism: Goethe and, 65; Wordsworth and, 111, 126

German Romanticism: Goethe and, 46, 55; Pushkin and, 272; Stendhal and, 178

Giannoli, Xavier, 303

Gide, André, 173

Glinka, Mikhail, 258, 262

God: Goethe and, 52, 58, 63–64; Hegel and, 100–102; Manzoni and, 215–16; Rousseau and, 39; Wordsworth and, 136. *See also* sacred

356

INDEX

Godunov, Boris, tsar, 264
Goethe, Johann Wolfgang, 7, 38, 41–74;
 Hegel and, 79; life of, 42–48; Manzoni
 and, 200, 222–23; Rousseau and,
 30; Stendhal and, 178; Wordsworth
 and, 107
Gogol, Nikolai, 257
Gothic, Austen and, 142, 150
Gounod, Charles, 64
Goya, Francisco, 6
Grecian urn, Keats' ode on, 245–51
Grigorev, Apollon, 258

happiness: Austen and, 156; Goethe and,
 51–53, 68; Keats and, 236–37, 243,
 248; Pushkin and, 262, 280; Rousseau
 and, 16, 34, 38–39; Stendhal and,
 174, 185
Hastings, Warren, 143
Haydon, Robert, 229
Hazlitt, William, 116, 229
Hegel, G. W. F., 2, 46, 52, 75–103;
 Goethe and, 45, 65; life of, 76–80
Heidegger, Martin, 101, 133
Heine, Heinrich, 56
Heloise, 27–29, 275, 279
Henry II, king of England, 70
Heraclitus, 82, 88
hero, Romantic: Balzac and, 302, 309;
 Goethe and, 53; Pushkin and, 263, 279
historical fiction: Manzoni and, 201, 204,
 221–24; Pushkin and, 265
history, 92–94; Hegel and, 75, 99, 103;
 Manzoni and, 210–21, 223–24
Hobsbawm, Eric, 3
Hogarth, William, 4
Hölderlin, Friedrich, 46, 77
Homer, 66, 230, 259
Howe, Irving, 181
Hugo, Victor, 3, 223, 288–89, 290,
 294, 305
human dignity: Balzac and, 300;
 Wordsworth and, 119–20

human nature: Austen and, 139, 143;
 Rousseau and, 22, 24, 26; Wordsworth
 and, 131
Hume, David, 1, 20
Hunt, Leigh, 229, 230
Hutchinson, Mary, 108, 111–12
Hyperion (Keats), 234
hypocrisy: Balzac and, 309; Pushkin and,
 269; Stendhal and, 180–95

"I": Hegel and, 89–90, 95, 98; Kant and,
 83–84
idealism: Fichte and, 78, 84; Goethe and,
 65; Hegel and, 92; Wordsworth and,
 111, 126
illness: Balzac and, 294; Goethe and, 43;
 Hegel and, 77; Keats and, 227, 239,
 243; Manzoni and, 217–21; Rousseau
 and, 18–19, 35
imagination: Goethe and, 71; Keats and,
 233; Romanticism and, 78
Imbonati, Carlo, 199–200
immortality: Keats and, 244; Wordsworth
 and, 128–31
independence. *See* freedom; liberty
individual: Goethe and, 49; Hegel and,
 101–2; Rousseau and, 25, 27
Industrial Revolution, 4; Balzac and, 293;
 Stendhal and, 181–82
inequality, 4; Rousseau and, 10–11, 21–3
innocence. *See* simple life
Italy: Goethe and, 45; Manzoni and,
 197–98, 212–22; Stendhal and, 177,
 178–80
"It is a beauteous Evening" (Wordsworth),
 108–9

James, Henry, 286, 342n5
Jena, 7, 44, 65, 78–9
Jerusalem, Karl Wilhelm, 49
Johnson, Samuel, 32, 142, 158, 292
Jones, Robert, 107
journalism, Balzac and, 305–6
Joyce, James, 133

357

judgment, Austen and, 148–49, 155–56, 160, 162, 168

July Revolution, 5, 179, 180, 285–86

Kant, Immanuel, 75, 90; Hegel and, 77–79, 82–86

Karamzin, Nikolay, 260

Karl August, duke, 44, 45, 48

Keats, John, 105, 110, 225–55; life of, 226–34, 253–55; Wordsworth and, 124

Kestner, Johann Christian, 43–44, 49

knowledge, Hegel and, 85, 92–99, 103

Lake District, Wordsworth and, 106–7, 111

Lamb, Charles, 229

Lampedusa, Giuseppe Tomasi di, 202, 337n68

language(s): Austen and, 143; Goethe and, 41, 49; Hegel and, 95; Manzoni and, 197–98, 202, 204, 222; Pushkin and, 257, 259, 269; Rousseau and, 28; Wittgenstein and, 91, 95; Wordsworth and, 105, 110, 115, 121

lawgiver, Rousseau and, 26–27, 29

Leibniz, Gottfried, 83

Lermontov, Mikhail, 257

Lethe, 242

letters: Balzac and, 292; Goethe and, 49; Heloise and, 27–28; Keats and, 253–54; Pushkin and, 275, 279; Rousseau and, 30; Stendhal and, 190–91, 192

Levasseur, Thérèse, 17–21

Levi, Primo, 220

Lewis, C. S., 160

liberty, 5; Hegel and, 77; Pushkin and, 261–62, 264; Rousseau and, 19, 21–27. See also freedom

life: Balzac and, 291; Goethe and, 42, 52; Manzoni and, 221; Rousseau and, 25, 38; Stendhal and, 184; Wordsworth and, 125, 127

limitations, Hegel and, 76, 86, 89

"Lines Written a Few Miles above Tintern Abbey" (Wordsworth), 110, 124–28

L'Innominato (character), 210–11, 214–16

literary criticism, Manzoni and, 223

literature: Austen and, 147; Balzac and, 289, 301–8; in Romantic era, 7; Russian, 257–58

Locke, John, 83

logic, Hegel and, 76, 86–92

loss: Keats and, 227, 238–41; Wilde and, 310–11; Wordsworth and, 106, 112–13, 118, 128

Lost Illusions (Balzac), 288, 290, 301–8

Lost Souls. See Splendeurs et misères des courtisanes

Louis XV, king of France, 18

Louis XVI, king of France, 4–5, 108

Louis XVIII, king of France, 178

Louis Napoleon, emperor of France, 6, 293

Louis-Philippe, king of France, 6, 179, 293

love: Austen and, 152; Goethe and, 53, 72; Keats and, 233–37, 243, 248; Manzoni and, 202; Pushkin and, 269, 275; Rousseau and, 11–12, 14–15, 27–30; Stendhal and, 174–75, 184–85, 191–95, 198. See also affairs; passion

Lukács, Georg, 223

Luke, David, 65

Luther, Martin, 215

Lyrical Ballads (Wordsworth), 105–6, 110, 111, 114

manifestos: Austen and, 143; Keats and, 230; Manzoni and, 204; Wordsworth and, 110, 114

Mansfield Park (Austen), 146, 159–62

Manzoni, Alessandro, 197–224; life of, 198–203

Marcus Aurelius, 93–4

Marguerite de Valois, 189, 193

Marie Antoinette, queen of France, 5, 108

358

INDEX

Marlowe, Christopher, 55, 57
marriage: Austen and, 147–48, 150–51, 152, 156–57, 159, 163–64, 167–68; Balzac and, 288, 293, 294, 298; Goethe and, 47; Manzoni and, 200, 202, 205, 208; Pushkin and, 265–68; Wordsworth and, 108, 111–12
Marx, Karl, 291
master/slave dynamic, Hegel and, 98–99
McMurtry, Larry, 224
meaning: Goethe and, 61; Wordsworth and, 106, 127, 131, 133, 136
mechanical universe, Goethe and, 61
memory: Stendhal and, 175; Wordsworth and, 106, 125–28, 131, 136
Mephistopheles (character), 57, 59–64, 65–66, 68, 70, 72–73
Mérimee, Prosper, 179
metanarrative, Manzoni and, 203–4
metaphysics: Hegel and, 81, 86–92; Kant and, 90
Meyerbeer, Giacomo, 6
"Michael" (Wordsworth), 120–24
Milan: Manzoni and, 212–14, 217, 219; Stendhal and, 178–80
Miller, Arthur, 325n13
Milton, John, 42, 107, 112, 225
mind, Wordsworth and, 136–37
Mitchell, Stanley, 274
mobs, Manzoni and, 213–14, 220
Molière, 181
moment: Goethe and, 59; Rousseau and, 38–39, 134; Wordsworth and, 131, 133–34, 136
Mondella, Lucia (character), 204–22
monism, Hegel and, 89
Montaigne, Michel de, 30–1
Montaigu, comte de, 16–7
Monza, Nun of, 210–12, 214
Moore, Michael, 197
morality: Austen and, 140, 157, 160–61, 164, 166, 168; Balzac and, 297–99; Hegel and, 101; Pushkin and, 280;

Stendhal and, 174; Wordsworth and, 118, 125–26
Morland, Catherine (character), 146–51
Mozart, Wolfgang Amadeus, 19, 42, 64, 266
music: Goethe and, 48; Keats and, 242, 246, 247–49, 253; in Romantic era, 6; Rousseau and, 16–17, 18–19, 34; Shakespeare and, 130; Stendhal and, 177, 187; Wordsworth and, 126, 133
Musset, Alfred de, 179
Mussorgsky, Modest, 258, 264

Napoleon Bonaparte, emperor of France, 5; Balzac and, 287–88; Goethe and, 41, 47–48; Hegel and, 79; Manzoni and, 201; Stendhal and, 176, 178, 182; Wordsworth and, 113
Napoleonic wars, 5, 47
naturalness. *See* simple life
natural religion, Rousseau and, 11, 20
nature: Austen and, 168; Goethe and, 51–52; Hegel and, 76; Keats and, 251–53; Manzoni and, 201; Rousseau and, 12, 14–15, 19–20, 34, 39; Schelling and, 78; Wordsworth and, 106, 107, 119–20, 124–28, 132–37. *See also* state of nature
negative capability, Keats and, 232, 242–43, 253
Neurath, Otto, 85
Newton, Isaac, 42
Nicholas I, tsar of Russia, 264, 267, 280, 282
Nietzsche, Friedrich, 41, 47, 48
nightingale: Coleridge and, 110; Keats and, 242–45
nihilism, Goethe and, 59, 72–73
nobility: Balzac and, 286, 288, 303, 306–7; French Revolution and, 4; Goethe and, 45; Manzoni and, 198; Pushkin and, 258; Rousseau and, 11, 19; Stendhal and, 180, 187
noble lie, Rousseau and, 26

The Wisdom of the Romantics

nominalism, Aristotle and, 87
Northanger Abbey (Austen), 142–43, 144, 146–51
nostalgia, Rousseau and, 11, 24
nothingness, Hegel and, 88
noumena, Kant and, 84
La Nouvelle Héloïse (Rousseau), 11–12, 20, 27–30, 49, 274
novel(s): Austen and, 139–71; Balzac and, 285–311; Manzoni and, 197–224; Pushkin and, 274; Stendhal and, 173–95; Wordsworth and, 107

O'Brian, Patrick, 224
obsession, Keats and, 238–41
odes: Keats and, 241–53; nature of, 241; Wordsworth and, 128–31
"The Old Cumberland Beggar" (Wordsworth), 119–20
Onegin, Eugene (character), 268–80
"On First Looking into Chapman's Homer" (Keats), 230
opera, 6, 333n8, 337n68; Goethe and, 64; Pushkin and, 258, 262, 264, 266, 281; Rousseau and, 18–19, 34; Stendhal and, 187
oppression: Manzoni and, 208, 213; Rousseau and, 22, 27
order: Austen and, 161; Hegel and, 94; Wordsworth and, 132–33
ordinary people: Austen and, 139–40; Balzac and, 294; Manzoni and, 201–2, 204; Pushkin and, 271, 274; Wordsworth and, 105–6
other, Hegel and, 89–90
Ovid, 46, 69–70, 107, 262

Padre Cristoforo (character), 207–10, 220–21
Paine, Thomas, 108
paranoia, Rousseau and, 11, 20–21, 37
Paris: Balzac and, 296, 303–5; Manzoni and, 200; Rousseau and, 36–37; Stendhal and, 179, 187–91

Parmenides, 82, 88
particulars, Hegel and, 87, 95
Pascal, Blaise, 42, 60–61
passion: Austen and, 167; Goethe and, 49–51, 53–54, 67; Keats and, 234–37, 248; Romanticism and, 78; Rousseau and, 27–30, 38–39; Stendhal and, 181, 184, 190, 193, 198; Wordsworth and, 114–15
pathetic fallacy, 114
patriarchy, Austen and, 147, 150
Paul I, tsar of Russia, 259
perception, Hegel and, 85, 96–97
Père Goriot (Balzac), 285–86, 290, 294–301
personifications: Keats and, 252; Wordsworth and, 115
Persuasion (Austen), 167–71
Peter the Great, tsar of Russia, 258
phenomenology, Hegel and, 90–93
Philip IV, king of Spain, 217
philosophy, 80–82; Hegel and, 75–103; Kant and, 78; Wordsworth and, 136
Pico della Mirandola, 31
plague, Manzoni and, 217–21
Plato, 26, 81, 86–88
Plutarch, 12, 32
poetry: Balzac and, 309; Goethe and, 42, 46, 48, 67, 73; Keats and, 225–55; Manzoni and, 199, 224; Pushkin and, 257, 262, 265, 268–80; Shakespeare and, 225; subject matter of, 105–6, 114–24; Wordsworth and, 105–37
political issues, 4–6; Goethe and, 46–47, 65–66; Pushkin and, 261; Rousseau and, 10, 22–27; Wordsworth and, 113
Poltava (Pushkin), 265
Ponchielli, Amilcare, 337n68
power: Austen and, 163, 165; Goethe and, 69; Manzoni and, 210–12; Pushkin and, 267; Rousseau and, 25
practical reason, Hegel and, 98
The Prelude (Wordsworth), 106, 107, 111, 112, 132–37

360

INDEX

Price, Fanny (character), 159–62
Pride and Prejudice (Austen), 144, 145, 154–59
process: Hegel and, 81, 96; Romanticism and, 3
progress through reason, Rousseau and, 18
property, Rousseau and, 22–23
prose: Pushkin and, 257, 265; Wordsworth and, 115
prostitution, Balzac and, 310
Proudhon, Pierre-Joseph, 6
Proust, Marcel, 41, 302–3
public opinion. *See* society
publishing, Balzac and, 289–90, 292–93
Pugachev, Yemelyan, 267–68
Pushkin, Alexander, 257–83; Balzac and, 293; life of, 258–68, 280–83

"The Queen of Spades" (Pushkin), 281

Racine, Jean, 179
Radcliffe, Ann, 142
Raevsky, Nikolay, 262
Rastignac, Eugene de (character), 174, 290, 296–99, 300–301, 304
realism: Balzac and, 285–86, 291, 301, 310; Keats and, 250; Plato and, 87; Pushkin and, 274; Stendhal and, 174, 181
reality: Hegel and, 81, 86, 90–1, 102–3; Kant and, 83–84; Keats and, 240, 245
reason: Austen and, 154, 159; Hegel and, 91, 100–1, 103; Plato and, 86; Rousseau and, 27
The Recluse (Wordsworth), 110–11
recollection, Wordsworth and, 131
The Red and the Black (Stendhal), 173–95
refusal, power of, Austen and, 148, 151, 156–57, 161
Reign of Terror, 5, 77, 108
religion: Goethe and, 51–52, 58; Hegel and, 77, 102; Keats and, 249; Manzoni and, 200, 205–6, 209–10, 215–16, 218, 220; Rousseau and, 11, 12, 15,

19, 20, 26, 39; Stendhal and, 186, 192; Wordsworth and, 126, 136
Renaissance, versus Romantic era, 30–1
Rênal, Mme de (character), 182–87, 192–95
representative democracy, Rousseau and, 24–25
"Resolution and Independence" (Wordsworth), 120, 124, 129
restraint: Austen and, 152–53, 164–65; Wordsworth and, 123–24
Reveries of a Solitary Walker (Rousseau), 12, 21, 27, 38–9
revolution(s): 1848, 6, 293; Manzoni and, 213; poetry and, 73; Pushkin and, 264; Romanticism and, 4–6; Rousseau and, 27; science and, 7; Stendhal and, 194. *See also* French Revolution
Reynolds, John, 229
Richardson, Samuel, 49
Rimsky-Korsakov, Nikolai, 258, 266
Robespierre, Maximilen, 108
Roman Elegies (Goethe), 46
Romanticism: Balzac and, 301, 309–10; dating of, 3, 9; definitional issues, 1–3; Goethe and, 46, 55, 61; Keats and, 232, 250; Pushkin and, 272, 274, 276; Stendhal and, 173–74, 178, 192–93
Rossini, Gioachino, 6
Rousseau, Jean-Jacques, 3, 5, 9–39, 71; Goethe and, 49; Hegel and, 77, 99; life of, 12–21; Stendhal and, 176, 188; Wordsworth and, 134
Rubempré, Lucien de (character), 301–11
"The Ruined Cottage" (Wordsworth), 110, 116–19
Ruslan and Lyudmila (Pushkin), 262
Russia: Balzac and, 293; Napoleon and, 5, 178; Pushkin and, 257–83

sacred, 2; Goethe and, 42, 70; Wordsworth and, 112, 115–16, 121, 136
Salieri, Antonio, 266

salvation: Goethe and, 71–72; Keats and, 250–51

Sand, George, 179

Sanditon (Austen), 146

Schelling, Friedrich, 56, 77–79

Schiller, Friedrich, 47, 178

Schopenhauer, Arthur, 65

Schubert, Franz, 48

science: Goethe and, 48, 67; Hegel and, 81, 85, 91–92; in Romantic era, 7

Scott, Walter, 139–40, 201, 204, 232, 289

self: Goethe and, 60; Hegel and, 89–90, 98–99; Montaigne and, 31; Rousseau and, 31, 38

self-consciousness: Hegel and, 98; Stendhal and, 190

self-interest: Austen and, 154; Rousseau and, 22, 24

Sense and Sensibility (Austen), 144, 145, 151–54

sense-certainty, Hegel and, 94–96

sensibility: Austen and, 151–54, 167; Goethe and, 49–50; Keats and, 242; Rousseau and, 10–12, 16, 27–30, 33, 37–38; Stendhal and, 187; Wordsworth and, 114, 120–24. *See also* emotions

Seven Years' War, 43

Severn, Joseph, 229, 254–55

sexuality: Goethe and, 46, 62; Keats and, 236–37, 239; Rousseau and, 13, 15, 17, 28, 34; Stendhal and, 183

Shaffer, Peter, 266

Shakespeare, William, 151, 222, 225, 255, 333n2; Balzac and, 286, 294, 297, 299–300, 342n5; Goethe and, 43, 61, 63, 73; Johnson and, 32; Keats and, 226, 243, 244; Manzoni and, 207; Stendhal and, 179; Wordsworth and, 107, 130

Shelley, Mary, 67

Shelley, Percy Bysshe, 105, 228, 229, 231

simple life: Austen and, 149; Rousseau and, 10, 16, 29, 32, 34; Stendhal and, 184–85

sincerity. *See* authenticity

skepticism, 99

"Sleep and Poetry" (Keats), 230–31

Smith, Adam, 21

The Social Contract (Rousseau), 11, 20, 24–26

society: Austen and, 147–48, 150–54, 156, 159, 164–66, 170; Balzac and, 288, 291–92, 295–301, 304, 309; Goethe and, 47, 51; Manzoni and, 200, 207; Pushkin and, 265, 267, 268–72, 276, 281; Rousseau and, 11, 17–19, 21–22, 24; Stendhal and, 174, 177, 180–81, 184–88, 193–94, 198

Socrates, 80, 242

sonnets: Keats and, 229; Wordsworth and, 124

Sorel, Julien (character), 174–75, 180–95

The Sorrows of Young Werther (Goethe), 7, 30, 44, 48–55, 274

soul: Goethe and, 52; Marlowe and, 57; Wordsworth and, 129–30. *See also* communion of souls

Spenser, Edmund, 107

Spinoza, Benedict de, 43, 58, 92

spirit: Hegel and, 76, 92–103; Keats and, 249; Wordsworth and, 106, 107, 126–27

Splendeurs et misères des courtisanes (Balzac), 308–11

Starobinski, Jean, 27, 28

state of nature, Rousseau and, 10, 22, 24

steam engine, 4

Stendhal, 173–95; life of, 175–80; Manzoni and, 200

Stoicism, 99

Strawson, P. F., 84

Sturm und Drang movement, 44, 47

subjectivity: Goethe and, 64; Hegel and, 89; Romanticism and, 3, 78

sublation, term, 89

sublime: Rousseau and, 28, 29; Wordsworth and, 124–26

suicide, Goethe and, 49, 54–55

INDEX

synthesis, Hegel and, 87–90, 92
systematic thought, Hegel and, 79, 81–82, 91, 103

Tacitus, 12
Talleyrand, Charles Maurice de, 185
Tchaikovsky, Peter Ilyich, 258, 281
teleology, Hegel and, 93
theater: Goethe and, 43, 45, 48; Pushkin and, 263; Schiller and, 47; Stendhal and, 176–77
theology, Hegel and, 77
Thucydides, 217
"Tintern Abbey" (Wordsworth), 110, 124–28
Tolstoy, Leo, 223, 224, 258, 266, 281
Tramaglino, Renzo (character), 204–22
Trilling, Lionel, 160
truth: Hegel and, 80, 85, 91; Keats and, 232–33, 246, 250; Wordsworth and, 131
Turgenev, Ivan, 257–58
Turner, J. M. W., 6
Twain, Mark, 75

understanding: Hegel and, 97–99; Kant and, 83; Wordsworth and, 127
unhappy consciousness, Hegel and, 99
universals, Hegel and, 87, 95–96
urbanization, 4, 293

Vallon, Annette, 108
Vautrin (character), 287, 290, 297–98, 308–11
Vendler, Helen, 248, 249, 251
Verdi, Giuseppe, 202, 203
Virgil, 224
Visconti, Francesco Bernardino, 211
Voltaire, 36
Vorontsov, Mikhail, 263

Vulpius, Christiane, 45–46, 47, 65

wager, Goethe and, 60–61
Wagner, Richard, 310
walking: Keats and, 233; Pushkin and, 265; Rousseau and, 14, 19–20, 34, 39; Wordsworth and, 107, 111
war: Manzoni and, 201, 212, 217; Romanticism and, 4–6; Stendhal and, 177
Warens, Mme de, 14–16, 19, 34
Wars of the French Revolution, 5, 108
Watt, Ian, 55
way of life: Balzac and, 291; Goethe and, 62; Manzoni and, 203; Pushkin and, 262; Rousseau and, 16, 23, 34, 37
Wellbery, David, 52
Werther (character), 48–55
Wilde, Oscar, 50, 285, 306, 310–11
Wissenschaft, term, 81. *See also* science
Wittgenstein, Ludwig, 2, 88–89, 91, 95
women: Austen and, 139–71; Balzac and, 287, 289, 292, 296, 298–99, 303–4, 306; Goethe and, 62–64, 68–69; Hegel and, 79–80; Keats and, 233–34, 238–41, 253–54; Manzoni and, 200, 202; Marlowe and, 57; Pushkin and, 259–60, 266–67, 273–77, 281–82; Rousseau and, 14–15, 17–18, 33; Stendhal and, 177–78, 183, 198; Wordsworth and, 108, 111–12
Wordsworth, Dorothy, 107–11, 113, 127
Wordsworth, William, 76, 105–37, 225; Keats and, 229, 232; life of, 106–13
world spirit, Hegel and, 76, 100–103
Wulf, Andrea, 7

Zhukovsky, Vasily, 260
Zola, Émile, 286, 342n5

363